Reiner Pomm

Clausewitz goes global
-
Carl von Clausewitz in the 21st Century

Clausewitz goes global

Carl von Clausewitz in the 21st Century

Commemorating the 50th Anniversary of the Clausewitz Society

Edited for the Clausewitz Society by
Reiner Pommerin

2014

Carola Hartmann Miles-Verlag Berlin

CIP-Kurztitelaufnahme der Deutschen Nationalbibliothek:

Reiner Pommerin (ed.), Clausewitz goes global.
Carl von Clausewitz in the 21st Century, Paperback der 2011 veröffentlichten Hardcover-Ausgabe, Berlin 2014

ISBN 978-3-937885-78-0

Titelbild: Scheiblich; Bild S. 8: Brenne-Wegener
Herstellung und Verlag: Books on Demand GmbH, Norderstedt

© Carola Hartmann Miles-Verlag,
(www.miles-verlag.jimdo.com; email: miles-verlag@t-online.de)

Alle Rechte, insbesondere das Recht der Vervielfältigung und Verbreitung sowie der Übersetzung, vorbehalten. Kein Teil des Werkes darf in irgendeiner Form (durch Fotokopie, Mikrofilm oder ein anderes Verfahren) ohne schriftliche Genehmigung des Verlages reproduziert oder unter Verwendung elektronischer Systeme gespeichert, verarbeitet, vervielfältigt oder verbreitet werden.
Printed in Germany

ISBN 978-3-937885-78-0

Content

	Page
A Golden Anniversary with Bright Prospects for the Future *General Lieutenant (ret.) Dr. Klaus Olshausen, President of the Clausewitz Society*	9
Clausewitz in a Global World *Colonel (res.) Prof. Dr. Reiner Pommerin*	11
A Fixed Star in a Galaxy of Quotes – Clausewitz and Austria *Hofrat Dr. Manfried Rauchensteiner*	14
Tailoring Ends to Means: Clausewitz in Belgium *Prof. Dr. Bruno Colson and Lecturer Dr. Christophe Wasinski*	31
The Western Master and Bible of War: Clausewitz and his "On War" in China *Prof. Dr. Yu Tiejun*	42
Observations and Verdict of a Lonely Clausewitzian Convert: "Vom Kriege" in Denmark *Brigadier General (ret.) Michael Hesselholt Clemmesen*	60
Clausewitzian War Theory and the Defence Doctrines of Small States: Case Finland *Colonel a. D. Dr. Pekka Visuri*	85

XXIst Century's Clausewitz in France   107
Prof. Dr. Hervé Coutau-Bégarie

The Reception of Clausewitz in Germany   122
Lieutenant Colonel (ret.) Prof. Dr. Freiherr Claus von Rosen and Colonel Dr. Uwe Hartmann

Clausewitz and 21st Century Israeli Military Thinking and Practice   150
Prof. Dr. Avi Kober

Clausewitz and Italy   173
Prof. Dr. Virgilio Ilari, Luciano Bozzo and Giampiero Giacomello

Clausewitz in the 21st Century Japan   203
Takeshi Oki

Clausewitz and the Netherlands   210
Lecturer Drs. Paul Donker

Clausewitz and Norway – Staring at a Distant Sun   239
Lieutenant Colonel Dr. Harald Høiback

Clausewitz in a Post-Communist State: A Case Study of Slovenia   263
Prof. Dr. Vladimir Prebilič and Dr. Jelena Juvan

Clausewitz, 'the People in Arms' and the Liberation Struggle in South Africa: Can they be linked?   287
Commander Dr. Thean Potgieter and Dr. Francois Vreÿ

Clausewitz, Spain and the 21st Century 311
Brigadier General (ret.) Dr. Alonso Baquer

Clausewitz in Sweden 320
Prof. Dr. Lars Erikson Wolke

Clausewitz in Switzerland 328
Oberst i Gst. Dr. Roland Beck

Clausewitz in America today 341
Prof. Dr. Christopher Bassford

Authors 356

Index 368

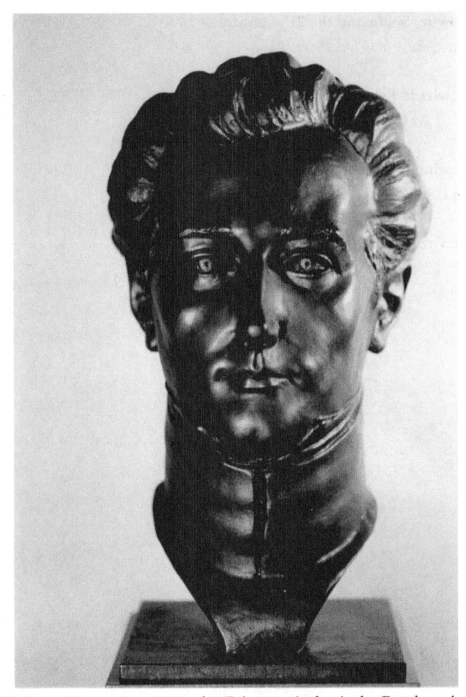

Carl von Clausewitz – Büste der Führungsakademie der Bundeswehr,
Clausewitz-Kaserne, Hamburg

A GOLDEN ANNIVERSARY WITH BRIGHT PROSPECTS FOR THE FUTURE
Klaus Olshausen

The year 2011 marks a milestone in the development of the Clausewitz Society and in the evolution of military thought in contemporary Germany and the wider world. Our organization looks back on a half century of labor towards the goals of excellence in strategic studies and professional development. Six years after the start of the new German Federal Armed Forces ("Bundeswehr") in the wake of the Second World War, an enlightened group of former officers of the pre-1945 general staff of the armed forces founded this society. In close connection with the new Bundeswehr, these men were guided by a spirit grounded in timeless ethical standards for soldiers in their desire to contribute to the further strengthening of the Federal Republic of Germany and its peace and security in a time of danger.

The society came into being in November 1961 as an independent, non-partisan and non-profit organization. Ours is a society of officers, many on General Staff/Admiral Staff service, as well as personalities who have distinguished themselves in the further promotion and support of the objectives of the Clausewitz Society. At present, there are some 1,000 members, the majority officers, active, retired and reserve; increasingly also personalities professionally active in politics, advanced study, economy and the media. Our Honorary President is General (retd.) Wolfgang Altenburg the former Chief of Defence of the Bundeswehr. He completed his active service as Chairman of NATO's Military Committee in Brussels.

The Clausewitz Society draws useful conclusions for the present that are informed by the insights and principles of the soldier and military scholar Carl von Clausewitz. This effort eschews merely a historical retrospective of Clausewitz and his era. We refrain from solely offering a detailed analysis of his works in a narrow sense. Rather, the labor of this society interprets contemporary political and strategic challenges through the lense of Carl von Clausewitz's thought while further examining which of his principles and insights remain relevant today in their timeless quality. Such a critical analysis is all the more urgent in dynamic strategic and security-political questions of the early 21st century. At the same time, this labor enriches and preserves the positive intellectual legacy of the General Staff. In a time of a arduous defence against transnational terrorism and the struggle against insurgents in UN mandated crisis management operations a special work of Clausewitz on small wars (the guerilla war of his time) gains renewed relevance.

The Clausewitz Society promotes its objectives three times a year with its cycle of meetings: the "Berlin Colloquium" in cooperation with the "Bundesakademie für Sicherheitspolitik" (Federal College of Security Studies); the "Annual General Meeting" in conjunction with a security-political conference together with the "Führungsakademie der Bundeswehr" (German Armed Forces Command & Staff College); and "The Forum" at different locations throughout Germany and in Switzerland. In addition, there are numerous events hosted by the Regional Chapters, the Switzerland Section and the Clausewitz-Table in Bremen. Since 2005 the society has published a yearbook, which contains contributions selected from the three main events and other parts of the society's work. The organization further supports scholarly work in the field of Clausewitz research and publications concerned with questions of security policy. In this field the society supports the recently founded Clausewitz Network of Strategic Studies (CNSS) of young officers of General-/Admiralstaff, academics and students of international politics. In our globalized world, with complex and complicated security challenges and serious crisis, the above efforts reflect and analyse - like in our own endavours - many functional or regional topics that employ methods and instruments based on the insights and methodolgy offered by Clausewitz. Since 2008, these selected issues of our conferences comprised such themes as the crisis region near & middle East; the future security and defence strategy and policy of NATO and the EU; the legitimization of military operations in the 21st century; the new capabilities, eduction & training requirements as well as command & control of modern armed forces amid (multi)national employments and warfare in crisis response operations. All topics underscore the forward looking approach of this society in the past and present.

The volume at hand emerged, then, from the present and emerging challenges that our society has sought to address in the recent past and in five decades until now. With this book we wish to extend our hand to our friends and partners in the world and hope, thereby, to encourage cooperation with military and academics who have already, or might well, include the work of Clausewitz into our common security policy analysis, policy advice and decisionmaking within our respective national and mulitinational responsibilities.

CLAUSEWITZ IN A GLOBAL WORLD
Reiner Pommerin

"Presenting Clausewitz's main ideas as bullet points on a Power Point slide is thus prone to convey the wrong ideas, both of the man and of his thoughts" (Harald Høiback).

This Festschrift commemorates the 50th anniversary of the foundation of the Clausewitz-Society in the Federal Republic of Germany of 1961. This volume follows the intentions of the Clausewitz-Society as described by one of its former presidents: "to view the current tasks of politics and strategy as reflected in the insights of Carl von Clausewitz and thus examine which of the principles and insights formulated by Clausewitz are still important today and are thus endowed with an enduring validity". The board and the members of the Clausewitz-Society therefore supported the idea to examine how and when the works of Clausewitz have been interpreted in selected countries of our world; further, the goal here has been to analyze the role that Clausewitz's thought still plays in these countries. Each article surely deserves the reader's full attention. Therefore, I do not intend to bore the reader with a lengthy introduction. By contrast I will only briefly mention some aspects of general interest.

Soon after *"On War"* had been published in 1832, a handful of military scholars and officers in foreign countries commented on Clausewitz. This fact may be due to the reality that the German language played a bigger role in scholarship and sciences before the turn of the 19th century. In Sweden for example Clausewitz was only translated in 1991, because most Swedish officers were expected to read and understand German. But not all officers in Europe and in more distant parts of the world could read German as well. Bits and pieces of Clausewitz's were translated quite early, like for example his *"The Campaign of 1812"*, which was published in English in 1843. The first translation of *"On War"* took place in the Netherlands in 1846. The first French translation of the book was made in 1849 by an officer of the Belgian Army, where French was the only official language in the 19th century. But as had been the case in his native Germany, the interest of international strategists and military theorists in Clausewitz's work began at a modest level.

Only after Helmuth von Moltke had praised Clausewitz in the context of the German victories in the unification wars in the 1870's did the interest in

Clausewitz outside of Germany increase and led to more translations of his *"On War"* into foreign languages. To give some examples: The first and only credible, non-émigré full translation of the book into English was published in 1873 by a British Colonel, while in the United States of America there was no evidence of any reading of *"On War"* before the 1890s. In 1907 the first Japanese translation was declared confidential and published only within army circles, where it was widely read by officers. However, the Japanese translation soon made its way to China where in 1911 parts of it were translated into Chinese, but without mentioning the name of Clausewitz as its author. A complete Chinese translation of the Japanese text of *"On War"*, which included the author's name, was printed 1915, followed by many other editions in China. In Spain the text remained unavailable in translation until the beginning of the Second World War, but surprisingly there existed a Spanish paper edition owned by the Circulo Militar Argentino in Buenos Aires. In Italy a translation of *"On War"* had to wait till 1942. In Norway the volume has never been translated completely and only a very abridged version was published in 1972.

After the First World War, though interest in military theory declined dramatically in many countries. After the Second World War and during the long period of the Cold War the decline of military theory in general and Clausewitz in particular became even more significant. Interestingly this was the time when the management side and also the union side of many capitalist enterprises began to read Clausewitz. Their interest was based on the demand for prescriptive model of strategy, namely how to perform in business. The end of the Cold War and the collapse of the Warsaw Pact and then the Soviet Union changed the situation and originated a lively reading and broad discussion of military theory. This development led almost everywhere to a revival of theoretical studies in war and warfare, which of course, included Clausewitz, whose thoughts can even contribute to an understanding of asymmetric wars.

All articles of the Festschrift underscore the observation that, beside the difficulty of reading *"On War"*, the rest of Clausewitz's works, seem to have had little impact on military education and thought even into the present. As often as the fixed star in a galaxy of quotes, the sentence "war is simply a continuation of political intercourse, with the addition of other means" may have globally been cited, it did not automatically reflect a true reception and understanding of Clausewitz's thought.

To a large extent in professional military education of the world's nations, Clausewitz remains compulsory reading for officers. The reason still adheres that Clausewitz is a strategic mind who gathered experience in all dimensions of modern strategy. The articles of the Festschrift prove that elements of Clausewitz's theory are relevant today; some of them have proven of even greater relevance. Practically at almost all Naval-, Air Force-, Army Academies, Staff Colleges and Academies in courses of Higher Staff or General Staff Education of all countries of our eighteen contributors, Clausewitz's work is not only on the shelves of the libraries, but actively read in curricula devoted to the theory and practice of war in its most critical aspects. Even where his thought is not as popular or overshadowed by such other strategists and military thinkers as Antoine Henri Jomini or Sun Tzu, for example, at least some chapters of Clausewitz's works or articles on Clausewitz are used for military education on all levels. One is not surprised to read that even in one of the youngest and smallest states in NATO Europe, in the Republic of Slovenia, Clausewitz has made his way into military education. However, although not influential in every country, Clausewitz cuts across ideological and cultural divides and continues to stimulate debate.

While for most authors included here many of Clausewitz's basic theoretical ideas are still relevant, some also point to considerable aspects of his thought, which do need some addition, updating or adaption. Clausewitz, however, could not react to developments, changes and capabilities, most of which have taken place after his death, like the importance of intelligence, the role played by morality in war or material factors like technology or logistics and the fact that wars have taken a strong attritional form involving non-military-dimensions.

After reading the Festschrift one only can agree with one author's remark: "Clausewitz offers considerable potential for today's politics and military, far more than the title of the principle work 'On War' would lead one to expect at first sight".

I am pleased to have the opportunity to thank those who have aided the project. Firstly, I thank my colleagues, comrades and friends from Africa, America, Asia and Europe who supported the idea for this reader and finished their papers in time. Without their help this Festschrift could never have been printed. On a more personal level I would like to thank my fellow members of the Clausewitz Society whose trust and support made this publication possible. Finally, for her generous aid with this book through the publication process, I am grateful to Carola Hartmann and the Miles Verlag.

A FIXED STAR IN A GALAXY OF QUOTES - CLAUSEWITZ AND AUSTRIA*

Manfried Rauchensteiner

It was 30 years ago. During a lecture on military and war history at the Maria-Theresian Military Academy in Wiener Neustadt, I asked the question: "As an educated officer, which three books would you pick for a small library?" The answer was simply surprising. Erwin Rommel's "Infanterie greift an" (Infantry Attacks) ranked first. Clausewitz reached a disputed second place, but only with some prompting. I continued to ask this question in the following years. The answers were similar.

Now, in the case of the officer candidates, several things probably came into play: For no obvious reason, the book by Rommel was quite popular. This was maybe connected to the fact that for about one year from 1938 on, Rommel was commanding officer at the former Austrian military academy which had been transformed into an officer cadet school of the infantry. But what could be mistaken for a hint of neo-Nazism turned out to be just ignorance, because hardly any of the officer cadets had even a glimpse at "Infanterie greift an". Also, it should be conceded that the future officers were still in their wild years. A much more trivial reason was, of course, the fact that until their classes in military and war history, they had never heard of Clausewitz and only got into touch with "Vom Kriege" (On War) in their lecture hall for the very first time. Sure enough, even after the lectures, only very few of them actually read Clausewitz.

What could merely pass as a military anecdote still has a far-reaching implication, because even in the seventies of the 20th century, Clausewitz's name was known in Austria, but not his works. His name was rarely mentioned in universities, and literature seemed to almost ignore him.

---

* In memoriam of Werner Hahlweg.

But actually, things did not necessarily have to be this way at that time. There was something like a first attempt of coming to terms with Clausewitz. However, also here the context needs to be taken into account: Still in 1975, the habilitation of a historian with the (additional) specialization in military history was downright prevented at the University of Vienna, let alone at the other Austrian universities.

Here, demilitarization and re-education which was promoted by the US occupying power in the first place obviously went so far and had such a lasting effect that habilitation regulations made it impossible to pursue a career in military history at Austrian universities at that time. So in a way, studying Clausewitz was officially banned.

Of course, outside universities, especially in the Austrian Armed Forces, the situation was completely different. Instead, another phenomenon, a thoroughly Austrian tradition prevailed: a certain aversion to humanities and social sciences. Primary subjects taught were the classical military subjects of tactics, operation and strategy supplemented by well-dosed portions of war history which for a long time was mainly illustrated by examples of World War I and World War II. Nevertheless: The overall situation gradually changed.

There is no doubt that Werner Hahlweg played a special role in this. Before World War II, Hahlweg also studied in Vienna and attended courses at the Institut für österreichische Geschichtsforschung (Institute for Austrian Historical Research) to pursue studies in historical auxiliary sciences, and even after the war, he remained committed to Vienna. Rather than his short-lasting marriage in Vienna, the reason for his affiliation to this city was the fact that he had access to the body of sources and literature of the Vienna War Archive's library, which made him return to the Stiftskaserne army barracks year after year. Consequently, his reputation within the scientific community and in the end also within the Austrian Armed Forces increased. Shortly after the formation of the Armed Forces, Hahlweg published an article in the magazine "Landesverteidigung"[1] (National Defense) and several others in the highly reputed and long-established Austrian military journal "Österreichische Militärische Zeitschrift".[2]

So he became the major source of inspiration in the Austrian military journal where Clausewitz developed into a recurring topic. It seemed natural to address warfare theory, to launch a series on operational thinking in Austria in the 19th and 20th centuries[3] and to make reflections on warfare an explicit category within Austrian military literature. Therefore the relatively large audience of the journal was driven to study this subject more thoroughly and to familiarize themselves with pertinent international research as done, for example, by Peter Paret. There was no way of getting around Clausewitz.

And ever since, he has remained in the focus of interest. A kind of first heyday of Clausewitz was at a conference in Vienna in 1987. The Austrian military attaché in Bonn at that time, Brigadier Otto Heller, himself a member of the German Clausewitz Society, conveyed the idea of organizing a conference in Vienna and became the initiator. The Austrian Commission for Military History and the Austrian Society for Political-Strategic Studies (chaired by Prince Karl Schwarzenberg at that time) were the hosts. The well-attended event took place in the great ballroom of the Association of Industrialists at Schwarzenbergplatz in Vienna and was dedicated to an "Intellectual Trilogy of the 19th Century and its Significance for the Present": Clausewitz, Jomini and Archduke Charles of Austria.[4] Apart from well-known researchers as Werner Hahlweg, Dietmar Schössler and Daniel M. Proektor, also American (John E. Tashjean; Michael D. Krause), Swiss (Daniel Reichel) and Hungarian (Jozsef Zachar) scholars, as well as Andrée Türpe of the Humboldt University were among the speakers. Presentations on Archduke Charles of Austria and the "Limited War" were given by me.

Comparing these historical personalities made it possible to identify common ideas, differences as well as different schools of thought. There was Jomini, who initially dominated the discourse on war and, through his vision of the consequences from passing the natural limits in wars, laid the foundation for a school of thought that had been particularly dominant in the US for a long time. There was Clausewitz, whose influence on strategies and actions on European armies came to bear much later albeit much stronger. And then there was idealistic Archduke Charles of Austria, who considered obtaining a favourable peace the ultimate goal of war. Incidentally, the latter became a classic in fields the other two did not "specialize in". This was maybe also the reason for Friedrich Engels to describe Charles of Austria as the most influential practitioner and theoretician in the field of mountain warfare.[5]

Since all of the three heroes of military history and theory of war and eponyms of the conference in Vienna had bequeathed the world with an abundance of reading material, it was inevitable that the speakers focused on individual aspects of the concepts and the works and tagged them with separate codifications. Here of course, it was necessary to explain the historic intellectual positions at an early stage, because the statements on the nature of war by Archduke Charles of Austria and by Clausewitz differed greatly. Charles of Austria formulated that: "War is the most horrible thing a state or a nation may suffer … To obtain a favourable peace must be the ultimate goal of every war, for only a favourable peace is permanent and only through a favourable peace can the happiness of nations be ensured and thus the purpose of government fulfilled."[6] This was an idealistic approach which was still strongly influenced by the age of enlightenment. This was also quite emotional. The other one, Clausewitz, provides a sober and multifaceted analysis. Hence, it does not come as a surprise, when he surpassed his Austrian contemporary in terms of both precision and arbitrariness. His demand of an "order of reason for the purpose of peace" which already should be established at the beginning of a war bears a remote resemblance to the phrase coined by the Habsburg Archduke 25 years earlier.

The comparison within the scope of the mentioned conference also revealed a relatively clear picture of the significance and of the reception history regarding Clausewitz, Jomini and Archduke Carl. Of course, the latter is more deeply rooted in the Austrian consciousness. At least among those interested in history, a basic knowledge can be presumed, even if the exact dates and quotes do not immediately spring to one's mind. And many would at least recognize his image due to the equestrian statue of the Archduke which was erected by his great-nephew Emperor Franz Joseph at the newly built Imperial Forum, later renamed Heldenplatz (Heroes' Square), in front of Hofburg Palace in 1860. At least the statue sparks interest and may raise the question "Who is that?" (Up to the present day, the words engraved on the pedestal of the statue „Dem beharrlichen Kämpfer für Deutschlands Ehre" (To the persevering fighter for Germany's Glory) have led to controversies).

There is no such monument of Clausewitz in Vienna. Unlike in Berlin, Hannover, Bremerhaven and dozens of other German cities, also no street and no square in Austria has been named after the German military philosopher, let alone a hotel bearing his name. Measured against his public presence, the Habsburg Archduke thus surpasses Clausewitz and Jomini by far. But this lead drastically melts away when searching for useful quotes by Clausewitz and Charles (Jomini shall be excluded in the following). Charles of Austria was a man of practice. He was a military leader and organizer and thus, in a way, combined the roles of Scharnhorst and Boyen. But he was also a very thoughtful and productive writer, of course with the reservation that "Grundsätze der höheren Kriegskunst für die Generäle der österreichischen Armee" (The Art of War - Basic Principles for Generals of the Austrian Army) - his only work intended to be passed on and used for training purposes - did not contain any notable philosophical approaches. This rather applied to "Grundsätze der Strategie" (Principles of Strategy)[7]. But they suffered the same fate as most of the Archduke's works: they were published only after his death. Reportedly, he had tried to publish his works earlier, but the printing was prevented by the Austrian censoring board. Consequently, the prince did not publish his manuscripts and only passed them on to his sons to serve their military education.

Also Clausewitz did not live to see the publishing of his great work, which was amongst others due to the fact that he only considered parts of the manuscript "On War" ready for publishing. Many others of the Prussian military philosopher's works were never published or only used in classrooms.

Most writings of Archduke Charles were published on behalf of his sons at the end of the 19th century. Some of the hitherto unpublished works can be only found in the Archduke's heritage archived in the Hungarian state archives in Budapest. It took a while until the scattered smaller pieces of Clausewitz's oeuvre were published in one anthology, but by now, all of them should be available.

For the conference in Vienna in 1987, "On War" was a sufficiently profound source, and maybe it was this very conference that led to the breakthrough and paved the way for the triumph of the Clausewitzian. They definitely pushed Jomini and Archduke Charles into the background – even in Austria.

At this point, the Österreichische Militärische Zeitschrift should be mentioned once more. In the following years, it consequently published articles on Clausewitz and thus consolidated his standing. Franz Freistetter, editor-in-chief of the Österreichische Militärische Zeitschrift, wrote about Lenin's remarks on Clausewitz's "On War"[8]. Daniel Proektor wrote about Clausewitz and the present.[9] The Chinese Yuanlin, Zhang wrote about the Chinese edition of "On War" by Carl von Clausewitz[10]. Thomas Rid published an essay on the reception of Clausewitz by the American Forces.[11] And even if the name of Clausewitz did not appear in the title, he was still present, e.g. in Gustav. E. Gugenau's "Zum Primat der Politik" (On the Primacy of Politics).[12] With these publications, the journal did not only live up to its reputation as one of the leading military journals in the world, but obtained an almost unique position, because it was the only publication in Austria discussing general war theory and Clausewitz in particular. It must be admitted that subject of the investigations was not whether or not central statements of Clausewitz could be applied to the army's daily routine or to international peacekeeping and peacemaking missions of the *Bundesheer* – which would have been a quite interesting topic. But the essential questions were and are being raised. And answers are given.

It is no coincidence that new research fields have emerged through applying Clausewitz's concepts and theories to the present world. It is not only about reception history Hahlweg is focussing on, but also about how statements by Clausewitz are mirrored in different models and different forms of recent conflicts. This was done in a similar way as Jörg Kohlhoff did in his Volume "Vom Krieg gegen Terrorismus" (On War against Terrorism)[13] or Eva Strickmann who wrote about Clausewitz and the war in Ruanda (1990-1994)[14]. Also in Austria, this approach is pursued. The broad definition of state-on-state wars opened up a vast field and already answered the question of whether or not the current forms of individual and collective use of force were covered by Clausewitz's formulations. Particularly in Austria, special examples and references were available. On the one hand, Austrian soldiers have participated in United Nations peacekeeping operations since 1960 and have gained some experience also in peace enforcing missions. But on the other hand even more relevant examples and corresponding deductions could be drawn from the years of fighting in Yugoslavia, where no state-on-state war in the classical sense was waged. Acts of violence were the characteristic element and the most repelling individual atrocities and also the siege of Sarajevo were about unlimited use of force and enforcing the will on the enemy. The fact that this enemy often turned out to be the civil population, moved this conflict towards terrorism, as in this case state terrorism which can be encountered every day. With the very broad interpretation by Hahlweg, according to which revolutions, but also economic issues, trade wars, technological attacks and terrorism are just facets of a greater whole, the individual phases of conflicts can be categorized. It is obvious that force uses technological progress as an instrument. But the question that had to be brought up time and time again was: which kind of policy was meant to be continued by military means? Correspondingly, for terrorist attacks the question is whether discontent with positions and developments or hatred against a person, an ethnic group, a religion or a social system are sufficient to be considered a policy.

Fortunately, Clausewitz drew a line at the other end of the scale, when he established the postulate on the utmost use of force. The use of all available "utmost means" of force, however, has not been an option so far. But this is probably only a matter of time.

The increasing interest in Clausewitz not only became visible within the routine duty of the Austrian Armed Forces and in essays. The increased presence of Clausewitz can be even more felt in doctrine, and teaching at the academies of the Austrian Armed Forces.

At the Theresian Military Academy in Wiener Neustadt – an advanced technical college since 1997 – the times when Rommel's "Infantry Attacks" ranked first in the library of the educated officer belong to the past. Every year, the officer cadets in their 3rd year have to write a thesis comprising some dozen pages. For this dealing with Clausewitz is almost unavoidable. Despite a working method that can be rather considered a lesson in reasoning and in spite of the focus on the present - as prescribed by the curriculum and the occupational image - the results can be sometimes quite interesting. The practical approach is also appreciated by the institution and lecturers, because the actual requirements certainly go beyond a mere hermeneutic discourse. Markus Stiebellehner, for example, addressed current issues regarding wars and conflicts between states and analyzed the arising questions in the light of Clausewitz.[15] Not only do some vague formulations, for example that of the "classical concept of state" and the fact that the author labels "On War" as "theory" show that the prospective officer tried to build a reference framework for his thesis, but also, more importantly, they are proof of a not truly Austrian phenomenon: the tendency of tailoring Clausewitz to one's needs in order to facilitate the use, interpretation and exploitation of him. The frequent use of quotes seems opportune as they can be conveniently resold.

When taking a closer look at Stiebellehner's interpretation, it becomes apparent that he effortlessly enhances Clausewitz's definition of state-on-state wars and also that of Hahlweg. Based on the deductions of Gustav Gustenau, he not only includes sovereign states, but also autonomous political communities and as a third category elements that are neither sovereign nor autonomous.[16] The latter (probably) are on their way to stateness and due to their civilisatory stage make use of the "lowest level of conflict resolution": low intensity conflicts and "latent war".[17] With this interpretation and under the precept that nowadays also liberation movements are considered legal entities under international law, it was easy to prove that Clausewitz was still up-to-date. And so, especially in the military, a common and sensible reduction of statements was possible, through which issues as the totality of war or the use of the available utmost force could be avoided. But for the normal curriculum at a military academy, a certain job-oriented interpretation and a solid presentation of smaller aspects of a larger concept should definitely suffice.

Of course, in 2001, the military academies went beyond this basic goal, because in that year, the diploma course "Military Command and Control" organized a symposium on different aspects of war. In the first place, the presentations were tailored to the professional image of the officer and focused on current theatres of operation as Lebanon and the Balkans. But it also provided an opportunity to listen to Herfried Münkler lecturing on Clausewitz and the new wars.[18]

Now, holding such a symposium did not actually belong to the central tasks of the "basic training" for officer cadets. But at the National Defense Academy in Vienna, an increasing devotion to Clausewitz could be observed within the scope of the general staff training.

Although Clausewitz had already been an integral part of the curriculum in lectures on the operational leadership, it was at the end of the seventies and entirely in the eighties when the history of war theory became a central subject of teaching. And the examples of war history which had dominated up to this time and which had been used and reused were gradually stripped from their generic meaning. Instead, the lectures were oriented towards Hahlweg's "Klassiker der Kriegskunst",[19] "Makers of Modern Strategy"[20] published by Peter Paret and the compendium "The Art and Practice of Military Strategy"[21] which was also compulsory for the curriculum at the National Defense University in the US. Clausewitz is extensively addressed in all of these works. In addition, Sun Tsu, Mahan and Herman Kahn were taught. At the Austrian National Defense Academy of course, the "Austrian" cycle with authors as Lazarus Schwendi, Montecuccoli, Archduke Charles of Austria, Maximilian Csicserics, Alfred von Waldstätten, Ludwig von Eimannsberger and others received at least the same attention as international writers. And as a matter of course, this was concluded with Emil Spannocchi. But this was just one chapter of time characterized by the intent to provide a general albeit rather superficial overview.

In the meantime, a noticeable reduction has taken place, while individual military theorists are addressed more intensively. And Clausewitz has gained more and more ground.

Obviously, there were several reasons for this increased attention and interest paid to Clausewitz. First of all, after the disappearance of the threat resulting from a bipolar world order that was definitely considered an eminent danger, a new approach to the theory of war had to be identified, and an adaptation to the new emerging areas of conflict was required. And in this process, the disintegration of states, especially of Yugoslavia, which was seen as a destabilization process, was in the focus rather than peacekeeping missions of the Austrian Armed Forces. Furthermore, and similar as in many other western (and eastern) states, forms of terrorism became a prevalent subject that could not only be empirically analyzed but also opened doors to theoretical and even speculative approaches. In the end, also the consolidation of Austria's policy of neutrality, reaffirmed in 2000, played a role. As if by coincidence, in search of an answer, the Austrian National Defense Academy again bumped into Clausewitz. As so often, also practical reasons came into play. Two general staff officers in succession who were familiar with Clausewitz became commandants of general staff officer courses. One of them was Lieutenant-Colonel (GS) August Reiter who after his general staff training attended the German Bundeswehr academy for a year where he was "fed" with Clausewitz. The other, Lieutenant-Colonel (GS) Sascha Bosezky, attended the German Command and Staff College and was awarded the Clausewitz Certificate for his outstanding work.

It should be mentioned, however, that Reiter's and Bosezky's work was facilitated by a foundation that had been laid before. Already in 2001 during the 16th course at the Austrian National Defense Academy, a quite demanding Clausewitz seminar of several days had been conducted.[22] Some general findings, brought up by Wolfgang Peischel, culminated in the statement: "If the current expert knowledge becomes obsolete quicker and quicker, then it makes less and less sense teaching it to officer cadets. It seems to make much more sense to develop abilities like abstract judgment and to teach expert knowledge 'on the job' immediately before the respective mission." And: "You have to learn to distinguish which lessons should be learned and which not."

This seminar of 2001 became the basis for the 17th and 18th general staff courses. In the last course which ended in 2010, the shift of contents and questions raised was more than evident. "Trattato della guerra" (Montecuccoli) was no longer discussed, instead there were Sun Tsu, Carl von Clausewitz, A. Jomini, Mahan and Corbett, Douhet, Mitchell and Warden, Ma Zedong, Võ Nguyên Giáp, Liddel Hart, Triandaffilov and Richard Simpkin as well as military thinkers addressing Islamism and fundamentalism. Austrian military thinkers and writers were perhaps mentioned, but they were not subjects of the seminar papers.

Despite the variety of authors, Clausewitz was given an essential role which was also underlined by the fact that one course participant could write his military-scientific paper on Carl von Clausewitz's notion of strategy in the light of Kant's critique of reason.[23] The author of this thesis, Alexander Klein, described his approach as a discourse on the conceptual history with the objective of facilitating the understanding of terms as tactics, operations, military strategy and strategy and of precisely illustrating the historical development of these terms. With his interpretation, Klein wanted to improve comprehensibility and readability of Clausewitz by referring to Kant's critique of pure reason. This should be achieved by an equation: The author argues that to Clausewitz, a battle meant the same thing as aesthetics to Immanuel Kant. On the next level, strategy is equated with analytics and politics with dialectics.[24]

Klein defines war as a notion of reason, because the objective of war is to break the enemy's will and thus surpasses the quality of a mere physical application of force. When the consideration of military components by policy and military political consultancy are seen as the consequence of the statement "war is the continuation of policy by other means", then one can tell that this has still not been sufficiently implemented. In Austria, it thus was very obvious that political parties and the government largely ignored possibilities and requirements of the Armed Forces. But in Austria of the seventies and eighties, area defense, which was seen as the point of departure for all military actions, was interpreted in the sense of Clausewitz, because here, the intention was to defend a central area as long as possible or to weaken the conquering forces in a raid-type combat with heavy losses until the political goal of securing the remaining basic sovereignty was achieved. The military however wanted policymakers to act "reasonably" in a military sense. And there were several occasions when this was not the case. Most probably both sides were responsible for the gap between political purpose and military objective.

On a higher level in turn, according to Klein, a war of conquest for exclusively material reasons was unreasonable and bound to fail. "If the political level forgets that it is responsible for breaking the enemy's will, which is only possible, if the war is thought through to the end, then this war cannot be won".[25] Again, this conclusion which Klein primarily connects to Adolf Hitler and the German Wehrmacht but which can also be associated with the US Vietnam syndrome and maybe more recently with the problems in Afghanistan is a modern interpretation of Clausewitz. Of course this is also a dilemma of the people interpreting him: In the end, they are historians, because most conclusions can only be drawn in retrospect and may lead to statements as "here action was taken according to Clausewitz", or "in this case, his postulates were completely ignored." But what if one consequently and consciously follows Clausewitz's postulates and still fails? In this case the element of friction according to Clausewitz's definition just needs to be considered more strongly. The bottom line of Klein's paper is: Clausewitz analyses the political system and correspondingly, studying Clausewitz makes one recognize the actions required for organizing the military in his sense.[26] From a certain point of view, the demand to give the Chief of the General Staff the authorities of a commander with absolute power, as Clausewitz projected it, definitely makes sense. Of course this kind of request is a product of huge optimism or a utopia. Thus the pertinent sections seem like an attempt to give the paper some practical value and to justify the demand for more power for the highest Austrian military through statements by Clausewitz and Kant.

The heritage of Clausewitz cannot only be found within the military or military-owned journals, even if these clearly and obviously are the most dominant and competent actors in this field. Indeed, there are other sectors, in which attempts to implement Clausewitz's theories were made. This of course leads to the vast field of auxiliary constructions. Ludwig Regele for example tried to prove that in the twenties and thirties of the 19th century Habsburg Archduke Johann had built huge fortresses in line with the concepts of Clausewitz.[27] It is only natural that Clausewitz witnessed the Tyrolean uprising and also commented on it, and of course, Archduke Johann was concerned with defense issues and as director of the engineers corps he also felt responsible for the construction of several big fortifications, in particular the one called "Franzensfeste" on the Schabser plateau in the Puster valley in the Tyrolean south. But to conclude that, as opposed to Schlieffen and the younger Moltke, Johann considered defense-based warfare as the better strategy, in line with Clausewitz, and that this was the reason for him to plan and build fortifications, is a little far-fetched. It is very likely that Johann never read a single line of "On War", as to him dealing with military issues was rather a necessity than a passion.

And it also seemed to be unavoidable that even pacifists quoted Clausewitz. An Austrian example for this phenomenon is Paul Wenzel's essay "Die Friedenskunst". Mit Clausewitz' Kriegsregeln den Frieden gewinnen" (The Art of Peace. Winning Peace with Clausewitz's Rules of War).[28] But at this place, this essay shall not be commented any further.

Far more important are the papers written at Austrian universities or by academics. Three observations can be made: Military history and also intellectual discourses on the theory of war have become respected subjects at universities. This and the inclusion of Clausewitz's concepts and theories approximately coincided with his already described reputational gain in the Austrian military environment. It can also be assumed that the applicability of the intellectual discussions' outcomes was not as imperative at the universities as within the military.

However, at least a part of the substance offered in teaching and scientific writing does not qualify as the pure doctrine: rather it is the sum of read and analyzed contents. There are empiric studies, essays on Clausewitz's biography or – most common – attempts to link and explain modern conflicts with Clausewitz. But first, let us stick to the facts:

At the University of Innsbruck, a guide for students, journalists, civil servants, and other people interested in the "basics on the changing faces of war and its manifestations" was composed that dealt with Mao, Che Guevara and also with Clausewitz.[29] This deliberately small-sized volume by Irene Etzersdorfer addresses the changeability of war. So the statement "war is a chameleon" is nothing new.

She argues that at the beginning of modern times, war was "nationalized". Today, new forms of the condotta, asymmetrical wars, have replaced state-on-state wars. Where the state is weak, the political power shifts from the state to the people. The words on Clausewitz seem to be an introduction rather than an interpretation. And whether he is in appropriate company might be questioned as well.[30]

A philosophical diploma thesis on Clausewitz, approbated at the University of Klagenfurt, is even shorter and also has little substance[31]. It is limited to just a few quotes on war as the continuation of national policy, on war as the advanced form of the duel, limitation of force and their absence and on the phenomenon of friction. At the end, the author briefly concludes that the observations and analysis on war made by Carl von Clausewitz – even if more than 200 years old – are still valid today.[32] You don't have to write a diploma thesis to realize this.

Much more important than the mentioned attempts at the subject is Christian Stadler's essay on Clausewitz in the volume "Krieg" (War) which addresses fundamentals and contains a profound and inspiring interpretation of the 1st book, even if only of a few key sentences.[33] It certainly contains concrete facts and is a philosophical essay which does not digress to modern armies or the Austrian Bundesheer. It deals with the notion and nature of politics which are characterized by being made by free "and on principle responsible creatures" that are "diametrically opposed or even hostile to each other". The political purpose, however, is often obstructed by the focus on the military strategic goal. Stadler sees the tendency to perceive war as absolute as a warning, and the apparent general removal of limitations as dangerous error. Making the enemy defenceless was always the primary goal. But in the end, the masses will "determine the nature of politics". With this, Stadler probably has arrived in the 20th or even 21st century.

Beyond interpretations of Clausewitz written by philosophers and political scientists, it is still the historians who provide a useful approach for research. Unfortunately, historians too often tend to draw on monocausal explanations. Whether this makes sense or not must be decided on a case-by-case basis. But this approach is still more plausible than a superficial presentation of some of Clausewitz's thoughts and can be used to project great historic decisions and processes onto one or more central statements of Clausewitz. In this context, the works of Martin Müller should be mentioned who started with a diploma thesis on the Austro-Hungarian warfare against Italy and later wrote a dissertation on the Austro-German offensive in Italy of October and November 1917 and the Michael offensive in France in 1918. Clausewitz is only mentioned when the author refers to the dual terminological concepts of Clausewitz as the main emphasis was on strategy and tactics. The limited terminological concepts were not important for the dissertation, but the word "annihilation" became the pivot of the paper. The concept of annihilation was the focal point of Martin Müller's thesis and he subsequently, even if not necessarily, added the subtitle "Eine Clausewitz-Studie" (A study on Clausewitz).[34]

He might have done this to allude that - at least for the mentioned offensives - Clausewitz would have come into play. But neither the offensive in Italy in 1917 nor the one at the German western front in 1918 were meant to be test exercises for the strategies and tactics described by Clausewitz in his books. Only in retrospect one could draw conclusions to the extent that some ideas might be in line with Clausewitz's concepts or the offensive was based on the concept of annihilation. But this can be said about any major offensive during the war, and this would apply to the thinking not only of German general staff officers, but also of the Entente Powers and the US Forces which at that time had more or less consequently followed the tradition of Jomini. Without any doubt, annihilation was the military goal. And irrespective of where this desire for a devastating victory was rooted: According to the "Dogma of the Battle of Annihilation" (Jehuda Wallach) the consequence must be something like a nuclear holocaust.

Finally, the Canetti Symposium in Vienna at the end of 2004 is worthwhile mentioning.[35] Starting out from Canetti's „Masse und Macht" (Mass and Power), among others, Thomas Macho, Martin von Creveld, Lutz Unterseher and Ulrike Kleemeier gave their presentations. The latter dwelled on the topic: "Das Denken des Krieges. Überlegungen zu Clausewitz" (Reasoning of War. Thoughts on Clausewitz). Thus, the organizer stuck to an established and proven pattern: When discussing Clausewitz, it is always advisable to include German scientists in the debate, especially someone like Ms. Kleemeier, because they always give fresh impetus to the debate. And this closes the circle back to Werner Hahlweg.

The fact that until the sixties of the 20th century, a Clausewitz reception was non-existent in Austria because he was ignored until then resulted in Hahlweg having to make something like a new start. This is why a Clausewitz renaissance was neither possible nor necessary. Actually Clausewitz continuously gained in importance. And this not through indisputable pontifications as is sometimes the case in ecclesiastical history, but in a much simpler and more basic way: Clausewitz is being read, received and interpreted. Hence, he is more than a fixed star in a galaxy of quotes. Fifty years ago, this was unthinkable.

Notes:

[1] Clausewitz, „Österreich und die preußische Heeresreform 1807-1812" in: *Landesverteidigung. Österreichische Militärische Zeitschrift*, 2nd year (1962), pp. 83 - 88. Revised version of a lecture held within the scope of the Austrian Military Society in Vienna on 18 October 1960.

[2] Werner Hahlweg, „Militärwesen und Philosophie. Zur Genesis der methodischen Grundlagen des Werkes ‚Vom Kriege' des Generals von Clausewitz" in: *Österreichische Militärische Zeitschrift*, issue 5/1976, pp. 395-398; „Philosophie und Militärtheorie im Denken und in den Aufzeichnungen des Generals von Clausewitz" in: *Österreichische Militärische Zeitschrift*, issue 1/1988, pp. 31-35.

[3] Manfried Rauchensteiner, „Zum ‚operativen Denken' in Österreich 1814 bis 1914" in *Österreichische Militärische Zeitschrift,* issue 2/1974, pp. 121-127; issue 3/1974, pp. 207-211; issue 4/1974, pp. 285-291; issue 5/1974, pp. 379-384; issue 6/1974, pp. 473-478 and 1/1975, pp. 46-53; „Zum ‚operativen Denken' in Österreich 1918-1938 in: *Österreichische Militärische Zeitschrift,* issue 2/1978, pp. 107-116.

[4] The presentations of the conference on Clausewitz, Jomini, Erzherzog Carl were published by Gesellschaft für politisch-strategische Studien (Vienna), by Clausewitz-Gesellschaft e.V. and by Landesverteidigungsakademie in Vienna in 1988.

[5] Frederick Engels, "Mountain Warfare in the Past and Present" in *New York Daily Tribune,* MECW Volume 15, p. 164.

[6] „Grundsätze der höheren Kriegskunst für die Generäle der österreichischen Armee, Vienna 1806" in: *Ausgewählte Schriften weiland seiner kaiserlichen Hoheit des Erzherzogs Carl*, vol. 1, Wien 1893, pp. 1-85.

[7] Archduke Charles of Austria, „Grundsätze der Strategie, erläutert durch die Darstellung des Feldzuges von 1796 in Deutschland, 1. Teil" in *Ausgewählte Schriften*, vol. 1, pp. 221-343. (Part 2, Ausgewählte Schriften Bd. 2, fills the entire volume, but only covers the story of the campaign).

[8] Issue 6/1964, pp. 409-414.

[9] *Österreichische Militärische Zeitschrift*, issue 2/1988, pp. 139-143.

[10] *Österreichische Militärische Zeitschrift* , issue 3/1990, pp. 229 f.

[11] „Vom künftigen Kriege. Zur Clausewitz-Rezeption der amerikanischen Streitkräfte" (On Future War. On the Reception of Clausewitz in the US Forces) in: *Österreichische Militärische Zeitschrift*, issue 2/2004, pp. 181-186.

[12] *Österreichische Militärische Zeitschrift*, issue 3/1994, pp. 253-258.

[13] Subtitle: Im Spiegel der Lehre des Generals Carl von Clausewitz, Neckenmarkt 2007.

[14] Eva Strickmann, *Clausewitz im Zeitalter der neuen Kriege: Der Krieg in Ruanda (1990- 1994) im Spiegel der „wunderlichen Dreifaltigkeit"*, Glienicke 2008.

[15] Markus Stiebellehner, *Krieg und Konflikt im Rahmen der klassischen Staatenkonzeption sowie unter besonderer Berücksichtigung der Theorie von Carl von Clausewitz*. Diplomarbeit Militärische Führung (Diploma thesis), Wiener Neustadt 2001.

[16] Gustav E. Gustenau, Zum Begriff des bewaffneten Konfliktes, in: *Österreichische Militärische Zeitschrift*, issue 1/1992, p. 48f.

[17] Stiebellehner, *Sicherheit als prioritäre Staatsaufgabe*, p. 81.

[18] Printed in: Armis et litteris 18: *Beiträge zum modernen Kriegsbegriff*, ed. by Theresianische Militärakademie, Wiener Neustadt 2001, pp. 155-168.

[19] *Klassiker der Kriegskunst*, ed. by Werner Hahlweg, Darmstadt 1960.

[20] *Makers of Modern Strategy from Machiavelli to the Nuclear Age*, ed. by Peter Paret with collaboration of Gordon A. Craig and Felix Gilbert, New Jersey 1986.

[21] Ed. by George Edward Thibault, Washington D.C. 1984.

[22] I would like to thank Brigadier August Reiter very much for providing the seminar documents. I would also like to express my gratitude to Brigadier Reiter and Leutenant-Colonel Bosezky who took the time for extensive talks with me.

[23] *Strategie und System. Der Strategiebegriff bei Carl von Clausewitz im Lichte der Kantischen Vernunftkritik*. Military-scientific paper, 18th general staff officer course, also diploma thesis at the faculty „Grund- und Integrativwissenschaftliche Fakultät" of the University of Vienna, 2010.

[24] Klein, *Strategie und System*, pp. 126-143.

[25] *Ibid*, p. 154.

[26] *Ibid*, p. 165f.

[27] Ludwig Regele, Erzherzog Johann, „Carl von Clausewitz und das Festungswesen" (Archduke Johann, Carl von Clausewitz and Fortifications) in *Der*

Schlern. Monatszeitschrift für Südtiroler Landeskunde, 75th year, issue 4, Bozen 2001, pp. 237-248. (Monthly Review of South-Tyrolean Regional Studies)

[28] Ed. St. Michael (Stmk) 1982.

[29] Irene Etzersdorfer, *Krieg.* (War) *Eine Einführung in die Theorien bewaffneter Konflikte*, Wien-Köln-Weimar 2007. (An Introduction into the Theories of Armed Conflicts)

[30] See: Critique by Martin Meier in *Militärgeschichtliche Zeitschrift*, 68th year (1968), issue 1, p. 135f.

[31] Stèphan Martin Binder, *Clausewitz und seine Folgen.* (The Aftermath of Clausewitz), Diploma thesis Universtiy of Klagenfurt, 2004.

[32] Even the corrector of the paper seemed to have overlooked the incorrect dates and grammatical mistakes (of the German thesis).

[33] Christian Stadler, *Krieg* (Grundbegriffe der europäischen Geistesgeschichte, ed. Konrad Paul Liessmann), Wien 2009, p. 76-85.

[34] Martin Müller, *Vernichtungsgedanke und Koalitionskriegführung.* (The Concept of Annihilation and Coalition Warfare). *Das Deutsche Reich und Österreich-Ungarn in der Offensive 1917/1918. Eine Clausewitz-Studie*, Graz 2003. (The German Empire and the Austro-Hungarian Empire in the 1917-18 Offensive: A Study on Clausewitz. Published in German)

[35] Krieg. Die unentrinnbare Doppelmasse. Referate auf dem 17. Internationalen Kulturanthropologisch-Philosophischen Canetti-Symposion, 4th-7th November 2004, ed. John D. Pattillo-Hess, Vienna 2005. (Papers delivered at the 17th International Canetti Symposium in Vienna).

TAILORING ENDS TO MEANS: CLAUSEWITZ IN BELGIUM

Bruno Colson and Christophe Wasinski

Clausewitz was in Belgium for the last Napoleonic campaigns. To his beloved wife Marie von Brühl he wrote letters from Hasselt, Tournai, Aalst, and Oudenaarde in 1814, from Bastogne and Ciney in 1815. He said his admiration for the towns, the gothic churches, the city hall of Leuven and Brussels' park[1]. Although this book is not about the Napoleonic wars, it is not without some interest to note the physical presence of Clausewitz on the Belgian battlefields of 1815, at Ligny and Wavre. As far as the reception of Clausewitz's works in Belgium is concerned, it has only been touched in a general way[2]. The first French translation of *Vom Kriege* was made by an officer of the Belgian Army, where the only official language was French in the 19th century[3]. Belgian military thought between 1830 and 1914 has not been thoroughly explored yet but we know that the first French book substantially devoted to Clausewitz was also by a Belgian officer, Charles de Savoye[4].

If there was a specific and enduring Belgian view of Clausewitz, it was built by the later General Emile Galet, who was the classmate and the personal adviser of King Albert I. In 1913-1914 he was professor at the War College in Brussels. Thinking about the difficult strategic position of a small neutral country between two great powers in a context of rising tensions, he developed what he called a principle: "*the proportionality existing between the means or forces one can rely upon and the aim one has in view*"[5]. Galet relied upon the following sentence from *Vom Kriege*: "*A prince or general who knows exactly how to organise his war according to his object and means, who does neither too little nor too much, gives by that the greatest proof of his genius*"[6]. In his recollections of the 1914 campaign, Galet repeated this sentence to explain the conduct of King Albert at the head of the Belgian Army and it was the only quotation he made from Clausewitz in this book[7]. In his course at the War College, Galet gave another quotation around the same theme, this time with the example of Frederick the Great of Prussia[8]. In a third quotation, Galet slightly modified the text by saying that "*it is very difficult in the present state of Europe, for the most talented general to gain a victory over an enemy equal his strength*". Clausewitz had written "*double his strength*"[9].

Galet's reading of Clausewitz formed the cornerstone of Belgian strategy during the First World War. As commander in chief, Albert I managed to keep his small army in being and refused to participate in the murderous offensives of the Allied powers until there was a clear prospect of success. In the fall of 1918 he committed his army to the final and victorious attack. In 1919 Galet, now a lieutenant colonel, was nominated at the head of the Royal Military Academy. In 1926, as a general, he became Chief of Staff of the Army. His ideas had been vindicated by the First World War and they formed the backbone of a specific Belgian school of strategy. Generals Prudent Nuyten and Raoul Van Overstraeten were his pupils and his followers, the second one becoming the military adviser of King Leopold III as Galet had been the one of Albert I[10]. After the Second World War, this school of thought persisted in the teaching of Henri Bernard, a former officer and resistant, whose lessons in military history printed their mark on several generations of Belgian officers. For Bernard, the first principle of military art was the one of *"proportionality of means and ends"*[11]. Napoleon had failed to conform to it in the Waterloo campaign. To trace Clausewitz's reading in Belgium in the 21st century, we will consider first the military teaching at the Royal Military Academy[12]. We will then turn to civilian universities with programmes in history and political science. Finally there will be a survey of current research and publications, military and civilian.

At the Royal Military Academy (RMA), Clausewitz appears mainly in the course entitled *"History of the art of war till 1945"*; currently hold by Professor Luc De Vos. This course is divided into three parts: *"Introduction to the history of modern wars"*, *"The First World War"* and *"The Second World War"*. The teaching is given, in Dutch as well as in French, in the second year of bachelor in social and military sciences. A substantial part of it is devoted to the main military thinkers. Luc De Vos clearly states in his introduction that his course owes much to the ones given by his predecessors Raoul Van Overstraeten, Henri Bernard and Jean-Léon Charles[13]. The vision of Clausewitz is thus in the national tradition established by Galet but it is also more elaborated than what we mentioned earlier. In a first chapter devoted to theory, concepts and definitions, Clausewitz is given with Jomini as a co-founder of the widely spread *"principles and rules of the military art"*. It is true that Clausewitz, mainly through his teaching to the crown prince of Prussia, was hold as a believer in rules and in some regards contributed to some of the basic statements about war. But he certainly would have rejected his association with sets of rules and principles.

His main objective in writing *Vom Kriege* was precisely to deride the ones who like Jomini believed in such firm and immutable rules[14]. The end of the page reveals the origin of this vision of Clausewitz as it mentions explicitly the transmission of Galet's ideas about Clausewitz through Van Overstraeten and Bernard to the present and the establishment of rules and principles like the one about the proportionality of means and ends. This principle is indeed given as the first one to be observed and this is clearly the Belgian tradition which goes on. De Vos elaborates around it and stresses, besides the question of numbers, other factors such as logistics, the quality of training, time, space, command and the will to fight. Non military aspects also matter, especially the economy and politics. Irrationality can also supersede rationality[15].

The section about military thinkers naturally devotes some pages to Clausewitz. As in the preceding section, he is associated with Jomini. One must never forget that the latter was much earlier studied in military academies, including the Belgian one, and there appears to be still a remnant of this privileged position. Although this section wrongly denies the intellectual relationship between the two thinkers, who actually read their mutual books and cited each other more than once, it rightly stresses their differences of approach. For Clausewitz, moral forces were of primary importance in war. Struck by the example of Napoleon, he advocated the necessity to concentrate on the destruction of the armed forces of the enemy without secondary moves, even if there was a human price to pay. Clausewitz is modern, says De Vos, because he put war within the wider context of the evolution of politics and society[16]. This section on military thinkers relies quite rightly upon the classical syntheses of Michael Handel and Peter Paret, mentioned in the bibliography[17].

Clausewitz comes back in chapter II, devoted to the evolution of the waging of war in the western world. As the philosopher Johann Fichte, he noticed the evolution of war to a more violent form, due to the growing implication of the population. The march began towards what would be called "*total war*" by General Erich Ludendorff after the First World War[18]. In chapter IV, "*War, propaganda and the media*", Clausewitz is quoted to show that the achievement of surprise, an essential component of strategy, needs a blackout on information. But he also insisted on the support of public opinion and was particularly aware of the moral effect of victory or defeat[19]. Students at the RMA can meet Clausewitz again in their 1st and 2nd years of master in social and military sciences. An optional "*Introduction to Strategic Studies*" presents a more in-depth analysis of classical strategic thinkers. A special attention is given to what is still relevant for understanding recent wars. The validity of Clausewitz's concepts is tested in relation to present-day conflicts. As Clausewitz advocated, the future officer is invited to think by himself in a critical way before taking a decision[20]. Besides the *Masters of War* by M. Handel mentioned earlier, the bibliography of the course includes recent titles in English and French[21].

Clausewitz could also be met at the Advanced Staff Course of the Royal Military Academy. This one year formation is given by military and civilian professors on six modules (world politics, strategic studies, Belgian foreign and security policy, collective defence and security, geopolitics, and strategic analytical model) to already experienced officers[22]. The name of Clausewitz is firstly mentioned in the world politics module to highlight the connexion of war as a continuation of politics. Students could also meet Clausewitz in more specialized lectures, depending on the service they are part of. For the Land Component, after a formation at the US Army Command and General Staff Course, Major Steven Van Den Bogaert has decided to insist on the importance of Clausewitz in his Belgian lectures[23]. The thinking of Clausewitz is seen as more relevant than the "Jominian approach" to grasp the current and complex dynamics of warfare. Concerning the air component, Dr. Joseph Henrotin has been asked to provide lectures on contemporary airpower theories and concepts[24]. When mentioned in these lectures, Clausewitz is considered as particularly relevant to underline the importance of the fog of war, in spite of the proliferation of electronic technologies supposed to reduce it to its minimum level in air warfare. Dr. Joseph Henrotin also considers the possibility to adapt the Clausewitzian trinity in order to add technology as a fourth dimension to it.

One must also acknowledge that the various military libraries are rather well furnished regarding Clausewitz. Numerous editions of his works in German, French, Dutch, English and also studies on Clausewitz can be found at the documentation centres of the Royal Army Museum, of the RMA in Brussels and at the Central Library of the Ministry of Defence at Evere, close to NATO headquarters. These libraries can easily be used by university fellows, as the authors of these lines can attest. University libraries are also rich in Clausewitz's writings, especially the French translations. This is not so much the case as far as recent studies on Clausewitz are concerned. To conclude, Clausewitz seems to be widely known among the Belgian officers and his books are frequently borrowed in military libraries[25]. Some officers are said to be intensive readers of his work and even to go back to it again and again before operational departure. On the other hand, it also seemed that Clausewitzciting is sometimes lived as a compulsory attitude aimed at marking the belonging to a social group. Not much better, sometimes Clausewitz is also said to be quoted when an officer is lacking relevant ideas in his/her speech.

Now, let's turn towards the Belgian academic education. Clausewitz is sometimes mentioned during lectures on introduction to political science or on security studies in several Belgian universities[26]. In the field of International Relations, one must especially take into consideration the course "*Stratégie et sécurité internationale*" by Michel Liégeois at the University of Louvain[27]. In this course, Michel Liégeois discusses, among other Clausewitzian concepts, the primacy of politics, the trinity and the culminating point. His teaching also compares Clausewitz with Sun Zi and makes use of the works of B.H. Liddell Hart, Edward N. Luttwak and Martin van Creveld to illustrate the debates concerning the evolution of strategy. The teaching in military history at the University of Namur, the only one among the Belgian universities, should then be mentioned. It is of course less developed than at the RMA in terms of hours of teaching. It matters for three European credits transfer system (ECTS) in place of six at the RMA. Optional for students in their 3rd year of Bachelor in History, the course is entitled "*War and Strategy in Late Modern History*" and is given in French by Professor Bruno Colson[28]. One of the first aims is to induce students to do research in military history. Main archival sources and major secondary works are presented, with case studies taken from the late modern history of Belgium (1792-1945). One hour is devoted to Clausewitz in the chapter about the evolution of strategic thinking from 1815 to 1914. Current debates between academic historians and political scientists about Clausewitz are mentioned. As this course is new, the comments of political scientists could in the future be located in the course of "*History of Political Ideas*", now given by Christophe Wasinski who also speaks about Clausewitz to students in Political Science (3rd year of Bachelor).

Research and publications on Clausewitz are more numerous in the French-speaking part of Belgium and are most of the time made in close cooperation with French colleagues and publishers. Besides his article on the first French translation of *Vom Kriege*, Bruno Colson has organized an exhibition at the University of Namur on military thinking from Machiavelli to Clausewitz, with an illustrated guide book[29]. He is familiar with Clausewitz not only since his 1986 article but also since his first doctoral dissertation which was about Jomini's reception in the United States[30]. As he specialized in military thinking in and about the Napoleonic wars, he mentioned Clausewitz in several publications[31]. He published three articles devoted to him, one of them being the text of his intervention at the Clausewitz conference organized at Saint-Cyr-Coëtquidan in October 2007[32]. As a member of the editorial board of the journal *War in History*, he wrote a review article about recent books on Clausewitz[33]. His current research includes a *Napoleon's On War*, regrouping with due reference to their origin the various sentences of Napoleon on war, following the books and chapters of Clausewitz's magnum opus[34]. Another book is in progress on the battle of Ligny, June 16, 1815, with the under-title *Napoleon versus Clausewitz*. This battle was indeed one of the four major ones where Clausewitz was physically facing the Emperor and the only one of them where he was wearing a Prussian uniform.

Christophe Wasinski began researching on Clausewitz for his master's thesis at Brussels' University. His work assessed the influence of Clausewitz in the United States from 1945 until 1999[35]. Then, he extended his interest to other strategic authors in order to complete a doctoral dissertation about the representation of self and other in strategic thinking. The published the results of this dissertation, however, he took some distance with the current opinions concerning Clausewitz[36]. The researches done on Clausewitz since the 1970s have had the tendency to transform him into an intellectual hero. As it is argued in some passages of Wasinski's book, it would also be wise to reconsider Clausewitz not only as completely exceptional but also, under some lights, as representative of purely classical strategic thinking[37].

Bruno Colson and Christophe Wasinski are also members of the "Réseau multidisciplinaire d'études stratégiques" or RMES (Multidisciplinary Network in Strategic Studies)[38]. Other members of this network, that brings together civilian scholars from different French-speaking universities or from the Royal Military Academy and the Royal High Institute for Defence, have shown a great interest for Clausewitz. This is for example the case in the writings of Joseph Henrotin (see also above), the head of the editorial team of the French magazine *Défense et Sécurité Internationale*. Although not directly dedicated to Clausewitz, most of the books of Joseph Henrotin make use of numerous concepts inherited from the Prussian officer[39]. This is also the case of some texts written by other members of the network, like Alain De Nève and Tanguy Struye de Swielande[40].

In another category are the books of Thierry Derbent[41]. Published by the independent Aden editions, they strongly focus on the connexions between Clausewitz, Marxism and revolutionary warfare. Derbent is particularly interested by the socialist-communist genealogy of Clausewitz: Ernesto "Che" Guevara, Vo Nguyen Giap and Lenin. Actually, it must be said that Derbent is a pseudonym for Bertrand Sassoye, a former active member of the Belgian Communist Combatant Cells (CCC). Sassoye and other members of the CCC were responsible for several bombings in the mid-eighties. He was released in 2000 after having been detained fourteen and an half years in jail[42]. Lastly, and far less sulphurous, are two books published in Brussels by the Editions Complexe in 1987. The first one was a reprint of the translation of Clausewitz's 1812 campaign in Russia and the second one a volume gathering Raymond Aron's articles on Clausewitz[43].

In conclusion, Belgium is certainly a place where Clausewitz is present, as he was in 1814 and 1815. At the centre of the European Union, Belgian military and university institutions are open to intellectual debate in other countries, especially in France, Britain and the United States. As such, members of their research communities contribute to the international publications and conferences about the great Prussian thinker, albeit modestly due to the dimensions of Belgium. Another problem is the specific Belgian view on and use of Clausewitz in the 21st century. As the teaching at the RMA can testify, the traditional accent on proportionality between ends and means, taken from Clausewitz by Galet, is still relevant. As it contributes to NATO military operations in Afghanistan, Belgium measures its commitment to what it estimates possible. This is truly common sense and one could say there is no need for Clausewitz in this regard. But Clausewitz has always been cited as an intellectual authority and the insistence of the Belgian government on its limited means was already frequent during the Cold War, as it was stressed by King Albert I during the First World War. Open to the reading of Clausewitz and to the necessary burden-sharing with its allies, Belgium still retains the Clausewitzian lesson that to exist politically a country cannot commit too much of its military forces to the same theatre of war.

Notes:

[1] *Karl und Marie von Clausewitz: Ein Lebensbild in Briefen und Tagebuchblättern*, ed. Karl Linnebach, Berlin, Martin Warneck, 1925, pp. 367, 369, 371, 373, 375; Clausewitz (C. von), *Schriften, Aufsätze, Studien, Briefe*, ..., ed. Werner Hahlweg, I, Göttingen, Vandenhoeck und Ruprecht, 1966 and II in 2 vol., 1990, II-2, p. 177-179.

[2] Jean-Michel Sterkendries, "Clausewitz et la pensée militaire belge", *Actas. XVII Congreso internacional de ciencias históricas*, Madrid, International Commission of Military History, II, 1990, pp. 173-179.

[3] Bruno Colson, "La première traduction française du *Vom Kriege* de Clausewitz et sa diffusion dans les milieux militaires français et belge avant 1914", *Revue belge d'Histoire militaire*, 26, 1986-5, pp. 345-364.

[4] Charles de Savoye, *Règlement sur le service des armées en campagne annoté d'après les meilleurs auteurs qui ont écrit sur l'art militaire*, 2^d ed., Paris, Dumaine, 1866; Benoît Durieux, *Clausewitz en France. Deux siècles de réflexion sur la guerre 1807-2007*, Paris, Institut de Stratégie comparée (ISC)-Collège interarmées de Défense (CID)-Fondation Saint-Cyr-Economica, 2008, pp. 71-73.

[5] Musée royal de l'armée, Brussels (MRA), A 16 184, Ecole de guerre, Cours de tactique [stratégie] du commandant Galet, 1913, p. 6.

[6] [Clausewitz], *Hinterlassene Werke des Generals Carl von Clausewitz über Krieg und Kriegführung*, 10 vol., Berlin, Dümmler, 1832-1837, I, p. 198 (*Vom Kriege*, book III, chapter 1); english version from *On War*, ed. J.J. Graham, London, Trübner, 1873.
(http://www.clausewitz.com/readings/OnWar1873/BK3ch01.html).

[7] Emile Galet, *S.M. le roi Albert commandant en chef devant l'invasion allemande*, Paris, Plon, 1931, p. 85.

[8] MRA, A 16 184, Cours de tactique [stratégie] du commandant Galet, 1913, p. 19.

[9] *Ibid.*, p. 30; [Clausewitz], *Hinterlassene Werke*, I, p. 231 (*Vom Kriege*, book III, chapter 8
(http://www.clausewitz.com/readings/OnWar1873/BK3ch08.html).

[10] J.-M. Sterkendries, "Clausewitz et la pensée militaire belge", p. 176.

[11] Henri Bernard, *La campagne de 1815 en Belgique ou la faillite de la liaison et des transmissions*, with maps, Brussels, Imprimerie médicale et scientifique, 1954, pp. 3 and 75.

[12] We thank Luc De Vos, Jean-Michel Sterkendries and Alain De Nève for the information provided on the RMA curriculum.

[13] Luc De Vos, *Introduction à l'histoire des guerres modernes*, Brussels, RMA, 2008-2009, p. 4.

[14] *Ibid.*, p. 14. This page also mistakenly says that Clausewitz served for a time in the Austrian Army.

[15] *Ibid.*, p. 15.

[16] *Ibid.*, pp. 31-32.

[17] Michael I. Handel, *Masters of War: Sun Tzu, Clausewitz and Jomini*, London, Frank Cass, 1992; Peter Paret, ed., *Makers of Modern Strategy from Machiavelli to the Nuclear Age*, Oxford, Clarendon Press, 1986.

[18] L. De Vos, *Introduction*, p. 98.

[19] *Ibid.*, p. 143.

[20] http://cost.rma.ac.be/index.php?option=com_content&view=article&id=85&Itemid=3&lang=fr

[21] John Baylis, *Strategy in the Contemporary World: An Introduction to Strategic Studies*, Oxford, Oxford University Press, 2006; Hervé Coutau-Bégarie, *Traité de stratégie*, 5ᵉ éd., Paris, ISC-Economica, 2006 (forthcoming translation by Oxford University Press); Rupert Smith, *The Utility of Force*, London, Penguin Books, 2006.

[22] See general description provided on:

http://cost.rma.ac.be/index.php?option=com_content&view=article&id=42&Itemid=13&lang=en.

[23] Personal email from Major Alain Vanhee, Monday, August 23, 2010.

[24] Joseph Henrotin, *L'airpower au 21ᵉ siècle: enjeux et perspectives de la stratégie aérienne*, Brussels, Bruylant, 2005.

[25] Anonymous comments collected in August 2010.

[26] Personal emails from Thierry Balzacq (concerning his Introduction to Political Science at the University of Namur, FUNDP), February 16, 2010 and from Tom Sauer (concerning his lectures on International Security at the University of Antwerp), February 11, 2010. Phone conversation with André Dumoulin (concerning his lectures on Security Theories at the University of Liège), August 16, 2010. Barbara Delcourt, Lecturer on Security Theories at the University of Brussels, added that she decided to drop the reference to avoid limiting herself to a familiarly mundane speech concerning Clausewitz (personal email, February 11, 2010).

[27] Personal email from Michel Liégeois, February 15, 2010. M. Liégois, *Stratégie et sécurité internationale*, UCL, Louvain-la-Neuve, 2009-2010, especially pp. 36-63.

[28] The expression in French is "époque contemporaine" which is larger than "contemporary history" as it begins with the French Revolution in 1789.

[29] B. Colson, *L'art de la guerre de Machiavel à Clausewitz dans les collections de la Bibliothèque universitaire Moretus Plantin*, Namur, Presses universitaires de Namur, 1999.

[30] B. Colson, *La culture stratégique américaine. L'influence de Jomini*, Paris, Fondation pour les Etudes de Défense nationale-Economica, 1993.

[31] B. Colson, "Camon ou l'exégète de Napoléon" in Hubert Camon, *La guerre napoléonienne. Les systèmes d'opérations, théorie et technique*, Paris, ISC-Economica, 1997, pp. 5-17; abridged edition of Antoine-Henri Jomini, *Précis de l'art de la guerre*, Paris, Perrin, 2001; *Le général Rogniat, ingénieur et critique de Napoléon*, Paris, ISC-Economica, 2006; "Austerlitz vu par les stratèges et les tacticiens", in *Austerlitz. Napoléon au cœur de l'Europe*, Musée de l'Armée-ISC-Economica, 2007, pp. 371-405; "La place et la nature de la manœuvre dans l'art de la guerre napoléonien", in Christian Malis (ed.), *Guerre et manœuvre. Héritages et renouveau*, Paris, Economica-Fondation Saint-Cyr, 2009, pp. 118-140.

[32] B. Colson, "La stratégie américaine de sécurité et la critique de Clausewitz", in *Stratégique*, 76, 1999-4, pp. 151-164; "Perché è importante leggere Clausewitz", *Contemporanea. Rivista di storia dell'800 e del'900* (Universita di Bologna), XI-2, April 2008, pp. 301-305; "Clausewitz, le retour d'expérience et l'histoire", in Laure Bardiès and Martin Motte (ed.), *De la guerre ? Clausewitz et la pensée stratégique contemporaine*, Paris, ISC-Ecoles de Saint-Cyr Coëtquidan-Fondation Saint-Cyr-Economica, 2008, pp. 349-359.

[33] "Clausewitz for Every War. Review Article", forthcoming in *War in History*. Books under review include: Antulio J. Echevarria, *Clausewitz and Contemporary War*, Oxford University Press, 2007; Andreas Herberg-Rothe, *Clausewitz's Puzzle: The Political Theory of War*, Oxford University Press, 2007; Hew Strachan, *Carl von Clausewitz's On War. A Biography*, Atlantic Books, 2007; Hew Strachan and Andreas Herberg-Rothe (ed.), *Clausewitz in the Twenty-First Century*, Oxford University Press, 2007; Benoît Durieux, *Clausewitz en France. Deux siècles de réflexion sur la guerre 1807-2007*, Economica, 2008; Peter Paret, *The Cognitive Challenge of War: Prussia 1806*, Princeton University Press, 2009.

[34] Written in French, the book is going to be published in the year 2011.

[35] Christophe Wasinski, *Clausewitz et le discours stratégique américain de 1945 à nos jours*, Paris, ISC-Les Stratégiques (electronic document available on www.stratisc.org/CW_TDM.htm). See also: Id., "Paradigme clausewitzien et discours stratégique aux Etats-Unis 1945-1999" in *Stratégique*, 78-79, 2000-2/3, pp. 75-119; Id., "Culture stratégique, dispositifs rhétoriques et concepts clausewitziens dans la pensée stratégique américaine", in Laure Bardiès et Martin Motte (ed.), *op. cit.*, pp. 43-72.

[36] Id., *Rendre la guerre possible: la construction du sens commun stratégique*, Bruxelles, Peter Lang, 2010.

[37] *Ibid.*, pp. 122-124.

[38] See: www.rmes.be

[39] Joseph Henrotin (ed.), *Au risque du chaos: leçons politiques et stratégiques de la guerre d'Irak*, Paris, Armand Colin, 2004; *L'airpower au 21ᵉ siècle (op. cit.)*; *La technologie militaire en question: le cas de l'armée américaine*, Paris, Economica, 2008; *La résilience dans l'antiterrorisme: le dernier bouclier*, Paris, L'Esprit du Livre, 2010.

[40] Alain De Nève and Joseph Henrotin, "La *Network Centric Warfar*: de son développement à *Iraqi Freedom*" in *Stratégique*, 86-87, March 2006, pp. 53-76; Tanguy Struye de Swielande, "L'asymétrie instrumentale et ontologico-stratégique dans l'après guerre froide", *Arès*, vol. XXI, n° 54, October 2004, pp. 107-115.

[41] Thierry Derbent, *Clausewitz et la guerre populaire*, Brussels, Aden, 2004 and *Giap et Clausewitz*, Brussels, Aden, 2006.

[42] R.P., "Bertrand Sassoye, l'illuminé sincère'", *La Libre Belgique*, June 6, 2008. (www.lalibre.be/actu/belgique/article/425977/bertrand-sassoye-l-illumine-sincere.html); Marc Metdepenningen, "Bertand Sassoye instruit les militaires de Saint-Cyr", *Le Soir*, June 26, 2008 (//archives.lesoir.be/bertrand-sassoye-instruit-les-militaires-de-saint-cyr_t-20080626-00GP41.html).

[43] Clausewitz, *La campagne de 1812 en Russie*, introd. by Gérard Chaliand, Brussels, Complexe, 1987; Raymond Aron, *Sur Clausewitz*, introd. by Pierre Hassner, Brussels, Complexe, 1987.

THE WESTERN MASTER AND BIBLE OF WAR: CLAUSEWITZ AND HIS "*ON WAR*" IN CHINA
Yu Tiejun

Introduction

Since Clausewitz's *On War* was published in 1832, it has been translated into many languages such as English, French, Japanese, Russian, and Chinese, etc., and circulated widely around the world, greatly impacting the world's military history. It is exactly one hundred years ago when Clausewitz was first introduced into China. Ever since then, Clausewitz was generally regarded as the most famous Western military thinker and *On War* was viewed as the cannon of Western military science, no matter it is at the times of the Republic of China or People's Republic of China. Though the times have changed a lot, and the Revolution of Military Affairs (RMA) is overwhelmingly sweeping China as in other countries, Clausewitz and his *On War* still holds an indispensable position in the Chinese military thinking, education, strategic planning and policy implementation.

This chapter will first examine the history of Clausewitz being introduced into China, and then analyze the role that Clausewitz plays in the formation of Mao Zedong's military thought which is still a dominant and orthodoxy framework and an essential part of the current military strategic thinking in China. In the following part, I will discuss Clausewitz and *On War* in contrast to Sun Tzu and *the Art of War*, trying to show how Chinese understand and interpret Clausewitz's *On War*. In the next part, I will focus on the relevance of Clausewitz to China in theory and practice. I will conclude this chapter with a brief discussion of the prospect of Clausewitz's military thought to China.

Journey of a Century: the Translation and Spread of *On War* in China

The first Chinese version of *On War* was published in 1911, titled *Dazhan Xueli*.[1] It was mainly translated by the Military Consultant Department of the Qing Government from the Japanese version of *On War*. This first Chinese version was not a complete one and was not openly published to the public audience, but only circulated in a small circle for research reference. Nevertheless, it is the first time that Clausewitz (though even his name was not mentioned) and his *On War* was introduced to China. In the preface of this Chinese version, the translators said, "This book is composed of many chapters. It is deeply thought, richly elaborated and clearly illustrated. It is completely different from those superficial military books in general, and thus should be an indispensable reference for our military comrades. Everyone should own a copy."[2] From this, we can see that *On War* was highly evaluated and was regarded as an unusual book from the very beginning.

In 1915, *On War* was re-translated from a Japanese version of *On War* and openly published for the first time in two volumes by Beijing Wuxueguan Shuju, still titled *Dazhan Xueli*. In the prefaces to this version, Clausewitz was acclaimed as a master military philosopher, and the posthumous *On War* was the best military work of Germany. According to the translator,[3] the book was based on Clausewitz's lifetime war experience, clearly and fully elaborated on the relationship between strategy and policy, and far surpassed the military works in China and other countries in its depth and thoroughness.[4]

In the following decades, *On War* had been re-translated and republished for many times,[5] especially during the Chinese War against Japan in 1930s and 1940s, when China was facing a hard time and military studies were urgent and highly demanded. These translations had been based on Japanese, Russian, English or German versions of *On War*. A very popular Chinese version at this time is *Dazhan Xueli* translated by Huang Huanwen, a veteran researcher of military thought. Although this version is not a complete and literal translation but only an abridged version with essential text and translator's summary, it has been very popular for several reasons. Firstly, Huang's translation was concise and easy to understand. He reorganized and streamlined *On War* according to his own understanding and provided some annotation, thus reducing the difficulty of reading Clausewitz for the average people. Secondly, in this version there were a short biography of Clausewitz and several prefaces very useful to help readers understand Clausewitz from different perspectives. *On War* was acclaimed as "not only military, but also scientific…not only scientific, but also philosophical; not only philosophical, but also psychological; not only psychological, but also of art and literature."[6] In the following editions of this version, book remarks praising Clausewitz and *On War* by statesmen and generals like Lenin and A. G. von Schlieffen were also included. The book was regarded as a world well known masterpiece and was included in the famous Commercial Press Series in 1944.[7]

The most important and the best Chinese version was published from 1964 to 1965 in three volumes after PRC was established.[8] In 1960, under the instruction of the Central Military Commission of the CPC and with the leadership of Marshal Ye Jianying,[9] the Academy of Military Sciences (AMS) of the People's Liberation Army (PLA) began to organize a team to translate *On War* into Chinese. In order to guarantee the quality of translation, AMS, with the help of the Publicity Department of CPC, mobilized the best and brightest of China's German academies. Except for the military researchers from AMS, the translation team also included nine excellent German translators from the Ministry of Foreign Affairs and Xinhua News Agency and 10 top professors and experts on German literature and philosophy from the universities and other cultural and educational units around the country. Mainly based on the *On War* published in 1957 in East Germany with reference to the Russian, Japanese, French, English and several previous Chinese versions, the new version proved to be a very successful enterprise after three years of hard work.[10] It is a complete and high quality translation with more than 200 endnotes explaining the historical background and military terminology, and indexes of names of people and places mentioned in *On War* with brief introduction. This version was published by the Publishing Bureau of the PLA General Staff Department and internally distributed for PLA officers' use. To make it more user-friendly, in 1977, AMS also published an abridged version of *On War*, heavily condensing the three volumes to a slim book, but still for the internal use.[11] It was until 1978 that the complete AMS version became openly published by the Commercial Publishing House of China, and then in 1985 by Jiefangjun Press with minor revision. The most up-dated edition was published in 2005. Although there are many other translations of *On War* before and after this version, the AMS translation is still regarded as the best Chinese version of *On War* today.

In the early of 1980s, the General Staff Department of PLA listed the *On War* as a must read for the high-ranking officers to improve their level of military thinking.[12] This is a big push to the development of study of Clausewitz's military theory and the spread of *On War*. Many books and hundreds of articles on Clausewitz and *On War* have been published in China in the past three decades corresponding with the Reform and Opening up policy taken by PRC since 1978.[13] Except for the effort of translation, annotation and publication of *On War*, a dozen of research monographs and edited volumes have got printed,[14] and at least four biographies of Clausewitz have been published in China.[15] In *China Military Encyclopedia*, Clausewitz was emphasized in almost every related sub-field.[16] In the military education system, Clausewitz was an indispensable part for generations of military officer corps of almost all levels. Clausewitz's military thought was praised as the apex of the capitalist military thought, an essential part of the development of Mao Zedong's military thought, and still relevant to the strategic thinking and military doctrine of contemporary China.

In terms of translation, publication, spreading, studying and persisting influence, it is not exaggerated that in China there is no other foreign person or writing in the military field that could compete with Clausewitz and his *On War* in the past century.[17]

Clausewitz's Influence on Mao Zedong's Military Thought

There are many reasons why Clausewitz's *On War* has been so widely spread and received so much attention in China for the past century and is still viewed as the bedrock of Western military science in the nuclear and information age. Except for his comprehensive, profound and systematic examination of war, the huge and enduring impact of Clausewitz in China should also be understood from the role he played in the development of Lenin and Mao Zedong's military thought.

Similar to the situation in the former Soviet Union, Friedrich Engels who had a particular interest and expertise on the military studies was usually the first to be cited in the discussion of Clausewitz in China. Engels praised Clausewitz to be the first-rate figure in the Prussian military academies, and "the world-widely recognized authority on the military aspects, like Jomini."[18] In his correspondence with Marx, he wrote, "Now I am reading Clausewitz's *On War*. A remarkable way of philosophizing about the question, but the book itself is very good."[19] Marx replied with equal approval. However, neither Engels nor Marx paid attention to the concept of "War as the Continuation of Politics by others means" which was stressed and highly acclaimed by Lenin later. "This dictum," Lenin wrote, "was uttered by one of the profoundest writers on the problems of war. Marxists have always rightly regarded this thesis as the theoretical basis of views on the significance of any war."[20] He further explained, the character of every war was "not determined at the point where the opposing armies take their stand, [but by] what policy is carried on by the war, what class is conducting the war and what objectives it is pursuing on the course of it."[21] Lenin had studied *On War* very seriously and left behind him lots of reading notes. These reading notes had been edited and published as a book in China in 1978.[22]

In the case of China, Clausewitz's popularity did not start from Mao Zedong, as we have seen above, but there is no doubt it was reinforced by Mao's appreciation of the Prussian strategist. In the Yan'an era when the Long March of the Red Army had ended, Mao Zedong began to conclude the revolutionary experience and think about the future of Chinese strategy facing the new situation of the Resistant War against a militarily stronger Japan and Nationalist KMT regime. Clausewitz entered Mao's vision in the early of 1930s when he was still at Jiangxi,[23] but it was at Yan'an that Mao began to study Clausewitz. He wrote to General Guo Huaruo, suggesting him to read Clausewitz if he wanted to study strategy at the end of 1937.[24] He himself also began to read *On War* and wrote down some reading notes. In 1938, Mao Zedong even organized a weekly study group on Clausewitz's *On War* at Yan'an, enrolling some comrade generals to listen to He Sijing's interpretation of Clausewitz's *On War* from a German text, followed by a group discussion.[25] According to the recalling of a participant, Mao Zedong was an enthusiastic listener and a serious note-taker at that time, and had talked on issues like concentrations of forces. Mao Zedong himself also mentioned at several different occasions after PRC was established that he has read *On War* in order to conclude the experiences of Chinese revolutionary war. Mao Zedong also expressed his disagreement with Stalin's remark on Clausewitz that he was a "representative of the hand-worker era" who had nothing to teach the industrial age, saying that one should not stop reading Clausewitz because Germany was defeated in the Great Wars.[26]

The influence of Clausewitz on Mao Zedong could be found in some works of Mao Zedong during this period. In *On Protracted War* delivered in May 1938, Mao for the first time cited Clausewitz's views like "war is the continuation of politics" and "the law of probability" while making some important theoretical innovations based on his rich practices of revolutionary war. "War is the continuation of politics.' In this sense war is politics and war itself is a political action;" Mao wrote, "But war has its own particular characteristics and in this sense it cannot be equated with politics in general… When politics develops to a certain stage beyond which it cannot proceed by the usual means, war breaks out to sweep the obstacles from the way… It can therefore be said that politics is war without bloodshed while war is politics with bloodshed."[27]

Regarding "law of probability," in Chapter one of *On War*, Clausewitz argued, "not only its objective but also its subjective nature makes war a gamble," and "absolute, so-called mathematical, factors never find a firm basis in military calculations."[28] In this case, Mao pointed out, "We admit that the phenomenon of war is more elusive and is characterized by greater uncertainty than any other social phenomenon, in other words, that it is more a matter of 'probability.' Yet war is no way supernatural, but a mundane process governed by necessity… (W)hatever the situation and the moves in a war, one can know their general aspects and essential points. It is possible for a commander to reduce errors and give generally correct direction, first through all kinds of reconnaissance and then through intelligent inference and judgment."[29] In the eyes of Chinese commentators, these arguments were considered as having made Clausewitz's original accounts deeper, more complete and scientific.[30] In this event, Clausewitz functioned as a link in the development of Marx-Leninist and Mao Zedong's military thought, a status that no other foreign military theorist enjoyed or could compete for.

Mao Zedong's military thought is still the guideline of China's military strategy and military doctrine today. It may be reasonable to draw a conclusion that so long as Marx-Leninism and Mao Zedong thought remain the orthodoxy ideology in China, Clausewitz and his *On War* will keep on enjoying a privileged and unparalleled position compared with other Western military thinkers in the future.

Clausewitz and *On War* as a Counterpoise to Sun Tzu and *The Art of War*

In China, Clausewitz and *On War* is often juxtaposed with Sun Tzu and *The Art of War*, called "Zhongxi Shuangbi" (Sino-Western Twin Jades).[31] The former is extolled as the Western Master and bible of war and the other is adored as the Eastern Sage and treasure of military art. However, in terms of time, geographic conditions, culture, writing style, and book length,[32] the gap between Clausewitz's *On War* and Sun Tzu's *The Art of War* could hardly be wider. But as the representatives of the West and the East in military thinking, people cannot help being curious about comparing the two masters of war: Did they say anything different? And if they did, on which points? Who is more convincing? Why they are different? Do they share anything fundamentally? Who is better and on what matters? These questions arise naturally in a comparative study. This kind of comparison is much valuable, because "it demonstrates the basic unity of the study of strategy and war, and also allows us to better understand these works on their own terms: each can be viewed from a broader perspective, and issues that would otherwise be obscured can be clarified."[33]

When comparing Clausewitz and Sun Tzu, British strategist Liddell Hart's seemingly paradoxical comments in his foreword to *The Art of War* translated by Samuel Griffith are well known. On one hand, he observed that Clausewitz's *On War* "…did not differ so much from Sun Tzu's conclusions as it appeared to do on the surface," and on the other hand he asserted that "Sun Tzu has clearer vision, more profound insight, and eternal freshness" and suggested that "Sun Tzu's realism and moderation form a contrast to Clausewitz's tendency to emphasize the logical ideal and 'the absolute'…".[34] Liddell Hart's preference to Sun Tzu and depreciation of Clausewitz may result from his biased understanding of Clausewitz, his distaste for Clausewitz's writing style, or that he was happy to find there was a consonant from Sun Tzu to his "indirect strategy." But he admitted anyway that "(a)mong all the military thinkers of the past, only Clausewitz is comparable."[35]

Liddell Hart's commentary on Sun Tzu and Clausewitz has been welcomed and echoed among Chinese Clausewitz experts.[36] However, there is no consensus regarding the comparison of *The Art of War* and *On War*. Zhai Dongsheng and Shi Yinhong have used Clausewitz's war theory to criticize Sun Tzu. Based on Clausewitz's argumentation that war by nature is a trinity of violence, probability, and policy instrument, they examined Sun Tzu's related observations, and draw a conclusion that there existed an unwarranted confidence and optimism about war in Sun Tzu's writing. It seems that the authors regarded Clausewitz as more convincing.[37]

In contrast, Xue Guoan, a professor of PLA's National Defense University asserted that although Sun Tzu and Clausewitz enjoyed some commons like concentration of forces, combination of the defensive and attack, and emphasis of generalship, generally speaking, there are more differences than similarities between the two masters in war view, strategic thinking, and military doctrine. According to Xue, Sun Tzu appreciates rationality while Clausewitz extols violence; Sun Tzu seeks strategy while Clausewitz emphasizes forces; Sun Tzu stresses changes while Clausewitz thinks much of rules.[38] Xue attributed these differences to the different military culture and way of thinking between the East and West, advocating both sides should learn from each other.

Niu Xianzhong, a prominent Taiwanese strategic scholar compared *The Art of War* and *On War* and draw a conclusion that they are both immortal masterpieces but with different characteristics, and they are more essentially complementary than contradicted. In the view of Niu, the biggest advantage of *The Art of War* lies in its clarity, while the biggest weakness of *On War* is its obscurity. Clausewitz emphasizes the relationship between war and politics while Sun Tzu attaches more attention to the relationship between war and economy; Clausewitz likes historical examples while Sun Tzu thinks more of geographical factors; when talking about military genius, Clausewitz ranks "courage" the foremost virtue while Sun Tzu chooses the "wisdom" as the most important quality of the commander; Sun Tzu stresses intelligence and surprise attack while Clausewitz dwells more on "friction" and "the fog of war". Nevertheless, Niu Xianzhong still thinks, in general, there are more similarities than differences between Sun Tzu and Clausewitz.[39] And there is no gulf between the East and West in strategic thinking, though Chinese usually like to put Clausewitz in the East-West division.

Niu Xianzhong's finding was shared by Michael Handel. After conducting a comprehensive, structural and rigorous comparison between *On War* and *The Art of War*, Handel more persuasively proved that despite their apparent differences in terms of time, place, cultural background, and level of material/technological development, all had much more in common than previously supposed. The logic of waging war and of strategic thinking seems universal as well as timeless.[40]

The Continuing Relevance of Clausewitz to China in Theory and Practice

Since *On War* was published for the first time in Germany in 1832, almost 180 years have past; since it was translated into Chinese, 100 years has past. The military setting has changed so fast, with RMA occupying the central stage of military affairs around the world. Under such circumstances, are those points expressed by Clausewitz in his *On War* still viable and useful? Isn't it already anachronistic considering we have entered the so-called nuclear, information, and space age, and we have so many fancy theories, models, technologies, and war machines? In short, is Clausewitz still relevant to us nowadays? This is not a new question. At the beginning of the last century, this kind of question had already been raised in his motherland Germany and other European countries,[41] and it has been continuously asked afterwards.

In China, the majority answer to this question is: some of Clausewitz's arguments may be out-of-date in the new military environment, but his general theory on war and his dialectic way of thinking are still relevant. In China, the following arguments of Clausewitz are usually regarded as innovative, insightful, and valuable, and continued to be part of China's military strategic thinking, though the list may not be complete:[42]

- War is the continuation of politics by other means.

- War is a paradoxical trinity - composed of primordial violence, hatred, and enmity; of the play of chance and probability; and of its element of subordination, as an instrument of policy. These three tendencies are like three different codes of law, deeply rooted in their subject and yet variable in their relationship to one another. People's task is to develop a theory that maintains a balance between these three tendencies.[43]

- Destroying the enemy's forces and preserving our own forces, these two efforts always go together; they interact. They are integral parts of a single purpose.[44]

- Theory cannot equip the mind with formulas for solving problems, nor can it mark the narrow path on which the sole solution is supposed to lie by planting a hedge of principles on either side. But it can give the mind insight into the great mass of phenomena and of their relationships, and help people to seize on what is right and true.[45] Because age had its own kind of war, its own limiting conditions, and its own peculiar preconditions, the theorists must scrutinize all data with an inquiring, a discriminating, and a classifying eye. He must always bear in mind the wide variety of situations that can lead to war. If he does, he will draw the outline of its salient features in such a way that it can accommodate both the dictates of the age, and those of the immediate situation.[46]

- The moral elements are among the most important in war. The effects of physical and psychological factors form an organic whole, which is inseparable by chemical processes. The principal moral elements are: the skill of the commander, the experience and courage of the troops, and their patriotic spirit.[47]

- As an important war phenomenon, a popular uprising is a broadening and intensification of the fermentation process known as war.[48]

- Defense and attack are interdependent, interactive, mutually inclusive and conversable. The defensive form of war is not a simple shield, but a shield made up of well-directed blows.

- There is no higher and simpler law of strategy than that of keeping one's forces concentrated.[49]

Like many other countries, lots of debates remain around Clausewitz and his *On War* in China. These debates may simply arise from the abstractness of *On War*. Liddell Hart's comment on Clausewitz may be a little bit biased and exaggerated, but at least on one point he is right: Clausewitz's thought is obscure, and his argument "often turned back from the direction which it seemed to be taking."[50] In addition, *On War* is a posthumous work and it was not finished before Clausewitz died, so there are some places in *On War* appearing incoherent or even contradictory. But a more important reason may lie in that different people tend to interpret Clausewitz differently.

In the past three decades, Chinese scholars have debated on the intellectual sources of Clausewitz's war theory, on his categorization of "absolute war and real war,"[51] on his argument that "war is the continuation of politics by other means," on the "law of probability,"[52] on the war purpose of "destroying the enemy's forces and preserving our own forces," and on the problem of "the defensive form of warfare is intrinsically stronger than the offensive."[53] There was an especially hot debate on the viability of "war is the continuation of politics" under the nuclear condition. Some scholars completely denied the viability of the argument, some doubted or partially denied the viability, and still others insist on the universal viability.[54] These debates, like Peter Paret said, "Remind us once more of the manner in which Clausewitz formed and refined his ideas. They also suggest the vitality of these ideas, which never coalesced into a finite system, but led to hypotheses that ... have shown the capacity for continuing growth that Clausewitz believed to be the mark of true theory."[55]

For the Chinese military professional nowadays, Clausewitz has not only theoretical implication, but also practical significance. Some of them have begun to apply Clausewitz's concepts and way of thinking to shape their arguments in recent years. For instance, when analyzing the purpose of the US conduct of war in Iraq, Su Enze, a retired major general questioned whether those American generals had forgotten Clausewitz's dictum that "war is the continuation of politics by other means", because according to Clausewitz, military purpose cannot take place of the political purpose of a state, but what the US army had done in Iraq seemed to have simply violated the principle.[56] Another major general Jin Yinan cited Clausewitz's analysis of the reasons why the Prussian army failed in 1806, asserting that the most deadly damage to a nation is the lack of enterprising spirit.[57] Li Yong examined "the fog of war" under the condition of high technology, arguing that the development of military technology may eliminate the traditional "fog of war," but under the new technological situation, the new "fog of war" will arise from the new technology, information explosion and pollution. The commanders have to face a new dilemma when making a strategic decision.[58] Still others have utilized Clausewitz's observation on the military virtue to explore the significance, contents, and means to develop the personality of military virtue among the officer corps.[59] These efforts show that Clausewitz remains rather relevant in the new setting in China.

Unfortunately, though Clausewitz lost none of his popularity in China today, the related research on Clausewitz is still limited in several aspects. Firstly, the study of "Clausewitz Studies" is not enough, especially those civilian scholarships from other countries. For instance, the four seminal essays included in the English version of *On War* which were written by Peter Paret, Michael Howard, and Bernard Brodie have barely been mentioned in China. And some excellent studies on Clausewitz like Michael Handel's *Masters of War*, Raymond Aron's *Clausewitz: Philosopher of War*, and Peter Paret's *Clausewitz and the State*, have not yet been seriously introduced into China even though some of them have been published for decades.[60] One reason for this may lie in the scarcity of communication between China and other countries in the field of Clausewitz studies, the lack of exchange between military scholars and civilian scholars in China, and the rarity of civilian scholars who work on Clausewitz.[61] This situation needs to be changed. Otherwise it may impede the improvement of China's research level and limit the further knowledge accumulation in the studies of Clausewitz. China needs to open its door to the outside world while encourage and strengthen the communication between the military and civilian scholars domestically in the field of Clausewitz studies.[62]

Secondly, the focus of Chinese Clausewitz studies should be moved to how to apply his war theory and strategic thinking to the real world instead of merely canonic reinterpretation. Methodologically, Clausewitz extremely stressed the importance of studying historical examples and approaching reality in the course of establishing his theory. With the rise of China and the increasing of China's strategic practices, Clausewitz should be more applicable and gain more audience.

Conclusion

In the preface of the AMS version of *On War*, it says "*On War* written by Carl von Clausewitz, the Prussian military theorist in the 19th century, is a classic of capitalist military theory. It reflects the progressive tendency and innovative spirit in the military thought of the capitalists at the early stage. It has put forwards some correct point of views regarding the nature of war, and greatly pushed the development of military thought. Thus this book is still extolled in the military of the capitalist countries ... Owing to the time limit, some views expressed in the book are no longer correct. Some views, especially those specific issues on the military doctrine are no longer coincidental with the objective reality. However, the author is the first military strategist who consciously made use of dialectics to study war, and draw some conclusions still viable ... Therefore, this book is not only a great help for our study of capitalist military thought, but also beneficial for us to study the general problems of war." [63]

If we put the ideological tone aside, this remark still viably holds today. Considering the role of Clausewitz and his *On War* playing in the system of Mao Zedong's military thought, its complementing value to Sun Tzu and *the Art of War* - the traditional way of strategic thinking in China - and its persistent relevance to contemporary strategic thinking, there is almost no uncertainty here that his influence will stay large in the foreseeable future. With the rise of China facing an increasingly complicated international environment and new challenges of RMA, Clausewitz will still be a source of theoretical inspiration and practical guide. Clausewitz's knowledge is still vital to survival, and *On War* will remain an extraordinary book for Chinese readers. The problem is how to combine the new reality with the philosophical thinking of Clausewitz in a new environment and make it more applicable, especially in a Chinese context.

Notes:

[1] *Dazhan Xueli* [*Theory of Great War*], Lujun Jiaoyu Yanjiushe Yiyin [Translated and Published by the Army Education and Research Society], 1911.

[2] *Ibid.*, Preface.

[3] The translator, Qu Shouti, had participated in the translation of the first Chinese version of *On War*. He was a graduate of Beiyang Army Crash School, and then became an instructor at Baoding Army College, two of the earliest and prominent military colleges in modern China.

[4] Gelusaiweizhi [Clausewitz], *Dazhan Xueli* [*Theory of the Great War*], Qu Shouti tran., Beijing: Beijing Wuxueguan Shuju [Beijing Military Science House Publisher], 1915.

[5] For a more detailed examination of the evolution of Chinese versions of *On War*, see Xia Zhengnan, "Kelaosaiweici *Zhanzhenglun* zai Zhongguo de Liuchuan" [The Spread of Clausewitz's *On War* in China] *Zhongguo Junshi Kexue* [*China Military Science*], No. 5, 2004.

According to Xia Zhengnan's study, there are 33 Chinese versions of *On War* until 2005, see Xia Zhengnan, *Jiedu Zhanzhenglun* [*Interpreting On War*] (2nd edition), Beijing: Jiefangjun Chubanshe [The PLA Press], 2005, pp. 680-682.

[6] Kelaosaiweici [Clausewitz], *Dazhan Xueli* [*Theory of the Great War*] (vol.1), Huang Huanwen ed. and tran., Guilin: Guofang Shudian [National Defense Bookstore], 1941, p. 9.

[7] Kelaosaiweici [Clausewitz], *Dazhan Xueli* (or *Zhanzheng Lun*) [*Theory of the Great War, or On War*], Huang Huanwen ed. and tran., Shanghai: Shangwu Yinshuguan [The Commercial Press], 1944.

[8] Kelaosaiweici [Clausewitz], *Zhanzhenglun* [*On War*] (PLA Academy of Military Sciences translated), Beijing: PLA General Staff's Publishing Bureau, 1964-1965.

[9] At that time, Marshal Ye Jianying was the President of the AMS. See Song Zi, "Yeshuai Zhidao Women Fanyi Zhanzhenglun" [Marshal Ye Instructed Us to Translate *On War*], *Zhongguo Shehui Kexuebao* [*China Social Science Newspaper*], January 6, 2011, p. 9.

[10] Xia Zhengnan, *Jiedu Zhanzhenglun* [*Interpreting On War*], p. 21.

[11] The remaining parts include the nature of war, the theory of war, strategy in general, the engagement, the principles of defense and the attack, and war plan.

Kelaosaiweici [Clausewitz], *Zhanzhenglun* (abridged)[*On War*], Beijing: Zhongguo Renmin Jiefangjun Junshi Kexueyuan [PLA Academy of Military Sciences], 1977.

[12] *Ibid.*, p. 22.

[13] A good summary of the literature on Clausewitz study, see Xia Zhengnan, *Jiedu Zhanzhenglun* [*Interpreting On War*], pp. 680-693.

[14] Among the most notable works are Xia Zhengnan, *Kelaosaiweici Zhanzheng Zhexue Yanjiu* [*Study of Clausewitz's War Philosophical Thoughts*], Beijing: Jiefangjun Chubanshe [The PLA Press], 1989; Wu Qiong, *Zhanzhenglun Quanshi* [*Interpreting On War*], Beijing: Huawen Press, 2001; Xia Zhengnan, *Jiedu Zhanzhenglun* [*Interpreting On War*] (2nd edition), 2005; and Wu Qiong and Xia Zhengnan, eds., *Lun Kelaosaiweici Zhanzhenglun* [*On Clausewitz's On War*], Shanghai: Shanghai Jiaoyu Chubanshe [Sahnghai Education Press], 1999.

[15] Two of these biographies are translated works written by German authors, two are written by Chinese scholars. See Fulanci Fabian [Franz Fabian], *Kelaosaiweici Zhuan* [*Clausewitz*], The Foreign Military Research Department of AMS tran., Beijing: Zhongguo Duiwai Fanyi Chunban Gongsi [China Foreign Translation and Publishing Company], 1984; Weilian feng Shilamu [Wilhelm von Schramm], *Kelaosaiweici Zhuan* [*Clausewitz*], Wang Qingyu et al., trans., Beijing: Shangwu Yinshuguan [The Commercial Press], 1984; Xue Guoan, *Kelaosaiweici Zhuan* [*A Biography of Clausewitz*], Shijiazhuang: Hebei Renmin Chubanshe [Hebei People's Press], 1997; Xia Zhengnan, *Kelaosaiweici* [*Clausewitz*], Kunming: Yunnan Jiaoyu Chubanshe [Yunnan Educational Press], 2008.

[16] In the new edition of *China Military Encyclopedia*, Clausewitz and his *On War* is present in the sub-field of Military Philosophy, Foreign Military Figures, Foreign Military Works, Mao Zedong's Military Thought, and Military Scientific Research, etc. See the related volumes published by Zhongguo Dabaike Quanshu Chubanshe [Encyclopedia of China Publishing House] in 2006-2007.

[17] In the Western military science, Jomini is usually regarded as standing on the same foot with Clausewitz. But Jomini's position and influence in China is obviously less prominent than Clausewitz. Jomini's *Summary of the Art of War* was not fully translated into Chinese until 1986, and related literature is far less than Clausewitz. The author has used "Kelaosaiweici (Clausewitz)" and "Ruomini (Jomini)" as the keywords to search the CNKI electronic journal database, and got a result of 447 entries related to "Clausewitz" and 10 entries re-

lated to "Jomini" during the period from 1980 to 2010 (searched on January 7, 2011).

[18] *Makesi Engesi Junshi Wenji* [*Military Writings of Marx and Engels*], Vol. 1, Beijing: Zhanshi Chubanshe [Soldier's Press], 1981, p. 258.

[19] *Makesi Engesi Junshi Wenji* [*Military Writings of Marx and Engels*], Vol. 5, Beijing: Zhanshi Chubanshe [Soldier's Press], 1981, p. 495.

[20] *Liening Junshi Wenji* [*Military Writings of Lenin*], Beijing: Zhanshi Chubanshe [Soldier's Press], 1981, p. 231.

[21] *Ibid.*, p. 333.

[22] Liening [Lenin], *Kelaosaiweici Zhanzhenglun Yishu Zhailu he Pizhu* [*Excerpts and Annotation of Clausewitz's On War*], Beijing: Renmin Chubanshe [People's Press], 1978.

[23] Song Zi, "Yeshuai Zhidao Women Fanyi Zhanzhenglun"[Marshal Ye Instructed Us to Translate *On War*]

[24] General Guo Huaruo is a prominent military theorist and strategist of PLA and a renowned expert on Sun Zi. In December 1937 when Mao Zedong wrote to him, he was helping Mao Zedong in Yan'an to write on strategy against the Japanese aggression. General Guo was the vice president of the AMS from 1973 to 1982.

[25] He Sijing, a famous Marxist intellectual who was a graduate of the University of Tokyo and an expert on German philosophy and theory of law. He died in 1968 during the Cultural Revolution of China.

[26] See Xia Zhengnan, *Jiedu Zhanzhenglun* [*Interpreting On War*], pp. 23-24.

[27] *Selected Military Writings of Mao Tse-tung*, Beijing: Foreign Languages Press, 1967, pp. 226-227.

[28] Clausewitz, *On War*, pp. 96-97.

[29] *Selected Military Writings of Mao Tse-tung*, p. 238.

[30] Xia Zhengnan, "Mao Zedong: Junshi Bianzhengfa Sixiang zhi Jidachengzhe" [Mao Zedong: A Master of Military Dialectic Thought], *MaoZedong Sixiang Yanjiu* [*Studies of Mao Zedong Thought*], No. 1 (1996), pp. 87-88; Yang Xin, "Shilun Mao Zedong Junshi Zhanlue Siwei Chansheng de Kexuejichu" [On the Scientific Foundations of the Birth of Mao Zedong's Military Thought], *Junshi Lishi Yanjiu* [*Military History Studies*], No. 2 (2002), p. 26.

[31] I have used "Kelaosaiweici (Clausewitz) and Sun Zi (Sun Tzu)" as keywords to search the CNKI journal article database, and found 52 related entries from 1980-2010 (searched on January 7, 2011). There are some monographs on this topic, see for instance, Xue Guoan, *Sunzi Bingfa yu Zhanzhenglun Bijiao Yanjiu* [*The Art of War and On War: A Comparative Study*], Beijing: Junshi Kexue Chubanshe [Military Science Press], 2003. This approach has been shared by some Western scholars. See Michael I. Handel, *Masters of War: Classical Strategic Thought*, 3rd edition, London: Routledge, 2001. The first and second editions of the book were published in 1992 and 1996, respectively.

[32] *The Art of War* was written in the 5th century BC while *On War* was published in 1832; *The Art of War* has only over 5,000 Chinese characters or fewer than 40 pages in English translation while *On War* is close to 600 pages long or over 690,000 Chinese Characters in translation.

[33] Handel, *Masters of War*, p. 4.

[34] B. H. Liddell Hart, "Foreword," in Sun Tzu, *The Art of War*, translated and with an introduction by Samuel B. Griffith, Oxford: Oxford University Press, 1963, pp. v-vi.

[35] *Ibid.*, p. v.

[36] Niu Xianzhong, *Zhanluejia* [*The Strategist*], Nanning: Guangxi Shifan Daxue Chubanshe [Guangxi Normal University Press], p. 150; Zhai Dongsheng and Shi Yinhong, "Dui Sunzi de Kelaosaiweicishi de Pipan" [A Clausewitzian Criticism of Sun Tzu], *Zhanglue yu Guanli* [*Strategy and Management*], No. 5 (2003), p. 30.

[37] Zhai Dongsheng and Shi Yinhong, "Dui Sunzi de Kelaosaiweicishi de Pipan" [A Clausewitzian Criticism of Sun Tzu], pp. 30-35.

[38] Xue Guoan, *Sunzi Bingfa yu Zhanzhenglun Bijiao Yanjiu* [*The Art of War and On War: A Comparative Study*], pp. 206-226.

[39] Niu Xianzhong, *Zhanluejia* [*The Strategist*], p. 149.

[40] Among the aspects of *On War* and *The Art of War* compared by Handel are "their frameworks; methodologies and styles; positions on the primacy of politics in the formulation of strategic policies and the decision to go to war; and analyses of a field commander's responsibilities compared with those of a political leader. Also examined are their evaluations of intelligence and deception; quantitative superiority; the relationship between the offense and the defense;

friction; chance, luck and uncertainty in war; and the rational calculus of war." See Handel, *Masters of War*, p. 21.

[41] Michael Howard, "The Influence of Clausewitz," in Clausewitz, *On War*, p. 35.

[42] See, Xia Zhengnan, *Kelaosaiweici Zhanzheng Zhexue Yanjiu* [*Study of Clausewitz's War Philosophical Thoughts*], pp. 334-335; idem, Xia Zhengnan, *Jiedu Zhanzhenglun* [*Interpreting On War*], pp. 7-16.

[43] Clausewitz, *On War*, p. 101.

[44] *Ibid.*, p. 112.

[45] *Ibid.*, pp. 698-699.

[46] *Ibid.*, pp.717-718.

[47] *Ibid.*, pp. 216-218.

[48] *Ibid.*, p. 578.

[49] *Ibid.*, p. 240.

[50] Liddell Hart, "Foreword," p. vi.

[51] Ni Lexiong, "Dui Kelaosaiweici Junshi Xueshuo de Jidian Kanfa" [Several Points on Clausewitz's Military Doctrine], *Xueshu Jie* [*Academics in China*], No. 2 (2002), pp. 155-162.

[52] Li Jijun, "Mao Zedong Junshi Sixiang de Tedian he Lishi Diwei"[The Characteristics and Historical Position of Mao Zedong's Military Thought], in Li Jijun, *Junshi Lilun yu Zhanzheng Shijian* [*Military Theory and War Practices*], Beijing: Junshi Kexue Chubanshe [Military Science Press], 1994, pp. 40-53; Wu Qiong, "Mao Zedong Junshi Sixiang yu Zhanzhenglun zhong de 'Gairanxing' Lilun" [Mao Zedong's Military Thought and the Law of Probability in *On War*], *Nanjing Zhengzhi Xueyuan Xuebao* [*Journal of Nanjing College of Politics*], No. 4 (1987), pp. 56-62.

[53] Kong Lingtong, et al, "Fangyu shi 'Yizhong Jiaoqiang de Zuozhan Xingshi'" [The Defensive Is 'a Stronger Form of Warfare'], in Wu Qiong and Xia Zhengnan, eds., *Lun Kelaosaiweici Zhanzhenglun* [*On Clausewitz's On War*], pp. 219-235; Guo Weitao, "Fangyu shi Yizhong Jiaoqiang de Zuozhan Xingshi Ma?" [Is the Defensive a Stronger Form of Warfare?], in Wu and Xia, eds., *Lun Kelaosaiweici Zhanzhenglun* [*On Clausewitz's On War*], pp. 223-225.

⁵⁴ See three papers in Wu and Xia, eds., *Lun Kelaosaiweici Zhanzhenglun* [*On Clausewitz's On War*], pp. 52-83.

⁵⁵ Peter Paret, "The Genesis of *On War*", in Clausewitz, *On War*, p. 28.

⁵⁶ Su Enze, "Buyao Wangle Kelaosaiweici" [Don't Forget Clausewitz], *Zhongguo Huofangbao* [*China National Defense Newspaper*], August 14, 2007, p. 6.

⁵⁷ Jin Yinan, "Shenme shi Minzu de Zhimingshang" [What is a Nation's Deadly Damage], *Jiefangjun Bao* [*Jiefangjun Daily*], February 9, 2010.

⁵⁸ Li Yong, "'Zhangzheng Miwu' Bing Wei Sanqu" ["Fog of War" has not Disappeared Yet], *Zhongguo Guofangbao* [*China's National Defense Newspaper*], July 18, 2002.

⁵⁹ Xu Xing, Wude Renge [The Personality of Military Virtue], *Junshi Lishi Yanjiu* [*Studies of Military History*], No. 3 (2003), pp. 144-152.

⁶⁰ Michael I. Handel, *Masters of War: Classical Strategic Thought*, 3rd edition, London: Routledge, 2001; Raymond Aron, *Clausewitz: Philosopher of War*, N.J. Prentice-Hall, Inc., 1985; and Peter Paret, *Clausewitz and the State*, Oxford: Clarendon Press, 1976.

⁶¹ In China, most of the writings on Clausewitz have been done by military scholars or scholars who used to work in the military. There are few exceptions like Shi Yinhong at Beijing and Ni Lexiong at Shanghai.

⁶² Within the author's reading limitation, the earliest and also the only literature review on foreign studies of Clausewitz and *On War* is Zhang Yuanlin, "Guoneiwai dui Kelaosaiweici jiqi Junshi Sixiang Yanjiu Zongshu" [A Comprehensive Review of Foreign Studies on Clausewitz and his Military Thought], in Wu Qiong and Xia Zhengnan, eds., *Lun Kelaosaiweici Zhanzhenglun* [*On Clausewitz's On War*], 1999, pp. 320-334. Many important researches had been absent. In contrast, a Japanese scholar has done a much more comprehensive and up-dated historiography of Clausewitz. See Yasuyuki Kawamura, "Historiography: For the Study on Clausewitz," *The Journal of Strategic Studies* (Japan), No. 1, 2003, pp. 111-171.

⁶³ Kelaosaiweici [Clausewitz], *Zhanzhenglun* [*On War*], Vol. 1, pp. I-II.

OBSERVATIONS AND VERDICT OF A LONELY CLAUSEWITZIAN CONVERT: "VOM KRIEGE" IN DENMARK

Michael H. Clemmesen

"Vom Kriege" was read and used in Denmark immediately after its publication. Danes have a new both elegant and accurate translation into the national language and during the years since that translation references to the work appear from time to time in the public debate about security and defence affairs to legitimise the contribution. A webpage - www.clausewitz.dk - is available for all interested, and Claus Eskild Andersen, major and MA, employs it as a notice board to inform about new international publications and as a venue to inspire debate.

In spite of all these positive facts and the efforts a number of academically minded army officers over the last three decades, the theory of Carl von Clausewitz has never been integrated into how the Danish armed forces or the national defence politicians think or act.

This paper follows the creation of a Danish advocate and his failed efforts to spread the gospel.

The first century

The realm of the old Danish King Frederick VI covered Denmark as well as the Duchies of Schleswig, Holstein and Lauenburg, when "Vom Kriege" appeared as the first three of the ten volumes "Hinterlassenes Werk des Generals Carl von Clausewitz" published by his wife, Marie von Clausewitz, née Gräfin Brühl, from 1832 to 1834. The cultural and academic life in Copenhagen then was directly inspired by events in the northern part of the German Federation, and especially by what happened in Berlin. Thus the small community of military intellectuals in the Danish capital read both this theoretical work and the historical studies immediately after their publication during the next five years.[1] In 1837, Captain August Baggesen[2] discussed Clausewitz's definitions of tactics and strategy in a long article in the military periodical: "Militairt Repertorium". In a footnote to the article Baggesen praised the works of Clausewitz as some of the latest and most "beautiful" additions to the military literature. Unfortunately the review that Baggesen promised was never published.

The predecessor of the present Royal Danish Defence College, "Den kgl. militære Højskole", meaning the Royal Military University, had been established in 1830 to educate officers for the General Staff and the scientific branches of the army: the artillery and the engineers. The lectures given during the first seven years of teaching were published. Baggesen's job was to teach Military History and the Art of Warfare, and his lectures from 1834 show familiarity with Clausewitz's publications. During the academic year 1836-37 First Lieutenant Johan Steenstrup,[3] the lecturer of fortress warfare, used the part of Book 7 about attack on fortresses in his teaching.[4]

However, in spite of this early, direct familiarity with Clausewitz, the officer education in Denmark thereafter mirrored what happened elsewhere. It became heavily influenced by Jomini's more easily applied, prescriptive, narrowly tactical-operational texts that had been inspired by his more narrow study of Napoleon's operational manoeuvres and battles.[5]

After the defeat by Prussia and Austria in 1864, the Danish Army needed and sought support and its main inspiration became France. It was to that power that the army looked for professional views. However, during the last decades of the 19th century pessimism about the army's chances with its only semi-militia trained conscripts and leaders in open clashes with the well trained, long national service German forces meant that the professional focus became dominated by officers of the scientific branches. They argued successfully that the only way that Denmark could survive the next war was by concentrating on the construction and manning of a modern Brialmond type fortress around Copenhagen. The construction work ended in 1894 and with supplementary field works created in 1914-16 it formed the base of the Neutrality Guard during World War I.

At that time the army had broadened its search for support and inspiration. With the German-British confrontation worsening after 1905, Great Britain was identified by the Danish Army General Staff as the most likely reinforcing power and links to the British Army were developed before and during the Great War supplementing the French inspiration. During the first decade after having received North Schleswig via a referendum supervised by British and French forces close relations were maintained with both Entente armies. They would assist if Germany misbehaved. Their doctrines during the Inter-

War period were dominated by the massive artillery support, scientifically managed tactics of the "bataille conduite". Within that framework Clausewitz's views about the character of combat were irrelevant.

However, in the 1930's, as it became increasingly clear that Denmark would have to defend itself without any hope of outside assistance, the Danish Army started to seek new inspiration. This came from the German Army. The new Chief of the General Staff, Major General Ebbe Gørtz[6], had realised the quality of Ludwig Beck's "Heeresdienstvorschrift 300/1. Truppenführung" from 1934 with its emphasis on combined arms tactics and delegation of authority, which mirrored Clausewitz's understanding of the reality and requirements of tactical combat. Like the "Reichswehr," the Danish Army needed a doctrine that enabled it to fight against forces of superior strength. Key ideas from the German manual appeared in the new formation level basic tactical manual "Feltreglement I, B" that was published in 1943, only a couple of months before the German occupation force dissolved the remains of the Danish armed forces.

The next three decades

As the Swedish Army was similarly stimulated by German Army doctrine, the many Danish regular officers that received Swedish training in the Danish Brigade in Sweden in 1944-45 came back indirectly inspired by German military thinking. Thus, when the Danish Army was rebuilt in the 1950s within the NATO framework with Anglo-American assistance, the 1943 manual was reprinted for use. With NATO's increasing emphasis on the nuclear battlefield, however, the focus of the replacement "Feltreglement I" from 1963 became how to fight at brigade level in a mobile defence supported by tactical nuclear weapons.[7]

This continued until the German Federal Army launched its new "Heeresdienstvorschrift 100/100 Führung im Gefecht" in 1974 with its emphasis on defence within a limited terrain zone with conventional weapons. Due to the necessary close integration of Danish and German land forces defending south-eastern Holstein, the Danish army doctrine had to be adjusted. This happened during the next decade and, like the German manual, it emphasised forward positional defence with conventional weapons. Consequently, any future thinking about warfare after a nuclear release would concentrate on the impossible issue of how to use nuclear fire-power fighting amongst your own population in a situation where NATO conventional forces had failed to contain an invasion and the enemy would respond in kind.

This article's author was born in 1944, entered the army in 1964, was commissioned into the combat arm in 1968 and served in armoured units during the following decade only interrupted by a year's UN service in Kashmir and Pakistan in the mid-1970s. Troop service continued until he entered the Army General Staff Course in 1978 that was followed by the Joint Staff Course. Thus practical service rather than theoretical critical meditation filled most of his time until about 1980. Till that time he remained rather unaware of the renaissance of Western professional military studies that had started in the U.S. land forces in the early 1970s in reaction to the Vietnam defeat. The American reforms were driven by a determination to develop the framework and tools for a potentially decisive victorious campaign with conventional weapons in Europe. It was the movement that set the scene for the first broad Anglo-Saxon discovery of "Vom Kriege" and the immediate success of the elegant translation of the book by Michael Howard and Peter Paret.

Via Howard to Clausewitz

For this author, the seed leaf of conversion had been planted several years before. By coincidence his class in the Military Academy was directly influenced by the three very different officers that would drive, inspire or lead different reforms of the Danish army during the next two decades. His cadet class director and tactics teacher was the junior of the three, Major Kaj Vilhelm Nielsen.[8] Nielsen sought professional insight in a step by step way and drove implementation with stubborn energy and diligence. The military history lecturer of the class was the former tactics teacher, Major Helge Kroon.[9] Kroon had served in the Resistance during the war and entered the army after Liberation. He was - and remains - brilliantly independent minded, charming, impatient with fools and totally disrespectful of formal authority. It was Kroon's teaching and inspiration that started the author on the track that ended with writing this article. The trigger was one of his teasing comments on the author's compulsory military history study. The subject was Crete 1941 and as the outcome had been impossible to explain in any other way this author had suggested in his conclusion – without being able to support it by references – that the reason had been the fundamental difference in leadership doctrine between the German and Austrian attackers and the British and Dominion defenders. Kroon had challenged the author to document his argument better.[10]

Later, in 1979, the publication of the first volume of F. H. Hinsley's official intelligence history highlighted the need for a good explanation because it documented that General Freyberg had some access to information from Enigma decrypts about the German invasion plans and this added to the pressure on my conscience to find a credible explanation of the outcome.[11]

The third of the three officers was the far more distant head of the Tactics Department, lieutenant colonel Nils Berg.[12] Berg was a highly sophisticated conceptual thinker, too theoretical to impress the cadets. Even before his commissioning in 1943 Berg had entered the Danish Resistance, he was arrested, sent to Neuengamme in 1944 and from there quickly dispatched to slave in the flooded mining corridors of Porta Westfalica. When incapable of further work the tall formerly strong man was returned in the winter of 1945 as nearly dead to Neuengamme. He only survived due to evacuation in Swedish Count Folke Bernadotte's White Busses. After the war he built up his health mapping the then still uncharted wild, mountainous East Greenland. His main contribution thereafter had been to inspire and formulate modern pedagogic and leadership principles for the army[13] as well as the creation of an academically and professionally balanced regular officer education.[14] His last position before retirement in 1978 had been as Military Academy commandant.

By that time the author had - by chance and good fate - been guided in an attractive direction. Looking for additional academic stimulation, he had used his spare time from 1974 to 1981 in a part-time history study at the Copenhagen University passing the exams of the then formally five years master programme. The chosen final subject had been the "Theories of War that influenced the 20th Century",[15] with the focus on the role of Clausewitz's theory on understanding of war of various Marxist-Leninists. At the end of the 1970's his university studies were temporarily interrupted by the accelerated learning and professional inspiration of the Army General Staff course in 1978 under the then Lieutenant-Colonel Jørgen Lyng,[16] which focused on the application of the new German and U.S. conventional war-fighting doctrines. Lyng was inspired by the new, 1976 edition of the U.S. Army Field Manual 100-5 "Operations" with its emphasis on flexible and constantly accurate dosage of the defender's combat and fire support element to contain and defeat the onrushing tank formations of the Warsaw Pact forces. The manual's battle management doctrine of "Active Defence" suited the talents of the highly intelligent and scientifically minded course director.

The army course was followed in 1979 by the newly created Joint Staff Course. It was directed by Kaj Vilhelm Nielsen, now lieutenant colonel, who was also responsible for lecturing strategy, assisted by Commander Hans Jørgen Garde.[17] As an external lecturer, Nielsen had been responsible for the strategy lessons in the Army General Staff Course since the early 1970's from his position as military history lecturer at the Military Academy. He had replaced Kroon in 1967. After taking over Nielsen had immediately started a reform of the Academy's military history course, inspired by Michael Howard's 1961 emphasis[18] that the subject should be taught in width, depth and context to become relevant to the development of a military professional. It had been Kroon who had discovered Howard's article and realised the applicability of the approach[19], but it was to be Nielsen who started using it systematically in his teaching.

Via Howard's inspiration the teaching mirrored Clausewitz's view of the role and limitation of military history in the development of the military professional. Nielsen had taken over editing the joint services periodical, "Militært Tidsskrift", (the Military Review) in 1963, and he modernised the journal and used it in an extended effort to heighten the professional level of his fellow officers. In 1974, he published a shortened version of Howard's 1973 Chesney Memorial Gold Medal lecture "Military Science in an Age of Peace" in the review,[20] and during the next years its pages became the place where officers and academic historians debated the use and abuse of military history.[21]

Nielsen's strategy lectures through the 1970s were based on Edward Mead Earle's "Makers of Modern Strategy. Military Thought from Machiavelli to Hitler"[22], and according to one of his students, his favourite lecture had been based on Hans Rothfels' chapter "Clausewitz".[23] The 1979 Joint Staff Course included a thorough discussion of the pulsing credibility crisis in nuclear deterrence and war-fighting doctrines as well as lectures about the development of military theory in the 19th and 20th centuries based on the chapters of Earle's anthology.

The author's first general staff officer posting after the two staff courses was in the Long Term Planning element of the Defence Staff. The small joint group of seven officers was formally responsible for developing force structure options and materiel alternatives at a 15 to 20 years horizon for later political discussion. As neither the individual armed service chiefs nor the joint defence leaders or the Ministry of Defence wanted an open minded presentation of alternatives, the planning element was deliberately blocked from doing what it had been created to do. It was often used by the Chief of Defence Staff as his personal pool of staff officers, writing speeches, drafting minutes from Defence Staff policy meetings and being employed as the Chief of Defence Liaison Group to the NATO Commander of the Baltic Approaches. The author's main experience from the period was a clear understanding of the total lack of an effective dialogue between the military professional chiefs and the national political leadership. The leading politicians considered the defence forces as a (minimum) contribution to the Alliance. They controlled the economy, burden of conscription and regional distribution of garrisons. The military leaders on their side considered that the force structures and readiness level should be left for the professionals to decide in a bargaining between the Army, Navy, Air Force and Home Guard.

The work as speech writer happened to lead to a visible role in the heated public debate about Western security and nuclear policies that followed the Alliance decision to deploy Intermediate Range missiles in various European member states. That again led to the author's selection to the Board of the Danish government Commission of Security and Disarmament Affairs during the first three years of its existence.

The work in the Long Term Planning Group was followed by two years from 1982 to 1984 as assistant military history lecturer in the Military Academy. The Academy military history then was conducted according to the Michael Howard-inspired guidelines introduced by Nielsen in the late 1960's. The "width" was done by covering the development from the Greeks until the latest wars in the Middle East, the "context" by linking the teaching as much as possible to the teaching in subjects like tactics, political science and military psychology. However, even if each cadet was supposed to develop an understanding "in depth" by writing a study of a battle or campaign, the programme never allowed him the time necessary to build up a proper understanding of how different factors interacted in the case.

Nielsen had also given military history a clear role in the advanced education of army officers in the General Staff Course. Since his time in the late 1970's, the head of the Danish Defence College Strategy Department became responsible for guiding the military history course in the Army General Staff

Course in the College. Besides a couple of initial general lectures and leading visits to selected First and Second World War battlefields such as Verdun, Sedan and Arnhem, the task consisted of guiding and criticising the students as they presented a case supposed to illustrate the actual subject topic of formation tactics teaching in the course. An example from the Eastern Front in World War II would highlight the principles of e.g. positional defence or a delaying action.

In his new Joint Staff Course he had tasked the students to give short lectures during a battle field tour of Normandy. However, even this regular exposure of the best officers to military history rarely succeeded in inspiring them to go on reading military history to support their further professional development.

The Danish translation

Clausewitz's influence in Denmark was the fortunate result of the lack of suitable employment for the many talents of Nils Berg, now a retired colonel. Berg may have known "Vom Kriege" superficially, however his main professional field had been different, and it was only his acknowledged lack of a proper post-retirement project that led him to accept the challenge of Major John Erling Andersen[24] and myself in Andersen's office in the Academy early in the 1980's to write a Danish translation.[25] Nils Berg's precondition for accepting the task had been that both I and Kaj Nielsen acted as control readers in the process and contributed to the publication, I by writing a short biography focusing on Clausewitz's interaction with the ideas of his time, Nielsen with a chapter about the philosophy and theory of war. Berg knew about Nielsen's interest in Clausewitz from his time as Academy Commandant, and because Nielsen had marked Clausewitz's 200 years' anniversary in October 1980 by a number of articles in the "Militært Tidsskrift", including two translated contributions by Werner Hahlweg.[26]

Both the process of translating and finishing the book "Om krig" - and the published result in 1986 became highly satisfactory for those involved in the project. Berg's combination of being an infantry officer, an accomplished independent conceptual thinker in a different field, a natural scientist as geodesist/geographer, and a comprehensive linguist made him the ideal translator and interpreter of Clausewitz's work. Even after his traumatic and brutal KZ-experience he nourished a deep love of German culture and literature. His deliberate use of late 19th century archaic Danish created a both elegant and accurate version of the flow of Clausewitz's arguments and parallels. The translation benefited from the proximity of the two Germanic languages.

The author's support work in the translation of "Vom Kriege" started during the two years period spent as lecturer at the Military Academy and was concluded during the ensuing troop service as subunit commander in an armoured battalion on the island of Zealand. For the author, the combination of the involvement in the translation, reading and lecturing and the total of a ten years period of troop duty[27] led to what was a full "conversion" to a Clausewitzian view of the limitations of theory, of the necessary politico-military interaction, of the society and context dominated chameleon of war, of the often fundamental difference of the phenomenon of war at the levels of the government, the field commander and the people, as well as of the chaotic character of combat influenced, as it is, by friction and chance.

The author's first intellectual activity after conversion was what might be called a pilgrimage to the battlefield of Maleme in Crete in summer 1986 to complete his analysis of the May 1941 events. When walking through the olive groves on what was once the New Zealander occupied slopes on the high ground over-looking the airstrip and along the road back to the brigade reserve's area, the reasons for the quick Axis tactical success became obvious. With so little fire support combat became decided by low level infantry combat. The British side wanted to manage the battle in an optimal way and waited for the thus necessary intelligence picture before ordering the units into counter attack. Understanding the normal chaotic character of combat, the Axis commanders and tactical leaders were trained to show initiative and act without orders. Even very high levels of losses did not hamper their action significantly. While the New Zealanders waited, the German air assault troopers and mountain infantry had plenty of time to bypass positions and get reinforcements. Thus the revisited case could become - and was - narrated in a way that made the result both obvious and generally relevant.[28]

The Clausewitzian prism combined with a close-up observation of how the Danish and other NATO forces worked in the mid-1980s. It exposed very serious weaknesses to the fresh convert. In command post exercises from the levels of the periodic WINTEX NATO-wide events down to the battalion the emphasis was on learning and drilling the application of procedures or doctrine. The actions of the Warsaw Pact enemy were always scripted as inflexible. He was always assumed to act in a schematic and fully predictable way. Even field exercises were conducted without free play; the umpires were not employed to ensure that good tactical behaviour was rewarded with success, and that unprofessional and stupid acts and decisions led to local defeat. Tactics had ceased to be the proper use of the equipment with an in-depth understanding of strength and limitations in relation to that of the enemy. It was not ensured that subordinate leaders and their units were used according to the known level and quality of cohesion and training. Exercises often were reduced to become a matter of demonstrating knowledge of the tactical manuals or, in NATO manoeuvres, Alliance solidarity and political correctness.

The root of the problem has been aptly identified by Sir Michael Howard back in 1961: "It is not surprising that there has often been a high proportion of failures among senior commanders at the beginning of any war. These unfortunate men may either take too long to adjust themselves to reality, through a lack of hard preliminary thinking about what war would really be like; or they may have had their minds so far shaped by a lifetime of pure administration that they have ceased for all practical purpose to be soldiers."[29]

National and NATO war planning was rarely if ever tested in realistic, free play, classical war games. If this was the result of a conscious decision, it was probably because such tests would demonstrate the lack of real realism in the member states' over-selling of the combat readiness of their units. One example: It was assumed and reported that the Danish Jutland Division could mobilise from cadre to full war strength and deploy to Holstein to be ready to fight in a couple of days. This was in spite of a situation where even the best, the semi-regular, units and their commanders and command cadres had never been through the demanding, realistic training for war that could weed out the unqualified and physically and mentally faint-hearted. Even this best half of the division missed the kind of training that could have developed the cohesion and tested the use of equipment in a way absolutely essential if the defending and therefore tactically surprised party should be able to withstand the shock of fire and assault without breaking, when the war started. It was assumed without question that the enemy would allow us and our overseas reinforcements the time to mobilise, deploy and dig-in before launching the offensive. We had to make this assumption as we never developed the ability to fight in the mobile meeting engagement against superior enemy forces that the Warsaw Pact formations went on training for. It was also assumed that the enemy would regard nuclear weapons in the same way we had done since the late 1960s and therefore abstain from early use.

An advocacy develops

The critical view that developed as a result of the "conversion" resulted in two types of reaction. Within one's own field of command or staff officer responsibility it was possible to change to conduct two-side, free play field and command post exercises that ensured a more realistic learning, also by experiencing failure through insufficient practical understanding to avoid friction. To some extent it was possible to include plans for realistic post-mobilisation training in the unit mobilisation plans, thereby highlighting the requirement and solution to both superiors and subordinates. However, the clear realisation of the weaknesses also led to intensive studies and an attempt to educate others to achieve a general improvement.

Clausewitz's model in Book 8 for political-military interaction flowed together with personal observations from the Danish political-military situation and inspired a number of analytic articles[30], where the superficial exercise and planning activities led to critical contributions to "Militært Tidsskrift".[31]

The public debating and publication activity of the author led to an invitation to become a member of the "Danish 1988 Defence Commission", a group combining the political parties' parliamentary defence policy spokesmen, the professional joint defence leaders (the senior one being Jørgen Lyng, now lieutenant general, Chief of Defence Staff soon designated next Chief of Defence), senior diplomats and academic security policy experts. The Commission was chaired by the new dynamic Permanent Under Secretary of the Defence Ministry, Michael Christiansen, and it had been established to conduct a fundamental review of the defence structures to achieve a better mission focus as well as an improved balance between structure and budget. The author had been invited because members of both government and opposition parties rather unrealistically hoped that he would be able to catalyse change.

The Commission was tasked with reporting on the threat, the Defence Force missions, allied reinforcement options and thereafter make a recommendation about the future organisation of defence to Parliament that could form the basis for the future organisation and budget. Without knowledge of the history of the previous 20th century Danish defence commissions, one might have assumed that this very Book 8-like combined political-military decision group - and the success of work of the 1988 Commission - had been inspired by the recent publication of Clausewitz's work. In reality, however, the commissions were never established with the primary aim of providing strategic understanding and guidance. They were created to achieve the highest possible level of consensus at the lowest possible budget level in periods when the domestic political situation or a major change in either the international economy or the external security framework made it relevant.

The success of achieving a high level of dialogue and consensus in the 1988 Commission was made possible by the changing domestic political situation and the personalities involved, not least the chairman. However, the result was meant to focus and balance the Danish Cold War defence contribution to NATO, so when the Commission report was ready at the end of 1989, it was fast becoming anachronistic.[32]

From 1988 onwards the time had come for the author to spread the gospel. Early that year he started as head of the Joint Operations Studies Department at the Royal Danish Defence College, and three years later he replaced John E. Andersen as Director, Joint Staff Course and head of the Strategic Studies Department on Andersen's promotion to colonel. Andersen had taken over from Kaj Vilhelm Nielsen three years earlier.

As the study of force doctrine and structure was an Operations Department field, applying Clausewitzian insights in the lecturing on the friction and pitfalls of politico-military decision-making in those fields could start immediately. The pedagogic method was to start by explaining how the ideal process would produce a force structure and doctrine that both mirrored the requirements and which could adapt in a flexible way to changing needs. Thereafter cases were used to demonstrate how this process normally failed to do so due to the difficulty of understanding the capabilities and proclivities of both allies and the potential enemy. The normal risks included both "mirror imaging"- believing that others read the options as we did - and the "colonel's fallacy" - a fixation with the worst case. The teaching also underlined the importance of the fundamental difference of priorities and views of the politicians and the leading military, of the tendency to delay or avert decisions on the politician's side, and a wish to keep control of the development among the military leadership. The teaching highlighted the importance of deliberate or subconscious roots in the organisational behaviour of the individual services, of service cultures, of bureaucratic and management fashions, and maybe even in some cases a difference in security policy paradigm between the politicians and leading military.

Later as head of the Strategy Department, the author became responsible for the lecturing of Military Theory. During the previous years the new "Makers of Modern Strategy from Machiavelli to the Nuclear Age" edited by Peter Paret[33] had replaced Earle's vintage edition as the main textbook, and the teaching now had the form of lectures based on the articles of that anthology about Jomini, Mahan, Liddell Hart, the Air Theorists, the Marxist-Leninists, Mao, the nuclear theorists and – Peter Paret's own – about Clausewitz.

The teaching now changed. The author would lecture on the context and implications of each theory that the student would now know from the reading of selected parts of the theorist's work as well as seminar discussions on the basis of that reading. The treatment of each theory would end with a plenary debate. The level of preparation and learning would be controlled by small tests to motivate the students to read enough to participate in the debates. Ten years later, when the author was responsible for lecturing military theory in the Baltic Defence College in Tartu, Corbett's theory would join Mahan's, Soviet Operational Art development teaching would replace the Marxist-Leninists, the discussion of the interaction of total war and geostrategic theories in the early 20th century would be added as well as a discussion of development of the joint, amphibious warfare doctrine.

As Nielsen and Andersen before him, the author was also responsible for the military history teaching in the Army General Staff Course as head of the Defence College Strategy Department. Initially he had used the model of his predecessors, having the students giving positive World War II illustrations to support the tactics teaching in spite of his understanding that this added very little to the student's professional insight. However, in the last course before the author departed for service in the Baltic States, the student contributions were changed, so that his role thereafter was to find and explain the factors that made the historical case operation plan collapse partly or fully in implementation, making it necessary to adjust or improvise at low level to achieve the objective of the operation or abandon it. The purpose was to open the eyes of the students to the limits of theory, to the normally chaotic character of combat, of the inevitable role of friction and chance in war as well as to how friction could be foreseen and its influence somewhat limited by simplicity in plans, delegation of authority, realistic training and the commanders' and staff officers' practical experience.

The effects of these endeavours of inspiring others by advocating a more Clausewitzian understanding of war and warfare will be dealt with later.

The author left the Danish Defence College for Riga late spring 1994. His service until 1997 was as Danish Defence Attaché to the three Baltic States with the mission and significant resources to support their defence development on the way to NATO. His observations soon led him to realise that the precondition for any real effect of Danish and other assistance was a shock-start of the development by the creation of a Western type staff officers corps - and a group of civil servants in the Defence Ministries - that could both plan and implement. He gained Baltic States and international support for the idea and developed and commanded the Baltic Defence College in Tartu in South Estonia from 1998 until retirement end 2004.

The main College activity was the 11 months Senior Staff Course. According to the August 2002 briefing to visitors, the mission was pure Clausewitzian: "The course should develop professional, active, hard working, honest, positively critical, independent minded General Staff officers of the best classical (German), international standard … After the course they should be prepared for continuous self-development, using self-study and the experience from command and staff positions". As one of his tools, the author used his military theory and doctrine development lectures. The College journal, "The Baltic Defence Review", was employed in a more general educational effort to develop understanding of why deep changes were necessary.[34]

In 2004 it had been realised that there was a need to take one further step to make a development towards effective staff structures and an effective politico-military interaction. Therefore a small "Higher Command Studies Course" was developed for Baltic and other East European officers and civil servants with a potential for promotion to top level. The mission according to the June 2004 pre-course briefing was to: "… educate selected senior officers and civil servants to initiate and lead implementation of a dynamic peacetime development of armed forces as well as for decision-making and leadership positions during their state's participation in war and military operations other than war". As the author planned and directed this first course himself as his last project before retiring, the key pedagogical tool became in-depth comparative studies of selected cases of peace- and wartime innovation.[35]

Confronting reality

From New Year 2005 the author was back in Denmark, a country involved in an unpopular low intensity war in Iraq and soon to become involved in the politically less controversial stabilisation of South Afghanistan. Denmark had been involved in Afghanistan very early, participating both in the winter 2002 special force operations southeast of Kabul and in ISAF activities in the capital and later in the provinces.

As a Clausewitzian the author would have expected that the Danish government had made a thorough, national, independent politico-military analysis of the nature and issues of a conflict. Before deciding to make its armed forces available, it would weigh the possibilities and limitations of the military instrument – in concert with other tools in the state inventory – in that specific situation. Due to the never predictable character of war, participation in the conflict was likely to bring significant risks. To a Clausewitzian, the armed forces' leadership has a direct responsibility to understand all professionally related issues. It also should be heard about the potential risks and benefits as well as role and composition of military and other contributions. The Chief of the Armed Forces of even small, potentially contributing states like Denmark must seek information that allow advising the government about total necessary force levels and required strategies in missions such as the post-invasion stabilisation of Iraq. The same applies to strategic issues like the essential integration of Pakistan in any counter-insurgency effort in Pashtun majority areas of Afghanistan. The Chief should never accept a political tunnel vision in his advice. Only by a full, independent, professional analysis can he minimise the risk that lives of his soldiers are sacrificed unnecessarily as the cannon fodder to allied mistakes or ambitions. He should be qualified to outline the military options, e.g. the use of air power or more boots on the ground, as well as the need for an integrated, multi-agency effort with long periods in the mission for all key cadres. He should highlight the force organisation and training essential for minimising the risks of large numbers of combat stress invalids.

The government should insist on getting this full and clear contribution in advance from the chief (and his supporting intelligence and other experts) and should replace the general or admiral immediately if he fails to do so. The Chief is responsible for being heard, and if ignored, he should if necessary resign to increase the chance that the politicians would listen to his successor and understand that they carry the full risk of ignoring professional advice. This not to undermine the government's right to decide.

The small state politicians should be conscious of the seriousness of not only the decision to contribute but also of how that contribution is organised. The pre-intervention analysis should form the basis not only of the decision to participate, but also for pre-decision negotiations with the leading state, normally the U.S., and the state forming the framework for the Danish contribution, normally the UK. Good preparation might give real influence and minimise risks, because both the leading and framework states need the small state force contributions. It might also clarify the criteria for the end of the small state force contribution in advance. However, if advice and preconditions for participation are ignored, the small state would probably benefit from limiting their offer to non-military assistance.

The only case known to the author where a Clausewitzian type interaction formed the decision basis of a significant military deployment was Prime Minister Poul Nyrup Rasmussen's then controversial choice in 1993 to send a main battle tank squadron to join the Nordic UN battalion protecting the Tuzla enclave in northern Bosnia. It was the result of a direct consultation with his Chief of Defence, Jørgen Lyng, in a situation where the Foreign and Defence Ministers disagreed with each other.

Nothing in the information now available either to the public or to the author about the decisions to send Danish force contributions to Afghanistan in 2001, 2002 and 2006 and Iraq in 2003 indicate that the decisions were informed by an independent analysis and Clausewitzian-type consultations. On the contrary the contributions seem to have been motivated by the commendable wish to show a symbolic support to Denmark's main allies. However, this does not necessarily rule out the thorough and tough discussion based on a national scrutiny of options. After all the situation was fundamentally different from 60 years earlier, when the government of occupied Denmark sanctioned that a volunteer unit would join other nations in the struggle against Communism on the Eastern Front. Now Denmark had the full freedom of choice, and with Donald Rumsfeld in charge of the Pentagon a significant improvement in the professional decision base level was achievable for all.

The present situation has deep roots. The historically alert person may remember that Danish history during the 150 years since the adoption of a democratic constitution has been characterised by a disastrous lack of politico-military dialogue with the periods 1905-09, 1910-13 and 1949-58 as the only relatively bright spots.[36] The best illustration of the total dysfunctional relations is the years 1852-63 and during the 1864 war with Prussia and Austria. The events and results of that war were so hard for the nation to face that it had to spin the historical narrative to make Denmark the victim. The painful reality had to wait for the autumn 2010 book to be presented in a balanced way.[37]

Let us move to the author's direct personal experience. When developing the military theory lecturing in the Baltic Defence College, the interaction with the students was fundamentally helpful, the feedback making it possible to improve the substance of this element from one course to the next. Even if some of the positive character of the students' feed-back might have been influenced by the fact that the lecturer was a general and the College Commandant, it does not give a full explanation. The Baltic and other East European students arrived with a hunger to learn their profession, and they accepted that not all teaching should be easily and directly usable in their follow-on job.

However, when the now mature military theory course was used by the now retired author lecturing to the Danish Joint Staff Course students that it had originally been designed for in the early 1990s, the reaction was fundamentally negative. Navy and air force students reacted against the relevance of "military" theory, the name itself indicating that it was army dominated. They also objected to what they saw as another indication of army bias: the fact that Mahan and Douhet were not presented as being at the same level as Clausewitz. Naval officers reacted against what they saw as the presentation of the Clausewitzian Corbett's writing as more sophisticated than Mahan's. The very influential curriculum text of the latter had been used where it logically belonged: for the discussion of the geo-strategic theorists.

To meet the students' concerns the name of the course was thereafter changed to "Strategic Theories", and the definition of strategy used was that of the modern Clausewitzian political scientist, Colin Gray,[38] who considered that "Strategy is the bridge that relates military power to political purpose". An additional Mahan text, "The Naval War College"[39], was added to the curriculum. In it he presented his Nelsonian - and very Clausewitzian - educational and tactical leadership philosophy. Mahan underlined the requirement for delegation of command authority. To adjust to the wish of the air force students, the modern precision air power theory of John A. Warden, III was included. The final step to adjust the course without breaking it was to separate theories about how to fight from the theory about the character of war and combat.

However, even these changes did not lead to a more positive reception. The students considered background knowledge about the context of a specific theoretical text irrelevant: the time, the theorist's background and purpose of writing. It became increasingly clear that the majority only considered theory relevant if it was directly usable and prescriptive. It is unclear if the change of reception from 1994 to ten years later is related to the fact that the number of students at the Joint Staff Course has been increased by about 40 percent, while at the same time the average educational levels - including historical knowledge and language skills - of officers undergoing basic training have been considerably reduced. On giving up Clausewitzian type theory lecturing, the experience led to the author's essay, "The lessons of Napoleon for lesser men" for the XXXV CIHM Congress in Porto in 2009. The conclusion was basically that a professional officer corps apparently needed and still need a Jominian-type prescriptive "scientific", battle management-like theory that can be directly formulated into a doctrine that becomes dogma by bureaucratic implementation.

The general professional military paradigm had also changed during the period. Following the renaissance in the 1970s and 1980s mentioned early in this article, American military thinking had regressed into the formalistic "Operational Art" discussions in the 1990s that was unrelated to any strategic requirements in real wars. Warfare theory thereafter was reduced to the "Netcentric" management of strikes a la Warden against scientifically selected targets chosen for effect in relation to multiple "Centers of Gravity". The emphasis was on quick arrival in the theatre assuming that the cancer of any political-military problem could be removed by a quick operation. Thereafter, the forces could return home from the victorious small war. Buzzwords that stalled and replaced independent critical analysis followed each other every four years. One sided punishment made possible by "Information Dominance" replaced traditional two sided war. Friction no longer hampered the smooth operations of the surgical strike machine. With a few years' delay, the – now partially anachronistic – buzzwords that guided the "Transformation" to the "Revolution in Military Affairs" reached NATO and were adopted in a somewhat confused and diluted form. When that happened, the uncritically progressive Danish staff course lecturers had already been preaching copies of the latest one-dimensional gospel to their students for months.

The teaching about the difference between the ideal force structure and doctrine development and the reality of historical cases is no longer given. It was stopped even earlier than the military theory course as it confused the students and the lecturers implicitly communicated a critical attitude to how our professional and political superiors take decisions. The message also implied that a hard self-critical effort would be required of the best of the future staff officers.

The same had immediately happened after the author's 1994 departure to the study in the army course of why plans failed due to friction, chance and unexpected enemy action in support of the teaching of formation tactical doctrine. This was the case even if such a focus had become ever more relevant due to the fact that the general (rather than mission) level of practical command experience of the students was becoming far lower now than in previous decades. Use of positive historical case illustrations is both the normal approach and far easier. However, it does not promote insight in the way that Clausewitz realised that the reading of military history could give to the aspiring field commander.

The only way to inspire enhanced understanding thereafter seemed to be to write. As a result the author has spent the latest few years writing new studies of politico-military decision-making with the purpose of creating more accurate narratives than those previously available.[40] However, even if the fraternity of active Clausewitzians remains very small in Denmark and their influence on the decision-makers and armed forces trifling, one doctoral student made a highly relevant contribution late last year, when he defended his dissertation and received his Ph.D. degree in political science from Aalborg University. Jeppe Plenge-Trautner's thesis: "Beliefs and the Politics of Modern Military Interventions. An analysis of how pre-conceptions about the nature of war and armed conflict shape the democracies' generation, use and direction of military force"[41] argued in a fully convincing way that a person's (and reality an organisation's common) "War Concept", is the prism through which he will see everything relating to war and the military. In the Western Democracies the political leaders tend to define war according what Trautner labels a "Liberal" war concept: "The underlying ideal of Liberal thinking is that warfare essentially represents a failure of politics. Once war has begun, Liberals argue, an emotion driven and largely irrational 'logic of war' displaces a peacetime rationality of co-operation for mutual benefit. …"[42]

The modern Western Militaries on the other hand, tended to adhere to what he labels the "MilTech" war concept: "(T)he Mil-Tech war concept proposes that the scope for rationality in warfare is much larger than what Liberals would allow for: Capable soldiers and well equipped armed forces are able to see through the 'fog of war', and to direct wars in detail; abilities which hinge on technological superiority and thorough planning of military operations.

While Mil-Techs are more confident in the ability and good judgment of soldiers than Liberals they fully agree with Liberals on the overall importance of the supremacy of civil politicians at the strategic level; Mil-Techs just advise that civilians should not meddle in what is most safely handled by soldiers, and that civilians thus should refrain from interfering in Operational and Tactical Level matters."[43]

The latter concept is purely Jominian and neither of the two concepts will assume that a close and constant political control of the military instrument is either relevant or necessary. This tends to make Trautner's (discretely held, own) Clausewitzian war concept an orphan, and thus explains the roots of the authors experience after his conversion.

It is good to understand the reason why "Vom Kriege" will always be more quoted than accepted in Denmark and other western democracies - why a generation of advocacy since conversion was doomed to failure.

If one goes through the key Danish professional military and naval periodicals from the last century and reads samples from every decade it become evident that the volume, the quality and the independent analysis have deteriorated gradually. This development was accelerated since the seventies where the national contribution to NATO settled into its more or less final Cold War form. So even if the renaissance in military thinking taking place in the U.S. during the 70s and 80s was interesting to follow and understand in a general way, there was no reason to integrate its conclusions into the military culture. Seen from a small Alliance member all the new stuff was meant to enhance deterrence by making the force posture more convincing, it was not introduced to fight wars, and the drastic reduction in combat readiness that had been decided by the Danish government in the late 60s remained in place during the rest of the Cold War. The cadre of forces that were only meant to act as a symbolic contribution to deterrence copied the Nordic societies developing new happy balance between work and private interests, family etc. Even for the career officer, the commitment to his profession became forever more limited. Professional studies were restricted to periods in formal courses where you could absorb the latest ideas. The continuous studies that are essential in any profession became rare, and thus the officers' ability to develop, present and defend any independent insight in print.

Therefore the Clausewitzian elements of the military renaissance never struck roots in Denmark beyond the occasional quotation, and when the enlightenment froze and collapsed in the 90s in America in the Pavlovian search for an appropriate silver bullet reaction to the 1991 Gulf War, the Danish military profession had not been absorbing enough resilient wisdom from Howard or Clausewitz to avoid being reduced to parrot the latest Pentagonese or management buzzwords.

If you are a small state it is ridiculous to be a Clausewitzian anyway, is it not? After all they are "… not to make reply, Theirs not to reason why, Theirs but to do & die, …"[44] So we stayed pragmatic, loyal, avoided strenuous independent thinking, and contributed (perhaps with symbolic cannon fodder) when the (maybe necessary) small wars came.

Notes:

[1] One of the sets of all ten volumes of the *"Hinterlassenes Werk"* from 1832 to 1837 acquired for use by the Danish Army elite ended in the book collection of the Centre for Military History of the Royal Danish Defence College. The different owner unit stamps in the book makes likely that this specific set was bought for use by the artillery officers.

[2] Frederik Ludvig August Haller Baggesen (1795-1865), son of the famous romantic poet Jens Baggesen, Major General in 1854. Among his publications is an analysis of the military geography of Denmark, published in German 1845-47.

[3] Johan Christian Vogelius Steenstrup (1795-1870). He ended his career as Major General.

[4] For this description of the early knowledge of Clausewitz in Denmark, see: Nils Berg, "Introduktion" in *Carl von Clausewitz, Om Krig. III. Kommentar og Registre,* Copenhagen 1986, pp. 831-833.

[5] As late as 1906 the chapter on Strategy in the Military Academy textbook about the Art of War was totally Jominian in its definitions and purpose of strategy and tactics, see: Kaptajn Jacobi: *Krigskunstens Udviklingshistorie. Til Brug ved Undervisningen af næstældste Klasse.*

[6] 1886-1976. Promoted to lieutenant-general in 1941 and served as army chief until the dissolution of the armed forces in 1943 and again after the 1945 Liberation.

[7] S.C. Volden, *Danske hærordninger efter 2. Verdenskrig i nationalt og internationalt perspektiv*, Karup 2007. Michael H. Clemmesen, "Den massive gengældelses lille ekko. De taktiske atomvåbens rolle i dansk forsvarsplanlægning i 1950'erne. In: Carsten Due-Nielsen, Johan Peter Noack og Nikolaj Petersen: *Danmark, Norden og NATO 1948 – 1962*, Copenhagen 1991.

[8] 1927-2001. Editor of *Militært Tidsskrift* 1963-1988. Military History lecturer at the Military Academy 1967-1976. Head of the Department of Strategy at the Royal Danish Defence College 1976-1988.

[9] Lieutenant Colonel Helge Kroon (1924-)

[10] Michael Clemmesen: *Kreta, Maj 1941*. Hærens Officersskole. Juni 1966, Margin comment p. 10: "Kilde?"

[11] F. H. Hinsley, E.E. Thomas, C.F.G. Ransom and R. C. Knight: *British Intelligence in the Second World War.* Volume I. London 1979, pp. 417-421.

[12] Colonel Nils Berg (1916-2000).

[13] Published as: Hærkommandoen: *Ledelse og uddannelse. Militær pædagogik*. Copenhagen 1969.

[14] Initially introduced as a sketch in "Det militærvidenskabelige grundstudium. Et essay." (The Basic Academic Military Science Course. An Essay). In *Militært Tidsskrift*, January 1966.

[15] Københavns Universitet. Det humanistiske fakultet. Eksamensadministrationen. Sommer 1981. Michael Hesselholt Clemmesen. Opgivelser til prøve i område nr. 7: *Krigsteorier i det 20. Århundrede*.

[16] Later Chief of Defence, general Jørgen Lyng (1934-).

[17] Later Chief of Defence, admiral Hans Garde (1939-1996).

[18] In: "The Use and Abuse of Military History". In: *The RUSI Journal*, 1961.

[19] Interview with Helge Kroon on 6.8.2010.

[20] *Militært Tidsskrift*, October 1974.

[21] For one example see: Knud J. V. Jespersen, "Debat: Hvad skal vi med militærhistorie? Et gensvar." In: *Militært Tidsskrift*, April 1980.

[22] Princeton 1970.

[23] Interview with Andersen on 10.8.2010.

[24] (1937-). Now retired colonel. Then the senior military history lecturer at the Academy.

[25] Most likely a day in early 1983.

[26] Militært Tidsskrift, October 1980.

[27] After the squadron command in a formation staff in Zealand followed by command of a regular infantry battalion in Bornholm and of a reserve tank battalion in the Jutland Division.

[28] "Kampene ved Maleme i maj 1941 – og nogle tanker på grundlag af deres forløb", in *Militært Tidsskrift*, July/August/September 1987.

[29] In the already mentioned RUSI Journal article: "The Use and Abuse of Military History".

[30] A selection: The book: *Jyllands Landforsvar fra 1901 til 1940*, Copenhagen 1982. The article: "Forsvarsforliget af 1984: Tilblivelse og Konsekvenser", in *Dansk Udenrigspolitisk Årbog 1984*, Copenhagen 1985. The article: "Dansk forsvar fra omkring 1890 til 1918 – en skitse med fynsk perspektiv". In: *Militärhistorisk Tidskrift* 1985, Stockholm 1986. The booklet: "Værnskulturerne og Forsvarspolitikken", in *Politica*, Aarhus 1986. The article: "Udviklingen i Danmarks forsvarsdoktrin fra 1945 til 1969", in *Militärhistorisk Tidskrift* 1987, Stockholm 1987. The article: "NATO – sikkerhedspolitikkens folkekirke", in *Udenrigs*, 2/1988. The article: "Den massive gengælselses lille ekko. De taktiske atomvåbens rolle i dansk forsvarsplanlægning i 1950'erne", in Carsten Due-Nielsen, Johan Peter Noack og Nikolaj Petersen: *anmark, Norden og NATO 1948-1962*, Copenhagen 1991. The article: „Efterkoldkrigstidens danske forsvarspolitik", in *Dansk Udenrigspolitisk Årbog 1992*, Copenhagen 1992. The article: "Denmark in the shadow of German Military Might. The Hostage of its Geographical Position in Times of International Turbulence and Rapid Technological Change, 1864-1945", in Göran Rystad, Klaus-R. Böhme and Wilhelm M. Carlgren: *In Quest of Trade and Security: The Baltic in Power Politics, 1500-1990, II: 1890- 1990*, Lund 1995. The article: "The Politics of Danish Defence 1967-1993", in Carsten Due-Nielsen og Nikolaj Petersen: *Adaptation and Activism. The Foreign Policy of Denmark 1967-1993*, Copenhagen 1995. The article: "Danmark i skyggen av Tysklands militære magt", in *Krigskunst og statssystem. Krig og maktpolitik i industrialismens tidsalder 1860-1918*, Oslo 2001. The article: "The Danish Straits in the Post Second World War Period" in *Revue Internationale D'Histoire Militaire, Edition Danoise, No 84*, Copenhagen 2004. Of more theoretical character should be added: The article: "Sun-tzu blandt krigsteoretikerne" in: Jens Østergård Petersen: *Krigskunsten*, Copenhagen 1989, and the article: "Krigs-

videnskabeligheden. Risikoen for det indlysende. Tidens sandheder i kritisk perspektiv", in *Det krigsvidenskabelige Selskab – 125 år*, Copenhagen 1996.

[31] The following "Militært Tidsskrift" articles critizise various departures from professionalism from a Clausewitzian point of view: "Om den lille professionelle hærs utilstrækkelighed", July/August/September 1982. "Om principperne for krigsføring og vort forsvar" July/August/September 1984." Om en af vore seriøse beskæftigelser: Operativ planlægning til bunds eller bureaukratiske korthuse med frasefyld", March 1985. "Om hærens mobiliseringsberedskab", April 1986, "Anvendelsen af historien i Hærens officersuddannelse", February 1987. "Egne forhold", October 1987. "Krigsrisiko, varsel og forsvarsberedskab", May/June 1988. "Vi kunne være draget afsted med kejserens nye klæder", April 1990. The sharpest critique of the erosion of proper tactical behaviour was: "Lidt landmilitær professionalisme – tak", in *Kentaur. Kamptroppernes Tidsskrift*, 5/1988. Much later followed two articles in *Militært Tidsskrift*: "De danske væbnede styrker i fremtiden – en skitse fra sidelinien", 2/2003 and "Om at glemme eller skamme sig over at være militær", 1/2009. The critique of the last listed article is developed further in the article "Kejserens nye klæder", in: Hans Mortensen (ed.): *'Helt forsvarligt?'. Danmarks militære udfordringer i en usikker fremtid*', Copenhagen 2009.

[32] For an analysis of this and the following Danish Defence Commission, see: Bertel Heurlin: *Riget, Magten og Militæret. Dansk Forsvar s - og Sikkerhedspolitik under Forsvarskommissionerne af 1988 og af 1997*. Aarhus 2004.

[33] Oxford and Princeton 1986.

[34] As a clear, example see the author's critical analysis of the situation from top to bottom in the Baltic Armed Forces after the NATO invitation: "The Path of Transition: from the Past towards Efficient Armed Forces", in *Baltic Defence Review*, No. 8, Volume 2/2002.

[35] BALTDEFCOL Higher Command Studies Course 2004 "Leadership of Transformation" 19th August 2004, themes: "AO 1.2 – Leaders of Innovation in Peace and Adaptation in War" and "AO 1.5 – Initiation, planning and management of force and doctrine development".

[36] Under the liberal Prime & Defence Ministers Jens Christian Christensen and Klaus Berntsen and during the first decade as a NATO member.

[37] Tom Buk-Swienty: Dommedag Als 29. juni 1864, Copenhagen 2010.

[38] His book: Modern Strategy, Oxford 1999, was included as a general strategy course textbook.

[39] North American Review, vol. 196 (July 1912).

[40] *Vilnakommandoet 1920-21. Vort første kontingent til en international fredsbevarende styrke – fra start til abort en lille måned før fødsel*, Copenhagen 2007. "The Danish Armed Forces 1909-1918. Between Politicians and Strategic Reality". Copenhagen 2008. "Bornholms forsvar 1893 til 1943 – københavnske ideer og bornholmsk realitet". In: *Bornholmske Samlinger*, IV. Række- 3. Bind, Rønne 2009. With Anders Osvald Thorkilsen: *Mod fornyelsen af Københavns forsvar 1915-18*, Copenhagen 2009. *Den lange vej mod 9. april. Historien om de fyrre år før den tyske operation mod Norge og Danmark*, Odense 2010. "Tunestillingen. Indenrigspolitisk middel og militær beskæftigelse", in *Første Verdenskrig ved Tunestillingen. Forsvarsvilje og hverdagsliv*, Greve 2010.

[41] Post-defence version of the thesis. Aalborg 2010.

[42] *Ibid.*, p. 28.

[43] *Ibid.*, p. 29.

[44] From *The Charge of the Light Brigade* by Alfred, Lord Tennyson 1854.

CLAUSEWITZIAN WAR THEORY AND THE DEFENCE DOCTRINES OF SMALL STATES: CASE FINLAND

Pekka Visuri

The article firstly reviews the basics of Clausewitz's theory on war and its relevance for the present security conditions in Europe. The interpretation of Clausewitz has been difficult because of his dialectical method and many contradictions in his unfinished book *On War*. For grasping the core ideas of Clausewitz's theory it is important to know the genesis of the book. His conclusions were mostly drawn from the Napoleonic wars, especially from the struggle of Prussia against France.

One of the main features in Clausewitz's theory was the emphasis he laid on the relation of defence to offensive. He argued that the defender has many favouring factors, beside the physical conditions also moral factors, e.g. better legitimacy and motivation to fight, in relation to the aggressor.

For explaining the small states' defence problems the case Finland has been studied and assessed. Finland defended her independence and national survival against the Soviet aggression in the Second World War. This positive experience made it possible after the war to continue with the proved defence system which was based on the civic army. During the 1960s Finland accepted a strategic-operational doctrine of territorial or area defence, which had many ideas offered by a neo-Clausewitzian theorist André Beaufre.

After the Cold War the discussions also in Finland have often concerned the relevance of Clausewitz's war theories in the post-modern conditions of the globalized world and especially in relation to the theories of high tech war-fighting, called RMA. After the wars in Afghanistan and Iraq the appreciation of Clausewitz seems to be growing again, and the consequences are interesting also for the small states like Finland.

The continuing relevance of the Clausewitzian war theory in the post-Cold War Europe has been proved. It is still a useful method for analysis of the security and defence issues of small states in the profoundly changing political landscape and military technical conditions of the world.

"The aggressor is always peace-loving (as Bonaparte always claimed to be); he would prefer to take over our country unopposed. To prevent his doing so one must be willing to make war and be prepared for it. In other words it is the weak, those likely to need defense, who should always be armed in order not to be overwhelmed. Thus decrees the art of war."[1]

"All warfare is based on deception."[2]

Introduction: Views on war theories in the post-Cold War era

The wars in the post-Cold War period have been often called "post-modern"[3] because they have many features which differ from the "modern wars" which are also known as "Clausewitzian wars". At the same time the term "revolution in military affairs" (RMA) has been used to describe the greatly increasing importance of the computerised information and precision guided technology in warfare. RMA, however, has turned out to be a rather confusing "acronym of choice in the US armed forces" covering a large scale of visions on future wars.[4]

Another well-known description for the development of military affairs has been presented in the book *War and Anti-War (1993)* by Alvin and Heidi Toffler. They used the terms "first, second and third waves of warfare" corresponding to agricultural, industrial and information societies which have their own specialised ways to wage war.

The Gulf War 1991 and the end phases of the Yugoslav wars in the 1990s, especially the Kosovo War 1999, seemed to prove that the RMA theories were correct. The precision guided weapons enhanced both effectiveness of the fire power and enabled striking against small targets without vast collateral damages. As the surveillance and communication technology improved the situational awareness remarkably it was no wonder that the American type military doctrines, "network centric warfare" etc, were totally overwhelming "traditional" strategy and battle doctrines.

However, the experiences from the wars in Afghanistan and Iraq 2001-2010 have again lowered expectations that high-technology together with network centric war-fighting could achieve a real revolution in military affairs, maybe "an end of the doctrine development". Instead, the interest to study classic war theories has grown as it happened during 1960s when André Beaufre and Raymond Aron applied Clausewitzian theories to the stalemated cold-war conditions in Europe. The aftermath of the Vietnam war in the late 1970s brought up a Clausewitz renaissance in the United States[5], so that we can now wait for a similar neo-renaissance, too.

The published debate on new revolutionary visions on war has been concentrated mostly on the US military policy. The United States is no doubt the leading world power and, therefore, it is important to observe her developments even if it cannot be followed straightaway by other countries. The security problems of smaller and poorer states are totally different. Their problems must be solved by other, much more cost-effective means than in a framework of that high technological military force which only the great powers must have and also can afford. A very important question for the small states is also the nature of their security policy which should be based on more peaceful means than the major powers are used to do.

The purpose of this article is to analyse the main features and continuing relevance of Clausewitz's theory for the defence policy and doctrines of the small states in the "post-modern situation" in Europe and in the globalized world politics. The emphasis is laid on the Finnish experience during the World War II and Cold War which has been building a basis for the present defence policy, too.

Genesis of the Clausewitzian theory on war and the problem of its further relevance

We can accept the thesis that the phenomenon war is always an expression of the culture of the respective societies. Therefore, also the theory on war which Carl von Clausewitz developed during and after the Napoleonic wars reflects, at the first place, the circumstances in Central Europe during the first two decades of the nineteenth century. Clausewitz was a "regimental officer" who grew up in the Prussian cultural milieu which was a mixture of enlightenment and romanticism. His compatriot was Karl Marx. Both wrote remarkable theories on politics, though from quite different viewpoints, and they both have roused very much confusion and false interpretations.[6]

For grasping Clausewitz's philosophy it is important to know his career and the genesis of his book *On War*.[7] Crucial was his experience during the Napoleonic wars, and the most important occasion was the failure of the Prussian troops in the battle by Jena and Auerstedt in 1806. Clausewitz had to analyse the reasons why the famous, well trained and disciplined professional army shaped by late Frederick the Great could not repel the offensive of the revolutionary French army which was organised on the basis of compulsory conscription. Only the genius of Napoleon was not a sufficient explanation for French success, even if it was one important factor. The reform movement of Prussian military in which Clausewitz had a remarkable role assumed then many features of the French civic army's organisation and tactics. Clausewitz saw also the importance of the state and society for an effective army.[8]

Already the battles of the first coalition against France in 1793 influenced Clausewitz's mindset about the war so much that he decided to begin war studies. He saw as 13 years old corporal a very confusing "real war" which differed totally from the disciplined "ideal war" for which the cadets were trained on the barrack fields in Potsdam.[9] Those impressions are well expressed in the introductory but very central part of his magnum opus *On War*, in the "book one" which is titled *On the Nature of War* (original German title: Über die Natur des Krieges). After the famous definitions of war and strategy Clausewitz raised the friction from the sidelines to a central explanation for many difficulties we know are connected with the warfare also today in Afghanistan and Iraq.

The appreciation of the present relevance of Clausewitz's theory is not an easy task, mostly because of his dialectic method. For example, his distinction between "absolute war" and "real war" has fascinated many interpreters who have found difficult to understand its real meaning for the nuclear age.[10] The same problem concerns generally theories on war and peace as well as definitions on aggression and defence. Clausewitz made apparently clear, "absolute" terms more relativistic by using controversial questions which were based on historical experience. For example, the quotation from the book *On War* which tells how "the aggressor is always peace-loving" is typical for Clausewitz's dialectics and was based on his personal experience as a prisoner of war after the lost battle in Jena and Auerstedt in 1806.[11]

An actual question now is e.g. the nature and meaning of "info-war". How does it relate to Clausewitz's concept on war? Another problem is to apply Clausewitz's war theories in the contemporary discussions about conflict and crisis management measures as well as the "war against terrorism".

The Essence of Clausewitz's views on strategy for application to new situations

A successful application of Clausewitz's theory for present and future conflicts depends on the findings of the real meaning of that theory, i.e. the ability to catch the core ideas presented by Clausewitz and their relationship to present and future circumstances. We know very well how much the opinions can change over time and according to environment. Clausewitz presents a theoretical menu for choice, and it demands a careful consideration, how to apply his findings to an actual situation.

Helmuth von Moltke, Alfred von Schlieffen and other German strategists before the WW I picked out the idea of the operational surprise and battle of annihilation. Yet, the way they used Clausewitz's theory was basically anti-Clausewitzian and resembled more the positivist principles of warfare presented by Antoine-Henry Jomini.[12]

Friedrich Engels, Vladimir Lenin and Mao Tse-tung found the analogy between war and commerce as well as connection of war and politics. Those Marxists changed Clausewitz's formula on "war as continuation of politics" to "politics for continuation of war" and applied the theory on war for making revolution and people's war.[13]

Michael Howard has emphasized the usefulness of Clausewitzian thinking in enlargement of the definition of strategy from pure operational military field to more comprehensive strategy. This is basically the same idea as in Liddell Hart's "grand strategy" but Howard wanted to define the term "strategy" proper to contain also the logistic, social and economic aspects in addition to pure military affairs. The reference to Clausewitzian "trinity" of people, army and government[14] explains the basis for this kind of reasoning.[15]

Neo-Clausewitzian theoreticians during the Cold War - and in the nuclear age - liked to point out the holistic way of thinking in Clausewitz's theory. Most famous and most important for Europeans, too, was André Beaufre whose "total strategy" responding to English "grand strategy" offered useful concepts also for small states. During the mid 1960s Beaufre and Aron argued that the nuclear weapons have not ceased the importance of seeking appropriate, practical strategy against the "nuclear stalemate" resulted from the deterrence, especially the doctrine of "mutual assured destruction". According to them there were also alternatives to the great power strategy which was based on massive nuclear deterrence and capability for mechanised warfare: "Strategy is a duel of wills". One variation of strategy supported also by Beaufre was the French independent nuclear doctrine of dissuasion which was developed during the 1960s.[16]

The Vietnam War showed the limits of massive (conventional) fire power without clear strategic aims, a systematic leadership and a firm political will. It also opened the way for new operative-strategic thinking in the USA, but the results were not seen until mid 1980s.[17]

Some neo-Clausewitzian theoreticians have applied the core ideas of the book *On War* for a rather universal theory on strategy. Edward Luttwak[18] picked up the anti-positivism and dialectics from Clausewitz to explain why "controversial logic" is the key for understanding strategy and warfare. According to Luttwak there is a different and controversial logic of action on the different levels of strategy, beginning from the bottom (technical level) upwards through tactical, operational and regional (theatre) strategy to grand strategy (security policy). Essential is the whole scope of actions and management of situations, where all elements of strategy influence each other. An action or a technological innovation can always be eliminated or circumvented by countermeasures on other levels of strategy. The point is that there can never be good universal strategies for all cases on all levels and sectors of strategy, but we must find a common ground for preparations in anticipating crises and have knowledge over the whole scope of strategy for choosing appropriate strategies for various cases and circumstances.

The influence of Clausewitz on small states' strategy during the Cold War and after

A path from Beaufre's total strategy and dissuasive deterrence went to "security policy" of the European neutral and non-aligned (N+N) countries during the late 60s. The strategy of conventional deterrence in those countries was "dissuasive" and "relative", as opposed to the "absolute" deterrence which was based on nuclear capabilities for a destructive retaliation.[19]

The aim of N+N countries was the same as the major powers had, i.e. to prevent war and aggression, but they tried to do it through a combination of policy of neutrality and a non-provocative defence system which had sufficient capacity to deter a potential aggression during a crisis or regional war. What could happen during a general war with nuclear arms was not so important because it was, in any case, too unpredictable and disastrous for all parties.

Another path starting from Clausewitz's theory and Beaufre's idea of dissuasion was the doctrine of territorial or area defence which was based on conventional, dissuasive deterrence.

Dissuasion (called in German "Abhaltestrategie") was a kind "deterrence by denial" which aimed to deter a potential aggressor by a "threshold against attack" over which it would be too risky to advance, because of big losses and waste of time compared with possible gains.

There was a long and passionate debate in Western Germany during the 1980s about "alternative strategies" or "non-offensive defence" (NOD) as a means of diminishing the dependence on nuclear weapons.[20] The ideas of NOD were basically the same as in the doctrines of territorial or area defence in neutral and non-aligned countries Austria, Finland, Sweden, Switzerland and Yugoslavia.[21]

Most interesting for the themes of this article are the differences presented by Clausewitz between offensive and defensive or between the aggressor and the defender. They are very much like the difference between tactics and strategy. We can well argue that many geographical and technical factors which Clausewitz saw as crucial for the superiority of defence against offensive are no more valid. The distances and the terrain obstacles are nowadays not so difficult to overcome as they were for the armies during the Napoleonic wars. Still, we have seen how a high-tech offensive force of the US military was eventually exhausted in the Vietnam War. The Americans were superior in the technical and mostly tactical fields, too, but they lost the war on the strategic level.[22]

The problems of war, or more generally armed conflicts, still remain. Is a "Clausewitzian war", i.e. a war between states, further possible in Europe? An answer by Clausewitz and the realistic school of political thinking is based on the nature of human mind. If it could be changed, then also the possibility of war could be diminished or even totally dismissed. However, the warning according to Clausewitz concerns the impossibility of foreseeing the developments if the men ever begin fighting each other. War as continuation of policy is an unpredictable phenomenon.[23] Escalation from conflict to crisis, from crisis to war and from local war to general war is always possible, if the very nature of human mind cannot improve and lead to more peaceful behaviour. In the real life of the post-Cold War Europe we have already seen wars between the successor states in the disintegrated Soviet Union and Yugoslavia.

The conditions and frequency of wars as well as the technique of warfare can change over time but we have no reason to be sure that either internal or inter-states wars cannot occur in the future Europe.

It is, however, most relevant to ask how the Clausewitzian theories on war could be applied to the peace-time security policy and crisis management, for example, in the context of the EU's foreign and security policy.

Defender versus aggressor: the human factor

A central point in the Clausewitzian philosophy is the importance of the human factor in strategy and warfare. This is also the key issue in the differences between great powers and small powers as well as between aggression and defence which do not depend on the actual conditions of Clausewitz's time.

The emphasis on the moral and other human factors was not original by Clausewitz; they were also the main element in Sun Tzu's theory.[24] However, it was Clausewitz who most clearly elaborated the effects of the human behaviour on strategic and war theories.

Clausewitz emphasized the human factor as a main source of escalation in war. According to him the beginning of war is not like a phenomenon of nature but an act of human behaviour in social context. "Two different motives make men fight another: hostile feelings and hostile intentions." We can influence the nature of war if we can regulate those factors. In the war a tendency to escalation prevails, i.e. the fighting, destruction, stress and other factors like those make both duelling parties ever more hostile to each other. On the other hand, in a 'real war', there are also many factors, e.g. weariness of the troops, fear, insufficient motivation, and lack of supply and other elements of friction, which restrain the escalation tendencies. These human factors also make defence superior over attack.[25]

Some military scientists have tried to assess the superiority of defence and come e.g. to relation 3:1 for the benefit of the defender. So the attacker should have at least three times more power against defender if he will make a breakthrough. This kind of calculation is, however, possible only when the opposing parties are rather similar and geographical or weather obstacles are not very much favouring one party. It is totally nonsense to define formulas on power relations between attackers and defenders if the parties are qualitatively asymmetrical, e.g. nuclear versus conventional forces, or in the case of sea power versus land power. According to Clausewitz also the human factor makes all calculations in war utterly uncertain. The computers can hardly eliminate this profound problem.

An interesting coincidence with the common thought on the superiority factor needed for successful attack is a statement by Napoleon that "moral is to material as three to one". A quite opposite view has been presented by a well-known proponent of mechanised warfare J.F.C. Fuller who stressed the importance of material "which forms 99 per cent of victory".[26]

Technological development has surely diminished the superiority of defence over attack, if not changed the whole relationship. Nuclear weapons are by nature offensive and nearly unlimited in their lethality. Only a threat of retaliation by a nuclear counter-attack is eventually the most effective defensive means against nuclear weapons. However, one of the most important lessons learned in the nuclear age has been the practical ineffectiveness of the weapons of mass destruction as real means of warfare. The nuclear strategy is full of controversies, for example, if we consider the roles of offensive and defensive measures. It seems to be true that the apparently offensive nuclear weapons are useful only as defensive deterrence means.

At present the attacker with high-tech conventional weaponry can see distant targets, move troops and weapons rapidly and destroy unveiled enemy forces by using accurate and lethal munitions. The most exposed are immobile objects of the command structure as well as communication lines.

However, there are many reasons to argue that the offensive capability of major powers cannot always be used effectively. First and foremost, it is the dependency of military power on economics, and, in return, a modern, a well functioning economy is dependent on freedom of information and access to foreign markets, and also at least to some degree on democracy in the society. These economic-societal factors do not favour aggressive and offensive strategy and warfare, especially if it demands very much resources and time, with large number of casualties, too. The wars in Afghanistan and Iraq have demonstrated this phenomenon clearly.

The general atmosphere at present is against initiating an aggression against a state. It is also forbidden in international law, though it is often difficult to say who is really aggressor and who is only defending national integrity and interests. Also coalitions and duties of collective security make the difference unclear, as we can refer to alliance warfare in the Second World War, Gulf War 1991 and Afghanistan from 2001. It seems to be ever more difficult to legitimise an offensive war domestically or internationally. This is a principal advantage for small states at least in the stable situation in Europe and in relatively small crises, but in a severe international crisis, not to mention a new world war, the ban of aggression is an insecure guarantee against major powers who are struggling for their basic interests and even their existence.

It has been a common sense that motivation is a crucial factor for the efficiency of troops in battle, even if it is not so easy to assess exactly. In the present conditions the moral of the army is far more important than earlier when the leaders saw their units and also the tight formations favoured the maintenance of discipline. The problem is now: which elements of motivation for national defence are still relevant and how the battle moral can be created in small states in front of the overwhelming great power forces? For explanation we can analyse some Finnish experiences from the last century.

Historical experience as a source of motivation: case Finland

Finland was until 1917 an autonomous Grand Duchy in the Russian Empire. The war of Finland's independence in 1918 was mostly civil war and caused deep societal traumas. Between the world wars Finland, however, was rapidly recovering from that aftermath and became a stable democracy, which was not usual in the rim states of the Soviet Union.

In the beginning of the Second World War in autumn 1939 the Soviet Union demanded some Finnish border areas near by Leningrad and a naval base westward of Helsinki. The Finnish Government mobilised rapidly the whole wartime army of 10 divisions with some 300 000 men and refused to give up state's territories.

The Soviet Union invaded Finland at the end of November with an army of nearly 30 divisions, totalling half a million men. They believed in short war and quick collapse of the Finnish defence power. The correlation of forces and resources was extremely unfavourable for the Finns. The Soviet Union of some 200 million inhabitants fielded against Finland at the end of the Winter War 60 mechanised and infantry divisions with almost unlimited stocks of material. Finland with four million people could at last mobilise 13 divisions, but they lacked heavy weapons and munitions.

The Finns repelled the attacks successfully during the first two months of war and they even destroyed several enemy divisions in the battles along the long eastern border of Finland. After many weeks's war of attrition the Red

Army eventually could achieve a breakthrough which pushed the front about 50 kilometres toward the city of Wiborg. There the front again stabilised, and both parties of war were ready to negotiate on ending of hostilities. The peace treaty which ceded the most parts of Karelia from the Finnish territory was made in Moscow on 13 March 1940.[27]

The tough defence of Finland against the Soviet aggression has been called "the wonder of Winter War". It was based on the firm determination of the people to repel the threatening occupation and forcing of the Stalinist Soviet system to Finland. The excellent battle moral was a result of the socio-economic consolidation in the 1930s and the effective preparation for a total war. General conscription and voluntary military training made it possible to build up a proportionally large army. It was trained with Finnish original tactical methods and equipped with such material, i.e. skis, tents and machine pistol "Suomi", which were practical in forest battles. Many tactical and organisational principles in the Finnish army were brought from Germany during the First World War and originated from the Prussian tradition.

Finland joined the war again in 1941 when Germany invaded Russia. That time the Finnish troops, together 16 army divisions, advanced over the Finnish border to the Soviet territory, deep into Eastern Karelia where the fronts remained until June 1944. Then the Red Army began a major offensive with 40 divisions which had 450 000 men, 800 tanks and 10 000 artillery pieces. The main thrust was again made from Leningrad towards Wiborg. After an advance of 100 kilometres and seizing of Wiborg the attackers were stopped in two weeks' fighting, some ten miles north of Wiborg. The battle moral of the Finnish troops was at first rather low, but it improved clearly as the army was withdrawn from east into the Finnish territory and began to defend the own homeland. The road to Helsinki became blocked and the Soviets had to interrupt their offensive in July without achieving a decisive breakthrough.[28]

After the fronts were stabilised Finland had soon a right time to get rid of war because the supporting power Germany was already going towards her final collapse. Also the Soviets saw that they had no chance to break the Finnish resistance without additional troops and, thereby, risking the advance to Central Europe. Field Marshall Mannerheim as president of the republic agreed on truce with the Soviet Government, and the Finnish-Soviet war ended on the 19 September 1944. Finland had to accept again the peace treaty made in Moscow 1940 with some additional area losses and forced leasing of a naval base in Porkkala near Helsinki, but the terms of peace were better than for example for Romania at the same time.[29]

The eventual success of the defence battle in summer 1944 was precondition for Finland to remain outside the Soviet bloc after the war. Finland had to establish good relations to the Soviet Union with a *treaty on friendship, co-operation and mutual assistance* 1948, but it was not a military pact and did not result to any military co-operation with the Soviets. The most important fact was that the society and legal system of the state overcame the war as intact. During the 1950s Finland got back the naval base Porkkala and could then step by step orient towards an intensive Nordic co-operation. In the 1970s Finland organised the Conference on Security and Co-operation in Europe and got a status as a member of the group of the neutral states.

The defence forces were organised on the well-proved principle of conscription with large land forces while the air defence remained relatively weak. The national defence doctrine was based on the territorial system which after the invasion of Czechoslovakia by the Warsaw Pact troops in 1968 was especially developed towards capability to repel also surprise attacks. Theoretically seen, the doctrine was clearly defensive and non-provocative while building a relatively effective conventional deterrence. The aimed dissuasive effect was similar as in Sweden, Switzerland, Austria and Yugoslavia.[30]

There was a difference in doctrines compared between the European neutrals and Israel during the Cold War. For geographic reasons Israel had to develop offensive armed forces which were capable to strike also pre-emptively and fight with mobile operations. The small countries between the military blocs in Europe preferred territorial defence because they had no possibilities to wage mobile war against the major powers. Yet, the tactics both in Israel and, for example, in Finland followed Clausewitzian principles of a flexible command.[31]

Soon after the Cold War Finland improved her air defence by purchasing modern anti-aircraft missiles and 64 US-designed fighter-aircraft F 18 Hornet. The land forces got a lot of tanks and other weaponry from the surplus stockpiles left by the DDR army (NVA). The geostrategic conditions around Finland had not so much changed as they did in Central Europe. Therefore, during the 1990s Finland kept relatively high preparedness for military defence despite the improving political atmosphere. Finland had also good reasons to continue the policy of military non-alliance even as member of the European Union from 1995.

A government report on defence policy (1997) stated that the basics of the defence system should be maintained but the wartime troops would be reduced somewhat, i.e. from 540 000 to 430 000 men. Also the new requirements for taking part in international peace-keeping duties had to be met with some improved rapid deployment troops. Still, there were maintained, together with the reserves, 22 operational army brigades with some 200 local defence units which were an effective force for the territorial defence. The defence expenditure were circa 1,5 % of GNP.

During the first decade of the 21th century Finland kept the defence system from the Cold War almost intact, with war-time troops of 350 000 men. However, the profoundly improved security situation in Europe made it already possible to reduce the defence readiness remarkably, but the potential for the mobilisation of large reserve troops was still maintained.[32]

A very important shift in the defence doctrine and readiness has been made with more emphasis onto the peace-time crisis management and duties where the military could be used as a reserve force for disaster management and other internal tasks. It was presented in the document *The Strategy for Securing the Functions Vital to Society* (2006). Also the cooperation concerning crisis management duties with EU member states and institutions has become very important.

As far as references to the Clausewitzian theories are concerned it is most remarkable that a consensus on the defence doctrine has been highly appreciated in Finland. Also the primacy of politics over military is secured by many means. They have contributed to a stable continuation of the security policy and defence system.

The Finnish defence doctrine has also other features of Clausewitz's theories. For example tactics has been learned according to the Prussian tradition, i.e. as "Auftragstaktik", and the Clausewitzian thinking has prevailed in strategy and leadership system, with only smooth recent changes towards American staff and administration procedures.

Views on the future defence and security problems of small states in Europe

Imaging the future wars and other conflicts has always been difficult. We have examples of fundamental errors, e.g. the overestimation of the offensive capability before the Great War.[33] The debate opinions were very much contradicting on the importance and implications of new technologies.[34]

One of the most influencing causes for the confusions in those debates has been the difficulty to make precise estimations over the importance of various factors in the latest wars. The Gulf War 1991 was very much showed in the media but the scientific analysis took time. After many years' research we have better knowledge on the details and basic factors which made the coalition forces so superior to the Iraq forces. Still, there have been long-living legends which overemphasize the high-tech capacity of American military and underestimate the human factors, i.e. tactics, motivation and leadership.[35] Most interesting is the observation that also in the air war against Iraq 1991 the "Clausewitzian friction" was very much influencing the results and we have no reason to assume that friction will be diminishing in the future.[36]

An interesting view was presented by George and Meredith Friedman (1998). They predicted that the American supremacy will prevail by using the most advanced technology. Especially the long-distance weapons basing on the space technology and capabilities for info-war should be superior. However, there would be a renaissance of the light infantry, too. That is the area in which also the small, technologically advanced countries can be effective. It is possible to produce with relatively low costs modern computerised weapons and effective means for communication and intelligence.

The post-modern crises and wars have various faces and unimaginable progress when they occur. Also the post-modern war is a political phenomenon as Clausewitz described his contemporary wars. I will argue that Sun Tzu was also right when he pointed out the human factors and especially deception as most important things in war. The wars in Yugoslavia from 1991 as well as wars in Chechenya, Iraq and Afghanistan have shown very well the continuing relevance of those arguments.[37] Those wars were very differing by nature so that also conclusions have been rather controversial.

Then came the "war against terrorism" which was declared in September 2001 by the US president George W. Bush and fought with high intensity and rapidly growing costs. The president explained the so called Bush doctrine in many speeches saying for example that pre-emptive strikes are legitimate against terrorists and their allies, adding that "the offensive is the best defensive". In spite of initial attempts to keep that war limited and clean it soon escalated both horizontally - to many areas of the world - and vertically - to comprise dirty methods and very high political and economic costs. It turned out to be some kind a post-modern world war, in which the United States and the allies have been fighting against many Asian movements and states without clear aims and exit strategies. The war has proved again the validity of the Clausewitzian term "friction" and the difficulties to foresee the developments in the armed conflicts.

According to the Clausewitzian tradition it is important to acknowledge that there are no universal solutions to the security dilemmas of different states. The defence policy of small countries must be in accordance with the aims of national security policy, foreseeable geostrategic circumstances and societal factors. That is why, for example, Finland has to maintain a defence system which is appropriate exactly to the Finnish circumstances and is not only a reflection of the international trends.

The most important thing also in future is maybe the cohesion of the society, as part of the so called Clausewitzian trinity of people, government and armed forces. As result of an analysis of cost-effectiveness in a crisis situation a major power hardly has good reasons to commit itself to a risky attack against a stable nation which has followed a non-provocative security policy and has a relative well armed civic army prepared to defend resolutely the independence of the state and the living conditions of the people.

There are still many problems as well as chances in application of the Clausewitzian theories to the changing conditions in Europe and in the world. At present the most important task for EU countries is to analyse the possibilities to improve the crisis management capabilities for external and internal affairs. There are too many and too complicated arrangements for example concerning counter-terrorism measures.

It would be useful to apply the Clausewitzian thinking to the planning practices in the area of crisis management and disaster mitigation. Starting from the thesis that a plan can be valid only until the first contact with the enemy we can develop a planning procedure which contains the basic emergency preparations including an adequate training and is flexible for rapid changes according to the actual situations.

The management of security crises and natural disasters is not the same thing as leading of traditional war operations but they both have common elements which make it possible to apply the Clausewitzian war theories to the emergency planning and management of crises also in the EU framework. This is maybe the most important heritage of Clausewitz's philosophy for the European states in the future.

Notes:

[1] Carl von Clausewitz, *On War*, Princeton University Press, p. 370. Original: Carl von Clausewitz, *Vom Kriege*, 1832. The references in this article are according to the English edition by Michael Howard and Peter Paret, Princeton University Press 1976.

[2] Sun Tzu, *The Art of War*, transl. by Samuel Griffith, Oxford University Press, 1963, p. 66.

[3] See e.g. Gray, Chris Hables, *Postmodern War. The New Politics of Conflict*, Routledge, London, pp. 21-22.

[4] Freedman, Lawrence, "The Revolution in Strategic Affairs", *Adelphi Paper 318,* 1998, p. 6.

[5] See e.g. Summers, Harry G., *On Strategy. A Critical Analysis of the Vietnam War*, Presidio Press edition 1995; Luttwak, Edward, *Strategy. The Logic of War and Peace*, Harvard University Press 1987; and Heuser, Beatrice, *Reading Clausewitz*, Pimlico 2002, pp. 168-178.

[6] Keegan, John, *A History of Warfare*, Pimlico, London 1993, pp. 12-22.

[7] The overview of the Clausewitzian theory is mainly based on the article Pekka Visuri, "Clausewitzian War and the Defence Problem of Small States" in *Collection of War Studies 1998: War – Vojna* (ed. Filip Tunjic, Ljubljana 1998).

[8] Makers of Modern Strategy from Machiavelli to the Nuclear Age, ed. by Peter Paret, Princeton University Press 1986, in references: Makers of Modern Strategy, pp. 110-168.

[9] Schramm, Wilhelm von, *Clausewitz. Leben und Werk*. Bechtle, Esslingen 1976, p. 58.

[10] The most comprehensive (neo-Clausewitzian) attempt has been made by Raymond Aron in *Penser la guerre Clausewitz*, Paris 1976 (English version Clausewitz: Philosopher of War, 1985). Aron described the nuclear war as "ab-

solute" and the period of crisis before it as "real war". A critical study on neo-Clausewitzian theory by Anatol Rapoport (1968: pp. 60-63) dislikes the quasi-rationalism which was based on Clausewitz and used in many American theories on nuclear war-fighting related to actual circumstances of the Cold War.

[11] See especially the description, how the prisoners of war the Prince August of Prussia and his adjutant Clausewitz were addressed by the victorious emperor Napoleon in the Castle of Berlin after the battle. Von Schramm, ibid., pp. 121-124.

[12] Howard, Michael, "The Infuence of Clausewitz", in Carl von Clausewitz, *On War*, Princeton University Press 1976, pp. 29-36 and Wallach, Jehuda, *The Dogma of the Battle of Annihilation. The Theories of Clausewitz and Schlieffen and their Impact on the German Conduct of Two World Wars*, Greenwood Press, Westport, CT 1986.

[13] Howard, ibid., pp. 43-44, Howard, Michael, *Clausewitz*, Oxford University Press 1983, pp. 66-73 and Rice, Condoleezza, "The Making of Soviet Strategy", in *Makers of Modern Strategy*, pp. 648-664.

[14] Clausewitz, ibid., p. 89.

[15] Howard, Michael, *Clausewitz*, Oxford University Press 1983, pp. 101-115.

[16] See Beaufre, André, *Introduction to Strategy*, London 1965, orig. *Introduction à la stratégie*, Paris 1963 ; Beaufre, André, *Strategy of Action*, New York 1967.

[17] Summers, Harry G., On Strategy. A Critical Analysis of the Vietnam War, Presidio Press edition 1995; Summers, Harry G., The New world Strategy. A Military Policy for America's Future, Touchstone, New York 1995, pp. 94-107.

[18] 1987.

[19] The term "total strategy" refers to a combination of political (diplomatic), economic, psychological and military means coordinated towards security objects of the nation. It contains the same idea as "security policy" (national security policy) had in neutral countries in Europe. See e.g. for Switzerland: Däniker, Gustav, *Dissuasion. Schweizerische Abhaltestrategie heute und morgen,* Huber, Frauenfeld 1987, pp. 30-34; for Austria: *Landesverteidigungsplan* 1985, pp. 19-21; for Sweden: Andrén, Nils, *Maktbalans och alliansfrihet. Svensk utrikespolitik under 1900-talet*, Norstedts juridik, Stockholm 1996, pp. 178-188; and for Finland: Visuri, Pekka, *Totaalisesta sodasta kriisinhallintaan* (Dissertation with English summary: From total war to crisis management. The evolution of defence doctrines in Western Central Europe and Finland 1945-1985), Otava, Keuruu

1989, pp. 205-212 and Visuri, Pekka, "Evolution of the Finnish Military Doctrine 1945 – 1985", *Finnish Defence Studies 1,* War College, Helsinki 1990, pp. 54-55.

[20] See e.g. Löser, 1981; Biehle, Alfred (ed.), *Alternative Strategien,* Bernard & Graefe, Ulm 1986; Pierre, Andrew (ed.), *The Conventional Defense of Europe. New Technologies and New Strategies,* New York University Press 1986; and Möller, 1991.

[21] See e.g. Stutz, Alfred, *Raumverteidigung. Utopie oder Alternative?* Neue Zürcher Zeitung, Zürich 1982.

[22] See Summers, Harry G., *On Strategy. A Critical Analysis of the Vietnam War,* Presidio Press edition 1995, pp. 1-7.

[23] Clausewitz, ibid., pp. 75-89.

[24] See e.g. Handel, 1992: pp. 101-154.

[25] Clausewitz, ibid., pp. 75-89.

[26] Gray, Chris Hables, *Postmodern War. The New Politics of Conflict,* Routledge, London 1997, p. 107.

[27] See e.g. Vuorenmaa, Anssi, "Defensive strategy and basic operational decisions in the Finland - Soviet Winter War 1939-1940", in *Aspects of Security,* 1985, pp. 74-96 and Tillotson, H.M., *Finland at Peace and War 1918-1993,* Michael Russel, Wilby Hall, Norwich 1993, pp. 121-192.

[28] See e.g. Tillotson, ibid., pp. 215-211.

[29] Polvinen, Tuomo, Between East and West. Finland in the International Politics 1944 - 1947, WSOY, Helsinki - Juva 1986, pp. 13-36

[30] See Visuri, Pekka, "Evolution of the Finnish Military Doctrine 1945-1985", *Finnish Defence Studies 1,* War College, Helsinki 1990.

[31] Kesseli, Pasi, In Pursuit of Mobility. The Birth and Development of Israeli Operational Art. From Theory to Practice. National Defence College of Finland. Publication series 1, N:o 6, Helsinki 2001.

[32] Finnish Security and Defence Policy 2009.

[33] Howard, 1991: pp. 97-112

[34] See e.g. Freedman, Lawrence, "The Revolution in Strategic Affairs", *Adelphi Paper 318,* 1998.

[35] See e.g. Biddle, Stephen, "Victory misunderstood", *International Security,* Vol. 21, N:o 2, 1996, and Cohen, Elliot, "Tales of the Desert", *Foreign Affairs,* Vol. 73, N:o 3, 1994.

[36] Watts, Barry, *Clausewitzian Friction and Future War,* McNair Paper 52, Institute for National Strategic Studies, National Defense University, Washington D.C. 1996.

[37] See e.g. Crawford, Beverly - Lipschutz, Ronnie, "Discources of War: Security and the Case of Yugoslavia", in Krause, Keith - Williams, Michael (eds): *Critical Security Studies,* UCL Press 1997, pp. 149-185.

Literature:

Andrén, Nils, *Maktbalans och alliansfrihet. Svensk utrikespolitik under 1900-talet,* Norstedts juridik, Stockholm 1996.

Aron, Raymond, *Clausewitz: Philosopher of War,* trans. Christine Booker and Norman Stone, Prentice-Hall, Eaglewood Cliffs, N.J. 1985; original: *Penser la guerre, Clausewitz,* Paris 1976.

Aspects of Security. The Case on Independent Finland, Revue Internationale d'Histore Militare 62, Commission Finlandaise d'Histore Militaire, Vaasa 1985.

Beaufre, André, *Introduction to Strategy,* London 1965, orig. *Introduction à la strategie,* Paris 1963.

Beaufre, André, *Strategy of Action,* New York 1967.

Biddle, Stephen, "Victory misunderstood", *International Security,* Vol. 21, N:o 2, 1996.

Biehle, Alfred (ed.), *Alternative Strategien,* Bernard & Graefe, Ulm 1986.

Clausewitz, Carl von, *On War,* orig. *Vom Kriege,* 1832, ed/trans. Michael Howard and Peter Paret, Princeton University Press, Princeton, New Jersey 1976.

Clausewitz, Carl von, *On War,* with an introduction by Anatol Rapoport, Penguin Books 1968.

Cohen, Elliot, "Tales of the Desert", *Foreign Affairs,* Vol. 73, N:o 3, 1994.

Crawford, Beverly - Lipschutz, Ronnie, "Discources of War: Security and the Case of Yugoslavia", in Krause, Keith - Williams, Michael, (eds. 1997): *Critical Security Studies,* UCL Press.

Däniker, Gustav, *Dissuasion. Schweizerische Abhaltestrategie heute und morgen,* Huber, Frauenfeld 1987.

Finnish Security and Defence Policy, Government Report, Helsinki 2009.

Freedman, Lawrence, "The Revolution in Strategic Affairs", *Adelphi Paper 318,* 1998.

Friedman, George and Meredith, *The Future of War. Power, Technology, and American World Dominance in the 21st Century,* St.Martin's Griffin, New York 1996.

Gray, Chris Hables, *Postmodern War. The New Politics of Conflict,* Routledge, London.

Handel, Michael, *Masters of War: Sun Tzu, Clausewitz and Jomini,* Frank Cass, London 1997.

Heuser, Beatrice, *Reading Clausewitz,* Pimlico 2002.

Howard, Michael, "The Infuence of Clausewitz", in Carl von Clausewitz, *On War,* Princeton University Press 1976.

Howard, Michael, *Clausewitz,* Oxford University Press 1983.

Howard, Michael, "Forgotten dimensions of Strategy", in *The Causes of Wars,* Unwin, London 1983.

Keegan, John, *A History of Warfare,* Pimlico, London 1993.

Kesseli, Pasi, *In Pursuit of Mobility. The Birth and Development of Israeli Operational Art. From Theory to Practice.* National Defence College of Finland. Publication series 1, N:o 6, Helsinki 2001.

Krause, Keith and Williams, Michael (eds.), *Critical Security Studies. Concepts and Cases,* UCL Press, London 1997.

Landesverteigungsplan, ed. by Bundeskanzleramt, Wien 1985.

Luttwak, Edward, *Strategy. The Logic of War and Peace,* Harvard University Press 1987.

Makers of Modern Strategy from Machiavelli to the Nuclear Age, ed. by Peter Paret, Princeton University Press 1986, in references: *Makers of Modern Strategy.*

Pierre, Andrew (ed.), *The Conventional Defense of Europe. New Technologies and New Strategies,* New York University Press 1986.

Polvinen, Tuomo, *Between East and West. Finland in the International Politics 1944-1947*, WSOY, Helsinki - Juva 1986.

Rice, Condoleezza, "The Making of Soviet Strategy", in *Makers of Modern Strategy*.

Schramm, Wilhelm von, *Clausewitz. Leben und Werk*. Bechtle, Esslingen 1976.

Strategic Review, 1/vol. 24 (1996) and vol. 25 (1997).

Stutz, Alfred, *Raumverteidigung. Utopie oder Alternative?* Neue Zürcher Zeitung, Zürich 1982.

Summers, Harry G., *On Strategy. A Critical Analysis of the Vietnam War*, Presidio Press edition 1995.

Summers, Harry G., *The New world Strategy. A Military Policy for America's Future*, Touchstone, New York 1995.

Sun Tzu, *The Art of War*. Transl. Samuel Griffith, Oxford University Press 1963.

Tillotson, H.M., *Finland at Peace and War 1918-1993*, Michael Russel, Wilby Hall, Norwich 1993.

The Strategy for Securing the Functions Vital to Society, Ministry of Defence, Helsinki 2006.

Toffler, Alvin and Heidi, *War and Anti-War. Survival at the Dawn of the Twenty-first Century*, Little Brown and Company 1993.

Visuri, Pekka, *Totaalisesta sodasta kriisinhallintaan* (Dissertation with English summary: From total war to crisis management. The evolution of defence doctrines in Western Central Europe and Finland 1945-1985), Otava, Keuruu 1989.

Visuri, Pekka, "Evolution of the Finnish Military Doctrine 1945-1985", *Finnish Defence Studies 1,* War College, Helsinki 1990.

Vuorenmaa, Anssi, "Defensive strategy and basic operational decisions in the Finland - Soviet Winter War 1939-1940", in *Aspects of Security*, 1985.

Wallach, Jehuda, *The Dogma of the Battle of Annihilation. The Theories of Clausewitz and Schlieffen and their Impact on the German Conduct of Two World Wars*, Greenwood Press, Westport, CT 1986.

Watts, Barry, *Clausewitzian Friction and Future War*, McNair Paper 52, Institute for National Strategic Studies, National Defense University, Washington D.C. 1996.

XXIST CENTURY'S CLAUSEWITZ IN FRANCE
Hervé Coutau-Bégarie

Clausewitz's glory has experienced highs and lows since the first publication of *Vom Kriege* in 1832, but it never waned completely and it is currently in an ascending phase. The turning point intervened in 1976, with the almost simultaneous translation by Peter Paret and Michael Howard in the Anglo-Saxon world and the master book of Raymond Aron, *Penser la guerre. Clausewitz*. But for France, it is only an episode in a very long history, which begun as early as the 1830s. It is no exaggeration to say that France was second election Earth of the Clausewitz work. Nowhere else, except of course in Germany, it was so extensively and so constantly commented, with significant deformation due to the relation with Germany, the long designated enemy.

This story was, so far, poorly understood. France did not produce the equivalent of well-known studies of Ulrich Marwedel or Christopher Bassford on the reception of Clausewitz. Things radically changed with the monumental Benoît Durieux's thesis *Clausewitz in France. Two centuries of reflection on war, 1807-2007*, published in 2009[1]. This master book replaced fragmentary annotations by a global picture on a remarkable scale.

Aron's Era

Clausewitz was *quasi absent* in the French strategic debate from the Second World War to the early 1970s. It was then a rediscovery, embodied in the emblematic figure of Raymond Aron, but Aron had some predecessors.

In 1967, André Glucksmann, who is not yet known as a "new philosopher", publishes *Le Discours de la guerre*[2]. Glucksmann is not a strategist and seems to have no knowledge of Clausewitz's predecessors or contemporaries[3] (Guibert and Jomini are absent), while he cites several contemporary writers. He retains from Clausewitz what may be useful for his demonstration, which borrows at least as much to Hegel, *Philosophy of history,* constantly cited. From the leftmost, and having not yet broken with it, he conducts in-depth Clausewitz and Mao comparison. It is difficult today to determine the influence of this book, which will be commented later, when the author came to fame for other reasons.

A totally unexpected figure rediscovers Clausewitz: Gérard Lebovici, cinema producer, show biz and Parisian nightclubs personality, who will be mysteriously murdered in 1984. Extreme-left businessman, he creates the publishing house Champ libre, which publishes anarchists, but also military authors. In 1973, after decades of absence, he reprints the *Précis de l'art de la guerre* by Jomini. And he undertakes the reprint, without any editing work, of forgotten Clausewitz texts translated at the beginning of the XXth century. It begins with *The campaign of 1814 in France* in 1972, followed by *Campaign of 1815 in France* the following year, *Notes on Prussia in its great catastrophe* in 1976, and finally by *The campaign of 1799 in Italy and Switzerland* in 1979. His death will not end in the existence of his publishing house, which will continue its activity under the name of editions Gerard Lebovici and then Ivrea.

There is a revival of interest for Clausewitz when Raymond Aron, the French specialist in international relations, begins his *magnum opus*. Aron explained his choice in his *Memoirs*[4]. While everyone expected a book on Marx, he wished to deviate somewhat from the registry of his previous works. Moreover, he wanted to write a genuine Treaty, he had no more practiced since *Paix et guerre entre les nations,* published in 1960, in which he quoted Clausewitz sparsely[5]. Originally, Clausewitz was the theme of lectures at the Collège de France, since a teacher must never repeat lectures and must propose a different topic every year. Aron returned to an author he had much frequented, but superficially. As often, the investigation gave rise to new questions and resulted in a much more ample book, published five years after the course. Aron wanted to apprehend Clausewitz in his own context, but also follow his posterity and discuss its validity in the nuclear age. The division of the book in two volumes: "European age" and "Global age", was not absolutely necessary in terms of volume (the two volumes are not larger than *Paix et guerre...*), but corresponded to a difference in content and even tone between the two volumes: the first follows the thinking of Clausewitz, the second takes a free approach: Aron expresses his ideas under the mask of Clausewitz.

The central thesis of the book is the affirmation of Clausewitz as a theorist of the war who was concealed by successive layers of doctrinaire Clausewitz, used by the military of each era to their needs. It absolves Clausewitz of the charges brought against him by Liddell Hart and his successors to be responsible for the transition to total war. The pivot is the intrinsic link between politics and war, conceived as instrument or continuation of the policy. Aron takes the famous sentence: *"war is the continuation of politics by other means"* which becomes, under his pen, the Formula, from which the entire work must be assessed.

Aron's fame was so great that the book is immediately received as a classic. It has a large international vogue: it is translated into English, Italian, German, and Portuguese. Reviews are numerous. At the forefront of defenders of Aron, his disciple Julien Freund gives to *Revue française de sociologie*, a penetrating and detailed comment, highlighting a background disagreement on the formula itself however: where Aron retains that war is the continuation of politics by other means, Freund prefers the translation "war is only the continuation of policy with other means". But there are also more critical reviews, such as politist Michel Dobry. However, their impact remains very limited and Aron's Magisterium will prevail during a generation, due to the prestige of its author and to the unique character of the work: articles in scientific journals can't compete with such a masterpiece; it will enjoy a monopoly up to the end of the century.

There is the crosswalk between Raymond Aron's book and the new English translation, published by Paret and Howard this year, which will definitely impose Clausewitz as the central strategic reference to the detriment of Jomini, who had been, until then, the hub of U.S. strategic culture[6]. Both Aron and Paret and Howard are pursuing the same goal: to present a modernized Clausewitz. The English translation therefore adopts the concepts that can be understood by the contemporary reader, in preference to those that would be more faithful to the original but less accessible; Aron wants to substitute for the militaristic Clausewitz a humanist Clausewitz. This will cause the very energetic reaction of an unknown German scholar, Professor Hepp. He denounces "the emasculation of Clausewitz", emphasizing the difference between Aron's Clausewitz and the historic Clausewitz who, in 1812, wrote an apology for Prussian militarism. Aron is injured by this review published in a German magazine and responds. But German has become a rare language, this criticism has little echo in France, where it is known only through the reply by Aron, published first in German in the same journal, then translated, partly in *Commentaire* and, much later, in *Stratégique*.

Aron's period will last up to the 1990s. Writings during this period fit virtually all in the lineage of Aron, although some differ somewhat. The main exception is Alain Joxe, whose strategy seminar at the École des hautes études en sciences sociales becomes the rallying point for the anti-aronians. It will give, in addition to the writings of Alain Joxe, Emmanuel Terray's book, ethnologist specialist in Africa, but curious of everything, who offers a new interpretation of the work of the Prussian master[7].

Clausewitz 2000

In the 1990s, the end of the Cold War and the collapse of the Soviet Union inevitably provoke a recomposition of French strategic thinking. Ailleret, Beaufre, Gallois, Poirier, the four generals of the apocalypse[8], have no real successors. There are many analysts, some of them accessing visibility in the media, but it is not sure that there are still real theorists. This does not, despite the recurring theme on the crisis of strategic thinking, preclude a rich and varied debate[9] in which Clausewitz is often called on different and even downright opposed registers. It is possible, using a formula long in vogue in intellectual Parisian circles, to talk about "burst" of Clausewitz French interpretation.

Historic Clausewitz

The historic Clausewitz takes advantage of the rise of French military history since the 1980s under the impetus of masters like André Corvisier, André Martel or Guy Pedroncini[10]. Even if they have not necessarily successors to their measurement, they sparked new fields of study, and among them the history of military thought. General Poirier, who is not himself a historian, comments Guibert and Jomini[11]. Jean Chagniot studied Folard[12]. Several authors have cleared the field, until then unknown, of naval thinking[13]. Clausewitz naturally benefits from this rediscovery of classics.

Firstly by the rediscovery of texts of unknown or forgotten. Reprints initiated by Gérard Lebovici, are continued by various authors. Gérard Reber, Professor of German civilization and Reserve Colonel, translated the two last volumes of *Hinterlassene Werke,* until then unpublished in French and covering the campaigns of the modern era, from Gustavus Adolphus to the Duke of Brunswick. This translation was initiated as part of a project of Clausewitz works, if not complete, at least very substantial, with *On War* in the translation of Neuens, all campaigns, the theory of combat, the principles of the strategy for the Crown Prince and the course on small war at the Kriegsakademie in 1810-1811, as well as a number of lesser-known texts, published in the three volumes of Werner Hahlweg. The Institut de Stratégie Comparée was the initiator for this project, which was to be published by Editions Economica in ten volumes. Disease of the editor and the failure of some promised funding led to successive delays that prompted Gérard Reber to publish separately these two volumes[14], with a preface by Beatrice Heuser. This separate publication condemned thereby definitively the project, which then aborted as had failed before him the Clausewitz Project in the

United States, not to mention multiple attempts of complete German works. The Institut de Stratégie Comparée, at least, published a translation of the *Theory of Combat,* a text which had been totally forgotten since the middle of the XIXth century[15]. The Institute hopes to start a translation of the course on small war. It is an important piece unknown due to its late discovery (it had been published only in 1966). Its volume (approximately 300 pages) represents a significant obstacle. Lieutenant-Colonel Lutz Müller, German student at the College Interarmées de Défense, proposed a valuable and meritorious, but unpublishable, first sketch of translation[16]. Thierry Derbent published some brief excerpts, a dozen pages[17].

Waiting to be published someday, this course is under scrutiny, due to the popularity of irregular strategies since the events of September 11, 2001 and asymmetric conflict in Afghanistan and Iraq that followed. The course has first undergone, besides Quiévrain, a post-marxist interpretation by Thierry Derbent, which undertakes to situate Clausewitz in a genealogy of the revolutionary war which include Lenin, Karl Liebknecht, Mao and Che Guevara. Clausewitz, with the idea of *Landsturm*, would be at the origin of this revolutionary war which won successes at XX[e] century and whose author, clearly of far-left, speaks with sympathy and even nostalgic. The task is difficult: even if Clausewitz was praised by Lenin and read by Mao, his ideas were not openly revolutionary. Indeed Thierry Derbent cites him as a tutelary figure, but then quotes him little. More interesting, because closer to the text, is exegesis proposed by Sandrine Picaud-Monnerat[18] who places it in the trend of small war in the XVIIIth century, i.e. the use of light troops in the service of the great war and not in opposition to it[19].

In addition to editing texts, the ISC launched an international research program on Clausewitz culminating in the publication of two issues of its magazine *Stratégique* in 2000 and 2009. The first begins with a "praise of Clausewitz" which clearly indicates the spirit. There are three groups of texts:

(1) Unpublished (in French language) or insufficiently known classics: in 2000, a German article in 1915 signed by Lucia Dora Frost on the strategic purpose in Clausewitz[20]; in 2009, a very important text by the great German strategist, a refugee in the U.S., Herbert Rosinski, on the structure of military strategy[21]; canvas of a lecture delivered at the Army War College in November 1954 and until then unpublished: it's a reflection on the general relationship between politics and war and an application of the theory of war: for Rosinski, Clausewitz "too closely focused on campaign and especially on their strategic component operations"; today, we must include "analysis of the organization of the war effort" (industrial mobilization, replenishment, logistics) and consider all dimen-

sions of operational strategy, i.e. land, naval, and air strategy. It's a penetrating, truly Clausewitzian, reflection, which remains perfectly faithful to Prussian master mind and method expanded to the new dimensions of contemporary strategy. The same issue also contains the response by Raymond Aron to Professor Hepp which was until then partially unpublished in French language[22].

(2) New epistemological studies: in 2000, a study by Gunther Maschke on the perennial problem of relation between war and politics[23]; a study by Hervé Guineret about Clausewitz and the problem of the method[24]; in 2009, an article by Corentin Brustlein on Clausewitz and the balance of offensive and defensive[25], which shows that Clausewitz remain infinitely superior to multiple American variations, over the past thirty years, around the security dilemma.

(3) Finally, historical studies: on an ignored but crucial predecessor to Clausewitz: Johann Friedrich Konstantin von Lossau[26]; on commentators of Clausewitz: Raymond Aron[27], Carl Schmitt[28], and Werner Hahlweg[29], and finally various studies on the reception of Clausewitz, in France, in the United States, in Hungary, in Italy, in the Netherlands, in Sweden and in China, to assess the exact audience and interpretation of Clausewitz that has been adapted to radically different contexts and cultures.

The purpose of this program is accumulating historical and theoretical materials that are necessary to understand in depth Clausewitz and his influence; to see how Clausewitz was received, but also used, the receivers subjugating classics in their own policy and foreign policy goals. The program is expected to continue over the next few years. Next goals are, possibly, a third issue of *Stratégique* and publishing texts out of print or not yet translated in French, including "The 1813 campaign until the armistice", currently unavailable (it is true that this is a booklet of circumstance, written in the heat of action, whose theoretical intake is thin enough) and especially Lossau's *On War,* whose French translation, published in 1819, had been lost: the common opinion believed that it had ever existed only in the too fertile imagination of General Bardin[30]. However, it exists, even in two versions, under cover of anonymity, and there are here major themes that Clausewitz will later develop. The publication of texts, the study of the dissemination and interpretation of the work is less spectacular than the great comments, but it is the prerequisite to real substantive work in the long term.

Military Clausewitz

Clausewitz was not much analyzed in War Colleges after 1945. It could be quoted by teachers or speakers, but it was cursive references, in support of not really Clausewitzian demonstrations. The appellation of a neo-Clausewitzian school, launched in the 1970s, had content for less fuzzy: under the label are grouped most of the analysts who refused a too technician approach of strategy, especially in vogue in the nuclear field to invade the strategic debate from the 1980s, with the themes of the revolution in military affairs, then the transformation. In the French case, the waning of Clausewitz was compounded by the fragmentation of teaching strategy. In War Colleges (of the Army, Navy and the Air Force) old chairs had disappeared in favor of teachings given by multiple speakers. This atomization of education could give a plurality of viewpoints, but contributed to the disappearance of any guideline. It was still in "recovery time" after a quasi erasure of the strategy from the mid-1960s to the mid 1980s, when fashion was in management and forecast, promotions from the École supérieure de guerre had practically no strategy conferences. Sign of growing uncertainty surrounding discipline, it was no longer defined in the glossary of joint forces which recognized, of course, a strategic level, but without any entry for strategy itself.

A mutation intervened in 1993, with the merger of War Colleges now grouped under a joint defense College (Collège Interarmées de Défense). A chair of geopolitics and strategy was established, but its holder was talking about the first, he was good connoisseur, and not the second, that was almost completely unknown to him. Lack appeared particularly badly in the second promotion, and the chair was split (1995-1996) in two separate chairs: geopolitics on one hand, and strategy on the other. Strategy thus regained its autonomy with an annual teaching course, for a limited time volume, but with a handout finally transformed into a book in 1999[31]. The *Treaty of strategy* often claims Clausewitz, quoted close to 200 times. Its purpose is to offer a strategy reader which gives first place to the human factor and not to the material factor. It distinguished several methods, including the historical method, whose Jomini would be the archetype; the geographic method, resulting in geopolitics and geostrategy; the material or realist method, that was embodied by the end of the XIXth century in French naval *Jeune École*, at the end of the XXth century in the school of the RMA; the philosophical method, Clausewitz is a pure representative, striving to understand the war rather than pretending to give keys to concretely conduct war.

The *Traité* favors the latter method, naturally combined with others, notably the historical method that provides an empirical validation. It's an attempt to suggest the complexity of contemporary strategy and the importance of thinking: doctrine remains paramount to technique, as the idea determines the orientations to be followed in the material choices. Very logically, more hardware investment is large, more intellectual investment must be proportionate to precede and accompany material choices. The Treaty keeps a classic view of strategy, understood as a dialectic between enemies using (or ready to use) force, against the new vision that would see strategy as the science of action in any sector of social life, and the idea of friction against the modernist school which transforms war in a purely technician process.

The CID in-depth studies of Clausewitz are rare. There are very few submissions, compared to 181 Clausewitzian subjects deposited in the Führungsakademie since 2003. Among them, Müller, "Schlieffen plan implemented up to the first battle of the Marne was consistent with the principles of strategy defined by Clausewitz?", 1997. Pierre-Yves Cormier, "Clausewitz stated that the war was none other than the continuation of politics by other means", 1998; A. Griffen, "Clausewitz today, 1998." Lieutenant-Colonel Serra, "What remains of the thinking of Clausewitz in nuclear deterrence strategies?", 1998. Then, apart Benoît Durieux, one expect close to a decade to find two Clausewitzian topics, due both to German students: Lutz Müller tries a first return course on small war, 2007; Carsten Wilhelm Schrehardt engages in a comparison of the teaching of Clausewitz in France and Germany today, 2010.

The most notable exception is Lieutenant-Colonel Benoît Durieux who submitted in 2001 a master on the receipt of Clausewitz in France until 1870, accompanied by a summary of *Vom Kriege* then released in book, on the model of the abstract general Palat published in 1921, but with a modern spirit[32]. Benoît Durieux then expanded his research to the submission of a thesis on the reception of Clausewitz in France in 2007, published the following year under the title: *Clausewitz in France, two centuries of reflection on war*[33]. It is undoubtedly one of the most interesting theses in military history and a major contribution to the history of the French military thought: under the aegis of Clausewitz, the author engages in an interpretation of all the themes developed by the French military writers since the middle of the XIXth century with a high scholarship. The investigation is probably exhaustive and almost definitive for land military authors, it can be supplemented for naval and air theorists. At least in the naval field, there are a few Clausewitzian voices, admittedly scattered, but not completely negligible. This author had proposed an interpretation of naval war based on the distinction between annihilation strategy, obtained by sea battle and attrition strategy, obtained by sea[34] blockade. Corbett and Rosinski[35] translations now provide French analysts bases for Clausewitzian interpretation of the maritime strategy. Work remains widely to do for air strategy, too often dominated by a technician approach.

The balance is not negative. However, it is true that the study of Clausewitz in French higher military education suffers from a cruel lack of institutionalization. There is no equivalent of Clausewitz-Gesellschaft or the Internationales Clausewitz Zentrum. Thinking about Clausewitz is always the result of individual initiatives and not a planned and systematic approach. *On War* is not a required reading at the CID. The only institutional record of the Prussian is, if we dare to say, the assignment of its name to a room of the CID (with a spelling to his name). It is not a rejection of the German master, but a demonstration, among many others, of the neglect of the military institution towards classics, whose study does not appear as a "burning obligation".

In this context, most notable is the symposium organized in 2007 by the schools of Saint-Cyr Coëtquidan on Clausewitz and contemporary strategic thinking. All French Clausewitzians (Benoît Durieux, Martin Motte, Christian Malis, Emmanuel Terray, Alain Joxe, Vincent Desportes, Hervé Coutau-Bégarie…) participated, as well as several foreign leading Clausewitzians: Hew Strachan for Britain, Bruno Colson and Christophe Wasinski for Belgium, Jean-Jacques Langendorf for Switzerland. This very rich conference marked the end of the Aron era, with the desire to break with certainly masterful analysis, but too tied to the personality of the commentator, to find a more historic Clausewitz, closer to the work itself. Against those who, once again, claimed the death of Clausewitz, the participants in the symposium were unanimous to emphasize the relevance of its themes, including friction, to analyze an increasingly shifting and uncertain contemporary strategic situation, with asymmetric conflicts which reveal the failure of a too close technological approach[36].

General Vincent Desportes, former Director of the Joint Defense College, is significant for this return of the Clausewitzian themes in policy debate. He participated in the Symposium of Coëtquidan and his books, including *Décider dans l'incertitude*[37], are very Clausewitzian with highlighting of friction, chance, and the necessity of not sticking to an American approach too tied to technology. Incomparable connoisseur of American strategic thinking, he attended to very closely during his long U.S. stays, he noted that Clausewitzian ideas[38] were able to overcome in United States because they were accommodated in the ambient technologism. It repeats a theme which is already developed by Bruno Colson, on the jominisation of Clausewitz[39].

Metaphysical Clausewitz

The big event of the first decade of the XXIst century is the advent of a new Clausewitz, largely unexpected and called, also, to a long posterity: the apocalyptic Clausewitz of René Girard[40].

Achever Clausewitz, published in 2007, is presented in the modest form of interviews. This is a book in which there is many more Girard than Clausewitz. Even more than in Aron, Clausewitz serves as pretext. Jean Guitton said, *"we pay tribute, classics, for ideas that they never had but we would not have had without them."* One such book is likely to generate what might be termed the Amadeus syndrome, namely the violent reaction of the specialist who does not accept being exceeded by a more talented newcomer. It seems wiser bowing to superior spirit and recognize René Girard's book is truly striking and presents a philologically fragile interpretation: it is intuition more than a real demonstration, but with unparalleled power. Grand master of strategic theory is the first time confronted with theology and metaphysics according to one scholar of comparable scale. True or false, the original hypothesis leads to an impressive result.

Girard proposes a religious interpretation of Clausewitz: *"it is completely hypocritical to see* On War *as a technical book"*[41]. *Vom Kriege* is an inspired book: *"Clausewitz is owned as all the great writers of resentment."* This is because he wants to be more rational than strategists who preceded him he fingers an irrational real. *"Then he pulls back and starts to not see"*[42]. As Aron, but for diametrically opposed reasons, Girard sees a radical hiatus between the chapter first book I and the rest of the book. But, where Aron sees the ultimate state of thinking which should inspire any final overwrite, Girard sees a meteoric intuition that the rest of the book would try to conceal. The formula which serves as a pivot to Aron: *"war as a continuation of the politic by other means"*, Girard overrides an apocalyptic formula: war as *"effort towards the external tenebras."* The idea of reciprocity is at the heart of the thesis: *"the modern wars are so violent because they are reciprocal: mobilization involves more people to become complete"*[43]. *"The interplay is such amplified by globalization, this global reciprocity where any small event can have some impact elsewhere on the globe, that violence is always one step ahead." "The policy runs behind violence"*[44]. This is why Clausewitz becomes the best guide to the accurate understanding of the contemporary world, beyond the narrow circle of strategists: *"because we are in a most positively violent universe that him and where some of his observations on the military thing became observations on the world, everything just"*[45].

Violence not war: war is no longer a ritualized institution as it was before the French Revolution, so it fills its traditional function of an evacuation pipe of violence; *"violence which produced sacred produces nothing more herself"*[46]. Absolute war is no longer an abstraction but becomes a reality: *"violence seems now deliberate, extreme ascent is served by the science or policy"*[47]. René Girard notes with reason the equivalence of illegal wars and regular war revealed by the attacks of September 11 and Iraq[48] U.S. response. He rejoins here the famous theory of Carl Schmitt on the end of the classic international law (*jus publicum europaeum*)[49]. Simply, where Schmitt sees a legal and ideological change, with criminalization of the enemy which prohibits any negotiated settlement, Girard identifies overall dysfunction: *"violence is today unleashed at the level of the entire planet, causing what apocalyptic texts announced: confusion between the disasters caused by nature and disasters caused by men, a confusion of the natural and the artificial"*[50].

This disruption is a sign of time and here Girard's message becomes truly apocalyptic: *"the apocalypse has begun"*[51]. And it goes very far in this direction since it does not hesitate to say that *"the global warming and the rise of violence are two absolutely linked phenomena"*[52]. Girard has some very harsh words on the willful blindness Westerners who refuse to see the coming disaster: *"Two global wars, the invention of the atomic bomb, several genocides, an imminent ecological catastrophe will not be enough to convince humanity, and Christians in the first place, as the apocalyptic texts, even though they had no value predictive, are related to disaster in course"*[53].

The strength of the warning is such that it is not possible to ignore it. Indeed, he occurs after many other updates in guard, variously reasoned, but convergent: on a more technique plan, disruption of war was analyzed by many recent authors, since General Le Borgne *(La Guerre est morte... mais on ne le sait pas encore,* 1990) to General Rupert Smith *(The Utility of Force,* 2007). In sociological terms, famous thesis Norbert Elias, set out in *The Civilisation of morals* and *The dynamics of the West* is undermined today by the debate around the brutalization or the ensauvagement of the world. In a long term perspective, Samuel Huntington *clash of civilizations* is excessive, but it does not invalidate his central thesis. There is no determinism in history, except demographic and trends in this area are overwhelming. On a metaphysical plane, or metastrategic to speak as Jean Guitton, apocalyptic process described by Girard is the logical culmination of a process initiated since at least two centuries.

The impressive nature of the message cannot however disguise superficial reference to Clausewitz. The starting point of Girard is clever, but untenable: If Clausewitz was really frightened by his vision of the outer darkness, he had to remove the offending, passage rather than attempting to drown in a demonstration of several hundred pages. From this point of view, this last interpretation of Clausewitz does not invalidate its predecessors; simply it adds an additional dimension, whose prophetic force equal as the exegetic fragility.

For nearly 200 years, France has worn cycles of high and low intensity attention almost constant to Clausewitz, sometimes dismissed but most often recognized as a master. One could almost speak of a Freudian couple attraction/repulsion, indifference was rare and brief. Each supposed death of Clausewitz was followed by a renaissance. Today, after the long period of the Magisterium Aron, who brought the French interpretation of Clausewitz in the international forefront, we are witnessing a new bubbling between diverging and even opposite trends. It cannot be said still in what direction the balance will tip. The only certain thing is that the figure of the Prussian master has not finished interweaving in French strategic debate.

Notes:

[1] Benoît Durieux, *Clausewitz en France. Deux siècles de réflexion sur la guerre,* Paris, ISC-Économica, 2008.

[2] André Glucksmann, *Le Discours de la guerre,* Paris, Éditions de l'Herne, 1967; rééd. en poche collection 10-18, 1973.

[3] What inspires him a comment at least ill-informed and casual: « before and after Clausewitz, that makes rigorous project, the books on theory of war are rare. Until 1945, a library file was enough", *Le Discours de la guerre,* Paris, 10-18, 1973, p. 273.

[4] Raymond Aron, *Mémoires. 50 ans de réflexion politique,* Paris, Julliard, 1983, p. 645.

[5] Christian Malis, *Raymond Aron et le débat stratégique français 1936-1966,* Paris, ISC-Économica, 2005.

[6] Bruno Colson, *La Culture stratégique américaine. L'influence de Jomini,* Paris, FEDN-Économica, 1993.

[7] Emmanuel Terray, *Clausewitz,* Paris, Fayard, 1999.

[8] François Géré, « Les quatre généraux de l'apocalypse », *Stratégique,* 53, 1992-1.

[9] Hervé Coutau-Bégarie, « La recherche stratégique en France », *Annuaire français des relations internationales*, I, 2000.

[10] *Histoire militaire de la France,* André Corvisier (dir.), Paris, PUF, 4 vols.

[11] Lucien Poirier, *Les Voix de la stratégie,* Paris, Fayard, 1985.

[12] Jean Chagniot, *La Stratégie de l'incertitude. Le chevalier de Folard,* s.l. Éditions du Rocher, 1997.

[13] Hervé Coutau-Bégarie (ed.), *L'Évolution de la pensée navale,* 8 vols, FEDN, puis ISC-Économica, 1991-2007; Michel Depeyre, *Tactiques et stratégies navales de la France et du Royaume-Uni de 1690 à 1815,* Paris, ISC-Économica, 1998 et *Entre vent et eau. Un siècle d'hésitations tactiques et stratégiques 1790-1890,* Paris, ISC-CFHM-Économica, 1998; Martin Motte, *Une éducation géostratégique. La pensée navale française de la Jeune École à 1914,* Paris, ISC-Économica, 2004.

[14] *Œuvres posthumes du général Carl von Clausewitz, Sur la guerre et la conduite de la guerre,* tome IX-tome X, Paris, La Maison du Dictionnaire, 2008.

[15] Carl von Clausewitz, *Théorie du combat,* Thomas Lindemann editor and translator, foreword by Hervé Coutau-Bégarie, Paris, ISC-Économica, 1998. A 2nd printing will be published in 2011, with the letters to Major von Roeder.

[16] Lutz Müller, *Carl von Clausewitz: Mes cours magistraux sur la petite guerre donnés à l'École de guerre en 1810 et 1811,* mémoire de DEA, École pratique des Hautes Études, 2007.

[17] Thierry Derbent, *Clausewitz et la guerre populaire, suivi de Lénine, Notes sur Clausewitz et Clausewitz, Conférences sur la petite guerre,* Bruxelles, Éditions Aden, s.d. (2005).

[18] Sandrine Picaud-Monnerat, « La réflexion sur la petite guerre à l'orée du XIXe siècle: l'exemple de Clausewitz (1810-1812) », *Stratégique*, pp. 97-98, December 2009 (first presented to XXXIe congrès international d'histoire militaire, Madrid, August 2005); « La petite guerre selon Clausewitz, à travers sa réflexion sur la guerre d'avant-postes », in Laure Bardiès et Martin Motte (dir.), *De la guerre? Clausewitz et la pensée stratégique contemporaine,* Paris, ISC-Économica, 2008.

[19] Sandrine Picaud-Monnerat, *La Petite guerre au XVIIIe siècle,* Paris, ISC-Économica, 2010.

[20] Lucia Dora Frost, « La finalité stratégique chez Clausewitz », *Stratégique*, 78-79, 2000-2/3.

[21] Herbert Rosinski, « La structure de la stratégie militaire », *Stratégique*, 97-98, december 2009.

[22] Raymond Aron, « À propos de Clausewitz: des concepts aux passions. Réponse à un critique belliqueux », *Commentaire*, 28-29, February 1985 (related to vol. II); « Réponse au professeur Hepp », *Stratégique*, 97-98, December 2009 (full text).

[23] Gunther Maschke, « La guerre, instrument ou expression de la politique. Remarques à propos de Clausewitz », *Stratégique*, 78-79, 2000-213.

[24] Hervé Guineret, « Clausewitz et le problème de la méthode », *Stratégique*, 97-98, December 2009.

[25] Corentin Brustlein, « Clausewitz et l'équilibre de l'offensive et de la défensive », *Stratégique*, 97-98, December 2009.

[26] Jean-Jacques Langendorf, « Clausewitz avant Clausewitz: Johann Friedrich Konstantin von Lossau », *Stratégique*, 97-98, December 2009.

[27] Christian Malis, « Aron-Clausewitz. Un débat continu », *Stratégique*, 78-79, 2000-2/3.

[28] David Cumin, « L'interprétation schmittienne de Clausewitz », *Stratégique*, 78-79, 2000-2/3.

[29] Jean-Jacques Langendorf, « Post tenebras lux. Werner Hahlweg », *Stratégique*, 78-79, 2000-2/3.

[30] It was known only by a mention in the *Dictionnaire militaire* by Bardin (1850).

[31] Hervé Coutau-Bégarie, *Traité de stratégie,* ISC-Économica, 1999; 2nd ed. 1999; 3rd ed. 2002, 4th ed. 2003; 5th ed. 2006; 6th ed. 2008; 7th ed. 2011.

[32] Benoît Durieux, *Relire De la guerre de Clausewitz,* Paris, Économica, 2005.

[33] Benoît Durieux, *Clausewitz en France. Deux siècles de réflexion sur la guerre, 1807-2007,* Paris, ISC-Économica, 2008, avec le soutien du Collège Interarmées de Défense et de la Fondation Saint-Cyr, 864 p., foreword by Hervé Coutau-Bégarie.

[34] Hervé Coutau-Bégarie, *La Puissance maritime. Castex et la stratégie navale,* Paris, Fayard, 1985.

[35] Julian S. Corbett, *Principes de stratégie maritime,* Paris, FEDN-Économica, 1993; Herbert Rosinski, *Commentaire de Mahan,* Paris, ISC-Économica, 1996.

[36] Laure Bardiès et Martin Motte (dir.), *De la guerre ? Clausewitz et la pensée stratégique contemporaine,* Paris, CREC-ISC-Économica, 2008.

[37] Vincent Desportes, *Décider dans l'incertitude,* Paris, Économica, 2007.

[38] Vincent Desportes, « Vie et mort de Clausewitz aux États-Unis », *Défense nationale,* 2002.

[39] Bruno Colson, « La stratégie américaine de sécurité et la critique de Clausewitz », *Stratégique*, 76, 1999-4, p. 163.

[40] *Achever Clausewitz,* entretiens avec Benoît Chantre, Actes Nord, 2007.

[41] René Girard, *op. cit.,* p. 13.

[42] René Girard, *op. cit.,* p. 14.

[43] René Girard, *op. cit.,* p. 51.

[44] René Girard, *op. cit.,* p. 54.

[45] René Girard, *op. cit.,* p. 111.

[46] René Girard, *op. cit.,* p. 11.

[47] René Girard, *op. cit.,* p. 57.

[48] René Girard, *op. cit.,* p. 129.

[49] Notably *Das Nomos der Erde;* French translation *Le Nomos de la Terre,* Paris, PUF, 1992.

[50] René Girard, *op. cit.,* p. 11.

[51] René Girard, *op. cit.,* p. 352.

[52] René Girard, *op. cit.,* p. 363.

[53] René Girard, *op. cit.,* p. 11.

THE RECEPTION OF CLAUSEWITZ IN GERMANY

Claus von Rosen and Uwe Hartmann

Introduction

The preface to Carl von Clausewitz's main work 'Vom Kriege' [On War], which was written by his wife Marie, contains his ambition "… to write a book that would not be forgotten after two or three years, and which anyone interested in the subject would at all events take up more than once".[1] This wish has been fulfilled. Clausewitz was and is to a large extent regarded as compulsory reading for the officer. Some 150 years after the first publication of the book 'Vom Kriege', the German Federal Minister of Defence at that time, Manfred Wörner, said that for him it would be "… inconceivable for an officer not to have read his 'Clausewitz'". However, a look at the history of its effect not only sheds some light on the matter but also reveals an unexpectedly large amount of shade.

Reception up until 1990

The history of the reception of Clausewitz's work in Germany from its publication in the year 1832 through to the second half of the 20th century has been described in detail by Werner Hahlweg and his pupil Ulrich Marwedel.[2] As long ago as 1836, Zedlitz published a biographical and literary outline of Clausewitz, which appeared in the pantheon of the Prussian army. However, the "sluggish" sales figures – publication of the first four editions did after all require just under 50 years – indicate that Clausewitz's work was not initially among the best-sellers. Outside of the narrow circle of military personnel[3], the book went largely unnoticed. And even inside the German officer corps, the prevailing theory was that of the French general Antoine-Henri Jomini (1779-1869), who Clausewitz had criticized fiercely in his writings, namely that of strategic thinking. Clausewitz himself would thus have been anything but satisfied with the reception of his main work.

In addition, changes in the contents of even the second and third editions show that gross misunderstandings accompanied the comprehension and adoption of Clausewitz's thoughts. However, at this time there were also attempts to shed a little more light on "Clausewitz". The year 1846, for instance, saw the Historical Department of the General Staff publish in the Militärwochenblatt [Military Weekly] a treatise on Clausewitz's influence on the structure of the Volkssturm and Landwehr [the territorial armies] and their establishment in East Prussia during January 1813. In 1878, the first Clausewitz biography appeared by Karl Schwartz, which also contained additional hitherto unknown documents. And in 1888, the Großer Generalstab [Great General Staff] published Clausewitz's "Nachrichten über Preußen in seiner großen Katastrophe" [News of Prussia in its great catastrophe].

Not until 1905, hence just under 75 years after the first publication of the "Hinterlassene Werke" [Posthumous Works], did a true Clausewitz boom emerge: in just 13 years, nine new editions appeared. The Chief of the Großer Generalstab, Alfred von Schlieffen, had become personally involved in the publication. At the same time a series of publications started up concerning Clausewitz and his life as well as his wife Marie. Lieutenant General Rudolf von Caemmerer in 1905, for example, wrote about Clausewitz in the series "Erzieher des Preußischen Heeres" [Educators of the Prussian Army]; Paul Creuzinger in 1911 produced an article about Hegel's influence on Clausewitz; Karl Linnebach in 1917 published "Karl und Marie von Clausewitz. Ein Lebensbild in Briefen und Tagebuchblättern" [Karl and Marie v. Clausewitz. A portrait of lives in letters and diary pages], an importance source - particularly from the biographical aspect.

During the interwar period, social scientists, above all, went to great lengths to provide new access to the work of Clausewitz. Especially representative of these works is the dissertation by the historian Hans Rothfels from 1920, in which he examined the relationship of politics and war in Clausewitz. At the same time he published Clausewitz's "Politische Schriften und Briefe" [Political writings and letters]. He thus considerably extended the view of Clausewitz's posthumous work. Walter Elze in 1934 examined the theory and didactic approach in the book 'Vom Kriege'. In 1936 the philosopher Walther Malmsten Schering opened up a view of Clausewitz's war philosophy. Finally, in a special edition of the Militärwissenschaftliche Rundschau [Military science review] of 1937, two letters with thoughts on defence were published for the first time. And between 1937 and 1943, in the small paper entitled "Strategie aus dem Jahre 1804 mit Zusätzen von 1808 und 1809" [Strategy from the year 1804 with addenda from 1808 and 1809], Eberhard von Kessel published

Clausewitz's card index from the time when he was a pupil of Scharnhorst at the Kriegsschule [War College].

During the years from 1933 to 1943, "Vom Kriege" was republished – after a break of 25 years. General Friedrich von Cochenhausen published two editions, and A. W. Bode even as many as five, which were declared a popular edition. Added to these came various abridged versions, such as that from Schurig or the version by Cochenhausen "um Veraltetes gekürzte Auflage" [abridged to remove the obsolete]. The "Clausewitz Katechismus" [Clausewitz catechism] by General Horst von Metzsch, first published in 1937, is a collection of quotations with brief annotations. Its high print run of more than 220,000 copies underlines the purely military exploitation interests prevailing at that time. The publishers were concerned with conveying in a brief and concise manner what were considered to be Clausewitz's most important theories so that readers would be able to make use of them in their professional activities. This abridging, profoundly unhistorical approach also applies to a similar collection, which Walter Faltz published as "Politisches Soldatentum" [political soldiering] in 1944.

During this time, some generally shorter biographies also appeared. In them Richard Blaschke and Walter M. Schering published some previously unknown texts by Clausewitz. In addition, a slightly novelistic genre emerged.[4] Overall, since the start of the 20th century, there has been an increasing conflict between the academic efforts to provide a comprehensive, critical view of Clausewitz's works, on the one hand, and a purely military interest directed to towards practical exploitation, on the other, accompanied by a romanticizing conception of Carl von Clausewitz as a person. The dominance of the interest in military exploitation together with the resulting abridged versions and misrepresentations may explain that, despite an apparently great demand for Clausewitz's work in the first half of the 20th century, both world wars were not conducted in the spirit of Clausewitz on the German side. The military historian Marwedel came to the conclusion "that the First World War was not waged according to Clausewitz because the way in which combat operations were conducted revealed a number of serious violations of his most elementary theories." And even the critical confrontation of the experiences of the First World War with Clausewitz's philosophy of war had, as Marwedel continued, only a slight influence on the conduct of the Second World War.[5]

After 1945, this realization led to intensive Clausewitz research in West Germany, the promoter of which, namely Walter Elze's pupil Werner Hahlweg, was at the establishment that later became the chair of "Militärgeschichte und Wehrwissenschaften" [Military History and Military Science] in Münster. Hahlweg dealt firstly with collecting and critically editing Clausewitz's writings. The 16th edition of "Vom Kriege" from 1952 thus offers the original text of the first edition for this first time after 120 years. Clausewitz's other "Schriften" [writings] were published by Hahlweg in the years between 1966 and 1990 in three substantial volumes, with a critique of the text and adapted to the form of the original. And to coincide with Clausewitz's birthday, Hahlweg compiled his "Verstreute kleine Schriften" [Scattered small writings] and made them accessible to a broader public. Secondly, he acted as a biographer of the works and produced a picture of Clausewitz during the period known as the "Deutsche Epoche" [German epoch]. Finally, he also provided the reader with a view of Clausewitz's thoughts on the "Kleine Kriege" [small wars] and their transferability to the new global picture of asymmetric wars. In doing so, he ascertained that the "Kleiner Krieg" as a popular war or war of total resistance of the then present-day had long exceeded the bounds of mere irregular military actions. Thus, as he claimed in 1980 with not unjustified pride, Hahlweg had through his "examination of the philosopher's thoughts in the field of interpretation and practical influence reached a new level." And he concluded: "In this respect the almost universal continuing attention to Clausewitz and his work, the intensification of the examination of his ideas, especially in the last two decades, may well be regarded as a Clausewitz renaissance; one gains the impression that only now is Clausewitz being understood in his actual meaning, particularly in the light of today's interdependent relations between society, politics, armed struggle, economics and the peace order.[6]

Parallel to this came further important stimuli from home and abroad for a new view of Clausewitz. Worthy of particular mention here are the educationalist Erich Weniger (1894-1961) with his article "Philosophie und Bildung im Denken von Clausewitz" [Philosophy and education in Clausewitz's thinking] from 1950, and Ernst August Nohn with his text "Der unzeitgemäße Clausewitz" [The anachronistic Clausewitz] from 1956. Peter Paret's book "Clausewitz and the State", which first appeared in the United States in 1976, was translated as "Clausewitz und der Staat" for the German book market in 1993; Raymond Aron's book "Penser la guerre, Clausewitz" [English version entitled Clausewitz: Philosopher of War] appeared in French in 1976 and in German as "Den Krieg denken" in 1980. And finally, in 1988, Panajotis Kondylis compared the theories of war in Clausewitz, Marx, Engels, and

Lenin. However, here it should be noted that the readership of these works was probably somewhat limited: the almost 20-year "delay" in the German edition of Paret's book is just as puzzling as the fact that the German translation of Aron's "Den Krieg denken" ended up in the bargain section at a very early stage. At the same time as Hahlweg's biographical works, biographies by Franz Fabian (1956) and Wilhelm von Schramm (1976) also came onto the German market. Friedrich Doepner shed a little more light on Clausewitz's family in "Die Familie des Kriegsphilosophen Carl von Clausewitz" [The family of war philosopher Carl von Clausewitz]. And in 1991 Dietmar Schössler enriched the German book market in a succinct yet still comprehensive biography "mit Selbstzeugnissen und Bilddokumenten" [with personal testimonies and documentary pictures].

Over the course of the years, a Clausewitz "School" established itself around Hahlweg and was more or less directly connected with him. It distinguished itself with numerous publications about Clausewitz and examined him from hitherto unseen perspectives. To mark the 200th birthday, Günter Dill published a collection of material on Clausewitz's main work, which bore the title "Clausewitz in Perspektive" [Clausewitz in perspective]. In it he compiled contributions that viewed Clausewitz as "a practitioner of warfare, a philosopher, a historian and a politician"[7]. New topics were covered by people such as the Marburg-based educationalist Heinz Stübig, who published an article on "Clausewitz in Yverdon. Anmerkungen zu seinem Pestalozzi-Aufsatz" [Clausewitz in Yverdon, notes on his Pestalozzi essay]. Helmut Gassen also dealt with Clausewitz from the educational viewpoint. Andrèe Türpe produced his doctoral thesis on Clausewitz, the philosopher of war (1977). In 1980 Colonel Klaus Buschmann published the monograph "Motivation und Menschenführung bei Carl von Clausewitz" [Motivation and leadership in Carl von Clausewitz], which appeared within the Bundeswehr [German Federal Armed Forces] as part of the Innere Führung [Leadership Development and Civic Education] series of publications. In 1984, the then Captain Erich Vad published his dissertation entitled "Carl von Clausewitz – Eine militärische Lehre. Untersuchungen zur Bedeutung Clausewitz' für die Truppenführung von heute" [Carl von Clausewitz – A military theory. Investigations on the importance of Clausewitz for today's military leadership]. In 1988, Peter Trummer, commissioned by the Studiengruppe für Internationale Sicherheitspolitik [Study group for international security policy], published the work "Clausewitz - heute. Den Krieg denken, um den Frieden zu sichern?" [Clausewitz today. The philosophy of war to secure peace?]. And in 1990, the psychologist Kurt Guss considered war from a psychological and pedagogical view as a unified whole. This interdisciplinary variety was characteristic of research into Clausewitz after the Second World War. It facilitated, as Hahlweg had said, the understanding of Clausewitz's theories and teaching, thus enabling them to be examined and assessed in terms of today's issues of politics and military power.

Since this time, various editions of the main work "Vom Kriege" have been published. The 17th to 19th editions, edited and annotated by Hahlweg, were published by Dümmler-Verlag and – in addition to the original version from 1832 – contain numerous supplementary texts. The latter included Clausewitz's preface and notice, the preface by the publisher of the first edition, the treatise "Übersicht und Entwurf zum Unterricht für den Kronprinzen" [Overview and draft of tuition for the crown prince] as well as a brief account of tactics and combat theory. These editions are still regarded as standards. In addition, a number of publishing houses produced – in some cases abridged – original texts of the eight books of "Vom Kriege" in paperback format or also in hardback. The editors included Marwedel, Wolfgang Pickert and Wilhelm Ritter von Schramm. And Gerd Stamp picks up on Mentzsch's thread by again publishing a more extensive collection of quotations with the promising title of "Clausewitz im Atomzeitalter" [Clausewitz in the atomic age].

A Clausewitz renaissance also occurred in the training and education of future leaders of the Bundeswehr. Since its foundation in 1957, the Führungsakademie der Bundeswehr [Command and Staff College of the German Federal Armed Forces] has also regarded itself as a stronghold of Clausewitz reception. Clausewitz has regularly been included in the training of future general and admiralty staff officers, as the former military history lecturer Othmar Hackl confirmed: Clausewitz was, according to Hackl, "one of the main subjects in the teaching of military history" at the Führungsakademie.[8] This generally took place in a lecture as part of the series "Geschichte der Strategie" [History of strategy], in which other strategic thinkers from the national and international arena were also presented. However, occasional seminars as compulsory options in defence history or also later in social sciences reached only few participants. The freedom of choice may have been a way of accommodating the course participants' wishes. In a comparison with thinkers such as Sun Tze or Jomini, they tended to regard Clausewitz as outdated, biased towards the army and difficult to read, if not incomprehensible. Nevertheless, quotations from his principle work were popular when keywords were required for lectures, presentations or meetings. In this manner, to mark the 25th anniversary of its foundation, the Führungsakademie also adorned its entrance area in the main building with a bust of Clausewitz and a quotation by him that appeared to embody the political spirit of the peace and security policy of that time. Accurately transcribed but taken completely out of context, this quotation merely records the incorrect and also thoroughly dangerous use of Clausewitz as a convenient supplier of quotations.

As an expression of academic ability, every participant attending the training course for the general and admiralty staff is required to produce a thesis. Of the 3,200 participants in the first 45 years, a mere 13 of them investigated topics directly dealing with Clausewitz and his work. This means that only one thesis every third or fourth year was dedicated to the Prussian general and military philosopher.[9] Ekkehard Guth, himself a military historian, was extremely generous when commenting on this: "The works of Carl von Clausewitz and his teachings have of course been used in some theses because his theories have left their mark even on today's post-war generation of general staff officers."[10] None of these works is among those honoured with the Clausewitz Medal of Honour by the Clausewitz-Gesellschaft [Clausewitz Society]. One exception was the course work produced by Thomas Will on "Operative Führung" [operational leadership], because it was later also accepted as a dissertation. It was set within the intellectual framework determined at that time by the editors of the army regulation HDv 100/100 (Field Manual) relating to the command of troops and their superior within the army command Major General Christian Millotat. The attempt – as already made by Moltke – to incorporate an operational level of command into Clausewitz's field of thought between strategy and tactics and hence transfer Clausewitz directly, as it were, to the battlefield was not, however, convincing.

In 1961, the Clausewitz-Gesellschaft [Clausewitz Association] was founded in West Germany, closely linked to the Führungsakademie der Bundeswehr. Essentially, it forms an amalgamation of active and former officers in the general/admiralty staff and had set itself the target of "preserving the intellectual legacy of the German general staff, particularly that of the General Carl von Clausewitz, and furthering its ideas which have a timeless validity."[11] Today its stated intention is to draw benefits for the present from the encounter with Clausewitz's thoughts: "This is not concerned with a historical review of Clausewitz and his period or even with a detailed exegesis of his work, but more with the attempt to view the current tasks of politics and strategy as reflected in the insights of Carl von Clausewitz and thus examine which of the principles and insights formulated by Clausewitz are still important today and are thus endowed with an enduring validity."[12] In the regional events of its groups, in colloquia and fora as well as at annual conferences it deals with general issues of security policy and military strategy. At regular intervals it publishes the results from this work. And the best thesis of every general/admiralty staff course at the Führungsakademie is honoured with the Clausewitz Medal of Honour.

Clausewitz was also received with acclaim in the former GDR. In Burg, Clausewitz's place of birth, his memory has been preserved through the naming of objects, such as a training centre, and by transferring the grave of Clausewitz and his wife from Breslau. In 1957, Ernst Engelberg and Otto Korfes published the principle work "Vom Kriege". In 1979 the Socialist Unity Part of Germany (SED) established a Clausewitz medal as part of the celebrations for his 200th birthday. Also to mark this anniversary, selected "Militärische Schriften" [Military writings] were published from his work. In this respect it is not surprising that, during the transition period to the united Germany, the Professor of Military History and Captain at Sea of the former Nationale Volksarmee (NVA) [National People's Army] Wolfgang Scheler, was also searching in Clausewitz for a "common intellectual source for the understanding of politics and war, of peace and military power, of the opportunities and limits of armed force". For the NVA he established that Clausewitz was "always called upon by those wishing to guide military thinking out of its state of torpor and develop it in line with new conditions". Nevertheless, the efforts of individuals to achieve recognition for Clausewitz and a fruitful transfer to the ideas of security policy and military thinking should hardly have exceeded "the narrow constraints of academic intellectual life".[13]

These self-critical thoughts of the former NVA officer are indeed not inappropriate for the West German academic community. Without question, the multidisciplinary, critical Clausewitz research stands as a beacon over the second half of the 20th century. It was and also continues to be suitable, as Dill ascertained, "as a means of taking up the dialogue with Clausewitz himself".[14] Yet it is particularly when the issue involves preparing the future generation of leaders, especially in politics and the military for the practice of strategic policy that the results of the Clausewitz research have barely been employed since Hahlweg. The number and quality of the theses at the Führungsakademie der

Bundeswehr on the topic of "Clausewitz" offer an extremely modest picture. And in the seminars and other teaching sessions, the trend has been towards simple, convenient selected texts that were primarily intended to serve as supporting arguments in everyday professional life. However, Clausewitz's aspiration for himself and for his work in terms of political and military practice is as follows: "It is not what we have thought that we consider to be a contribution to the theory but the way in which we have thought it."[15] Consequently, Hahlweg had emphasized "the philosophical method of the work 'Vom Kriege'" with its cognitive structures as one of the still unresolved core issues in the epilogue to the 19th edition.[16] Apparently there existed a deficit here that was capable of also having negative effects on the education and training of future leaders in politics and the military.

No empirical investigations exist on the extent to which Clausewitz is established in the consciousness of German society. A look at an Internet search engine with the number of hits it produces provides a certain amount of empirical evidence[17]: "Clausewitz" alone records 215,000 hits, "Clausewitz" and "Strategie" has 62,200 entries, "Clausewitz" and "Vom Kriege" still 39,000, and "Clausewitz" and "On War" as many as 101,000. The intention here is not to compare the number of hits with those for other important strategic thinkers. However, the relationships among the search strings are interesting: firstly, it becomes clear that the principle work appears almost three times more in the English translation than in the German version. Secondly, it is surprising that the more specific subject of "Strategie" records almost twice the number of hits as the work "Vom Kriege". Alongside this, the 79,400 entries for "Clausewitz-Gesellschaft" are astonishing: as large as the other hit rates may appear – Clausewitz with the German connotations appears almost paltry in comparison. As it is not possible to state who the interested parties in these topics are, a further look into the Internet is ventured. This reveals three Clausewitz barracks in Germany: in Burg, Hamburg, Nienburg – until a few years ago there was also a fourth in Oldenburg; Burg and Leipzig each have a Clausewitz-Hotel, and in Burg there is a secondary school, the former Erich Weinert Schule, which has been renamed the "Europaschule Carl von Clausewitz"; and clicking on "Clausewitz-Straße" yields 14,600 hits. In this context, it should be mentioned that the postal services in the GDR and the Federal Republic of Germany both issued a commemorative stamp to mark the 200th birthday. All this, as previously stated, has little conclusive power and yet the result of an empirical survey on the level of awareness of Clausewitz in society would presumably yield rather modest results.

New stimuli

The picture looks different in the academic debate: in the last two decades, four groups have formed that deal intensively with Clausewitz. A first group gathered in 1990/91 at the Universität der Bundeswehr Hamburg [University of the German Federal Armed Forces] around the sociologist Gerhard Vowinckel. Its members regarded Clausewitz as "a non-canonized classical exponent of social science". Uniting them was their surprise in the topicality, clarity of thought and academic usability of Clausewitz's thinking.[18] The works produced within the scope of a research colloquium displayed a surprisingly varied palette of social scientific approaches, inviting further studies. Unfortunately, there was no continuation of this colloquium.

Almost as a countermove, in 1995 Schössler founded the "Interdisziplinäre Forum für die Theorie und Praxis der Sicherheitspolitik, für Strategie und Streitkräfteforschung in der postkonfrontativen Periode" [Interdisciplinary forum for the theory and practice of security policy, for research into strategy and armed forces in the post-confrontational period] at the Universität der Bundeswehr München [University of the German Federal Armed Forces Munich]. This forum published Clausewitz studies, annual compendia and a collection of written works in the form of anthologies. In 1991 Schössler himself brought out a clearly structured and very readable academic biography in paperback format with personal testimonies and documentary pictures. Today the forum no longer exists; Schössler continues to be involved in this topic and, seizing on a notion by Clausewitz, recently published the "Grundriss einer Ideengeschichte militärischen Denkens" [Outline of a history of ideas in military thinking].

A third group formed in Berlin around the political scientist Herfried Münkler. His work "Das Bild des Krieges im politischen Denken" [The image of war in political thinking] takes an intensive look at Clausewitz's theory of war compared with other military philosophers such as Engels or Carl Schmitt. Münkler deals in particular with the partisan and guerrilla warfare as well as terrorism. In 2001, the philosopher Andreas Herberg-Rothe completed his habilitation[19] thesis under Münkler's supervision with his work "Das Rätsel Clausewitz. Politische Theorie des Krieges im Widerstreit" [The mystery of

Clausewitz. Political theory of war in conflict]. In her habilitation thesis, the philosopher Ulrike Kleemeier investigated the philosophical principles of the theory of war. And, more recently, Krzysztof C. Matuszek has emerged from Münkler's group with his dissertation "Der Krieg als autopoietisches System. Der Krieg der Gegenwart und Niklas Luhmanns Systemtheorie" [War as an autopoietic system. Present-day war and Niklas Luhmann's systems theory].

The fourth group resulted from the fortunate circumstance that the Commander of the Führungsakademie der Bundeswehr at that time, Admiral Lange, was committed to a substantial dissemination of Clausewitz's ideas in teaching. In 1999, he arranged for Paret to receive a special honour for his research on Clausewitz at the Führungsakademie. During his acknowledgement speech on "ways of approaching the work of General Carl von Clausewitz", Paret pointed out that a special focus of research on the "pedagogical Clausewitz" had evolved at the College.[20] The pedagogical views and statements represented an integral constituent in Clausewitz's political and strategic philosophy; ignoring these resulted by necessity in a reduction, a distortion or even a loss for the comprehension of the overall work. Clausewitz himself with the previously mentioned observation: "It is not what we have thought that we consider to be a contribution to the theory but the way in which we have thought it" had underlined that he regarded his studies on the campaigns less worth reading as an objective result but more as an example of how such studies can be made profitable – namely in the manner of "strict sciences". In general his principle work "Vom Kriege" and the theory of war elaborated within is a lecture, autodidactically for himself as well as for others.

Essential elements in Clausewitz's pedagogical thinking such as the nature of the matter, clarification of the circumstances, instruction, theories and methodological and methodical instruments are in a constant interplay with one another and serve one common aim, namely that of educating the individual by autodidactic means for his activity as a military leader. Clausewitz has thus developed a set of educational instruments which is appropriate for the objective of training military leaders for top positions and key roles. This set of instruments even stands up to present-day examinations in terms of educational science, particularly those directed from the field of adult education. The effectiveness of Clausewitz's ideas to date can therefore – also – be explained by virtue of their didactic structures.

Clausewitz himself was a successful educator and instructor. He gave intensive thought to educational issues, both as the head of Scharnhorst's office during the reform phase as well as in individual memoranda and essays. Pedagogically therefore, Clausewitz was not only in keeping the times, but stood at the forefront of educational progress along with other leading reformers. It may justifiably be said that their reform work was to a large extent an educational reform.

Discovery of the 'pedagogical Clausewitz' at the Führungsakademie der Bundeswehr had specific consequences. As long ago as 1995, Admiral Lange had ordered a 24-hour compulsory seminar for every member of the general and admiralty staff course. In addition, every participant received his own personal copy of "Vom Kriege". The seminar was arranged under the heading of "Clausewitz – den Krieg denken" [Clausewitz – philosopher of war] and was designed on interdisciplinary lines. Philosophical approaches were taken into account, and very specifically among them anthropology, dynamics, decision theory, gestalt theory, action theory, conflict theory, constructivism, educational science, phenomenology, functionalism, sociology and engineering. In twelve sessions it dealt directly with the principle work "Vom Kriege", in each case under a core heading and with a view to its importance for contemporary practical strategy. These seminars came to an end in 2007. Today "Clausewitz" is again (only) offered in seminars as compulsory options, e.g. on the topic of "intercultural competence"[21]. However, the lecture series on various approaches to strategy including that of Clausewitz continues to run.

In the years from 2002 to 2008, ten theses at the Führungsakademie der Bundeswehr were written on the subject area of "Clausewitz"; this is a threefold increase compared with the number in the first 45 years. During this period a number of notable and especially commended theses were produced. Hartmann's work from 1997 dealt with the topic of "Erkenntnis und Bildung. Philosophische Grundlagen der Kriegstheorie Carl von Clausewitz' und ihre Bedeutung für pädagogisches Handeln" [Discovery and knowledge. Philosophical principles of Carl von Clausewitz's theory of war and its importance for pedagogical activity]. It found its way into his book "Carl von Clausewitz: Erkenntnis. Bildung. Generalstabsausbildung" [Carl von Clausewitz: Discovery. Education. General staff training programme], which appeared in 1998. In this work, Hartmann reconstructed the contemporary philosophical and epistemological knowledge paradigms which Clausewitz was able to employ or by which he was influenced. It was specifically F.D.E. Schleiermacher's particular hermeneutics and dialectics as well as their astonishing agreement with Clausewitz's exposition that offer the basis, as Hartmann summarized, for a new "better Understanding of Clausewitz". However, Hartmann also investigated the principles of educational theory in Clausewitz and used these to evaluate learning and teaching at the Führungsakademie. Overall he drew a positive picture: "In principle ... the statement that Clausewitz's essential pedagogical ideas are specifically employed at the Führungsakademie der Bundeswehr (is) fully justified." Features he emphasized here were the general educational aspiration, the granting of self-study components, the open and critical discussion, the integration of theory and practice, the importance of personality development for the course participants and the educational travel. Nevertheless, he also made sixteen "proposals for improvement". Education should be understood as being more formal and less material. Tuition should be concerned with the development of intellectual and methodical competence as an overriding educational aim and a metacommunicative level of reflection. This would require an academic-intellectual approach he claimed: "Academic thinking in the actual military area of tactics, operations and strategy is a humanities-oriented way of thinking. Mastery of the methods of thinking in humanities (hermeneutics, dialectics) is an essential prerequisite for the development of intellectual-methodical competence. In turn it forms the prerequisite for performance-related skills in complex dynamic situations."[22]

Besides this, other works appeared by younger staff officers, the origins of which are also at the Führungsakademie der Bundeswehr. In 2005, Müller examined elements of systems theory in Clausewitz's work from a mathematical viewpoint. In 2007, during his further studies at L'Ecole Pratique des Hautes Etudes in Paris, he presented his master's thesis on "Clausewitz' Lehre über den Kleinen Krieg 1810-1811 an der Berliner Kriegsschule" [Clausewitz's theory on the Little War 1810-1811 at the Berlin War College]. The French participant in the course at the Führungsakademie der Bundeswehr Cohélèach dealt with Clausewitz from the viewpoint of economic theory. Taking the same perspective, Gieseler developed the "Elemente der Spieltheorie in Clausewitz' 'Vom Kriege'" [Elements of game theory in Clausewitz's 'On War']. And finally, several works seized on Clausewitz's teachings on the Kleiner Krieg and appraised them in terms of the current challenges through asymmetric warfare.

In 1999, the "Internationale Clausewitz-Zentrum" (ICZ) [International Clausewitz Centre] was founded at the Führungsakademie. Today it is in close contact with the economics and social sciences faculty of Potsdam University, where an International Clausewitz Institute is to be established. In the first eight years, the Centre held 49 events in the form of Clausewitz discussions, workshops and colloquia and also regularly reported on these events in the Clausewitz-Informationen [Clausewitz bulletins]. By far the majority of the events were concerned with general political and military topics, without establishing a direct reference to Clausewitz's theories, principles and ways of thinking.[23] The target which the Centre had set itself "to analyse the methodology … of Carl von Clausewitz's thinking in terms of its topicality and – in a second step – to apply it to today's global risks and conflicts in security policy", apparently remains largely neglected in these events. Instead, it appears to be concerned with applying what are termed the "timeless discoveries" of Clausewitz, such as the "wunderliche Dreifaltigkeit" [fascinating trinity] in politics and strategy. This approach is also in accord with the objectives of the Clausewitz-Gesellschaft, with which the ICZ is closely connected. As one of its set targets states: "This is not concerned with a historical review of Clausewitz and his period or even with a detailed exegesis of his work, but more with the attempt to view the current tasks of politics and strategy as reflected in the insights of Carl von Clausewitz and thus examine which of the principles and insights formulated by Clausewitz are still important today and are thus endowed with an enduring validity." The separation mentioned here of academic treatment and political and military practice as well as the wish to search and work with "enduring" or "timeless" discoveries is a contradiction in itself in connection with Clausewitz.

Outlook

What the four groups mentioned above share is their search for approaches to Clausewitz from the viewpoint of the humanities or social sciences. In contrast to some of the hard, open discussions of such issues in other countries, for a long time in Germany these new perspectives were only found in the more academically oriented groups. The same is true of approaches to Clausewitz from the fields of economics, natural sciences and technology. And the stimuli to adopt an understanding of war determined by sociology as a social system not only on the level of interaction and organization but on that of society in accordance with Niklas Luhmann have only become part of the German discussion in recent years.

Consequently, only now is it becoming really clear that Clausewitz - far ahead of his time and with only a premonition of the differentiation of the academic disciplines from the middle of the 19th century - developed a sociological theory of the functional social system of 'war' which contains a theory of strategic thinking and action. We find today's corresponding academic theory offered in Luhmann's functional-structural systems theory. The immediate link to Luhmann's theory, and especially to his comments on "Politik als Gesellschaft" [politics as society] and on the generalized communication medium "Macht"[24] [Power], has already been formulated by Clausewitz himself when he interprets war as a means of politics and - in his first definition in "Vom Kriege" - as an act of force. This means that on the basis of this general theory, individual discoveries by Clausewitz on power, complexity reduction and the reallocation of quotas on actions and expectations, on the concatenation of contact selections of experience and action, on paradoxes, uncertainty and indeterminability, on probability and degrees of freedom can be included in the development of theories from the medium range to the lessons of strategy, i.e. extending into the practice of theory and doctrine formation in education and teaching for leadership personnel. Similarly problems from experience, hence from the empirical knowledge of war - exactly in line with Clausewitz's understanding of historical example - can be treated differently and can be linked with different approaches to those used previously. This also enables answers which today's picture of war urgently needs, as shown in some cases by the very confused contributions on terrorism and asymmetric warfare.

Relatively independently of these four groups, a large number of works are also currently appearing from very different perspectives. Today's technology is leading to what one might actually call revolutionary changes in the publishing of Clausewitz's works. The principle work is now available as a copy on CD-ROM provided with the especially convenient search functions, and various publishers are now outbidding each other with low-cost reprints of the full edition of the "Hinterlassenen Werke" from the first half of the 19th century. Since 2005 the book "Clausewitz lesen!" [Read Clausewitz] by Beatrice Heuser has also been on the German market and this is well suited as an introduction and aid to understanding, without lapsing into the same mistakes of earlier collections of quotations.

The works of Olaf Rose – finally – provide the German reader with access to how Clausewitz was received in Russia (1991/1995). Due to Soviet secrecy, existence of the Clausewitz biography by the Soviet-Russian Clausewitz philosopher Swetschin (1997) and of his official Clausewitz translation remained concealed from German Clausewitz researchers until the end of the Cold War.

For some time, the subject of asymmetric wars has increasingly been approached from the viewpoint of Clausewitz. In 2002, for example, the Internationales Clausewitz-Zentrum ran a workshop dealing with the topic of "Kampf gegen den internationalen Terrorismus" [the fight against international terrorism], while the Bundesakademie für Sicherheitspolitik [Federal College for Security Studies] together with the Clausewitz-Gesellschaft held a colloquium on the same subject in 2003. Kohlhoff in 2007, on the basis of Clausewitz's teachings, raised the question concerning the possibilities to defend oneself against terrorism. And Claus von Rosen traced Clausewitz's basic elements of the Kleiner Krieg from the tactical, strategic and political view. In doing so, he discovered in particular, that Clausewitz as a strategist of insurrection was far more practical in the field of the New Wars than had hitherto been assumed. His theories on the Kleiner Krieg are directly connected with comments on "great" war. And the detailed comments on tactics and combat methods in the Kleiner Krieg can to some extent be directly applied to today's New Wars. Clausewitz's thoughts can therefore make an essential contribution to the understanding of asymmetric wars.[25]

A further new field is opening up in the comparison of economics and Clausewitz. In 2001, a translation from the English of a workshop report by the Boston Consulting Group appeared with the title "Clausewitz. Strategie denken" [Clausewitz on Strategy]. This report is intended as a reader for practitioners and theoreticians in industry and business in order to facilitate access to the topic of "strategy". As a collection of quotations it has the familiar failings of the random, largely uncritical eclectic. And in 2008, Jan Grünberg published "Strategie und Taktik nach Clausewitz und ihre Anwendung in mittelständischen Unternehmen" [Strategy and tactics according to Clausewitz and their application in medium-sized enterprises]. However, the connection between the theories of Adam Smith and Clausewitz has not yet been properly revealed.

Several works deal with "Strategisches Denken" [strategic thinking] in connection with Clausewitz. Alongside Peter Trummer's anthology from 1988 and Martin Kutz's observations from 2001 on the "Historischen Voraussetzungen und theoretischen Grundlagen strategischen Denkens" [Historical preconditions and theoretical principles of strategic thinking], Hartmann's works from 1998 are particularly important in this respect. He has demonstrated that Clausewitz has developed a new - comprehensive - paradigm for the theory of war with a claim to universality: In order to observe and understand as well as practically experience and deal with such complex-dynamic realities as war and actions in war as if in a complicating medium and in a space creating its own effect, this - according to Clausewitz - would have to be distinguished by an increase in complexity if it is to be appropriate to the subject. For this purpose Clausewitz is said to have connected to the two methods of thinking: hermeneutics and dialectics according to Schleiermacher. He thus contradicted all quantitative-mechanistic approaches of his time for dealing with the social phenomenon of war. At the same time, Hartmann has therefore also terminated the 100-year-old quarrel as to whether Clausewitz was inspired by Hegel or not. Clausewitz not only employed this method himself but also introduced it for the reader in his principle work within the generally unread Book II. In this he explains, admittedly in what for our present-day ears is a rather clumsy conceptual style, three special techniques: methodism, criticism and examples. Ultimately Clausewitz is concerned with the link between theory and practice. The three special methods are comparable with today's social-empirical methods such as the critical-empirical method, the ideal typology or the probability and decision theory. Current scientific theories and the like do of course extend beyond 'Clausewitz'; however, they have neither overhauled nor even discarded his principles.

The task is therefore to render Clausewitz's thought paradigm rewarding by education on how to think. Clausewitz's theory of war is a hermeneutic theory. It is to a great extent not a technology but a critical science of reflection. At the same time it offers a method of reflection. Due to the complex-dynamic reality of war, the theory offers space for individual talent and the "tact of judgement". Uncertainty should not be driven out by education committed to positive teaching contents; instead, the individual should be enabled to withstand uncertainty by training of the commonsense and character. A number of theses can be derived from this:

- Science is an open process which cannot be locked and has no Archimedean point. A criterion for scientific progress is the crosslinking of theoretical elements which is becoming increasingly dense.
- War as a subject of research is part of the real world and in turn of the socio-political world within.
- Historical relativity, changeability and polarity of the object call for methods capable of capturing this. They are hermeneutics and

dialectics.
- Theory of war is critical reflective knowledge not a positive theory based on laws and technology. In the field of tactics, however, methodism is a suitable access at lower levels of leadership.
- Understanding is a suitable method not only for the interpretation of texts or speeches but quite simply for the interpretation of social reality. This also includes war and warfare.
- Dialectics provides principles for truth-oriented communication. Dialectics does not necessarily look for the synthesis if the subject itself is characterized by polarity. Hermeneutics and dialectics are mutually dependent.[26]

This is what constitutes the "how" in thinking according to Clausewitz. It is said to be "extremely modern", if he is not still considered to be visionary. Learning and practice have to be consistent in the training of leaders. "If after the end of the East-West conflict, Clausewitz may have been rediscovered, his theory of war is nevertheless abridged to the contents affecting security policy and strategic operations, what remains lost is that which Clausewitz defined as his legacy for posterity: the epistemologically reflected methodology for solving complex-dynamic tasks."[27]

Concluding remarks

Is Clausewitz embedded in German consciousness today? Was the ball for a fresh reflection on an academic-practical examination of Clausewitz taken up in Germany at the end of the Second World War? As is all so often the case, there is no clear yes or no; after all, more than 50 years after Hahlweg's new approach a major gap still exists up to the present-day. On the one hand, numerous academic research studies exist with an impressive variety and breadth, the results of which are also of importance for political-military practice. However, the extent to which these studies have penetrated society or even the groups of decision-makers is probably rather small.[28] On the other hand, to a large extent an abridged acceptance of "Clausewitz" prevails, fed by a plain interest in exploitation; a practice-related examination of "Clausewitz" himself has barely taken place so far and is even categorically rejected by some decision-makers. Implementation of the new discoveries in political and military applications therefore still leaves much to be desired. This leads to the almost typical misunderstandings that have been occurring since the first publication of "Hinterlassene Werke" over 180 years ago until the present-day. These misunderstandings are extensive and are effective in terms of the question concerning the utility of Clausewitz's work in the very general sense, his theory of methods for understanding and thinking of war and warfare as well as the explanation of the social phenomenon of war as part of politics. They also affect the more special issues such as the theory of warfare, the continuation and effect of politics down to the last thin threads of warlike events or the applicability of the theories, not only to the air force and navy but also to the New Wars of today.

Nevertheless, Clausewitz offers considerable potential for today's politics and military, far more than the title of the principle work "Vom Kriege" would lead one to expect at first sight. Important steps in the academic preparation of this potential have already been taken in the last 60 years:

- for an understanding of the New Wars and the requirements they place on politics, society and the military by bringing back the scientifically value-free term "war" into the public debate and not restricting its use to either the so-called war between states or the asymmetric terrorism in the field of domestic politics;
- for the development of a strategic culture within the scope of the national and European alliance with a firmly established priority for politics;
- for the transformation of the Bundeswehr as a permanent reform: this process has itself a strategic dimension in the coordinated development of armed forces planning and is not merely to be understood as the organizational side;
- in pedagogical terms: Clausewitz is not part of history teaching; he is not a mine of attractive quotations and not a positive theory for "makers of systems" like Jomini but offers a school of thought aimed at reflexivity for the social system of war and warfare; this cannot only be experienced and acquired in a space for free academic thought;
- for continued research on the understanding of Clausewitz's approaches and their connection to further discoveries from the perspective of today's science. However, this must not only take place randomly and in groups acting mutually independently; a think tank of

this nature would not only befit society in the Federal Republic of Germany with science and politics and also the Bundeswehr in the homeland of Clausewitz, but instead, in times of increasing complexity in global society and politics with an increasing pace of change, it should presumably become a social necessity.

Notes:

[1] Clausewitz, Carl von, *Vom Kriege*, 18th edition, Berlin 1991, pp. 175-176.

[2] Hahlweg, Werner: „Das Clausewitzbild einst und jetzt", in: Clausewitz, *Vom Kriege*, pp. 1-172; the 19th edition additionally contains: Nachrede zur 19. Auflage, pp. 1253-1340; Marwedel, Ulrich: *Carl von Clausewitz. Persönlichkeit und Wirkungsgeschichte seines Werkes bis 1918*, Boppard a. Rh. 1978.

[3] Helmuth von Moltke's remarks that Clausewitz's Vom Kriege had been essential for his self-education und leadership skills significantly promoted the interest of contemporary and upcoming officer generations. See Hahlweg: „Das Clausewitzbild einst und jetzt", p. 64.

[4] Example given, Gerhard Scholtz: *Carl von Clausewitz. Bildnis eines deutschen Soldaten,* Berlin 1936; Gerhard Scholtz: *Reich mir Deine Hand. Carl und Marie von Clausewitz,* Heilbronn 1939; Paul Burg: *Feder und Schwert. Der Philosoph des Krieges Carl von Clausewitz,* Berlin o.J..

[5] Marwedel, Ulrich: *Carl von Clausewitz. Persönlichkeit und Wirkungsgeschichte seines Werkes bis 1918,* Boppard a. Rh. 1978, p. 2.

[6] Hahlweg, Werner: *Nachwort zur 19. Auflage „Vom Kriege",* p. 1331.

[7] Dill, Günter, „Vorwort", in Dill, Günter (ed.): *Clausewitz in Perspektive. Materialien zu Carl von Clausewitz: Vom Kriege,* Frankfurt/M., Berlin, Wien 1980.

[8] Citation in Marwedel, Ulrich: *Carl von Clausewitz. Persönlichkeit und Wirkungsgeschichte seines Werkes bis 1918,* Boppard a. Rh. 1978, p. VIII.

[9] All theses are listed in Führungsakademie der Bundeswehr/Clausewitz-Gesellschaft (ed.): *Generalstabsausbildung zwischen Gesellschaft und Militär. Das Jahresarbeiten-Archiv,* Herford und Bonn 1991. An assessment of these theses is given by Bald, Detlef and Wilhelm Nolte (ed.): *Ansichten und Einsichten. Militär, Staat und Gesellschaft im Spiegel ausgewählter Jahresarbeiten von Absolventen der Führungsakademie der Bundeswehr,* Bremen 1998.

[10] Citation in Bald, Detlef und Wilhelm Nolte (Hrsg.): *Ansichten und Einsichten. Militär, Staat und Gesellschaft im Spiegel ausgewählter Jahresarbeiten von Absolventen der Führungsakademie der Bundeswehr*, Bremen 1998, p. 121.

[11] Elble, Rolf: *Clausewitz in unserer Zeit. Ausblick nach zehn Jahren Clausewitz-Gesellschaft*, hrsg. im Auftrag der Clausewitz-Gesellschaft Darmstadt 1971, p. 7.

[12] Clausewitz-Gesellschaft e.V. (ed.): *Jahrbuch 2007. Eine Zusammenfassung von Beiträgen aus der Arbeit der Gesellschaft*. Band 3. Hamburg 2008, p. 255.

[13] Scheler, Wolfgang: *Clausewitz und das militärtheoretische Denken in der DDR* (http://www.sicherheitspolitik-dss.de/ap/ap04x055.pdf) (accessed 27 October 2010), p. 57.

[14] Dill, Günter, „Vorwort", in: Dill, Günter (ed.): *Clausewitz in Perspektive. Materialien zu Carl von Clausewitz: Vom Kriege*, Frankfurt/M., Berlin, Wien 1980, p. XXX.

[15] Clausewitz: *Hinterlassene Werke*, Band VII, Berlin 1835, p. 361.

[16] Hahlweg, Werner in: Clausewitz, *Vom Kriege*, pp. 1282, 1339-1340

[17] Accessed 14 August 2010.

[18] Introduction to Vowinckel, Gerhard (ed.): *Clausewitz – Kolloquium. Theorie des Krieges als Sozialwissenschaft*, Berlin 1993.

[19] Post-doctoral qualification showing ability to lecture and do research at professorial level.

[20] Details in Rosen, Claus von: „Carl von Clausewitz" in: Detlef Bald, Uwe Hartmann, Claus von Rosen (ed.): *Klassiker der Pädagogik im deutschen Militär*, Baden-Baden 1999, pp. 77-106.

[21] Souchon, Lennart in: Clausewitz-Gesellschaft e.V. (ed.): *Jahrbuch 2007. Eine Zusammenfassung von Beiträgen aus der Arbeit der Gesellschaft*. Band 3, Hamburg 2008, p. 226.

[22] Hartmann, Uwe: *Carl von Clausewitz. Erkenntnis-Bildung-Generalstabsausbildung*, München 1998, pp. 154.

[23] An overview of all conferences and presentations is provided by *Clausewitz-Information* 3/2007, pp. 59-81, and *Clausewitz-Gesellschaft* 2008, pp. 83.

[24] Niklas Luhmann: *Macht*, Stuttgart 1988; Niklas Luhmann: *Soziologische Aufklärung 1*. Aufsätze zur Theorie sozialer Systeme, Opladen 1974, p. 213.

[25] Rosen, Claus von: „Die heutigen Kriege – nach Clausewitz. Zum Verständnis der neuen Kriege heute" in: Helmut R. Hammerich, Uwe Hartmann, Claus von Rosen (ed.): *Jahrbuch Innere Führung 2010*, Berlin 2010, pp. 201-238.

[26] Hartmann, Uwe: *Carl von Clausewitz. Erkenntnis-Bildung-Generalstabsausbildung*, München 1998, pp. 138.

[27] Hartmann, Uwe: *Carl von Clausewitz. Erkenntnis-Bildung-Generalstabsausbildung*, München 1998, p. 160.

[28] As evidence may serve Naumann, Klaus: *Einsatz ohne Ziel? Die Politikbedürftigkeit des Militärischen*, Hamburg 2008.

Literature:

Aron, Raymond: *Clausewitz. Den Krieg denken*. Aus dem französischen von Irmela Arnsperger, Frankfurt 1980.

Bald, Detlef und Wilhelm Nolte (ed.): *Ansichten und Einsichten. Militär, Staat und Gesellschaft im Spiegel ausgewählter Jahresarbeiten von Absolventen der Führungsakademie der Bundeswehr,* Bremen 1998.

Blaschke, R.: *Carl von Clausewitz. Ein Leben im Kampf,* Berlin 1934.

Buschmann, Klaus: Motivation und Menschenführung bei Carl von Clausewitz, in: *Schriftenreihe Innere Führung*, Heft Nr. 3/1980, hrsg. vom BMVg Fü S I 4, Bonn 1980.

Caemmerer, R. von: Clausewitz; in Reihe: *Erzieher des Preußischen Heeres,* Bd. 8, Berlin 1905.

Clausewitz, Carl von: Hinterlassene Werke - über Krieg und Kriegführung in 10 Bd., Berlin 1832 bis 1837.

Clausewitz, Carl von: *Hinterlassenes Werk, Vom Kriege*. Edited by Werner Hahlweg. Bonn 1952 (16th); 1966 (17th); 1973 (18th); 1991 (19th edition)

Clausewitz, Carl von: *Nachrichten über Preußen in seiner großen Katastrophe*. Edited by the Großer Generalstab, Abt. Kriegsgeschichte, Heft 10, Berlin 1888.

Clausewitz, Carl von: *Politische Schriften und Briefe*. Edited by Hans Rothfels, München 1922.

Clausewitz, Carl von: *Über das Leben und den Charakter von Scharnhorst*, Berlin 1935.

Clausewitz, Carl von: Zwei Briefe des Generals von Clausewitz. Gedanken zur Abwehr. In: *Sonderheft der Militärwissenschaftlichen Rundschau,* Berlin 1937.

Clausewitz, Carl von: *Strategie - aus dem Jahre 1804 mit Zusätzen von 1808 und 1809.* Hrsg von Eberhard Kessel. Hamburg ^{3}1943 (1937).

Clausewitz, Carl von: *Der Russische Feldzug von 1812,* Wiesbaden 1953.

Clausewitz, Carl von: *Schriften - Aufsätze - Studien - Briefe.* Edited by Werner Hahlweg. Göttingen 1966 (vol. 1), 1990 (vol. 2.1), 1990 (vol. 2.2.).

Clausewitz, Carl von: *Historische Briefe über die großen Kriegsereignisse im Oktober 1806.* Neu herausgegeben und kommentiert von Joachim Niemeyer, Bonn 1977.

Clausewitz, Carl von: *Verstreute kleine Schriften.* Zusammengestellt bearbeitet und eingeleitet von Werner Hahlweg, Osnabrück 1979.

Clausewitz, Carl und Marie von: *Ein Lebensbild in Briefen und Tagebuchblättern.* Hrsg. u. eingeleitet von Karl Linnebach, Berlin 1917 (4. - 6. Tausend).

Clausewitz-Gesellschaft e.V. (ed.): *Freiheit ohne Krieg. Beiträge zur Strategie - Diskussion der Gegenwart im Spiegel der Theorie von Carl v. Clausewitz,* Bonn 1980.

Clausewitz-Gesellschaft e.V. (ed.): Clausewitz und das Neue Denken in Europa. Fachtagung der Clausewitz-Gesellschaft e.V.. *Militärgeschichtliches Beiheft zur Europäischen Wehrkunde. Wehrwissenschaftliche Rundschau.* Sonderausgabe. 5. Jahrgang, Freiburg 1990.

Clausewitz-Gesellschaft e.V. (ed.): *Jahrbuch 2007.* Eine Zusammenfassung von Beiträgen aus der Arbeit der Gesellschaft. Band 3, Hamburg 2008.

Clausewitz-Kolloquium: *Theorie des Krieges als Sozialwissenschaft,* Berlin 1993.

Cochenhausen, Friedrich v.: *Führertum. 25 Lebensbilder von Feldherren aller Zeiten,* Berlin 1930.

Cochenhausen, Friedrich v.: *Soldatische Führer und Erzieher.* Gesammelte Aufsätze. Hamburg ^{2}1942.

Creuzinger, Paul: *Hegels Einfluss auf Clausewitz,* Berlin 1911.

Dill, Günter (ed.): *Clausewitz in Perspektive.* Materialien zu Carl von Clausewitz: Vom Kriege - mit einer Einleitung von Günter Dill, Frankfurt/M., Berlin, Wien 1980.

Doepner, Friedrich: Die Familie des Kriegsphilosophen Carl von Clausewitz. In: *Der Herold,* Bd. 12, 30. Jg. 1987, Heft 3, pp. 53-68.

Elble, Rolf: *Clausewitz in unserer Zeit. Ausblick nach zehn Jahren Clausewitz-Gesellschaft,* hrsg. im Auftrag der Clausewitz-Gesellschaft, Darmstadt 1971.

Elze, Walter: Von der Lehre und der Lehrweise im Buch Vom Kriege von Clausewitz. In: *Durch Wehrhaftigkeit zum Frieden - Jahrbuch der Deutschen Gesellschaft für Wehrpolitik und Wehrwissenschaften,* Hamburg 1934, pp. 30-39.

Fabian, Franz: *Feder und Degen. Carl von Clausewitz und seine Zeit,* Berlin 1956.

Faltz, Walter: *Politisches Soldatentum. Carl von Clausewitz. Aus seinen Schriften,* Berlin, Leipzig 1944.

Führungsakademie der Bundeswehr/Clausewitz-Gesellschaft (ed.): *Generalstabsausbildung zwischen Gesellschaft und Militär. Das Jahresarbeiten-Archiv,* Herford und Bonn 1991.

Gantzel, Klaus Jürgen: Der unerhörte Clausewitz. Zur Korrektur gefährlicher Irrtümer – eine notwendige Polemik. In: *Arbeitspapier Nr. 5/2001 der Forschungsstelle Krieg der Universität Hamburg,* Hamburg 2001.

Gaßen, Helmut: Clausewitz' Buch Vom Kriege als Bezugspunkt pädagogischen Denkens im 20. Jahrhundert. In: *Wehrwissenschaftliche Rundschau 2/79,* pp. 49-51.

Gieseler, Marc: *Elemente der Spieltheorie in Clausewitz' „Vom Kriege". Ein Beitrag zu „Clausewitz aus wirtschaftswissenschaftlicher Sicht",* Hamburg (MS) 2010.

Groote, Wolfgang (ed.): *Große Soldaten der Europäischen Geschichte,* Frankfurt/M. und Bonn 1961.

Grünberg, Jan: *Strategie und Taktik nach Clausewitz und ihre Anwendung in mittelständischen Unternehmen,* Hamburg 2008.

Guss, Kurt: *Krieg als Gestalt. Psychologie und Pädagogik bei Carl von Clausewitz,* München 1990.

Hahlweg, Werner: *Carl v. Clausewitz. Soldat - Politiker – Denker,* Göttingen 1957.

Hahlweg, Werner (ed.): *Klassiker der Kriegskunst,* Darmstadt 1960.

Hahlweg, Werner.: *Typologie des modernen Kleinkrieges,* Wiesbaden 1967.

Hahlweg, Werner: *Guerilla: Krieg ohne Fronten*, Stuttgart, Berlin, Köln, Mainz 1968.

Hahlweg, Werner: *Lehrmeister des Kleinen Krieges. Von Clausewitz bis Mao Tse-Tung und Che Guevara*, Darmstadt 1968.

Hartmann, Uwe: *Erkenntnis und Bildung. Philosophische Grundlagen der Kriegstheorie Carl von Clausewitz' und ihre Bedeutung für pädagogisches Handeln*, Hamburg, Lehrgangsarbeit FüAkBw, Jg. 95H, 1997.

Hartmann, Uwe: *Carl von Clausewitz: Erkenntnis-Bildung-Generalstabs-ausbildung*, München 1998.

Hartmann, Uwe: *Carl von Clausewitz. Eine Einführung in seine Erkenntnis- und Bildungstheorie*, Eschede 1998.

Hartmann, Uwe: *Carl von Clausewitz and the Making of modern Strategy*, Potsdam 2002.

Herberg-Rothe, Andreas: *Das Rätsel Clausewitz. Politische Theorie des Krieges im Widerstreit*, München 2001.

Heuser, Beatrice: *Clausewitz lesen! Eine Einführung*, München 2005.

Kessel, Eberhard von (ed.), *Carl von Clausewitz, Strategie aus dem Jahre 1804 mit Zusätzen von 1808 und 1809*, Hamburg 1943.

Kleemeier, Ulrike: *Grundfragen einer philosophischen Theorie des Krieges: Platon, Hobbes, Clausewitz* 2002.

Kohlhoff, Jörg: *Vom Krieg gegen Terrorismus. Im Spiegel der Lehre des Generals Carl von Clausewitz*, Neckenmarkt 2007.

Kondylis, Panajotis: *Theorie des Krieges. Clausewitz - Marx – Engels - Lenin*, Stuttgart 1988.

Kutz, Martin: *Historische Voraussetzungen und theoretische Grundlagen strategischen Denkens*, Reihe WIFIS-Aktuell Nr. 21, Bremen 2001.

Linnebach, Karl: *Karl und Marie von Clausewitz*, Berlin 1916.

Niklas Luhmann: *Macht*, Stuttgart 1988.

Niklas Luhmann: *Soziologische Aufklärung 1. Aufsätze zur Theorie sozialer Systeme*, Opladen 1974.

Marwedel, Ulrich: *Carl von Clausewitz. Persönlichkeit und Wirkungsgeschichte seines Werkes bis 1918*. Hrsg. vom MGFA: Militärgeschichtliche Studien, vol. 25., Boppard a. Rh. 1978.

Matuszek, Krzysztof C.: *Der Krieg als autopoietisches System. Die Kriege der Gegenwart und Niklas Luhmanns Systemtheorie,* Wiesbaden 2007.

Metzsch, Horst von: *Clausewitz. Katechismus,* Berlin 1937, mit Ergänzungen von 1941.

Müller, Lutz Dieter: *Systemtheoretische Elemente im Werk von Clausewitz.* (Lehrgangsarbeit, MS) Hamburg 2005.

Müller, Lutz Dieter: *Carl von Clausewitz. Mes Cours Magistraux sur la Petite Guerre,* Donnes a L'Ecole de Guerre en 1810 et 1811.

Münkler, Herfied: *Gewalt und Ordnung. Das Bild des Krieges im Politischen Denken,* Frankfurt/M. 1992.

Naumann, Klaus: *Einsatz ohne Ziel? Die Politikbedürftigkeit des Militärischen,* Hamburg 2008.

n.n.: Errichtung der Landwehr und des Landsturms in Ostpreußen, Westpreußen am rechten Weichsel-Ufer und Litthauen im Jahre 1813. In: *Beihefte zum Militär-Wochenblatt pro Januar bis inclusive October 1846,* Berlin 1846.

Nohn, Ernst August: Der unzeitgemäße Clausewitz. Notwendige Bemerkungen über zeitgemäße Denkfehler, *Beiheft 5 der Wehrwissenschaftlichen Rundschau,* Frankfurt/M. 1956.

Oetinger, Bolko v., Ghyczy, Tiha v., Christopher Bassford (ed.): *Clausewitz. Strategie denken,* München, Wien 2001.

Paret, Peter: *Clausewitz und der Staat. Der Mensch, seine Theorie und seine Zeit,* Bonn 1993.

Paret, Peter: Wege der Annäherung an das Werk des Generals Carl von Clausewitz. In: Führungsakademie der Bundeswehr (ed.), *Akademie-Information Sonderheft,* Hamburg 1999.

Pickert, Wolfgang und Wilhelm Ritter von Schramm (ed.): *Carl v. Clausewitz. Vom Kriege. Als Handbuch,* o.O. 1963.

Priesdorff, Kurt v. (ed.): *Soldatisches Führertum,* 10 Bde., Hamburg 1936-1942.

Rose, Olaf: Carl von Clausewitz. Wirkungsgeschichte seines Werkes in Russland und der Sowjetunion 1836-1991 in: *Beiträge zur Militärgeschichte,* hrsg. vom MGFA, Nr. 49, München 1995.

Rosen, Claus von: Carl von Clausewitz. In: Detlef Bald, Uwe Hartmann, Claus von Rosen (ed.): *Klassiker der Pädagogik im deutschen Militär,* Baden-Baden 1999, pp. 77-106.

Rosen, Claus von: Die heutigen Kriege – nach Clausewitz. Zum Verständnis der neuen Kriege heute. In: Helmut R. Hammerich, Uwe Hartmann, Claus von Rosen (ed.): *Jahrbuch Innere Führung 2010,* Berlin 2010, pp. 201-238.

Rothfels, Hans: *Carl von Clausewitz. Politik und Krieg,* Berlin 1920, Reprint 1980.

Rothfels, Hans (ed.): *Carl von Clausewitz. Politische Schriften und Briefe,* München 1922.

Scheler, Wolfgang: Clausewitz und das militärtheoretische Denken in der DDR (http://www.sicherheitspolitik-dss.de/ap/ap04x055.pdf) (accessed 27 October 2010).

Schering, Walther Malmsten: *Die Kriegsphilosophie von Clausewitz,* Hamburg 1935.

Schering, Walther Malmsten (ed.): Clausewitz, Carl von: Geist und Tat. Das Vermächtnis des Soldaten und Denkers. In: *Auswahl aus seinen Werken Briefen und unveröffentlichten Schriften,* Stuttgart 1941.

Schössler, Dietmar: *Carl von Clausewitz - mit Selbstzeugnissen und Bilddokumenten,* Reinbek (Hamburg) 1991.

Schössler, Dietmar: *Clausewitz – Engels – Mahon. Grundriss einer Ideengeschichte militärischen Denkens,* Band 1, Berlin 2009.

Schramm, Wilhelm [Ritter] v.: *Clausewitz. Leben und Werk,* Esslingen am Neckar 1976.

Schwartz, Karl: *Leben des Generals Carl von Clausewitz und der Frau Marie von Clausewitz, geb. Gräfin von Brühl,* Berlin 1878.

Stamp, Gerhard (Hrsg.): *Clausewitz im Atomzeitalter. Auszüge aus seinem Werk „Vom Kriege",* Wiesbaden o.D. (1962).

Stübig, Heinz: Clausewitz in Yverdon. Anmerkungen zu seinem Pestalozzi-Aufsatz. In: *Paeagogica Historica* XVII/2; pp. 440-455, Gent 1977.

Souchon, Lennart (ed.): Carl von Clausewitz – Die Hauptlineamente seiner Ansicht vom Kriege. In: *Internationales Clausewitz-Zentrum. Clausewitz-Information 3/2007,* Hamburg 2007.

Swetschin, Alexander: *Clausewitz. Die klassische Biographie aus Russland.* Edited by Olaf Rose / Hans-Ulrich Seidt, Bonn 1997.

Trummer, Peter (ed.): *Clausewitz - heute. Den Krieg denken, um den Frieden zu sichern?* Im Auftrag der Studiengruppe für Internationale Sicherheitspolitik e.V. Mannheim, Mannheim 1988.

Vad, Erich: *Carl von Clausewitz - Eine militärische Lehre. Untersuchungen zur Bedeutung Clausewitz' für die Truppenführung von heute,* Münster 1983.

Vowinckel, Gerhard (ed.): *Clausewitz-Kolloquium. Theorie des Krieges als Sozialwissenschaft,* Berlin 1993.

Weniger, Erich: Philosophie und Bildung im Denken von Clausewitz. In: Walther Hubatsch (ed.): *Schicksalswege Deutscher Vergangenheit - Beiträge zur geschichtlichen Deutung der letzten hundertfünfzig Jahre,* Düsseldorf 1950, pp. 123-143.

Will, Thomas: *Operative Führung. Versuch einer begrifflichen Bestimmung im Rahmen von Clausewitz' Theorie „Vom Kriege",* Hamburg 1997.

Zedlitz, L. Frhr. v.: *Pantheon des Preußischen Heeres. Ein Biographisches Lexikon für Militär- und Zivilbehörden aus den besten Quellen,* bearbeitet im Verein mit einigen Freunden der Kriegsgeschichte des Vaterlandes, 2. Bd., Berlin 1836.

Clausewitz and 21ˢᵗ Century Israeli Military Thinking and Practice

Avi Kober

Clausewitz, along with Sun Tzu, is often considered one of the two greatest theorists of war. The special status he has earned is based on the assumption that he offers a universal, cross-time and place theory. And indeed, not only are elements of Clausewitz's theory relevant today; some of them have proven of even greater relevance. But Clausewitz has also been a target of criticism, with the critics' fingers often directed to the perceived gap between his theory and the nature of war and strategy in our time. For some of them Clausewitz is no more than a great interpreter of Napoleon's wars.

The question this chapter addresses is: Are Clausewitz's ideas still valid in Israeli 21ˢᵗ century military thinking and practice? Both the number and the varied nature of the wars Israel engaged in during the Cold War and in its aftermath make the Israeli experience excellent source material. The main argument here is that judging from the Israeli case, whereas many of Clausewitz's basic theoretical ideas are still relevant, considerable aspects of his thought need addition, updating, or adaptation. The chapter considers the argument from three angles: the nature of war, the study of war, and the conduct of war.

The nature of war

It seems indisputable that one of the greatest weaknesses of Clausewitz's theory is its narrow approach to war. Clausewitz essentially treated war as a confrontation on the direct battlefield, virtually ignoring developments and factors that took place in the rear or before war broke out. In addition, he underestimated war's material factors such as economy and technology. Israel, however, is testimony to the broader concept of war. It is true that until the 1970s Israel tried to achieve quick battlefield decision, among other reasons as a means of neutralizing the non-operational factors in war and strategy, but since then its wars have undertaken a strong attritional form involving non-military dimensions.

The following discussion deals with more specific aspects of Clausewitz's perception of the nature of war: the tension between the rational element of war and the forces of escalation; the extent to which low-intensity conflicts (LICs) challenge the Clausewitzian paradigm; the role played by intelligence; morality and war; and post-heroic warfare as a challenge to Clausewitz's perception of war.

The rational element of war vs. the forces of escalation

Clausewitz points to two basic elements in war. The first is the rational/calculative element, which treats war as a tool to achieve objectives. The second is the expressive/escalatory element, which although treated by Clausewitz as an ideal type of war, represents the inherent dynamics of military confrontation that sweep adversaries into spiraling escalation, almost regardless of their objectives or of any real cost/benefit calculation.[1] One can opt for violence out of a rational choice, believing that it could be tamed according to one's objectives, but once violence starts, it may soon feed on its own momentum.

The Arab-Israeli case is filled with examples of political considerations that have limited the scope of military operations. At the same time, there are examples of violence that went out of control. Most Israeli officials feared uncontrolled escalation that might lead to regular war or external players' intervention on the enemy's side. If already engaged in escalation, they usually wished to escalate to a level where the adversary would understand he cannot win, that is, to achieve escalation dominance. But Israeli success in these respects was limited and partial. Before the 1956 Sinai War, the 1967 Six-day War and the 1982 Lebanon War Israeli LICs deteriorated to HICs. In three wars of attrition Israel failed in preventing the intervention of players in the confrontations it was engaged in – when the Egyptians were drawn into the conflict with the Palestinians in early 1955, and again in 1967 into the conflict with Syria; and when the Soviets intervened in the Egypt-Israel 1969-70 War of Attrition.[2] As recently as 2006 Israel's political and military echelons initiated what proved to be a major retaliatory operation in Lebanon after some IDF troops were killed and kidnapped by Hezbollah, an operation that soon deteriorated into war.[3]

LICs: A challenge to the Clausewitzian paradigm?

The pervasiveness of LICs during the Cold War (some 80 percent of the conflicts during that period) and its aftermath (some 95 percent) has raised the question whether Clausewitz's theory has retained its descriptive and explanatory weight against the backdrop of this change in the reality of war. It has been argued that Clausewitz's theory is state-to-state, high-intensity conflict (HIC)-oriented, which allegedly makes it less relevant today. The fact is that Clausewitz *did* relate to the LIC context, which he called "popular war", after having observed such conflicts during Napoleon's campaigns in the Iberian Peninsula and Russia, although during his time they took on the form of guerrilla warfare rather than terror.[4]

Although Israel has engaged in LICs for so many years, until the late 1980s IDF military thinking, education, and training were geared toward HICs,[5] as LICs were perceived to be a relatively minor challenge. In recent years the combination of lack of intellectual tradition in the Israeli military establishment[6] and the pervasiveness of LICs has gradually produced fragmented, eclectic LIC thinking.

In its LICs Israel has applied at least two important aspects of Clausewitzian theory: first, the role played by attrition[7] (although Clausewitz did not confine attrition to LICs). After World War II attrition became a dominant feature of such conflicts, both as a type of war and as a strategy employed in war, particularly by the weak. The aversion to encounters of attrition among Israel's political and military elite and their preference for *blitzkrieg* notwithstanding,[8] since the early stages of the first intifada Israeli leaders have evinced a greater understanding of the importance of attrition.[9] Second is the role played by centers of gravity in popular uprisings outside the actual battlefield. Basically, Clausewitz preferred hitting centers of gravity on the direct battlefield, but he acknowledged the effect of targeting leadership and aiming at enemy public opinion while coping with a popular uprising.[10] Especially in the second intifada, Israel targeted Palestinian leaders; particularly effective was the campaign against Hamas's political and spiritual leadership.[11]

The role of intelligence

Not only was Clausewitz (unlike Sun Tzu and other thinkers and practitioners) skeptical of the value of intelligence in war; he even considered it a source of friction.[12] Yet notwithstanding the perpetual tension between reliance on intelligence as compared to reliance on military capability and force deployment, which entails considerable security expenses; repeated intelligence failures; problems stemming from lack of information on the one hand and too much information on the other; and questions regarding the credibility and reliability of intelligence estimates, it is hard to imagine military activity or political and military decision making without intelligence serving as a main source of information. In LIC, where the enemy is so elusive, it has in fact become a crucial factor. It seems, therefore, that Clausewitz judged intelligence too harshly.

One cannot ignore the contribution of intelligence throughout the years to Israeli counterinsurgency successes. In the second intifada, the IDF managed to implement a high degree of inter-service (military-police-Shin Bet) jointness, thereby improving the efficiency of its counterinsurgency activity. Joint Computerized Command Control Communications and Intelligence (C^4I) operation centers were established, working for the first time in IDF history as joint operational entities. The centers provided visual monitoring to all command levels, down to the tactical leaders and combat helicopters, with all being able to see the same evolving battle picture on their computer screens. The Shin Bet provided real time intelligence through its channels; the IAF extended and verified information through its unmanned aerial vehicles and other aerial platforms; and Field Intelligence supplied updated information from its observation units. Once the intelligence picture was complete, the field commanders could decide on the best way to carry out the mission, which was then monitored throughout by the C^4I command centers.[13] Intelligence also played a major role in targeted killing activities. Inter-service (ground forces-military intelligence-IAF-police-Shin Bet) activity allowed the IDF not only to identify the targets but also to shorten the sensor-to-shooter loop, that is, the time between identifying a target and hitting it, to real time or near real time.

Morality and war

Although as a human being and likely a sensitive man Clausewitz could not deny war's dangerous and costly nature, he did not hide his negative attitude towards "kindness" in war.[14] As a realist and a person who lived in a non-liberal, militaristic society, he was mainly interested in ensuring effectiveness on the battlefield. For him war was only one means among others, and he did not particularly care if force was applied as a first or rather last resort. His insistence on a rational use of force should not be interpreted as a moral stand, but as a utilitarian, pragmatic approach, whereby force must be tamed if it has to serve the political objective. Clausewitz also believed that once the expenditure of effort exceeded the value of the political objective, the objective must be renounced and peace must follow.[15] For him, however, peace meant no more than a situation in which no violence took place, rather than any ideal relationship between two parties. More recently, especially during the interwar period, military thought was dominated by British thinkers, who were highly inspired by a liberal democratic tradition. Since then, moral and legal aspects have played a major role in war.

As a liberal-democratic state, Israel saw moral and legal considerations become an integral part of its military thought and practice at two levels: first, as an international systemic constraint; and second, as a self-imposed domestic moral commitment. At the systemic level, criticism of Israeli counterinsurgency policy has stemmed not only from Israel's Arab enemies, but also from international organizations such as Amnesty International that have blamed it for using force indiscriminately and disproportionately, for continuously violating the basic rights of the local population, and for adopting a policy of targeted killing, which allegedly denied terrorists the right to a fair trial, claimed the lives of innocent people, provoked more killings of civilians as revenge, and complicated the peace process.[16]

A more recent, 21st century challenge has stemmed from so-called lawfare. Unlike criminal jurisdiction of an international tribunal that is exercised by an international organization such as the ICC, universal jurisdiction exercised by states that feel it is within their moral obligation to mankind to prosecute individuals who allegedly committed crimes outside the boundaries of the prosecuting state may have disastrous consequences for any state carrying out military actions. It essentially creates and imprisons defendants in their home countries, lest they be arrested once they step beyond their own borders. In recent years many Israeli commanders have refrained from traveling abroad to countries that apply such procedures.

Beyond the criticism stemming from the international system and without explicitly acknowledging it, issues of just war, discriminate use of force, proportionality, and civil liberties have penetrated into Israeli military thought and particularly counterinsurgency policy, even at the unit level. Israel's strong commitment to fight morally has been expressed *inter alia* by the development of doctrinal and technological means and information gathering methods that could considerably reduce collateral damage; the existence of a code of ethics, which was formulated by the IDF as a result of the ethical dilemmas Israeli troops faced during the intifadas; close control by the IDF's judicial authorities on targeted killing of terrorists and other operations in the territories; rules of engagement and methods of dispersing demonstrations that tried to ensure that loss of life or serious bodily injury was minimized; and occasional rules by the Israeli Supreme Court on matters such as discriminate use of force, torture, and human shields. In the early 1990s the Military Advocate General upgraded the international law unit, turning it into a department headed by a full colonel. The department is in charge of making sure that the IDF abides by the laws of war; of approving or prohibiting the use of methods such as targeted killing or controversial weapon systems; and of developing relations with governmental and non-governmental international organizations. Since the late 1990s military lawyers have become involved in operational aspects, something that might subordinate operational considerations to legal ones to the point of curtailing operational sophistication and freedom of action. And indeed, Israel has often restrained its behavior despite the fact that hitting civilian targets could have a greater punitive and deterrent effect.[17] As a result of the Goldstone report, in March 2010 the IDF announced a new officer job at the regiment level – humanitarian assistance officer – whose mission is to identify humanitarian problems that might occur as a result of fighting among civilians and to solve them in the course of the fighting.

Efforts to adhere to the highest moral standards and abide by the law, however, have occasionally failed, usually because Israel's LICs are waged under complex conditions, for example, the difficulty in distinguishing between combatants and noncombatants; stress among soldiers; intelligence failures; poor planning or performance; lack of professionalism and discipline; or murderous terror activity, such as the Palestinian suicide bombing campaign during the second intifada.

Israeli post-heroic warfare: A challenge to the Clausewitzian perception?

Western democracies engaged in asymmetrical wars have tried to bridge operational effectiveness and morality by opting for a "post-heroic" policy. By sparing not merely the lives of their own troops and civilians but also the lives of enemy civilians, they have not only complied with the principles of discriminate use of force and proportionality and respected the right to life, but they have also gained greater domestic and external legitimacy as well as sustainability in such wars.

Clausewitz criticized 18th century war for resembling a game with preset rules rather than real war. Conversely, had he lived to see post-heroic war, he most probably would have been puzzled, as for him war was nothing but a unique social phenomenon entailing killing on both sides. Moreover, for him sacrifice and destruction were justified as means for achieving operational effectiveness, and there was no point in preserving one's forces by avoiding bloodshed.[18]

Thinking and operating along post-heroic lines was introduced in the background of war in the late 1970s, first by Israelis and then by Americans, long before post-heroic warfare's first rule was formulated by Edward Luttwak. The explanation Luttwak offered was demographic, but in the Israeli case post-heroic warfare seems to have stemmed also from a combination of technological developments, liberal-democratic values, and the non-existential nature of the LICs Israel has been engaged in. A few examples will illustrate the extent to which the two post-heroic rules have influenced Israeli behavior.

Israel managed to sustain its presence in Lebanon for more than 20 years (1978-2000), basing it on strong public support. A major reason for that support was the fact that the death toll was relatively tolerable – some 25 soldiers each year. The death toll for Israeli civilians was also tolerable.[19] In 1997, however, post-heroic warfare's first rule – avoid casualties among your own troops – was broken, when a helicopter crash over the Galilee claimed the lives of seventy-three Israeli soldiers on their way to Lebanon. This was followed a few months later by the casualties inflicted on Israeli troops in Wadi Saluki in August 1997 (five fatalities) and the September 1997 elite commando unit operation in southern Lebanon (which cost twelve soldiers their lives). As a result of these incidents, the voices calling for a withdrawal from southern Lebanon, spearheaded by the anti-war Four Mothers movement, commanded much attention, and the door for the 2000 withdrawal was opened. In 1999, Chief of Staff Shaul Mofaz admitted that the IDF was relying on air activity against Hezbollah, rather than activities on the ground, so as to reduce Israeli casualties.[20]

During the Second Lebanon War, Cabinet members warned against a ground operation due to its likely death toll;[21] IAF fighter bombers flew at high altitude in order to avoid pilot casualties;[22] every casualty was reported to the chief of staff; and in one case an entire battle was stopped because of one casualty.[23] Chief of Staff Dan Halutz admitted that a "no-casualties" approach penetrated the Israeli military mentality as a result of the IDF's preoccupation with terror challenges.[24] According to IDF Chief of Human Resources General Elazar Stern, part of the explanation for the IDF's failure in the war was oversensitivity to casualties.[25] During Operation Cast Lead IDF troops advanced under the protection of a rolling barrage.

As for the second post-heroic rule, during the intifadas the IDF developed and used non-lethal and less lethal weapons, in order to minimize casualties among Palestinian civilians. Despite the suicide bombings during the second intifada, the IDF made an effort to uphold post-heroic warfare's second rule. Targeted killing, which became a major if controversial counter-terror method that was widely criticized, was to a great extent compatible with the notion of discriminate use of force, with the number of innocent civilians killed during these actions dropping consistently over the years.[26]

There are also two examples of post-heroic warfare's second rule from the village of Qana in southern Lebanon. In 1996, during the Israel-Hezbollah first war of attrition, Israel launched Operation Grapes of Wrath. Israeli artillery fire inadvertently killed 100 civilians in Qana, which forced Israel to stop the operation. During the Second Lebanon War, after 28 Lebanese civilians were killed in the wake of an IAF strike on a building in the same village, Israel declared a 48-hour suspension of air strikes over southern Lebanon in order to allow an investigation and time for civilians to evacuate the area.

The Study of War

Even a sworn military thinker like Clausewitz – for whom "the powers of intellect" played a significant role[27], especially in coping with challenges posed by uncertainty – believed that "in the art of war, experience counts more than any amount of abstract truths."[28] This skepticism notwithstanding, he believed that theory can and ought to provide commanders with the tools for becoming better commanders. But unlike his predecessor Frederick the Great or his contemporaries Antoine Henri Jomini and Dietrich von Bülow, he thought there was no point in offering predetermined principles or recipes for success on the battlefield, as every confrontation is unique. Instead, he perceived theory as a set of tools which every commander must use to tailor solutions suited to his own circumstances.

Clausewitz may have been satisfied with the skills IDF commanders demonstrated in coping with friction on the battlefield, but he surely would have been less satisfied with the tendency both to rely on improvisation and to underestimate the value of knowledge. And indeed, noteworthy improvisation by the IDF became a self-defense mechanism, which compensated for lack of professionalism.[29] Resourcefulness on the battlefield developed into a cult of escaping troubles upon their occurrence, instead of thinking systematically ahead.

Against this backdrop, it is easy to understand what underlay the attitude against the study of military history and theory articulated by Major General Gershon HaCohen, Commander of the IDF Military Colleges. "Isn't it possible that [Chief-of-Staff Moshe] Dayan was able to produce such a fascinating [operational] plan [for the 1956 Sinai War] precisely because he did *not* have to spend four years in studying Clausewitz and Jomini?" asked General HaCohen rhetorically.[30] At the same time, he admitted that General Norman Schwarzkopf, whose brilliant operational plan in the 1991 Gulf War he could not but praise, "had learned a lot" prior to that war.[31] Schwarzkopf himself was quite proud of that plan, and was eager to explain how a combination of the principles of war and Hannibal's indirect approach vis-à-vis the Romans during the Punic Wars served as his main source of inspiration.[32]

The tension between reliance on improvisation and theoretical and doctrinal tools has also been reflected in the IDF's command and control system. The IDF has been credited with a mission-oriented command system, but a good decentralized command can succeed only if it is based on a thorough education and training process whereby all commanders acquire the same set of professional tools, which they will later employ on their specific battlefield. This explains why the IDF's mission command gradually deteriorated over the years, until it became no more than lip service.

The Conduct of War

The following section examines both the anachronistic and the still relevant aspects of Clausewitz's thoughts on the conduct of war, as represented by the Israeli case. Generally speaking, Clausewitz's narrow approach to war also applies to his treatment of the conduct of war, which is reflected in some of the characteristics below.

Deeper political intervention in the conduct of war

The sensitivities and vulnerabilities of Western democracies involved in LICs, coupled with the existence of unprecedented effective sources of information and means of command and control at the political leadership's disposal, have stimulated the political echelon's direct involvement with operational and tactical matters, something that Clausewitz would have justified[33]. This involvement has gained the name "tacticization of grand strategy". This combination of sensitivities and command and efficient control and control means also explains why the Israeli political and military echelons have recently been heavily involved in the details of the military efforts to stop flotillas heading to Gaza in an attempt to break the blockade Israel imposed on the Hamas-governed Gaza Strip, which from a purely military point of view is no more than a tactical challenge.

The tactical echelon in turn has become more sensitive to the political repercussions of its activity, incorporating political considerations in its tactics-related decisions. Commanders engaged in LICs have often become "soldier-statesmen" rather than combat leaders, a process that could be dubbed as "grand strategization of tactics."[34] This reality was reflected by Prime Minister Ariel Sharon's meeting with a group of IDF colonels engaged in LIC in the West Bank and the Gaza Strip during the second intifada. "As a young officer, whenever I met with politicians, I spoke tactics, and they spoke strategy. With you, I speak tactics, while you speak strategy", Sharon said.[35] These processes are compatible with Clausewitz's recommendation that statesmen have a military understanding,[36] but also that the military understands the wider picture. They have only gained more relevance under LIC conditions.

The forgotten dimensions of strategy

Michael Howard's famous piece on the "forgotten dimensions of strategy"[37] criticized Clausewitz's focus on the operational dimension of strategy, arguing that it reflected a narrow and not sufficiently modern and material perception of the conduct of war. In Clausewitz's defense, however, it should be noted that the societal dimension is present throughout his work and that from his treatment of centers of gravity one learns that he did acknowledge the impact of actions beyond the actual battlefield, at the grand-strategic level of war.[38] Had Clausewitz lived today, he would most probably have been puzzled by the extent to which Western militaries have become committed to the "forgotten" technological dimension to the point of developing a cult of technology, something that is particularly reflected in RMA thinking.

The IDF has been no exception. Only a decade ago it still held a balanced approach with regard to technology, aware of the danger entailed in over-reliance on technology at the expense of the non-material human factor. In recent years, however, strongly inspired by technological developments and RMA, technology has started overshadowing the non-material aspects of Israeli strategy and tactics, becoming the main factor in military thought, buildup, and operations. To a state that has suffered from a strong sense of quantitative inferiority vis-à-vis the Arab militaries; a technology-based military has been very appealing as a force multiplier. Israeli LIC thinking too has often demonstrated the naive belief that the IDF's technological edge would enable it to cope effectively with irregular challenges at a relatively low cost, in terms of both casualties – which also suits post-heroic warfare principles – and the economic burden.

At what levels of war is war waged?
For Clausewitz there were two levels of war – strategy and tactics. One of the consequences of the broadening of war and strategy since his death has been the addition of two levels – the operational level and the grand-strategic level. Another development pertains to the relative weight of the levels: in wars of attrition and LICs the levels at the two extremes of the levels of war pyramid – tactics on the one hand and grand-strategy on the other – have become the most important. In LICs in particular, the strategic and operational levels of war are usually intentionally bypassed by the militarily weaker side in order to balance the militarily stronger side and divert the confrontation to those levels in which the weaker side has better chances of compensating for its weakness. The military encounters, therefore, usually take place at the tactical level, where they are limited in terms of forces, time, and place, whereas the objectives of those engaged in the conflict and sometimes also the targets they aim to hit tend to be outside the direct battlefield, at the grand-strategy level, with the enemy's society and economy constituting the center of gravity.

This phenomenon likewise applies to the Israeli case. In recent decades, the adversaries in the Arab-Israeli conflict – both states, like Syria, but particularly non-state players, like the PLO, Hamas, and Hezbollah – have adopted such an approach. At times when Israel felt that the enemy had pushed its patience too far, it was dragged into operating at the operational level, and sometimes even at the strategic level, e.g., Operations Accountability (1992), Grapes of Wrath (1996), and the Second Lebanon War (2006) against Hezbollah; and Defensive Shield (2002) and Cast Lead (2009) against the Palestinians. In most cases the confrontation ended with Israel imposing heavy damage on the other side.

The role played by airpower and sea power

Regrettably, one of the greatest weaknesses of Clausewitz's work is its continental orientation, which diminishes its external validity. It is true that airpower became a significant component of war only after Clausewitz's time, but sea power did play a central role in war before and during his time, and it is nonetheless missing from his work.

When it comes to Israel, airpower (and to much lesser extent sea power) has always been considered a necessary condition for battlefield decision, which Israel has traditionally achieved via its ground forces. In recent decades, as the IDF has become fascinated with RMA ideas, Israel has been swayed by the belief that technology now offers new opportunities for destroying the enemy with standoff precision fire while saving the lives of troops and minimizing enemy civilian casualties, and that airpower has become decisive on the battlefield. In 2002, still as IAF chief, General Dan Halutz referred to the IAF's capabilities: "Airpower alone can decide, let alone be the senior partner in such decision."[39]

In the Second Lebanon War the IDF's planners were so confident that airpower alone – or almost alone – could do the job[40], that they did not provide the government with any real alternative until the last stage of the war. Had the IDF been acquainted with the history of airpower, it would have known that no battlefield decision at the strategic level has ever been achieved from the air (Kosovo, which was so frequently referred to as a model of decision from the air, was a grand-strategic decision, achieved by denying Serbian *society* the ability to carry on the war – not the Serbian army, which remained almost unharmed). The fact that battlefield decision still needs boots on the ground keeps airpower and sea power in supporting roles that enable battlefield decision, without being able to achieve it on their own. This also keeps Clausewitz's focus on ground forces relevant.

Playing an important role in deterrence, airpower and sea power help prevent war no less than wage war. Since Clausewitz preoccupied himself with how to wage war, not how to prevent it, one would find this aspect of modern war missing from his work. In the Israeli case, strategic deterrence is heavily based on airpower and submarines, and its theoretical sources are not to be found in Clausewitz's work.

What happened to the commitment to achieve battlefield decision?
Although Clausewitz was neither interested in deterrence nor in early warning, elements that have constituted two legs of the Israeli security concept triangle, he was nevertheless highly interested in the third leg – battlefield decision. In recent years the IDF's commitment to battlefield decision in its Clausewitzian meaning, i.e., denying the enemy the ability to continue to fight has eroded significantly.

In an interview with a brigadier-general from the IDF's Planning Branch less than three years before the Second Lebanon War, the senior commander made a comment one would normally not expect to hear from a professional officer: "When I started my job, I found in the plans the phrase, 'defeating the Palestinians. I asked myself, what is that nonsense? Whom exactly are we supposed to defeat? What does defeat mean? We tried to think of alternatives to defeating the enemy. Initially I talked about a 'victory image', which is merely an appearance. It then became a matter of producing a victory show."[41] On another occasion Chief-of-Staff Moshe Yaalon expressed skepticism about the ability to land a decisive blow to a guerrilla organization like Hezbollah.[42] His successor, Dan Halutz, did not believe that a knockout was an option in the Second Lebanon War or that "defeating a terror organization" was achievable. He therefore thought battlefield decision was irrelevant.[43] During the 2000s, "burning an idea in the enemy's consciousness" became more important for IDF commanders than affecting its capabilities. Reflective of this approach was Chief of Staff Moshe Yaalon's statement during the second intifada that "[Israel must] burn into the Palestinian consciousness" that violence does not bring them political gains.[44]

In such a state of mind, it is no wonder that when the Second Lebanon War broke out then-Chief of Operations General Gadi Eisenkot said that defeating Hezbollah was unattainable.[45] "The military does not even pretend to achieve battlefield decision," was Foreign Minister Tzipi Livni's impression from the military's ideas aired during a Cabinet meeting held on July 31.[46] This attitude toward battlefield decision was also reflected in an edited volume published in 2004 by the IDF's publishing house titled *Low Intensity Conflict*, which projected skepticism about the chances of achieving battlefield decision in LICs.[47]

The impact of the firepower/maneuver ratio

One of the most powerful factors that have affected the conduct of war in our time has been the firepower-maneuver balance. Technology has made it possible to attack the enemy and transfer the war to its territory via fire, to bypass ground operations, to concentrate fire instead of forces, and to launch first strike and surprise the enemy within minutes. Some of these capabilities, which Israel has had at its disposal, have challenged some of Clausewitz's concept of the conduct of war.

Offense/defense. Unlike Clausewitz, Israel has traditionally preferred offense to defense, considering it the stronger form of war and a preferred strategy, given its narrow territorial margins and inability to absorb enemy attack on its soil.[48] During the course of its LICs, however, it gradually learned that in LIC contexts offense and defense were preferably applied in tandem, complementing each other.[49] The increased threats to the civilian rear and society's expectations to be effectively defended have left no choice but to invest in passive and active defense. None of these considerations, however, treated defense as the stronger form of war.

Remnants of indirect approach. For Clausewitz nothing could replace direct approach as a means for bringing about the enemy's collapse. The IDF, on the other hand, has preferred the indirect approach, in which it saw a very effective force multiplier. After the early 1970s, however, only little was left of the traditional Israeli indirect approach,[50] one important reason being the ascendancy of firepower over maneuver. Some Israeli military thinkers, however, believed in a fire-based substitute for Liddell Hart's indirect approach.[51]

The decline of the IDF indirect approach was exemplified during the 2006 Second Lebanon War. Had the IDF truly been committed to its sophisticated indirect approach tradition, its ground operations would have opened by quickly outflanking and encircling the enemy and using the element of surprise to capture the northern parts of southern Lebanon first. An indirect approach *à la* Sun Tzu or Liddell Hart would have caused confusion among the enemy ranks and might have brought about its psychological collapse much better than the Clausewitzian direct approach, which enabled Hezbollah to recover and stand strong. Instead of creating a top-down effect, IDF ground troops

163

were engaged in a Sisyphean effort to translate achievements in numerous battles into operational and strategic gains.

Concentration of fire instead of concentration of forces. The ability to concentrate or disperse rapidly long range and precise fire has made dilemmas of concentration versus dispersion of forces, typical of maneuver-oriented operations, much easier to solve. It has already caused the distinction between interior and exterior lines – which Clausewitz, like other military thinkers, discussed in his theory – to lose much of its relevance.

Another consequence of the ascendancy of firepower has been the narrowing of the gap between strong and weak. By concentrating rocket or missile fire on the stronger side's rear, as did the Palestinians and Hezbollah from the early 1980s to the 2000s, the weaker side has made technology a force multiplier. At the same time, as was proved during the Second Lebanon War, in counter-insurgency operations concentration of fire has a much smaller effect than ground maneuvers.

Lower likelihood of first strike. Clausewitz considered first strike, let alone strategic surprise, hardly feasible or effective.[52] This is understandable given the technological capabilities during his life time. With the dramatic technological developments that have taken place since his death, however, first strike became a central feature of strategy in general and in Israeli strategy in particular. The possibility of launching a destructive strike without exposing the preparations for it serves not only the initiator but also the defender, who is better equipped with immediate, near real time intercepting or retaliating options via firepower. This lowers the risk of being taken by surprise, and serves those like Israel that due to political reasons suffer from constraints on launching a first strike.

The role played by logistics. Clausewitz did not preoccupy himself much with logistics either as a national effort in the rear, which is supposed to support military operations, or as an effort on the direct battlefield, which is supposed to support maneuver. He simply did not believe it was a decisive factor. The ascendancy of maneuver, which reached its peak during the interwar period and in the Arab-Israeli wars in the 1950s and the 1960s, as well as the role played by *blitzkrieg*, has made logistics a critical factor.

This has been reversed, though, with firepower becoming dominant and maneuvers becoming less feasible and necessary. In the Israeli case, this explains why after years of faith in *blitzkrieg* and a logistics system that used to push supplies to the advancing combat units, in the years preceding the Second Lebanon War the IDF assumed that such a logistics system was obsolete. It has therefore been replaced by a more centralized system, which was based on modularly structured area-logistics units.[53] During the war, however, it became clear that the new system may have improved control over logistical resources and saved manpower and stocks[54], but at the same time, it crippled the combat units' logistical autonomy and countered operational art's logic and spirit. It is doubtful it would have met operational requirements had the war involved large scale ground maneuvers.

The emergence of the notion of diffused warfare

Some RMA-inspired Israeli thinkers believe that a fundamental shift has taken place in the conduct of war, from waging campaigns consisting of horizontal clashes between rival forces, which entail breaking through the opponent's layers of defense and proceeding along defined lines with distinct start and finish lines, to diffused confrontations that take place simultaneously on the entire battle space, distributing the force's mass among a multitude of separate pressure points, rather than concentrating it on assumed centers of gravity.[55] The notion of diffused warfare, which took hold of the IDF prior to the Second Lebanon War, contradicts the notion of concentration shared by theorists and practitioners for many generations. Moreover, it seems to have taken strategy back to the Clausewitzian idea of accumulating numerous tactical successes and translating them into operational or strategic achievements.

Other enthusiastically adopted RMA-inspired elusive notions, such as effect-based operations (EBO),[56] have also distanced Israeli commanders from the old but simple concept of center of gravity, which as part of the general idea of concentration has united military thinkers and practitioners for centuries, except for the dilemma of where and against what it would be best to concentrate forces.[57]

"Military genius"

IDF commanders have often demonstrated high adaptability to changing conditions on the battlefield.[58] Clausewitz would surely have found in them at least a grain of "military genius," which is based on intuition and "needs no theory."[59] At the same time he would have recommended that they not underestimate knowledge, which, according to him, also has practical dividends (as discussed above in reference to the study of war).

From Clausewitz's discussion of the commanders' performance in battle, it is obvious that he assumed their physical presence on the battlefield. In the 21st century, Israeli commanders' traditional skills of running battles by leading troops on the battlefield have been negatively affected by RMA. It strengthened their temptation to run battles from headquarters located in the rear and over plasma screens, as occurred during the Second Lebanon War.[60] This "may have changed the focus of our command," Chief of Staff Halutz admitted.[61] Yet as former Deputy Chief of Staff Matan Vilnai said, one can run MacDonald's using plasma screens, not a battle.[62] This practice was rectified in the wake of that war.

Can the stronger side win?

Like his successors Moltke and Engels but unlike most post-World War II theorists and practitioners, Clausewitz was quite optimistic regarding the chances of a well equipped, trained, and highly motivated regular army to defeat insurgents. The misfortunes great powers have experienced during the post-World War II asymmetrical conflicts, however, created the impression that non-state players are almost undefeatable.

The Israeli case seems to put the question in the right proportion. First, it may be true that liberal-democratic societies tend to suffer from chronic perseverance when conducting LICs, but this seems to apply only to those cases where their vital interests are not at sake. Israel's conflict with the Palestinians, however, does entail Israeli vital interests, as a result of which Israeli cost tolerance has been high. Moreover, the cost of Israel's LICs in terms of losses and quality of life has been mitigated by the moderate economic cost inflicted on Israel, as well as by the fact that the death toll was usually relatively limited. The more remote the LIC activity from the country's population centers and the greater the share of the lower classes in combat units, the less severely the threat was perceived by the Israeli society.[63] Second, given its LIC aversion, most of Israel's asymmetrical conflicts were imposed on it, therefore almost never igniting a significant public debate regarding their legitimacy. Third, in handling LICs, Israel, like other liberal democracies, can afford to conduct the conflict post-heroically. This does not merely imply constraints on going to war and on conducting it, but at the same time constitutes a way to overcome the society's aversion to war. Fourth, it is true that unlike in the past, weaker sides in our time also play in the technological ballpark, taking advantage of technology-based multipliers. It seems, though, that Israel, like other stronger adversaries, will always retain its technological edge.

The Israel-Palestinian balance sheet shows that in its military operations against the Palestinians Israel usually had the upper hand, and that the two intifadas ended because the Palestinian cost tolerance proved to be lower than that of Israel. Like Egypt and Jordan, the PLO eventually recognized the existence of Israel and decided to negotiate with it on the basis of a two-state solution. When one adds to this the relative quiet in the West Bank after the 2002 Defensive Shield operation, the quiet on the Lebanese border in the post-2006 Second Lebanon War period, and the relative stability on the Gaza Strip front following the 2009 Operation Cast Lead, the unavoidable conclusion is that asymmetrical conflicts do not necessarily end to the detriment of the strong.

Conclusion

Judging from the Israeli case, it seems that whereas many of Clausewitz's basic theoretical ideas are still relevant, considerable aspects of his work need updating and adaptation, something that Clausewitz would most probably have acknowledged and done himself had he lived longer or later.

As far as the *nature of war* is concerned, the tension between the rational and the expressive elements in war; the central role played by society in war; and the challenge of "popular war," which today is referred to as LIC, asymmetrical war, or insurgency have all retained their relevance. Clausewitz's approach to the *study of war* likewise carries a valuable, lasting message. He knew exactly what one could expect of a theory – not any recipes, rather a tool kit that helps the commander tailor solutions suitable to his particular conditions. Clausewitz's discussion of the *conduct of war* also offers at least three lasting principles: the right and the duty of the political echelon to intervene in military operations, if necessary, and the expectation of the military echelon to understand that there is a greater picture, wherein the military dimension is only one, though a very important, consideration; the importance of achieving battlefield decision; and the dialectic nature of the relationship between offense and defense.

But one cannot ignore those aspects that Clausewitz did not acknowledge or address. Absent from his treatment of the *nature of war* are some of the major features of modern war that have emerged after his death, particularly the broadening of war beyond the direct battlefield; the importance of intelligence; the role played by morality in war; and post-heroic warfare – the latter two applying to and characterizing mainly liberal democracies.

Clausewitz's treatment of the *conduct of war* also fails to represent developments, changes, and capabilities, most (though not all) of which have taken place after his death: the emergence of the operational and the grand-strategy levels; the centrality of the levels at the two extremes of the levels of war pyramid; "the forgotten dimensions of strategy" (technology and logistics); the role played by airpower and sea power; the firepower/maneuver ratio and its impact on the offense/defense balance, interior and exterior lines, the indirect approach, and *blitzkrieg*; and concentration of fire.

Notes:

[1] For the expressive/escalatory element see Carl von Clausewitz, *On War* (Princeton: Princeton UP 1976), pp. 76-77; C.R. Mitchell, *The Structure of International Conflict* (London: Macmillan, 1981), p. 26; Raymond Aron, *Peace and War* (New York: Doubleday, 1967), pp. 168, 967; Fred C. Ikle, *Every War Must End* (New York: Columbia University Press, 1971), p. 34; Colmar von der Goltz, *The Conduct of War* (London: Kegan Paul, Trench, Trubner, 1908), p. 5; Bernard Brodie, *War and Politics* (New York: Macmillan, 1973), Ch. 1; Robert Osgood, *Limited War: The Challenge to American Strategy* (Chicago: Chicago University Press, 1957), pp. 28-45.

[2] Avi Kober, *Israel's Wars of Attrition* (New York: Routledge 2009), pp. 143-69.

[3] Chief of Staff Dan Halutz's testimony before the Winograd Commission. http://www.vaadatwino.org.il/pdf/תמליל%20דן%20חלוץ.pdf, p. 50; Minister of Transportation Shaul Mofaz's testimony before the Winograd Commission, http://www.vaadatwino.org.il/pdf/תמליל%20שאול%20מופז.pdf, p. 43.

[4] See the chapter "The People in Arms" in Clausewitz, *On War*, pp. 479-83.

[5] Eliot A. Cohen, Michael J. Eisenstadt, and Andrew.J. Bacewich, *Knives, Tanks, and Missiles: Israel's Security Revolution* (Washington, DC: The Washington Institute for Near East Policy, 1998), p. 71; Avi Kober, "Israeli Military Thinking as

Reflected in *Maarachot* Articles, 1948-2000," *Armed Forces & Society*, Vol. 30, No. 1 (Fall 2003), pp. 153-4.

[6] Kober, "What Happened to Israeli Military Thought?"

[7] Clausewitz, *On War*, p. 93.

[8] Kober, *Israel's Wars of Attrition*, pp. 35-49.

[9] Ibid.

[10] Clausewitz, *On War*, p. 596.

[11] Avi Kober, "Targeted Killing during the Second Intifada: The Quest for Effectiveness," *Journal of Conflict Studies*, Vol. 27 (2007), http://www.lib.unb.ca/Texts/JCS/bin/get.cgi?directory=Summer07&/filename=jcs27art06.html

[12] Clausewitz, *On War*, p. 117.

[13] *Defense Update*, 26 April 2005.
http://www.defense-update.com/2005_04_01_defense-update_archive.html

[14] Clausewitz, *On War*, p. 75.

[15] Ibid., p. 92.

[16] Michael L. Gross, "Fighting by Other Means in the Mideast: A Critical Analysis of Israel's Assassination Policy," *Political Studies*, Vol. 51, No. 4 (December 2003), pp. 350-68; M. Gross, "Assassination: Killing in the Shadow of Self-Defense," in J. Irwin (ed.), *War and Virtual War: The Challenge to Communities* (Amsterdam: Rodopi, 2004), pp. 99-116.

[17] Amos Harel, "Avodot Patzar: Interview with the Military Chief Advocate," *Haaretz*, 18 September 2009.

[18] Clausewitz, *On War*, p. 98.

[19] Ofer Shelah and Yoav Limor, *Captives in Lebanon* (Tel Aviv: Yediot Aharonot, 2007) [Hebrew], p. 132.

[20] Interview on Israeli Radio, Channel 2, 6 October 1999.

[21] Ariella Ringel-Hoffman, "This Is Not How a War Should Be Conducted," *Yediot Aharonot Weekend Supplement*, 23 March 2007; Scott Wilson, "Israeli War Plan Had No Exit Strategy," http://www.washingtonpost.com/wp-dyn/content/article/2006/10/20/AR2006102001688 _pf.html

[22] Shelah and Limor, *Captives in Lebanon*, p. 244.

[23] Israeli Radio, Channel 7, 2 November 2006, http://www.inn.co.il/News/News.aspx/ 155971

[24] Amir Bouchbout, "Halutz's Swords Speech", http://www.nrg.co.il/online/1/ART1/506/ 032.html

[25] Israeli Radio, Channel 7, 2 November 2006. http://www.inn.co.il/News/News.aspx/155971; Yossi Yehoshua, "Declining Values," *Yediot Aharonot Weekend Supplement*, 13 July 2007.

[26] Kober, *Israel's Wars of Attrition*.

[27] Clausewitz, *On War*, p. 101.

[28] Ibid., p. 164. See also p. 186.

[29] Emanuel Wald, *Kilelet Hakelim Hashvurim* [The Curse of the Broken Vessels] (Tel-Aviv: Shoken, 1987) [Hebrew], p. 183.

[30] Gershon HaCohen, "Educating Senior Officers" in *Is the IDF Prepared for Tomorrow's Challenges?* BESA Colloquia on Strategy and Diplomacy, 24 July 2008, p. 28.

[31] Ibid.

[32] "Hannibal and Desert Storm," *BBC Time Watch production*, 2002.

[33] See Stuart A. Cohen, "Why Do They Quarrel? Civil-Military Tensions in LIC Situations," *The Review of International Affairs*, Vol. 2, No. 3 (Spring 2003), pp. 21-40.

[34] Bernard Boëne, "Trends in the Political Control of Post-Cold War Armed Forces," in Stuart Cohen (ed.), *Democratic Societies and Their Armed Forces: Israel in Comparative Context* (London: Frank Cass, 2000), pp. 73-88; Eliot A. Cohen, "Technology and Supreme Command," Ibid., pp. 89-103.

[35] *Yediot Aharonot*, 1 February 2002.

[36] Clausewitz, *On War*, p. 608.

[37] Howard, Michael. "The Forgotten Dimensions of Strategy," *Foreign Affairs*, Vol. 57, No. 5 (Summer 1979), pp. 975-86.

[38] Clausewitz, *On War*, p. 596.

[39] Amnon Lord, "The Air Went Out," *Makor Rishon*, 2 November 2006. http://www.makorrishon.co.il/show.asp?id=14091.

[40] Halutz's testimony before the Winograd Commission, p. 16.

[41] Interview with Brigadier General Eyval Gil'adi, *Yediot Aharonot Weekend Supplement*, 19 September 2003.

[42] Shelah and Limor, *Captives in Lebanon*, p. 129.

[43] Halutz's Testimony before the Winograd Commission, p. 25.

[44] *Haaretz Weekend Supplement*, 30 August 2002.

[45] Halutz's Testimony before the Winograd Commission, p. 54.

[46] Ringel-Hoffman, "This is not How a War Should be Conducted."

[47] Haggai Golan and Shaul Shai (eds.), *Low-Intensity Conflict* (Tel Aviv: Maarachot, 2004) [Hebrew].

[48] For the most compelling works on compellence, see T.C. Schelling, *Arms and Influence* (New Haven: Yale University Press, 1966), pp. 1-18; A. George and W. Simons (eds), *The Limits of Coercive Diplomacy* (Boulder: Westview, 1994). On deterrence-by-punishment as opposed to deterrence-by-denial, see G. Snyder, *Deterrence and Defense* (Princeton: Princeton University Press, 1961); Ami Gluska, *Eshkol, Give the Order!* (Tel Aviv: MOD, 2004) [Hebrew], p. 101.

[49] Kober, *Israel's Wars of Attrition*, pp. 50-71.

[50] Kober, "The Rise and Fall of Israeli Operational Art," pp. 185-6.

[51] Shmuel Gordon, *The Bow of Paris* (Tel Aviv: Poalim, 1997) [Hebrew], particularly pp. 320–2.

[52] Clausewitz, *On War*, pp. 198-9.

[53] Kober, "The IDF in the Second Lebanon War," p. 29.

[54] Amnon Barzilai, "[Chief of the IDF's Technology and Logistics Branch General Udi] Adam's Technological Revolution," *Haaretz*, 2 April 2004.

[55] Haim Assa and Yedidya Yaari, *Diffused Warfare* (Tel Aviv: Yediot Aharonot, 2005) [Hebrew].

[56] Allen W. Batschelet, *Effects-Based Operations: A New Operational Model?* (Carlisle: US Army War College, 2002).

[57] Edward A. Smith, *Effects Based Operations: Applying Network-Centric Warfare in Peace, Crisis, and War* (Washington, D.C.: Department of Defense Command and Control Research Program, 2002).

[58] Moshe Dayan, *Story of My Life* (Jerusalem: Edanim 1976) [Hebrew], p. 244; Tuvia Ben-Moshe, "Liddell Hart and the Israel Defense Forces: A Reappraisal," *Journal of Contemporary History*, Vol. 16, No. 2 (April 1981), pp. 369-91.

[59] Clausewitz, *On War*, p. 145.

[60] Sheath and Limor, *Captives in Lebanon*, p. 385.

[61] http://www.haaretz.co.il/hasite/pages/ShArtSR.jhtml?itemNo=755196&objNo=59745&returnParam=Y.

[62] Amira Lam, "We Betrayed our Constituency", *Yediot Aharonot Weekend Supplement*, 1 September 2006.

[63] Kober, *Israel's Wars of Attrition*, pp. 74-5.

CLAUSEWITZ AND ITALY

Virgilio Ilari, with Luciano Bozzo and Giampiero Giacomello[1]

> «It took the cultural poverty of the most part of the philosophers, their dull hyper specialization, their parochial mentality, tell it like it is, to explain the apathy, the aloofness towards books as Vom Kriege».
> (Benedetto Croce, *Azione, successo, giudizio*, 1934, p. 267.)

Military literature and Clausewitzian studies

Albeit cursory, the studies on Napoleon's first Italian campaign (*Der Feldzug von 1796 in Italien*[2]) and the 1799 campaign in Italy and Switzerland, as well as the 1828 short sketch of a *War Plan against France*[3], are proof that Clausewitz studied Italian strategy far more profoundly than Italian strategists had and have studied him.[4] As John Gooch severely but righty states, Italy simply "disregarded" Clausewitz.[5]

According to Brian Sullivan, Italy invented "the strategy of decisive weight"[6], playing her coalition power among the true Great Powers. This does not imply that *Vom Kriege* is useless for rulers whose unique concern is not to decide war but only to choose (or stress) allies. Chapter IX, the last chapter of the eighth book of the Treaty gives just a discerning and evergreen lesson on coalition warfare[7]. From another point of view, the Italian example may support the Clausewitzian theory on moral factors, demonstrating "the disastrous consequences that can attend the use of force as the principal tool of national strategy without the union of people, military and government that Clausewitz described as necessary for the successful prosecution of war"[8].

The Italians, however, are not the only rulers and military leaders who planned and fought their wars without paying more than lip service to *Vom Kriege*. "The American military experience of the past 25 years clearly demonstrates the need for the senior military leadership to move away from the concept of war as a problem in management and organization, back to the study of war on its higher levels as an art and a problem of leadership in which the role of intuition is paramount"[9]. Michael Handel wrote these naïve words (in reference to Vietnam and McNamara), in 1986, when Admiral William Owens was "lifting the fog of war"[10] and preparing the American way to *Blitzkrieg*, i. e. the way to impose oneself upon the enemy's will so rapidly to be free of waging war without both "adverse determination" and material, political or moral frictions.

This approach is not a mistake. The job of military establishments, in all countries and times, is of course to attempt to limit war "to a single solution, or several simultaneous solutions". Yet hardly, such a goal can be obtained, even in temporary and relative terms. However, as Clausewitz warns, reducing war to a single solution is only one of the three necessary conditions reaching "perfection in war": the other two being that "war [must] become a completely isolated act, which arises suddenly and is in no way connected with the previous history of the combatant states", and that "it contains in itself the solution perfect and complete, free from any reaction upon it, through a calculation beforehand of the political situation which will follow from it" (I, 1, 6). The mistake that is so commonly made is to act as if the first condition, technically possible, could take the place of the other two, historically impossible. Force cannot surrogate politics.

Adapting Alberico Gentili's acute statement on jurisprudence (*historia non est cur legat juris interpres*[11]), we might say *Vom Kriege non est cur legat miles*. In all times and countries, the task of the military is to plan, fight and "win" wars, not to understand war. Planning requires concrete numbers, not uncertainty; fight and victory (at least as they are seen from an armchair) require doctrines, not fortune or genius. Faced with *Vom Kriege*, military establishments cannot but exclaim "God does not play dice!", as did Einstein when facing the Heinsenberg principle of uncertainty. The Jominian reaction against Clausewitzian friction looks something like that of Bertrand Russell with regard to the incompleteness theorems of Kurt Gödel[12]. Once again Western military literature applies Jomini's concepts, thinking war as to be calculable and foreseeable simply because its natural approach is practical, subjective, and auto-referential. The concern here is not about war, however, but about warfare, "the art of war", "strategy", i. e. about the office and art of the General Captain, or what Wilhelm Rüstow called *Feldherrnkunst*[13].

Perhaps the story could have turned out to be quite different had Western military literature evolved from the idea of "ratio belli"[14] instead of "ars belli". Had it done so, the Western concept of strategy would be quite close to the Chinese *Zhan lüe xue* (战略学) or *celue* (战略)[15]. But the fact is that *Vom Kriege* is the only Western book that attempts to understand what

Clausewitz called the "nature" of war. Some of his detractors, indeed, believed to scrap him arguing that nature of war has "changed"[16]. The idea, however, that nuclear or asymmetrical[17] war are not simply chameleonic variations, but a completely different archetype, is perhaps less argued than Stalin's view that Clausewitz, insofar as he was "a representative of the industrial war age", became obsolete in the coming "machine age of war"[18].

Physics and Mathematics had not yet found a way to incorporate the complications introduced by Heisenberg and Gödel in a "unified theory of everything"; they have nevertheless revolutionized research and technology. The "geometric" or Jominian-minded military literature is a dramatic, fascinating collective work, a river of knowledge evolving and renewing itself. But it differs from science. Not, as Clausewitz curiously wrote, because the science would be exerted upon "inanimate matter" and the art of war "against a living and reacting force" (II, 3, 4), but simply because military know-how is relative to particular historical conditions, and cannot generate cumulative knowledge beyond its epoch. Only the effects of the particular wars on the historical process are cumulative, as are, on a shorter scale of time, the improvements in military technologies (ultimately because they depend on the scientific progress). Cumulative is history: histories are only repetitive.

Yes, military literature likes to peruse histories extracting arguments to support or beautify doctrines. Yes, Admiral Owens's label of "Revolution on Military Affairs" (RMA) is borrowed from a famous interpretation of the Renaissance art of war proposed in 1956 by Michael Roberts, which was refused by John Rigby Hale and revived in 1988 by Geoffrey Parker[19]. Yes, to study American experiences against Aguinaldo and Pancho Villa's guerrillas and to learn from Gillo Pontecorvo's film on the battle of Algiers were part of the US Army preparation for the Iraq War. Yes, the ideology or self-representation of this war was perhaps partly influenced by statements Victor Davis Hanson made on the Athenian origins of the Western warfare[20]. Yes, in *Seven Pillars of Wisdom*, Lawrence of Arabia warns us that "with 2000 years of examples behind us we have no excuse, when fighting, for not fighting well"[21]. But in the field of Mars we are not "dwarfs on the shoulders of giants". Clausewitz warns us that historical examples may be deceptive (II, 6), that principles, rules and predicaments excerpted from military history should be learned only for self-education (II, 2, 27), that rules ignoring the moral factors "are not only made for idiots, but are idiotic in themselves" (III, 3). Yes, Clausewitz messed in the field, the day after Waterloo. But Jomini sentenced that Russia would win the Crimean War, and to preserve his eternal principles he wished to stop the arms race as Joshua did the chariot of the sun.

Clausewitz deluded himself convincing himself to be able "to iron out many creases in the heads of strategists and statesmen". In this he failed, as Wilhelm Rüstow wrote back in 1857[22]. He succeeded in his subordinate objective, "at least to show the object of action, and the real point to be considered in War" (*Introduction* of 1827). What Scharnhorst and Gneisenau asked him was not to discuss their ideas, but to educate to war the *philosophes* – a task that was very hard to accomplish with warlike and bloody tribe as they are[23]. This was exactly what Clausewitz has done, even posthumously. He moved from *sagata* to *togata militia*, jubilated by his colleagues and welcomed by the *savants*, starting with Johann Wilhelm von Archenholz.

If in military literature Clausewitzians seem to be like Savonarolians in the Catholic pulpits, *franc-penseurs* unifluential upon establishments, they do have an edge as military historians. The *outillage intellectuel* deriving from *Vom Kriege* works better when writing the history of a war than for fighting it. The "culminating" or fateful point of a war can be detected more easily *post* than *ante eventum*: did Clausewitz realize that the victory of Smolensk was the culminating point of Napoleon's Russian campaign as *sudden* [ευθίς, *eythís*] as Thucydides tells us he realized the magnitude of the coming Peloponnesian war? But this concept is a powerful key in the hands of historians. Trafalgar, e. g., may appear to be, as Alfred Thayer Mahan genially suggested, the true "culminating point" of the entire World War of 1792-1815 – as long as was the aftermath. The theory of the culminating point looks something like what Santo Mazzarino, the greatest Italian historian of the past century, taught us to think as "a prophecy about the past"[24].

Secondly, *Vom Kriege* is not only a chapter of the history of military thought, but also a useful introduction to such a sophisticated discipline. One can leave aside the fact that Clausewitz, in few words, outlined the birth and development of military thought (II, 2, 1-11)[25], but we are indebted to him for his key lessons on the logical methods used by military scholars and their intrinsic limitations, namely found in *Vom Kriege*'s Second Book that Raymond Aron considered "une sorte de commentaire méthodologique ou épistémologique de l'oeuvre entière"[26].

Military history and history of military thought are not the only fields *Vom Kriege* sowed. Philosophy and Political theory, Psychoanalysis and Germanistics are as well: and these last four fields of study are by far preponderant in the Italian contributions. It is for this reason that Italian essays on Clausewitz continue to be separate from the studies conducted by the international mainstream, which pertain especially to military history. Italian essays form instead what Sextus Empiricus called a αμέθοδος ὕλη [*améthodos hyle*, "a forest without paths"][27]. The Italian contribution may be likened to a muddy river, in which, however, specks of gold may be found. The best contributions are "aspects of another 'job', of another intellectual praxis", as Luciano Canfora frames the early Greek literature on history and geography[28]. It means that they originate and circulate only in their own discipline, ignoring and being ignored by the rest.

However these are, if only, original lectures. But the *améthodos hyle* is mostly formed by naïve excursions stretching somewhat over the right of free examination. Some are valuable as private notes marking progress in self-education, but often the author simply ends up popularizing *Vom Kriege*, believing that, being the first among his friends or colleagues, he is too in his own country, if not in his century.

1875-1942: The reception of Clausewitz in Italy[29]

One can find mention of *Vom Kriege* neither in Mariano d'Ayala's Italian military bibliography (1854)[30] nor in the first and prominent treaty of military art published in Italy only two years after *Vom Kriege* was printed: written by Luigi Blanch (1784-1872)[31], the treatise was rather influenced by Jomini, whose books began to be translated in Italian as early as 1816[32]. Bearing in mind that translation was not indispensable at the time, French being then well known not only in Piedmont[33], but in all the Italy. Therefore, the fact that Clausewitz was almost ignored in Italy during the Risorgimento may not be imputed to a linguistic barrier; *Vom Kriege* was translated in French back to 1849-52 (by Belgian Major Jean N. Neuens) and in 1853 the *Commentaire sur le traité de la guerre de Clausewitz* by Edouard Nicolas de La Barre Duparcq was printed; in 1860, the latter published a treaty inspired namely to Blanch[34], whose *Della scienza* was in turn translated into French. In 1860 Carlo De Cristoforis (1824-1859), the next after Blanch among the most prominent military writers of Risorgimento, quoted Clausewitz seventeen times, while not including *Vom Kriege* in the list of books consulted (approximately forty). De Cristoforis, however, took nothing from Clausewitz, being rather obsessed by the principle of the mass, which he believed to have discovered first[35].

Despite that Wilhelm Rüstow served under Garibaldi[36], it seems he did not export *Vom Kriege* among Italian democrats of the Risorgimento. But in 1883 the Garibaldinian General Antonio Gandolfi quoted *Vom Kriege* for rejecting the criticism against the Two Worlds Hero, whose guerrilla generalship had been professionally discredited by dogmatic and Jominian-minded officers of the regular army[37].

As well known, the French-Prussian War was responsible for the fortune of *Vom Kriege*. In 1873 it was translated for the first time in English and in 1875 Niccola Marselli (1832-1899), an Italian officer educated in the Hegelian clubs of Naples, discussed the Clausewitzian ideas about moral factors in depth. Marselli, having abandoned idealism and converted to positivism, disagreed with the impossibility of creating a complete theory of war and asserted his faith in a positive science of War[38]. Nevertheless Marselli criticized the doctrinarism of Jomini and admired Clausewitz to the point where he considered him to be a precursor of positivism.

Despite the Prussian influence upon the Italian army[39] and Italy being in the Triple Alliance, Marselli's attempt at importing *Vom Kriege* into Italy's military culture was far too forced and superficial to succeed. Italian Marxists also paid no attention to Marx and Engels's Clausewitzian lectures that Franz Mehring (1846-1919) delivered them. It took half a century before a new Clausewitzian wave came forth into the Italian culture. When that time came, it was the Axis time.

In 1925 Colonel Emilio Canevari (1892-1966), a brillant officer from Viterbo who fell in disgrace during the Re-conquest of Lybia, began a new life as freelance journalist, publishing an anthology (*Marte*) of great captains and military writers with Giuseppe Prezzolini (1882-1982). Then Canevari became the military columnist (under the pseudonym of "Maurizio Claremoris") of *Il Regime Fascista*, the newspaper owned by Roberto Farinacci (1892-1945). In 1930 he published an essay on Clausewitz and Modern War (*Clausewitz e la guerra odierna*). It took four years, however, before a political detainee like Antonio Gramsci (1891-1937) could read a notice of the book. He commented in his notebook that *Vom Kriege* was not yet translated in Italian[40], that the only book in circulation was that of Canevari, and that Admiral Sirianni, in a paper, misspelled the Clausewitz's name writing «Clause*n*witz»[41]. Nevertheless the entry "Clausewitz" of the 1931 *Enciclopedia Italiana*, written by General Alberto Baldini, director of *Esercito e Nazione*, is clever, analytic and supported by a good international as well as Italian bibliography, including Marselli and Canevari[42].

One can only suppose that the book Canevari wrote also spurred the short intervention on Clausewitz written in the late 1933 by Benedetto Croce (1866-1952)[43]. The philosopher, however, does not quote Canevari: he indeed had a direct and better knowledge of *Vom Kriege* (in its 5th Edition of 1905) and of the relevant literature[44]. Croce agrees with Roques about the influence Machiavelli had on Clausewitz, refusing the supposed Hegelian imprinting[45]. According to him, the contrast between the "Generalstabs-Gelehrsamkeit" (staff pedantry) and "kräftige natürliche Denken" (thought naturally penetrant) made by Clausewitz in his study of the Russian campaign, brings to mind the superb Tolstoian picture of the Allied Council of War on the eve of Austerlitz, in which the Author contrasts the dozing of Hero Kutusov to the fatuous exposition of the plan made by the Austrian General Kalckreuth ("energetic and self-confident with his *marschiren, attackiren*"). According to Croce, "what Clausewitz states about the connection between theory and practice in war is the same in each other field; e. g. in poetry (just to take a distant example)". But it is impossible to summarize such an essay. Croce wrote also two notes on a quotation of the Italian novel *I Promessi Sposi* made by Clausewitz[46] and the influence the Kantian aesthetic had upon *Vom Kriege*[47].

Despite the fact that Canevari was nearly to be seen as a star, considering the extreme modesty of Italian Interwar military thought, there was nothing original in his approach to *Vom Kriege*, in that it reflected the exploitation of Clausewitz as the *Völkisch* Hero of Tauroggen during the Interwar period in Germany, while the true geniality of Clausewitz referred to the German Staff as a collective entity[48]. What Hew Strachan states about Walter Malmsten Schering, "the leading academic commentator of Clausewitz in Nazi Germany", and General Friedrich von Cochenhausen, the major propagandist of the Reichswehr and then Wehrmacht, can also be said of Canevari. They all agreed that "absolute war was an ideal construct, not a reality", and had some difficulty getting a handle on the new catchword of "total war"[49]. Indeed, in December 1937 (see *La Vita Italiana*) Canevari polemicized against the attempt philosopher Julius Evola made to found the totalitarian state, mixing the Schmittian *Begriff des Politischen* and the total war Erich Ludendorff had theorized. According to the rough Colonel, those are all

"Begriffi" (*sic*, in Italian) of German professors, which Hitler did not take seriously.

During the Second World War the old English translation of *Vom Kriege* was reprinted in Great Britain, and a new translation was published in the United States, as well as three selections, a commentary and a West Point study on Jomini, Clausewitz and Schlieffen. Moreover the editors of Princeton *Makers of Modern Strategy* commissioned the chapter on Clausewitz to a true specialist, the German Jewish historian Hans Rothfels (1891-1976)[50]. These seminal Clausewitzian studies were part of the Western intellectual mobilization against the Axis. In Italy, instead, the contemporary Clausewitzian issues were part of an apparent and propagandistic Germanization of the Italian Army, and marked the change from the "Parallel War" to the "Axis War" in 1941.

Suspected to have inspired Farinacci's reprimand that led Marshal Badoglio to resign, Canevari was pardoned by the new chief of staff Marshal Cavallero. He joined the Historical service of the Army Staff ("Ufficio storico"), led by General and Senator Ambrogio Bollati (1871-1950), to cooperate at the Italian translation of *Vom Kriege*. Bollati had experience translating, having already translated Hindenburg, von Bernardi and Falkenhayn, as well as many documents of the German State and Austrian War archives[51]. Paradoxically enough, there would be no written documents about the translation: according to the oral tradition of the Ufficio storico, the true translator was actually an academician and Bollati and Canevari only revised the military terminology. Quite surprisingly, the Google-books list of the Clausewitzian works published in all languages during the Second World War does not include the Ufficio storico translation, perhaps because it did not circulate outside the Army Staff. There are, however, two partial translations on the Google list that were both published by Le Monnier in 1942 and Sansoni in 1943[52]. There are only Italian editions of propagandistic pamphlets published in the Third Reich (in the Google list they are eight, from 48 to 199 pages in length, with titles as *Brevier*, *Kathechismus*, *Grundgedanken* and so on).

Italian contributions to the Clausewitz-Renaissance

The political misfortune of Clausewitz reached bottom when Hitler named after him the desperate plan to defend Berlin. Werner Hahlweg (1912-89) was, with his 1952 critical edition and his 1957 short biography[53], to restore him to the quietness of the military studies. In 1954 Gerhard Ritter (1888-1966) assessed the genesis of Clausewitzian thought from an historical perspective, and in 1961 General Ulrich de Maizière (1912-2006), the maker of the Bundeswehr, founded the Clausewitzian Society (Clausewitz-Gesellschaft). Initially, however, approval of *Vom Kriege* was limited to German scholars, as is proven by its anthological application to the nuclear era written by Gerd Stamp, a former ace of the Luftwaffe who was working for NATO at the time. In 1963, however, Carl Schmitt (1888-1985) brought Clausewitz back to the German tragic history, with his harsh comparison between the rebellion of General York at Tauroggen in 1812 and those of de Gaulle (1940) and Salan (1962)[54] and his critic of the Clausewitzian "Prussianism"[55].

In these two auroral decades, when outside Germany only Peter Paret worked on Clausewitz in original way[56], Piero Pieri was to popularize *Vom Kriege* once more in postwar Italy, beyond the circle of uniformed scholars. His 1955 study on Italian military writers primarily regards the connection between war and politics, but in the chapter about Marselli the Clausewitzian epistemology of the military science is also discussed[57]. In his 1962 *Storia militare del Risorgimento*, Pieri quoted, if only, some Clausewitzian *loci*, such as that "an attack exhaust itself in progressing" or the "result is proportionate to the risk assumed" (with regard to the Sardinian plans in 1848 and Garibaldi's caution at the battle of Velletri). Furthermore, he summarized the pivotal ideas of *Vom Kriege*, in four pages (157-160), using them to criticize Blanch and De Cristoforis[58].

Clausewitz was also quoted in Raimondo Luraghi's history of the American Civil War, one of the most valuable Italian contributions to military history, published in 1966[59]. Despite the fact that the Unionist Army was largely influenced by Jominian Generals, Mahan and Halleck, Luraghi considered the supremacy of the political authority that characterized the Union's high command to be "Clausewitzian", albeit he reported with some caution that President Lincoln would have been among the few Americans to have actually read *On War*[60]. According to Luraghi, whereas McClellan's concern to avoid risk contradicted Clausewitz, Grant's concern for logistics brings to mind the idea of the war as an act of commerce, in which battle is the spot payment; and Grant at Pittsburg Landing incarnated the Clausewitzian genius of war.

In the Sixties, Ernesto Ragionieri (1926-75)[61] and Clemente Ancona[62] contributed to the studies on the Clausewitzian lectures of Marx and Lenin, and Filippo Gaja, director of *Maquis*, the only military periodical of the Italian Left, published an integral translation of the Lenin notes on *Vom Kriege*[63]. In 1966 Gerhard Ritter's *Staatskunst und Kriegshandwerk*[64] and Gerd Stamp's *Clausewitz im Atomzeitalter* were also translated in Italian. It must be noted, however, that the translation of the title of this last misspells Clausewitz's name, "Clausewizt", an error that evidently was considered by publisher, if even noted, to be acceptable to Italian readers![65] Nevertheless it was just a popular magazine to publish a superb Clausewitzian bonsai of Lucio Ceva[66]. In 1969 *Politik und Strategie* by the Bundesmarine Admiral Ruge (1894-1985) was translated[67]: while the translations of the Glucksman potpourri[68] and of the Hahlweg *Krieg ohne Fronten*[69] were fall-outs of the Giangiacomo Feltrinelli's revolutionary obsessions. This first wave of the renewed attention to Clausewitz in postwar Italy culminated in 1970 with the paperback reprint (by Mondadori, one of major Italian publishers), of the 1942 translation of *Vom Kriege*, thus guaranteeing for the first time its countrywide circulation[70].

A century after the French-Prussian War, which secured the fortune of *Vom Kriege*, a new Western defeat, that of the United States in Vietnam, ensured the definitive foundation of the Clausewitzian studies. Just in 1976 the new English translation of Paret and Michael Howard, the two fundamental essays of Paret and Aron and a new essay of a student of Hahlweg[71] were published.

Looking with admiration to the East German military mass education, Colonel Rodolfo Guiscardo opened back to 1974 the nationalistic cult of Clausewitz[72]. In 1975 a small Maoist group included Volksbewaffnung in a manual for resistance against a coup d'état[73]. From 1976 Luigi Bonanate began quoting *Vom Kriege* in his essays on the international system[74] and the Italian military quarterlies echoed the Clausewitzian wave starting in NATO colleges[75]. But it was only in 1978 that the then Lt Colonel Carlo Jean brought *Vom Kriege* to the Italian Army[76]. That was part of a cultural process, which in the next decade led to the birth of the Military Center for Strategic Studies (CeMiSS).[77] Jean started his academic career editing two books (*Il pensiero strategico* and *La guerra nel pensiero politico*), both published by Franco Angeli in 1985 and 1987. In 1985 Lt Colonel Ferruccio Botti, initially paired with Ilari, began his research for systematizing the Italian military literature[78]. Commenting on the Italian reception of *Vom Kriege* (pp. 288), the authors noted its political ambiguity. In fact, while affirming the supremacy of politics, the Prussian General transplanted, for the first time, the theory of war from political theory to military literature. In doing so, he founded a new "strategic" - if not at all militaristic - vision of politics, thus legitimating rulers to subordinate the "political logic" to the "military grammar"[79]. In 1989 the Italian Army quarterly (*Rivista Militare*, then directed by Colonel Piergiorgio Franzosi, who, like Jean, was part of the Alpine troops) reprinted the 1970 edition of *Vom Kriege*, adding Jean's 1978 essay as the introduction; Mondadori later kept this structure for its following reprints. In 1990-93 Franzosi published also nine Clausewitzian studies by Colonel Quinzio[80], the Generals Vittorio Bernard[81] and Giulio Primicerj[82], among others[83]. There were also some would-be Clausewitzian guides for managers and traders[84].

A Clausewitzian renaissance occurred also in the field of the Italian philosophical and political studies. This renaissance of sorts was initially a fall-out of the popularity that Carl Schmitt had in Italy's Leftist culture at the time, and may be traced back to 1981, when *Theorie des Partisanen* was translated in Italian[85]. Umberto Curi [86], Pier Franco Taboni[87], Luciano Guerzoni[88], Massimo Mori[89], Ettore Passerin d'Entrèves[90], Michele Barbieri[91], Loris Rizzi[92], Anna Loretoni[93], Gianfranco Frigo[94], Federico Dalpane[95] followed. Mori, Barbieri, Rizzi, Loretoni, Jean and Luciano Bozzo held a seminar in 1988, at the Forum on Peace and War, Florence, on Clausewitz in the philosophical and political sciences[96]. Other Italian scholars discovered *Vom Kriege* through Aron[97]. In 1993 Nicola Labanca edited an abridged translation of the 1986 *Makers of Modern Strategy*[98] and Angelo Panebianco the 1978 *Philosophers of War and Peace* by W. B. Gallie (1912-1998)[99].

While Italian philosophers massacred *Vom Kriege*, the 1994 and 1995 essays of Christopher Bassford and Olaf Rose on its reception in English and in Russian[100] inspired in 1996 Andrea Molinari, a candidate for the ephemeral Italian PhD in military history, to propose a research project on the Clausewitzian reception in Italy. The PhD board (formed by the Universities of Turin, Padua and Catholic), however, rejected the proposal by a majority, on the ground that it was not consistent with the Italian approach to military history. Accidentally, some "splinters" of international debate on strategy and military history reach Italy too, but in a way reminding flotsam picked up ashore by prying natives. When that occurs, Italian publishers generally apply Gresham's law[101]. Therefore none of the fundamental contributions to Clausewitzian studies published in the last decade of the past[102] and in the first of the new Century[103] have been translated, with the only exception of some essays written by Andreas Herberg-Rothe[104], of Hew Strachan's scholastic biography of Clausewitz[105] and of two philosophical icons as *La guerre dans les sociétés modernes* by Julien Freund (1923-1993)[106] and *Achever Clausewitz* by René Girard[107].

The Italian books the present decade that discuss Clausewitz, are two manuals of strategic studies, written by General Jean[108] and Giacomello-Badialetti[109], a topic treaty of Admiral Sanfelice[110], a further reduced edition of *Vom Kriege*[111], and *excerpta* in two anthologies of political[112] and military writers[113]. Besides, Marco Menicocci unwittingly recycled the old thesis of Hegelian influence upon *Vom Kriege* that was rejected by Roques and Croce[114], Massimiliano Guareschi upended the *Fortsetzung* formula leveraging upon Foucault and Guattari[115], while Gian Mario Bravo quoted Clausewitz in a short history of militarism and pacifism that culminated in Norberto Bobbio[116] as did Paolo Ceola in an essay on contemporary war as a "labyrinth"[117]. According to Antonino Drago and Francesco Pezzullo the frequent recurrence of the double negative betrays the logical weakness of the Clausewitzian definitions[118]. In 2010 the Farefuturo Foundation inaugurated its new quarterly publishing the 1967 essay of Carl Schmitt on Clausewitz as a political thinker[119].

The most original among recent Italian lectures

As seen, Italian lectures on Clausewitz relate to the philosophical and political sciences rather than to strategic studies or military history, and their qualitative standard appears to have declined in the last decade. Some contributions would none the less deserve the attention of the international community of Clausewitzian students. The best is still, in our opinion, Gian Enrico Rusconi's essay on the collapse of the European balance in 1914, in which he defends, against Delbrück and Liddell Hart, the Clausewitzian rationality of the Schlieffen Plan, and attributes to the German government rather than to the German Staff the responsibility for the outbreak of the war[120]. In 1999 Rusconi published a new, and larger contribution[121], which is not only a much more detailed and penetrant biography of the Prussian General than Strachan's, but also a profound analysis of *Vom Kriege*, of its ideas and methods, as well as of its fortune and fate in historical perspective. Correcting the Schmittian vision of the Clausewitz's Prussianism, Rusconi investigates the "Prussian syndrome", which aimed to strengthen Germany without mining the European balance, and was absolutely incompatible with the Hitlerian subversion. Furthermore

Rusconi contributed a new, albeit partial, translation of *Vom Kriege*, with a wide and clever introduction[122].

The comparison between the Chinese Seven Classics and *Vom Kriege* made in 1998 by General Fabio Mini was also noteworthy. According to him, when analyzed from an Oriental point of view, the opposition between Jominian and Clausewitzian legacies vanishes and the latter appears to truly be the focal point of Western military thinking. According to Mini, the implementation of Clausewitzian theories by the Western armies made them appear mechanical, stiff and static while the Chinese classics seemed more human, flexible and dynamic. Mini notes also that when the Japanese strategy referred to the "Chinese" classics it was astonishing and successful, as in the Russian-Japanese War, while it was disastrous when following a "Clausewitzian" approach like in the Second World War[123].

Other good Italian texts included the 2006 Alessandro Colombo comparison between Clausewitzian and Grotian ideas of "limited war"[124], and the Clausewitzian interpretation that Jean made in 2002 of the War on Terror as "confrontation of strength" and "clash of wills", and where the moral factor is what is at stake ("to conquer hearts and minds")[125]. Not less important were, in the field of military history, the applications of Clausewitzian categories made by Luigi Loreto, namely in his 1993 essay on Caesar, in which, e.g., he employs the concept of friction to interpret the Caesarian *BG* VI and *BC* III as "the books of the *casus*"[126]. We owe him, in 2007, a masterpiece of the Italian military history (*The Great Strategy of Rome in the First Punic War*)[127], whose geniality aggravates his Liddell-Hartian sin. May Heaven forgive him!

Notes:

[1] This article had been discussed with Luigi Loreto, the leading Italian specialist of ancient military history, and submitted to Prof. Gian Enrico Rusconi, the Italian specialist of Clausewitz, and to Generals Carlo Jean and Fabio Mini, the most prominent Italian uniformed scholars in the early XXIst Century.

[2] C. v. Clausewitz, *Hinterlassene Werke*, IV, 342. This essay has still not been translated into Italian. French translation by Jean Colin, *La campagne d'Italie*, Paris, 1901 (Paris, Pocket, 1999, with a prefatory note by Gérard Chaliand).

[3] See Piero Pieri, *Storia militare del Risorgimento*, Torino, Einaudi, 1962, p. 788.

[4] Machiavelli's influence on Clausewitz is evident and well known, less so that of Montecuccoli. Elaborating on this topic is beyond the scope of this chapter, but we want to point out a particularly remarkable comparison of Clausewitz and Montecuccoli in Raimondo Luraghi, "Il Pensiero e l'Azione di Raimondo Montecuccoli" in Andrea Pini (Ed.), *Raimondo Montecuccoli: Teoria, Pratica Militare, Politica e Cultura nell'Europa del Seicento*, Atti del Convegno, Modena, 4-5 October 2002, pp. 19-30.

[5] John Gooch, "Clausewitz disregarded: Italian military thought and doctrine, 1815-1943", in *Journal of Strategic Studies*, Vol. 9, Issue 2&3, June 1986, pp. 303-324.

[6] Brian R. Sullivan, "The strategy of the decisive weight: Italy, 1882-1922", in Williamson Murray, MacGregor Knox, Alvin Bernstein (Eds.), *The Making of Strategy. Rulers, State, War*, Cambridge, Cambridge U. P., 1994, pp. 307 ss.

[7] See V. Ilari, "Guerre di coalizione e operazioni combinate", in N. Ronzitti (Ed.), *Comando e controllo nelle Forze di pace e nelle coalizione militari : Contributo alla riforma della Carta delle Nazioni Unite*, Milano, Angeli, 1999 (full version on www.scribd.com/doc/10972013/Coalizioni). This is one of the points in *Vom Kriege* largely ignored: f. e., according to Franco Apicella, an Italian General who worked a long time both at NATO HQs and in international staffs, Clausewitz would never have examined the issue of the unity of command"; see Apicella's "A proposito dell'unità di comando", 28 August 2002, in www.paginedidifesa.it).

[8] Sullivan, *op. cit.*, p. 307. On the other hand, General Jean suggests that the "Italian way in Peacekeeping", so appreciated in recent international operations, which relays on the Italian tradition of "Commedia dell'arte" and "arte di arrangiarsi" (the art of improvising on the spur of the moment), may be seen as *naturaliter* Clausewitzian (paraphrasing Molière, to be "Clausewitzian without knowing it"; or Antonio Gramsci's famous dictum: "the worker is a philosopher without knowing it"). For a substantially different view on Italy's peacekeeping, see Piero Ignazi, Giampiero Giacomello and Fabrizio Coticchia. *Italy's Military Operations Abroad: Just Don't Call It War*, Palgrave, Basingstoke and New York, 2011.

[9] Michael I. Handel (Ed.), *Clausewitz and Modern Strategy*, London and New York, Frank Cass, 1986, Introduction, p. 9.

[10] Admiral Bill Owens with Edward Offley, *Lifting the Fog of War*, Baltimore, Johns Hopkins Press, 2001. According to the Authors, the Network Centric Warfare, "this new revolution [in Military Affairs] challenges the hoary dictums about the fog and friction of war".

[11] See his V *dialogus de juris interpretibus*.

[12] Clausewitz also applied a different logical approach to his field of study, based on the so-called "couples philosophiques" (conceptual oppositions, or dichotomies). See Raymond Aron, *Clausewitz: Philosopher of War*, London, Routledge & Kegan Paul, 1983 (transl. from German orig., 1980), II, pp. 89-173.

[13] On literature about the Perfect General Captain: see Marcello Fantoni (ed.), *Il "Perfetto Capitano". Immagini e realtà (secoli XV-XVII)*, Roma, Bulzoni, 2001.

[14] As Luigi Loreto pointed out, the Caesarian equivalent to our "strategy", but also to our "warfare", are *ratio* et *consilium* (*BG* 1, 40, 8-9; *BC* 1, 72, 2). *Belli ratio* meaning "conduct of operations"; *nova vincendi ratio, alia ratio, haec ratio (novus genus pugnae)* "a new way to fight or to win" ("Pensare la guerra in Cesare", in Diego Poli (ed.), *La cultura in Cesare*, Roma, 1993, I, pp. 239-343). Caesar, *BC*, 1, *haec tum ratio (dimicandi) nostros perturbant, insuetos huius generis pugna*). However in two passages of the Tacitus's Histories *ratio* seems to imply "logic" of war: *obstabat ratio belli* (*Hist.* 4, 63): *ulcisci ratio belli* (*Hist.* 3, 51). In Cicero and Livius, namely in the form *ratio belli gerendi*, means both the cause (or pretext) for waging war and the way it is fought (as *ratio belli bene gerendi, belli administratio*). Quite surprisingly, this expression was not developed by the literature on the "Ragion di Stato", with the well known definition of war as the *ultima ratio regum*. Francesco Guicciardini uses it to mean "reason for war": "Lost the castle, I confess that *mutata fuit ratio belli gerendi*" (Lettera CLXXXII al Protonotario Gambara, Piacenza, 9 November 1520).

[15] Among his valuable contributions to Italian military culture, General Fabio Mini, former military attaché at Beijing, was to import the current international studies about Chinese strategic thought to Italy. See his *L'altra strategia. I classici del pensiero militare cinese dalla guerra al marketing*, Angeli, Milano, 1998. Id., *La Guerra dopo la guerra, Soldati, burocrati e mercenari nell'epoca della pace virtuale* , Torino, Einaudi, 2003; Id. *Guerra senza limiti, (LEG 2001)* his Italian editing of the work of the PLA Senior Colonels Qiao Liang and Wang Xiangsui who

were so Clausewitzian in their analysis of the Gulf war (1991) and so "oriental" in their prophecy about asymmetrical and terror wars.

[16] I. Duyvesteyn and J. Angstrom (eds), *Rethinking the Nature of War*, Frank Cass, London 2005. The most prominent among the Italian "Kaldorians" is Nicola Labanca, (*Guerre vecchie, guerre nuove). Comprendere I conflitti armati contemporanei*, Pearson Paravia Bruno Mondadori, 2009). Instead, from a Schmittian perspective, the concept of "new wars" appears a naive mystification of the "Imperial peace enforcing", and the "novelty" regards not the supposed "nature" of war, but the substantial shifting of the effective and formal War powers from the National States to the President of the United States, acting as the Roman universal emperor (see Ilari, "Debellare superbos", in *Palomar*, VIII, No. 3, july 2008, pp. 6-76, and online in www.scribd.com).

[17] Raymond Aron considered the strategy of Mao Zedong in the Chinese civil war to be *naturaliter* Clausewitzian (*Penser la guerre, Clausewitz*, Gallimard, Paris, 1976, II, pp. 96-116). On chameleonic continuity see also Hew Strachan and Andreas Herbert-Rothe (eds), *Clausewitz in the twenty-first century*, Oxford U. P., 2007 (particularly see the articles of Christopher Daase and Antulio J. Echevarria II on small wars and the nature of the War on Terror). Generally, Italian scholars are cautious about the asymmetrical meme. See Alessandro Colombo, "Asymmetrical Warfare or Asymmetrical Society? The Changing Form of War and the Collapse of International Society", in Gobicchi A. (ed.), *Globalization, Armed Conflicts and Security*, Rubbettino, Soveria Mannelli, 2004; Stefano Ruzza, "Il rapporto fra guerra ed asimmetria", in Walter Coralluzzo and Marina Nuciari (eds), *Conflitti asimmetrici. Un approccio multidisciplinare*, Aracne Editrice, Roma 2006, pp. 35-78; Ruzza and Ruggero Cucchini, Asimmetria e trasformazione della guerra. Spazio, tempo ed energia nel nuovo contesto bellico (in *Informazioni della Difesa*, n. 5/2007, pp. 32-37: Ruzza, *Asymmetric War or post–Westphalian War? War beyond the state*, in www.archive.sgir.eu. Ferruccio Botti, "Clausewitz e la guerra asimmetrica", in *Rivista Militare*, n. 5/2004, pp. 12-21. Id., "Dalla strategia aerea alla strategia spaziale: parte 2a Tra Clausewitz e Jomini: spunti per una teoria della guerra spaziale", in *Informazioni della Difesa*, n. 5, settembre-ottobre, 2000, pp. 42-49, and, more in general, his *L'arte militare del 2000 - uomini e strategie tra XIX e XX secolo*, Roma, Rivista Militare, 1998. In the Robert Redford film *Lions for Lambs* (2007), during a military briefing in Afghanistan, Lt. Col. Falco (Peter Berg) says: "Remember your von Clausewitz: 'Never engage the same enemy for too long or he will ...'", "adapt to your

tactics", completes another soldier (from Wikipedia, "Carl von Clausewitz (…) in popular culture").

[18] J. Stalin, *Works*, Vol. 16, Red Star Press Ltd., London, 1986 (Answer to a letter of 30 January, from Col.-Professor Rasin on Clausewitz and the questions of war and the art of war, 23 February, 1946).

[19] See V. Ilari, "*Imitatio, restitutio, utopia*: la storia militare antica nel pensiero strategico moderno", in Marta Sordi (ed.), *Guerra e diritto nel mondo greco e romano*, Milano, Vita e Pensiero, 2002, p. 269-381.

[20] For a penetrating dissection of Hanson's approach, which he inherited from Sir John Keegan, see Luigi Loreto, *Per la storia militare del mondo antico. Prospettive retrospettive*, Jovene, Napoli, 2006, pp. 191-99.

[21] In the film *Lawrence of Arabia* (1962), General Allenby (Jack Hawkins) contends to T. E. Lawrence (Peter O'Toole) that "I fight like Clausewitz, you fight like (Maurice de) Saxe". To which Lawrence replies, "We should do very well indeed, shouldn't we?" (from Wikipedia, "Carl von Clausewitz (…) in popular culture").

[22] Wilhelm Rüstow, *Die Feldherrnkunst des neunzehnten Jahrhunderts: Zum Selbststudium und für den Unterricht an höheren Militärschulen*, Zürich, Druck und Verlag von Friedrich Schulthess, 1857, p. 507: „Clausewitz wird viel genannt, ist aber wenig gelesen." ("C. is frequently quoted but seldom read").

[23] As Voltaire, who poetically antagonizes Guibert (*La Tactique et autres pièces fugitives*, Genève, 1774), but jealous of Berthold Schwarz's glory in the art of killing and impatient to overrun the Turks in the open Ukrainian plains, with the scythed chariots he had genially restituted (G. Hemerdinger, "Voltaire et son chariot de guerre", in *Revue d'artillerie*, 1934, pp. 587-607, quoted in Andrea Giardina, *Introduzione al 'de rebus bellicis'*, Mondadori Milano, 1989, pp. IX-XV: Ilari, *Imitatio*, p. 360).

[24] S. Mazzarino, *Il pensiero storico classico*, Laterza, Roma-Bari, 1974, I, p. 5, relating to Epimenides who "profethized about the past" (εμαντεύετο περ τ ν γεγονότον).

[25] Indeed, for however acute, the Clausewitzian observations in this field are not new. The reciprocal influence between tactics and fortification, e. g., as it was developed by a French contemporary of Clausewitz, Commandant Jean-Baptiste Imbert, in a study on Vauban published in 1835, was more precise

(*Communauté de principes entre la tactique et la fortification, démontrée à l'aide du dessin des « travaux de l'attaque, par le Maréchal de Vauban »*, Paris, Anselin, 1835).

[26] Raymond Aron, *Penser la guerre: Clausewitz*, Gallimard, Paris, 1976, I, pp. 285 ff. According to Stefano Bernini, "if Philosophy of war is not yet a definite discipline, Epistemology of war is a completely uncultivated field, except for the *On War* Second Book, however the least known of the treaty" (*Filosofia della guerra: un approccio epistemologico*, www.sintesidialettica.it). This author contrasts the Jominian "axiomatic" rationalism to Clausewitzian "empirical" one. See also V. Ilari, "Il problema epistemologico delle scienze militari. Una presentazione critica del saggio di Benedetto Croce sul 'Vom Kriege' di Clausewitz", in *Strategia Globale*, 1984, n. 2, pp. 171-180.

[27] "But, at last, would be that a limit? History can appear, to the classicist mind, as an *améthodos hyle*; and however it has a method and a sense, for Greek and Roman historians, method and sense differently depending the epochs and the authors (…) they consider the *améthodos hyle* dominated by fortune and virtue, and however they know how give a meaning and a soul to it" (Mazzarino, *Il Pensiero*, II2, pp. 376-77).

[28] Luciano Canfora, *Il viaggio di Artemidoro. Vita e avventure di un grande esploratore del'antichità*, Rizzoli, Milano, 2010, p. 9.

[29] This paragraph is based upon Ferruccio Botti and V. Ilari, *Il pensiero militare italiano dal primo al secondo dopoguerra (1919-1949)*, Rome, USSME, 1985, pp. 289-95. See also the John Gooch's paper quoted above and Botti, "À la recherche de Clausewitz en Italie: souvent cité, peu applique", in *Stratégique*, n. 78-79, 2-3, 2000, pp. 141-167. Much more about nineteenth-century Italian Clausewitzians one can find in other monumental books on the Italian military thought owed to our beloved friend Botti (*Il pensiero militare e navale italiano dalla rivoluzione francese alla prima guerra mondiale (1789-1915)*, 3 vols., I (1789-1848), II (1848-1870), III (1870-1915), tomo I (la guerra terrestre e i problemi dell'esercito), tomo II (la guerra marittima), Rome, USSME, 1995, 2000, 2006 and 2010. (pp. 1120 + 1192 + 1120 + 908). See also his "Note sul pensiero militare italiano dalla fine del secolo XIX all'inizio della 1a guerra mondiale", in *Studi storico-militari* 1985, pp. 11-124, 1986, pp. 51-208. Id., "Note biografiche e bibliografiche sugli scrittori militari e navali della prima metà del secolo XIX", in *Studi Storico Militari*, 1995, Roma, USSME, 1998, pp. 1-102. Voce: Italiens (Théoriciens), in Thierry de Montbrial e Jean Klein *Dictionnaire de Stratégie*, Paris, Presses Universitaires de France, 2000, pp. 320-323.

[30] Mariano d'Ayala, *Bibliografia militare italiana*, Torino, Stamperia Reale, 1854.

[31] Luigi Blanch (*Della scienza militare considerata nei suoi rapporti con le altre scienze e col sistema sociale*, 1834; 1869; 1939). See Luigi Parenti, "Luigi Blanch e la sua 'scienza militare'", in *Studi Storici*, Anno 35, No. 3 (July - September 1994), pp. 705-740. Andrea Zambelli (*La guerra*, 1839).

[32] *L'arte della guerra: Estratto di una nuova istoria militare delle guerre della rivoluzione di Francia del Barone Jomini,. Tenente generale, ajutante di campo di S. M. l'Imperatore di tutte le Russie, Prima edizione italiana coll' originale a fronte*, Napoli, 1816. *Vita politica e militare di Napoleone, raccontata da lui medesimo al tribunale di Cesare, Alessandro e Federico*, Livorno, tip. Vignozzi, 1829. *Sunto dell'arte della guerra o nuovo quadro analitico delle principali combinazioni della strategia, della grande tattica e della politica militare*, del Barone de Jomini, Generale in capo Ajutante Generale di S. M. l'Imperatore di tutte le Russie, prima traduzione dal francese fatta sull'ultima edizione di Parigi 1838, considerabilmente accresciuta, C[arlo] B[ertini], Napoli, dalla Stamperia dell'Iride, 1855. The latter (i. e. the *Précis*) was reprinted in 1864 at Agrigento, but the next translation (*Sommario dell'arte della guerra, 1837/1838*) came to light not before 2008 (ed. Rivista Militare), and was interrupted by the death of Colonel Botti, who was able to translate and comment only the first three chapters.

[33] In a sound and pro-Italian study on the Sardinian Army, the anonymous French author wrote: "toutes les écoles (d'artillerie) sont à l'arsenal, où il y a une Bibliothèque bien dotée et assez fournie d'ouvrages militaires, mais peu fréquentée" ("Notice sur l'Etat Militaire de la Sardaigne", in *Bulletin des Sciences Militaires*, VIII, janvier-juin 1830, N. 150, p. 372). The progress, in contemporary times, is that the Italian Military Libraries had directly wasted their books.

[34] Duparcq, *Histoire de l'art de la guerre avant l'usage de la poudre*, Paris, Ch. Tanera, 1860. The book includes (pp. 297-307) an essay of Blanch on the works of Duparcq (originally published in the monthly *Diorama* di Napoli) in which its *Commentaire* on Clausewitz is obviously mentioned.

[35] Carlo De Cristoforis, *Che cosa sia la guerra*, 1860; 1894; 1925.

[36] See Carlo Moos, "Streiflichter auf Wilhelm Rüstows Beziehungen zu Italien", in *Quellen und Forschungen aus italienischen Archiven und Bibliotheken*, 1985, a. 65, pp. 342-404. "Wilhelm Rüstow, Garibaldi stratega e l'ambiente zurighese", in *Garibaldi Generale della Libertà*. Atti del Convegno internazionale (Roma 29-31 maggio 1982), Ministero della Difesa – Comitato storico per lo studio della figura e

dell'opera militare del generale Giuseppe Garibaldi, Roma, USSME, 1984, pp. 235-294.

[37] A. Gandolfi, "Garibaldi Generale", in *Nuova Antologia*, XXXIX (1883), pp. 385-408. See Piero Del Negro, "Garibaldi e la guerriglia", in Aldo A. Mola (Ed.), *Garibaldi generale della libertà*, USSME, 1984, pp. 103-130.

[38] Niccola Marselli, *La guerra e la sua storia*, 1875.

[39] Georg Christoph Berger Waldenegg, "Die deutsche 'Nationale Mentalität' aus Sicht Italienischer Militärs, 1866-1876. Beschreibung, Rezeption, Schlussfolgerungen", in *Militärgeschichtliche Mitteilungen*, 1991, n. 2, pp. 81-106. Id., *Die Neuordnung des Italienischen Heeres zwischen 1866 und 1876: Preussen als Modell*, Heidelberg, Winter, 1992. It should be noted that Clausewitz is never quoted in the archive of the Staff Captain and later General Giuseppe Govone, who was military attaché at Berlin and signed the Prussian-italian alliance in 1866. Marco Scardigli, *Lo scrittoio del generale. La romanzesca epopea risorgimentale del gen. Govone*, Torino, Utet, 2006.

[40] Actually, this statement was not quite accurate, considering the excerpt from Vom Kriege chosen and translated by Colonel Oete Blatto (*Della guerra. Pagine scelte*, transl. by A. Beria and W. Müller, Torino, Schioppo, 1930).

[41] *Passato e presente*, Einaudi, Torino, 1954, p. 128. Gramsci quoted Clausewitz also about the attack which exhausts itself progressing (*Note sul Machiavelli, sulla politica e sullo stato moderno*, Einaudi, Torino, 1955, p. 153). The name is also misspelled (like "Clausevitz") in the entry of the semi-official *Enciclopedia Militare* (Il Popolo d'Italia, Roma 1930, III, p. 87).

[42] In *Enciclopedia Italiana*, Treccani, Roma, 1931, X, p. 550. On military entries of the Treccani encyclopedia, see Botti and Ilari, *Il pensiero, cit.*, pp. 295-305.

[43] Croce, «Azione, successo e giudizio: note in margine al *Vom Kriege*», in *Atti dell'Accademia di Scienze morali e politiche della Società reale di Napoli*, LVI, 1934, pp. 152-163 (=*Revue de Métaphysique et de Morale*, XLII, 1935, pp. 247-258). From a postcard addressed to Corrado Chelazzi (ASSR *Incarti della biblioteca*, 913/1933-34: see *Benedetto Croce in Senato*, Rubbettino, Soveria Mannelli, 2002: *Lettere a Giovanni Castellano 1908-1949*, Istituto Italiano di Studi Storici, 1985. ASR, LVI, 1934, pp. 152-163) it results that Croce wrote it in two days (27 and 28 December 1933). He later inserted it in his Last Essays (*Ultimi Saggi*, Bari, Laterza, 1935, pp. 266-279). The Clausewitzian essay was reprint in 1984 in *Strategia globale* No. 2, with a prefatory note written by Ilari ("Il problema

epistemologico delle scienze militari", pp. 171 ff.). Aron does not quote this essay in his Clausewitz of 1976, but in his *Memories* (p. 666 of the Italian edition) he reveals that he was stimulated to write on Clausewitz by the hard observation Croce made, which we have quoted as epigraph of the present study.

[44] In the paper only K. Schwartz, *Leben des Generals...*, Berlin, Dümmler, 1878, 2 vols. and P. E. A. Roques, *Le général de Clausewitz, Sa vie et sa théorie de la guerre, d'après des documents inédits*, Paris, Berger-Levrault, are quoted; but in the postcards also E. Palat, *La politique de la guerre d'après Clausewitz*, Paris, Lavauzelle, 1922, and R. von Caemmerer, *Clausewitz*, Berlin, Betet-Narbon, 1905, 2 vols, are quoted.

[45] Suggested by Colonel Creuzinger, *Hegels Einfluss auf Clausewitz*, 1911.

[46] Un ricordo dei "Promessi sposi" in una lettera del Clausewitz (comparison between the plague in Milan and the cholera epidemic in Poland), in *La Critica*, XXXII, N. 5 (III serie a. VIII) 20.9.1934, pp. 399-400 (= *Pagine sparse*, III, pp. 242-3).

[47] B. Croce, Riscontri tra l'arte della guerra e le arti belle nel Clausewitz, in Quaderni della "Critica", n. 2, agosto 1945, *Noterelle di estetica*, VII, p. 105.

[48] See Canevari, *Lo Stato maggiore germanico da Federico il Grande a Hitler*, Mondadori, Milano, 1942. Cfr. Milivoj G. Lazarević, *Od Šarnhorsta do Šlifena: sto godina Prusko-Nemačkog đeneralštaba*, Geca Kon, 1936 (Serbian translation of Friedrich von Cochenhausen, *Von Scharnhorst zu Schlieffen 1806-1906: 100 Jahre preussisch-deutsche Generalstab*, Auf Veranlassg d. Reichswehrministeriums, Berlin, 1933); *Karl fon Klauzevic: O ratu*, Geca Kon, 1939; 1940. Clausewitz, Carl von, *O Ratu*. Trans. Milivoj Lazarevic, ed. Lt Col Zdavko Serucar and Professor Stevan Menciger. Yugoslav military publishing house, 1951.

[49] Hew Strachan, "Clausewitz and the Dialectic of War", in Strachan and Andreas Herbert-Rothe (Eds), *Clausewitz in the twenty-first century*, Oxford U. P., 2007. P. M. Baldwin, "Clausewitz in Nazi-German", in *Journal of Contemporary History*, SAGE, London and Beverly Hills, Vol. 16, 1981, pp. 5-26. Jehuda L. Wallach, "Misperceptions of Clausewitz's *On War* by the German military", in *Journal of Strategic Studies*, Vol. 9, Issue 2&3, June 1986, pp. 213-239.

[50] Hans Rothfels, *Carl von Clausewitz: Politik und Krieg*, Berlin, Dümmlers Verlag, 1920. "Clausewitz" pages 93–113 from *The Makers of Modern Strategy* edited by

Edward Mead Earle, Gordon A. Craig & Felix Gilbert, Princeton, N.J.: Princeton University Press, 1943.

[51] Bollati was also the Author of one of the famous books (that his on the Italian intervention in the Spanish Civil War) missed from the Einaudi's Catalog after the fall of Fascism (Vittorio Messori, «Il giallo dei libri scomparsi», *Corsera* 11 luglio 1998).

[52] *La guerra (Vom Kriege), pagine scelte*, Firenze, Felice Le Monnier, 1942, 190 pp., translated by Luigi Cosenza and Giuseppe Moscardelli. *Pensieri sulla guerra*, Firenze, Sansoni, 1943, 107 pp. Transl. By Giacinto Cardona (reprinted by Editoriale Opportunity Book, Milano, 1995). Luigi Cosenza (1905-1984), a Neapolitan engineer and architect, was later a representative of the Italian Communist Party and his harangues in the municipal council against the housing speculation in Naples are one of the highlights in the Francesco Rosi's film, *The hands over the city*.

[53] Werner Hahlweg, *Clausewitz, Soldat–Politiker–Denker*, Göttingen, Münsterschmidt Verlag, 1957, 1969.

[54] Schmitt's *Theorie des Partisanen. Zwischenbemerkung zum Begriff des Politischen* (1963) provoked a passionate response of Raymond Aron (1905-1983), *Penser la guerre, Clausewitz*, Gallimard, Paris, 1976, II ("L'âge planétaire"), pp. 210-222. Ilari, "Riflessioni critiche sulla teoria politica della guerra di popolo", in *Memorie storiche militari 1982*, USSME, Rome, 1983, pp. 107-172.

[55] *Clausewitz als politischer Denker*. Bemerkungen und Hinweise. Beck, München, 1967, in „Der Staat", N. 4, anno 1967, pp. 479-502.

[56] Peter Paret, "Clausewitz. A Bibliographic Survey", in *World Politics*, Vol. 17, No. 2, Jan. 1965, pp. 272-285. Id., "Education, Politics, and War in the Life of Clausewitz", in *Journal of the History of Ideas*, Vol. 29, No. 3 (Jul. - Sep., 1968), pp. 394-408.

[57] Piero Pieri, *Guerra e politica negli scrittori italiani*, Firenze, Riccardo Riccardi Editore, 1955; Milano, Mondadori, 1975. See also Id., "Il rapporto tra guerra e politica dal Clausewitz a noi", in *Relazioni al X Congresso internazionale di scienze storiche*, Firenze, 1955, I, pp. 277-339.

[58] Piero Pieri, *Storia militare del Risorgimento*, Einaudi, Torino, 1962, p. 134 (people's war), 151, 157-60, 205, 425, 582-85. See also, Pieri, "Orientamenti per lo studio di una Storia delle dottrine militari", in *Atti del I Convegno nazionale di*

storia militare (Roma 17-19 marzo 1969), Roma, Ministero della Difesa, 1969, pp. 123-171.

[59] Raimondo Luraghi, *Storia della guerra civile americana*, Torino, Einaudi, 1966. Luraghi, a former commander of partisan bands during the Italian Resistance, criticized the John Brown action at Harper's Ferry as contradictory with the predicaments of Carlo Bianco di Saint Jorioz, a military writer of the Risorgimento, who Luraghi calls "the Clausewitz of the guerrilla" (p. 132).

[60] On the point see Bassford, *Cl. in English, cit.*, p. 50.

[61] Ernesto Ragionieri, "Franz Mehring", in *Studi Storici*, I, 2 (Jan.-March 1960), pp. 410-423.

[62] Clemente Ancona, "L'influenza del 'Vom Kriege' di Clausewitz sul pensiero marxista da Marx a Lenin", in *Rivista storica del socialismo*, 1965, pp. 129-154. Despite Hahlweg had already discussed this point ("Lenin und Clausewitz", in *Archiv für Kulturgeschichte*, XXXVI, 1955, 1 and 3), the Ancona essay was reprinted in German (Günther Dill, Ed., *Clausewitz in Perspektive*, 1980) and deeply discussed in the 1995 book of Olaf Rose on the Clausewitzian reception in Russia and Soviet Union. Lacking evidently of better candidates, Ancona was to redact the military chapter of the Einaudi History of Italy ("Milizie e condottieri". *Storia d'Italia Einaudi. I documenti.* V. Einaudi. Torino. 1973) as well as the "War" entry of the *Enciclopedia Einaudi* (6, 1979, pp. 996-1018, a pastiche of game theory and would be Marxism).

[63] Lenin, *Note al libro di Von Clausewitz "Sulla guerra e la condotta della guerra"*, Edizioni del Maquis, Classici del Marxismo N. 5, Milano, 1970, integral edition not included in *Opere complete*. Reprint in Lenin, *L'arte dell'insurrezione*, Gwynplaine, Camerano (AN), 2010. See also Enea Cerquetti, "Le guerre del Risorgimento italiano negli scritti di Marx ed Engels", in *Trimestre*, 1984, nn. 1-2, pp. 77-120.

[64] Ritter, *I militari e la politica nella Germania moderna*, Torino, Einaudi, 1966, I, pp. 57 ss.

[65] *Clausewizt (sic) nell'era atomica*, Milano, Longanesi, 1966 (however reprinted in 1982 in correct form by the same publisher). See Leonardo Tricarico, "Considerazioni su 'La guerra' di von Clausewitz", in *Rivista Aeronautica*, 1967, n. 11, pp. 1985-89.

⁶⁶ Lucio Ceva, "Napoleone a Tavolino (Il Grande Clausewitz è ancora attuale?)", in *Storia Illustrata*, reprinted in Scuola di Guerra Aerea (Ed.), *Letture scelte di dottrina e strategia*, 2a ed. (128), October 1981, pp. 109-116.

⁶⁷ Friedrich O. Ruge, *Politica e strategia. Pensiero politico e azione politica*, Firenze, Sansoni, 1969.

⁶⁸ André Glucksman, *Il discorso della guerra*, Milano, Feltrinelli, 1969.

⁶⁹ Werner Hahlweg, *Storia della guerriglia: tattica e strategia della guerra senza fronti*, Milano, Feltrinelli, 1973.

⁷⁰ Clausewitz, *Della guerra: con una cronologia della vita dell'autore e dei suoi tempi, un'antologia critica e una bibliografia* / bibliografia a cura di Edmondo Aroldi, Milano, Mondadori, 1970, 441 p.

⁷¹ Wilhelm von Schramm, *Clausewitz. Leben und Werk*, Esslingen, Bechtle, 1976. See Id., *Clausewitz. General und Philosoph*, Heyne, Munich 1982; Paret, *Clausewitz and the State* (Princeton U. P.); Aron (*Penser la guerre, Clausewitz*, 2 voll., Gallimard: German translation, Propyläen, Frankfurt a. M., 1981). M. Mori, *Aron interprete di Clausewitz*, Torino, Einaudi, Exc. from *Rivista di filosofia*, No. 6, Oct. 1976. pp. 532-540. Howard *Clausewitz*, Oxford U. P., 1983; Paret (Ed.), *Makers of Modern Strategy*, Princeton U. P., 1986, pp. 186-213; Michael I. Handel (Ed.), *Clausewitz and Modern Strategy*, London, Frank Cass, 1986.

⁷² R. Guiscardo, *Forze armate e democrazia: da Clausewitz all'esercito di popolo*, Bari, De Donato, 1974

⁷³ Vincenzo Calò (Ed.), *In caso di golpe. Manuale teorico-pratico per il cittadino, di resistenza totale e di guerra di popolo, di guerriglia e di controguerriglia*, "scritti di Clausewitz, Mao Tse-tung, il manuale del maggiore von Dach, testi delle Special Forces", Stella Rossa, Roma, Savelli, 1975.

⁷⁴ Luigi Bonanate, *Teoria politica e relazioni internazionali*, Edizioni di Comunità, 1976; Id. (ed.), *Politica internazionale*, La Nuova Italia, Firenze, 1979; *Guerra e pace: due secoli di storia del pensiero politico*, Milano, Angeli, 1994. *La guerra*, Roma-Bari, Laterza, 2005. See also S. Martina, *La guerra come oggetto scientifico: Karl von Clausewitz: uno studio sul pensiero clausewitziano dagli scritti minori al Vom Kriege*, tesi di laurea, Un. di Torino, SP, rel. Bonanate, a. a. 1989/90.

⁷⁵ Antonio Pelliccia, Clausewitz e la strategia politico-militare sovietica, Roma, Centro Cft A.M., 1976. Ugo Tarantini, "Clausewitz nell'era nucleare", in *Rivista Militare*, 1977, N. 2, pp. 11-16.

⁷⁶ Carlo Jean, "Teoria della guerra e pensiero strategico del generale Carl von Clausewitz", in *Rivista Militare*, 1978, n. 3, pp. 40-50 (=used as Introduction to *Della Guerra*, Rivista Militare, 1989, and later Mondadori reprints. Transl. as *Carl von Clausewitz's Theory of War and Strategic Thought*, Roma, Ed. Rivista Militare, 1989).

⁷⁷ Jean was supported by some young academician, who flavored these initiatives with naïve patriotism, and a megalomaniac idea to prussianize Italian Army, parroting Scharnhorst & Gneisenau. General Jean smiled, the Italian Staff did not even notice. See V. Ilari, "Gli studi strategici in Italia", tracing *inter alia* the history of CeMiSS and of the insertion of the strategic studies and military history into the *curricula* of Italian universities (this study is online at the site www.scribd.com with the title "strategic studies in Italy").

⁷⁸ Botti and Ilari, *Il pensiero militare italiano dal primo al secondo dopoguerra 1919-1949*, USSME, Roma, 1985. See also Botti, "Da Clausewitz a Douhet alla ricerca dell'arma assoluta. Wells, Ader e Douhet: chi fu il primo?", in *Rivista Aeronautica*, 1985, Nos. 1 (8), 4 (pp. 28), 6 (22); "Clausewitz e la strategia marittima, in *Rivista Marittima*, CXVIII., 1985, No. 2, pp. 80-88.

⁷⁹ Tracing the history of the label "global strategy", Ilari pointed out its militaristic implications (in Jean, Ed., *Il pensiero strategico*, 1985, pp. 21-63).

⁸⁰ Patrizio Flavio Quinzio, "Clausewitz: politica e guerra. Per una edizione a fascioli del `Della Guerra", in *Rivista militare* 1990, pp. 48-55.

⁸¹ Bernard, Vittorio. "La preparazione culturale dei capi militari nel pensiero di Clausewitz", in *Rivista Militare* 1990, pp. 2-9.

⁸² Giulio Primicerj (he also an Alpine!), "La vita e le opere di Karl von C.", "C. nel quarantennio di pace della Germania guglielmina", "C., il piano Schlieffen e la prima guerra mondiale", "C. negli anni di Weimar", "C., Ludendorff e il Fuhrer del Terzo Reich" (in *Rivista Militare*, 1990, No. 6, pp. 116-129; 1992 No. 1, pp. 81-91; 1992 No. 3, pp. 104-120; 1992, n. 6, pp. 122-134; 1993 No. 1, pp. 98-114).

⁸³ E. Vad, "Commiato da Clausewitz? Il nuovo pensiero nella politica di sicurezza" and E. Wagemann, "Ritorno a Clausewitz!", in *Rivisita militare*, 1991 No. 3, pp. 20-36. See also Admiral Falco Accame, "Il Vietnam, Clausewitz, Freud: appunti per una teoria della strategia", in *Punto critico*, No. 10, (11 March 1988), pp. 116-132.

[84] Mario Unnia, *Della guerra aziendale: Clausewitz riletto dal manager: come sopravvivere e fare carriera nelle ristrutturazioni aziendali*, Milano, Edizioni dell'Olifante, 1983; Antonio Bomberini, *Lezioni di cultura strategica e psicologica dei mercati per managers e traders: una rilettura critica de L'arte della guerra di Sun Tzu e de Il libro dei cinque anelli di Miyamoto Musashi in compagnia del Della guerra di Carl Von Clausewitz*, Desenzano del Garda, Borsari, 2003.

[85] *Teoria del partigiano. Note complementari al concetto di politico*, Milano, Il Saggiatore, 1981. In 2005, Adelphi published a new edition of the aforementioned translation (by Antonio De Martinis), with a slight change to the title (*Teoria del partigiano. Integrazione al concetto di politico*) and with an essay of Franco Volpi (1952-2009), a prominent Italian student of Heidegger.

[86] Umberto Curi, *Della guerra*, Arsenale Editrice, Venezia, 1982; *Pensare la guerra*, Dedalo, Bari, 1985 (reprinted with addenda in 1999); *Polemos. Filosofia come guerra*, Torino, Bollati Boringhieri, 2000.

[87] Pier Franco Taboni, "Filosofia e filosofie della guerra", in *Il Pensiero*, N. S. XXIV-XXV, 1983-84; Id., "Violenza in Clausewitz", in *Hermeneutica*, No. 4, 1985. Id., *Clausewitz. La filosofia tra guerra e rivoluzione*. Urbino, Quattroventi, 1990.

[88] Luciano Guerzoni, "Politica e guerra. Indissolubili?", in *Bozze*, (Bari, Dedalo), 1985, n. 1-2, pp. 9-46. Francesco Lamendola, Clausewitz mostra che per l'Occidente guerra e politica sono inseparabili, www.scribd.com (2010).

[89] Mario Mori, *La ragione delle armi. Guerra e conflitto nella filosofia classica tedesca (1770-1830)*, Milano, Il Saggiatore, 1984.

[90] Ettore Passerin d'Entrèves, *Guerra e riforme. La Prussia e il problema nazionale tedesco prima del 1848*, Il Mulino, Bologna, 1985, pp. 37-50 (critics to Mori, nt. 20).

[91] Michele Barbieri, "Clausewitz. Restaurazione della politica in guerra e politica delle armi", in *Scritti per Mario Delle Piane*, Napoli, ESI, 1986; Id. "La politica in Clausewitz", in *Studi Senesi*, C, 1988, Suppl. II, "Il problema Clausewitz: la letteratura monografica negli ultimi decenni", in *Archivio di storia della cultura*, V, 1992, pp. 261-312. Id., *Per un'estetica della politica: il primo Goethe*, 1996.

[92] Loris Rizzi, *Clausewitz. L'arte militare nell'età nucleare*, Milano, Rizzoli, 1987, a precise and exhaustive compte-rendu of the international Clausewitzian studies and their impact on the debate about the nuclear dissuasion.

[93] A. Loretoni, "C. von C.: La sicurezza dello Stato", in Quaderni Forum, 1989; "C. von C.: la teoria politica della guerra moderna", ne *Il Pensiero politico*, XXV, 1991, 3, pp. 376-396; *Teorie della pace. Teorie della guerra*, Pisa, ETS, 2005. According to her, the Clausewitzian political realism, insofar as it is based on structure rather than on experience, differs from neo-classic realism (as exempled by Morgenthau) and is more congruent with the neo-realism of Kenneth Waltz and the Rousseauvian internationalism.

[94] Ed. of Clausewitz's Letter on Machiavelli (1809) as an appendix to Fichte's essay, Gallo, Ferrara 1990, pp. 121-8.

[95] Federico Dalpane, "C. von C.: osservazioni sugli scritti 'minori'", in *Scienza & Politica*, No. 13, 1995, pp. 71-90; Id. "*Incertezza, azione e decisione in C. von C.*", in *Teoria politica*, XIV, 1998, No. 2, pp. 145-157; Id., *Guerra e incertezza*, Clueb, Bologna, 2001.

[96] «Quaderni Forum» n. 1 (*Carl von Clausewitz: lo stato e la guerra*), Seminario di studio Villa La Bicocca, 13 febbraio 1988. See also Pier Paolo Portinaro, "Carl von Clausewitz", in Bruno Bongiovanni e Luciano Guerci (Ed.), *L'albero della rivoluzione. Le interpretazioni della Rivoluzione Francese*, Torino, Einaudi, 1989, pp. 113-116.

[97] Rinaldo Falcioni, "Politica e guerra da Clausewitz ad Aron", in *Il Mulino*, 1984, n. 4, pp. 577-602. It. transl. (Mondadori) of the *Memoires* of Aron (1905-1983), with a preface of Alberto Ronchey. It. Ed. by Carlo Maria Santoro (1935-2002) of Aron *Sur Clausewitz* (Bruxelles, 1987: Il Mulino, Bologna 1991). See Jean and Rusconi in A. Campi (Ed.), *Pensare la politica. Saggi su Raymond Aron*, Roma, Ideazione, 2005.

[98] Nicola Labanca, "I due *makers of modern strategy*", in Peter Paret (cur.), *Guerra e strategia nell'età contemporanea*, Genova, Marietti, 1992, pp. 7-32

[99] W. B. Gallie, *Filosofie di pace e di guerra. Kant, Clausewitz, Marx, Engels, Tolstoi*, Bologna, Il Mulino, 1993 (Cambridge, 1978).

[100] Christopher Bassford, *Clausewitz in English. The Reception of Clausewitz in Britain and America 1815-1945*, Oxford U. P. 1994; Olaf Rose, *Carl von Clausewitz. Zur Wirkungsgeschichte seines Werkes in Russland und der Sowjetunion 1836 bis 1994*, Monaco, Oldenbourg Verlag, 1995.

[101] There are of course exceptions, as Gorizia's LEG which called on the expertise of specialist General Mini, but there are not enough of such examples to fill the gap. F. e., despite his valuable critics to the Western conduct of the War

on Terror, James S. Corum is known in Italy only for his 1992 study on the roots of Blitzkrieg, translated and prefaced by General Mini in 2004 (*Le origini del Blitzkrieg: Hans von Seeckt e la riforma militare tedesca: 1919-1933*, LEG, Gorizia 2004).

[102] Azar Gat, *The origins of military thought: from enlightenment to Clausewitz*, Oxford, Clarendon, 1989. Kurt Guss, *Krieg als Gestalt. Psychologie und Pädagogik bei Carl von Clausewitz*, 1990; Dietmar Schössler (*Carl von Clausewitz*, Rowohlt, Reinbeck bei Hamburg, 1991; Handel, *Sun Tzu and Clausewitz: The Art of War and On War Compared*, Strategic Studies Institute, U. S. Army War College, 1991. Alan Beyerchen, "Clausewitz, Nonlinearity, and the Unpredictability of War", in *International Security*, Vol. 17, No. 3 (Winter, 1992-1993), pp. 59-90; Martin van Creveld, *The Transformation of War* (New York, Free Press, 1991). K. M. French, a Marine Officer and former van Creveld student at Quantico, graduated himself with an interesting commentary (*Clausewitz vs the Scholar: Martin van Creveld's Expanded Theory of War*). Peter Paret, *Understanding war: essays on Clausewitz and the history of military power*, Princeton U. P., 1993. Lt Colonel Barry D. Watts, *Clausewitzian Friction and Future War*, McNair Paper 52, Institute for National Strategic Studies, 1996. Gert de Nooy (Ed.), *The Clausewitzian dictum and the future of the Western military strategy*, The Hague, London, Boston, Kluwer International (Nijhoff Law Specials 31), 1997. Emmanuel Terray, *Clausewitz*, Paris, Fayard, 1999.

[103] See e. g. Andreas Herberg-Rothe (*Das Rätsel Clausewitz. Politische Theorie des Krieges im Widerstreit*, Fink Verlag, 2001; *Clausewitz – Strategie denken*, Munich, 2003; Herfried Münkler, *Clausewitz' Theorie des Krieges*, Nomos Verlag, 2003; David J. Lonsdale, *The nature of war in the Information Age: Clausewitzian future*, London and New York, Frank Cass, 2004. Ralf Kulla (*Politische Macht und politische Gewalt. Krieg, Gewaltfreiheit und Demokratie in Anschluss an Hannah Arendt und Carl von Clausewitz*, Hamburg, Verlag Dr. Kovač, 2005; Beatrice Heuser (*Clausewitz lesen! Eine Einführung*, Oldembourg Verlag 2005; Hew Strachan and Andreas Herberg-Rothe (eds), *Clausewitz in the Twenty-First Century*, Oxford U. P. 2007.

[104] Andreas Herberg-Rothe, "Opposizioni nella teoria politica della guerra di Clausewitz", in *Scienza & Politica*, 9, n. 19, Trento 1998, pp. 23-45. Of the same Author, "Clausewitz eller Nietzsche", in *Res Publica* No. 54, Stockholm, March 2002, pp. 17-22; Clausewitz oder Nietzsche: Sul mutamento di paradigma nella teoria politica della guerra, in *Merkur*, n. 623, March 2001.

[105] *Carl von Clausewitz's On War. A Biography (A Book That Shook the World)*, Atlantic Monthly Press, 2007, trad. it. Roma, Newton Compton, 2007.

[106] J. Freund, "Guerra e politica da Carl von Clausewitz a Raymond Aron", in Id., *La guerra nelle società moderne* (1991), Lungro di Cosenza, Marco Ed., 2007, pp. 81-94.

[107] *Achever Clausewitz* (2007), whose title evokes the idea to bring him down rather than complete him (Ital. transl. Girard, *Portando Clausewitz all'estremo. Conversazione con Benoît Chantre*, a cura di Giuseppe Fornari, Milano, Adelphi, 2008).

[108] Carlo Jean, *Guerra, strategia e sicurezza*, (1997-2000); Id., *Manuale di studi strategici*, (2004, 2008), both published by Laterza (Roma-Bari).

[109] Giampiero Giacomello and Col. Gianmarco Badialetti, *Manuale di studi strategici. Da Sun Tzu alle "nuove guerre"*, Milano, Vita e Pensiero, 2009.

[110] Ferdinando Sanfelice di Monteforte, *Il dibattito strategico*, Soveria Mannelli, Rubbettino, 2010.

[111] Clausewitz, *Della Guerra*, Milano, Rizzoli, BUR ("Pillole"), 2009, pp. 121.

[112] Carlo Galli, *Guerra*, Roma-Bari, Laterza, 2004.

[113] Gastone Breccia (Ed.); *L'arte della guerra da Sun Zu a Clausewitz*, Torino, Einaudi, 2009, pp. cxxxvi-vii. After have told us that *Vom Kriege* disappointed him when he was wargaming Raimondo Luraghi's *American Civil War*, Prof. Breccia states that "is undoubtedly wrong to consider (Clausewitz and Jomini) two opposite poles of the 19th Century military thought".

[114] Posted 20 October 2002 in www.recensionifilosifiche.it.

[115] Massimiliano Guareschi, *Ribaltare Clausewitz. La guerra in Michel Foucault e Deleuze-Guattari*, Roma, Centro di Studi e Iniziative per la Riforma dello Stato, 2005.

[116] Gian Mario Bravo, "Dall'arte della guerra alle armi per la pace: da Machiavelli a Erasmo, ovvero, da Clausewitz a Bobbio", in Vincenzo Ferrari (Ed.), *Filosofia giuridica della guerra e della pace. Atti del XXV congresso della Società italiana di filosofia del diritto*, Milano, Franco Angeli, 2008, pp. 493-510.

[117] Paolo Ceola, *Il Labirinto. Saggi sulla guerra contemporanea*, Napoli, Liguori, 2002. Id., *Armi e democrazia. Per una teoria riformista della guerra*, Biella, 2006.

[118] Drago Antonino, and Pezzullo Francesco, "Logica e strategia. Analisi della teoria di K. von Clausewitz", *Teoria Politica* 16 (2000), pp. 164-174.

[119] C. Schmitt, "Clausewitz come pensatore politico. Osservazioni e riferimenti", in *Rivista di Politica*, I, 1, 2010, pp. 93-111, with G. Maschke's complementary notes (112-19), transl. by Luigi Cimmino (see his "Il limite del Clausewitz 'politico'", in *L'Indipendente*, 20 March 2005).

[120] Gian Enrico Rusconi, *Rischio 1914. Come si decide una guerra*, Bologna, Il Mulino, 1987 (see the chapter "Clausewitz è caduto sulla Marna?", pp. 147-164).

[121] Gian Enrico Rusconi, *Clausewitz il Prussiano. La politica della guerra nell'equilibrio europeo*, Torino, Einaudi, 1999.

[122] Clausewitz, *Della guerra*, Einaudi, Torino, 2009, 250 pp. Newly (but only partially) translated and commented by Gian Enrico Rusconi.

[123] Fabio Mini, *L'altra strategia*, Franco Angeli, Milano, 1998. Same idea in Gastone Breccia, he too a "Sunziist" ("Adieu Herr von Clausewitz", in *Limes* 6/2006).

[124] Alessandro Colombo, *La guerra ineguale. Pace e violenza nel tramonto della società internazionale*, Bologna, Il Mulino, 2006.

[125] Jean, "Clausewitz and bin Laden", in Lucia Annunziata and Marta Dassù (eds). *Conflicts in 21st Century*, Rome, Aspen Institute Italia, 2002, pp. 151-163. Quoted by Paolo Della Sala, in *Guanaca e-book 42* (http://lapulcedivoltaire.blogosfere.it).

[126] *Pensare la guerra in Cesare*, I, *cit.*, pp. 271-72.

[127] Luigi Loreto, *La grande strategia di Roma nell'età della prima guerra punica. L'inizio di un paradosso*, Jovene, Napoli, 2007.

CLAUSEWITZ IN THE 21ST CENTURY JAPAN
Takeshi Oki

In the 21st century Japan, the understandings of Clausewitz's thought on war vary from the practical to the academic and speculative. If a foreign student who is studying Clausewitz visits a Japanese bookshop, he would likely be astonished to see a book titled "To Understand Clausewitz's 'On War' with Cartoons". Such a phenomenon has its roots in the belief of ordinary Japanese people that Clausewitz's thought on war and strategy could apply to their business and daily life like Sun Tzu's.

On the other hand, how Clausewitz's theories should be understood in the post-Cold War age is seriously discussed in academic circles and Jieitai (Japan Self-Defense Force, JSDF).

The purpose of this article is to provide a general outline and background of the situation regarding the understanding of Clausewitz's thinking in Japan.

Historical Background

The first mention of Clausewitz in Japan is found in a letter from a scholar who was interested in western civilization, Shozan Sakuma, to the Statesman of the Late Tokugawa Shogunate Kaishu Katsu in 1859. "I received Clausewitz's book recommended by you. This book impressed me as being very interesting". It is not clear if Sakama could understand Clausewitz's ideas precisely. The Clausewitz book he had was a Dutch edition.

After the end of Shogunate and the Meiji Restoration of Tenno (The Emperor) Rule in 1868, the army of the new Japanese nation state was transformed. The model for the army changed from the French Republic's army - which had been a model of modern warfare for the Shogun's troops and the Japanese Army of the early Meiji era (reign of the Meiji Emperor lasted from 1868 to 1912) - to the Imperial German Army. The sweeping victory of the Prussian Army during the Franco-Prussian War made a great impression on the leaders of the Imperial Japanese Army, and they therefore sought to learn the secret behind the German Victory. They thought that secret was Clausewitz.

In 1886, an army officer who was studying modern strategy and tactics in Germany, Iyozo Tamura, later the chief of the army general staff, visited one of the great authors of modern Japan and who was also a military doctor, Rintaro Mori, in Berlin (Mori was also a resident student in Germany from Japan). Tamura was eager to learn the essential principles of "On War" from Mori, who was adept in many foreign languages, especially German.

After his return to Japan, Mori started a translation of "On War" into Japanese. Based on Mori's translation, Rikugun Shikan Gakko (the military academy) completed the translation of the entire volume in 1903. This first Japanese edition was confidential and published only within army circles, but it was widely read by army officers[1].

A Japanese military historian has pointed out that the translation of "On War" was urgently needed at that time. This was because Major Klemens Jacob Meckel, the German officer hired by the Japanese government as a lecturer to Japanese young staff officers, taught the elements of warfare only on the divisional level but not at the corps-army operational or strategic level[2].

The Japanese efforts to understand Clausewitz's thought bore fruit: victory over Russia in 1905 - or so it appeared. Many military theorists around the world regarded the Japanese as the foremost students of Clausewitzian theory, but in reality, the Imperial Japanese Army inclined more and more to the canonization of the operational understanding of Clausewitz. "On War" was not as a book on theory, but one on doctrine, which taught how operations and tactics were conducted.

Such a rigid understanding extended into the making of the Tosui Koryo (Principles of Command) in 1914. This Program was an extension of the Schlieffenlike Annihilation Strategy formulated before the First World War, and it was essentially a guide for conducting military operations. Thus Clausewitz's famous maxim that "War is not merely a political act, but also a political instrument, a continuation of political relations, a carrying out of the same by other means", was not seriously discussed in the Japanese Army any longer[3]. In the period between the two world wars, this excessive indoctrination of the staff officers continued[4]. As a result they pursued an overly "operation-oriented strategy" and brought the disaster of 1945 to their nation and country.

After Japan's defeat in the Second World War, the study of Clausewitz's theory in Japan was sluggish. There were several reasons. As is widely known, the post-war Constitution of Japan has forbidden the nation from the use of war as a political instrument. Assuming this Constitution is rigidly applied, Japan will never be able to conduct a war henceforth. Therefore, Clausewitz's ideas were regarded as useless. Moreover, it was judged in Japan in the late 1940s and 1950s when a pacifistic tendency took hold - just like the social trend in Europe after World War I - that the beginning of the nuclear war age brought the end to the Clausewitzian understanding of war. But some former army officers and several officers of Jieitai, Japan Self-Defense Force reexamined their understandings of Clausewitz's ideas in their own reflection on the defeat of World War II. In addition, military theorists whose thinking was based on Marxism-Leninism deepened their study of Clausewitz from their standpoints as well.

But the economic revival of Japan in 1960s changed the situation. From 1965 to 1969 three new translations of "On War" were published successively, and they were read by both the management side and the union side of many enterprises besides members of JSDF[5]. Apparently this Clausewitzian "civil needs" were based on the demand for an instrumental model of strategy, namely how to act in business wisely.

As pointed out in the introduction of the article, these tendencies - while military theorist and the officers study Clausewitz theoretically and systematically, there is also a public demand for the practical use of "On War" have continued up to this present day.

Coming of the New Age Scholars

However a new generation of scholars appeared in 1990's. Before the fall of the East European communist countries and the Soviet Union, the pacifistic tendency and the aversion to war, already mentioned above, dominated the academic world in Japan. Therefore the study of Clausewitz's ideas in the universities was discouraged, if not prohibited. But the end of the Cold War and the fact that nevertheless wars will never disappear, as exemplified by the conflicts in the former Yugoslavia, made the younger generation of Japanese scholars pay attention to Clausewitz again. They began to cooperate with the lecturers of Boei Kennkyuujo (National Institute for Defense Studies), Kanbu Gakko (the Staff Colleges of Japan Self-Defense Force) and Boei Daigakko (National Defense Academy). This would have been unimaginable in the 1960s or 1970s. Their new approaches greatly advanced the study of Clausewitz in

Japan and improved the understanding of Clausewitz's thought generally in the society with the publications of their works.

The author would like to point to the volume of essays, „Clausewitz and 'On War'"[6] in 2008 as an example of such a "new wave". Three foreign scholars (Martin van Creveld, Jan Willem Honig and Williamson Murray) took part in the project, but the other articles are all written by Japanese scholars.

In the part I "Clausewitz and 'On War'", Takichi Shimizu, one of the translators of "On War" in Japan, described the life of Clausewitz and Yasuyuki Kawamura explained the essence of "On War"[7].

The four articles in the part II "Clausewitz and his times" explored the age of the French Revolution and Napoleonic Wars, in which Clausewitz lived and developed his thoughts on war. After the introduction by Masaki Miyake that surveyed the German literature about Clausewitz, Takashi Araya discussed the transformation of wars (from limited war or cabinet war to unlimited war between nation states) in the French Revolutionary Wars and the Napoleonic Wars. Hiroto Maruhata reexamined the development of Clausewitz's thought on war through a study of the making of Prussian general conscription system and Tadashi Suzuki discussed the meaning of the military reform in Prussia after the defeat of Jena-Auerstedt, with an emphasis on the formation of Freikorps[8].

The articles in part III "the legacies of Clausewitz" took up the issue of the influence of Clausewitzian thought on military theorists in the 19th and 20th centuries. Hiroki Nakajima explored the understandings of Clausewitz in the Prussian-German army from Moltke the elder to Schlieffen, and pointed out the inclination of the German officers to use Clausewitz's thoughts. Jun Kozutsumi took the three examples of German generals and military theorists, Ludendorff, Seeckt and Beck, and discussed the influence of Clausewitz on them. Tomoyuki Ishizu compared Clausewitz and Liddell Hart and reached the conclusion that the latter inherited -- contrary to the widely accepted view -- the several elements of the Clausewitzian thinking[9].

In the last part "Clausewitz and wars of our days", Satoshi Nagasue discussed the relations between the Clausewitzian thought and technology through the example of air power[10].

Thus the studies of Clausewitz's thoughts in the 21st century Japan are extricating themselves from the peculiar situation formed by the social trends of post-war Japan and the volume edited by Shimizu and Ishizu showed that

Japanese academicians can develop new and "normal" approaches like colleagues of other countries. With the turning of the tide, it is expected that more positivistic studies of Clausewitzian thoughts will proceed in Japan. And this progress should help to improve the general understanding of Clausewitz in Japanese society that is rather inclined to the pragmatic interpretations.

Clausewitz in the educations of Jieitai Officers

Finally, the author would like to sketch how Clausewitz's thought is presented in the education of SDF Officers.

In Rikujo Jieitai (Japan Ground Self-Defense Force, JGSDF), Clausewitz is taught in Shiki Bakuryo Katei (the command and general staff course) for captains and majors and in Kanbu Kokyu Katei (the advanced command and general staff course) for colonels and lieutenant colonels of Rikujo Jieitai Kanbu Gakko (the Staff College of JGDSF). However Clausewitz is not presented as a separate subject, but as a part of the "Yohei Shiso Si" (The History of strategic Thoughts) along with Frederic the Great, Napoleon, Jomini, Moltke the elder and Liddell Hart. In the lectures, the Clausewitzian philosophical reflections on "what is war" and his understanding of war as a phenomenon, which is unable to predict, are emphasized[11].

Kaijo Jieitai (Japan Maritime Self-Defense Force, JMSDF) attaches importance to Mahan and Corbett and does not provide lectures on Clausewitz. In Koku Jieitai, Clausewitz is more appreciated than by the JGSDF, much more than JMSDF, because the U.S. Air Force, the most important partner of JASDF and the most progressive air force in modern air warfare, adopts the Clausewitzian thinking on war as one of the nucleus elements of its strategy. Therefore the officers of JASDF must understand Clausewitz's thoughts and are required to read "On War" repeatedly. Of course Clausewitz is lectured in all officer-education courses of the JASDF[12].

Notes:

[1] Yugo Asano, *Clausewitz to kindai nihon* (Clausewitz and the Modern Japan) 3-1, Rikusen Kenkyu (Studies of the Land Warfare), No. 328, 1981 (cite as Asano I), pp. 27-30.

[2] Ibid., p. 30. Cf.; Georg Kerst, *Jacob Meckel. Sein Leben, sein Wirken in Deutschland und Japan*, Göttingen 1970.

[3] Asano I, 33-35. Cf., Tohru Maehara, *Nihon rikugun e no Clausewitz no eikyou* (The Influence of Clausewitz upon Imperial Japanese Army) 1, Gunji-Shigaku (Military History Studies), Vol .19. No.1, 1983, especially pp. 20-25.

[4] Clausewitz's thoughts as a theory was not lectured even in Rikugun Daigakko (the military academy). Asano I, p. 34.

[5] Yugo ASANO, *Clausewitz to kindai nihon* (Clausewitz and the Modern Japan) 3-2, Rikusen Kenkyu (Studies of the Land Warfare), No. 329, 1981, pp. 11-14.

[6] Takichi Shimizu/Tomoyuki Ishizu (ed.), *Clausewitz to sensoron* (Clausewitz and 'On War'), Tokyo, 2008 (cite as S/I).

[7] Takichi Shimizu, *Clausewitz no shogai--Clausewitz to Napoleon sennso* (The Life of Clausewitz - Clausewitz and the Napoleonic Wars); Yasuyuki Kawamura, *Clausewitz no 'sensoron toha nanika* (What is Clausewitz's 'On War'), both in S/I.

[8] Masaki Miyake, *Doitsu ni okeru Clausewitz kennkyushi o chusin to site* (Introduction of the literature on Clausewitz focusing on the studies in Germany); Takashi Araya *Jyukyuuseikisyotou no yoroppa senryakukankyou to puroisen* (The European strategic environment and Prussia in the beginning of the 19th century); Hiroto Maruhata, *Clausewitz and the age of the general conscription system*; Tadashi Suzuki, *Puroisen Gunseikaikaku - gaikan to tenbo* (Prussian military reform - an outline and the prospect), all in S/L.

[9] Hiroki Nakajima, *Puroisen-doitsu gun to Clausewitz* (The Prussian-German army and Clausewitz); Jun Kozutsumi, *Sennryaku naki jidai no Clausewitz - Sennkanki no doitu o chusin ni* (Clausewitz in the era without strategy - With the emphasis on Germany between the World Wars); Tomoyuki Ishizu, *Clausewitz to Liddell Hart - 'Zettai senso' to 'Seigen senso' no sokoku?* (Clausewitz and Liddell Hart - An antagonism between 'Unlimited War' and 'Limited War'?), all in S/L.

[10] Satoshi Nagasue, *Clausewitz no sennryakugainen to air power* (Clausewitzian concepts of strategy and air power), in S/L.

[11] "Yohei Shiso si" Kyoiku Yotei Hyo (The curriculum of "History of strategic Thoughts"), Rikujo Jieitai Kanbu Gakko; The informations from the lecturer of Koku Jieitai Kanbugakko (the Staff College of Japan Air Self Defense Force); Maj.Gen. (ret.) Takashi Genda by E-Mail of October 12, 2010.

[12] Ibid. Cf., Takashi Genda, *Posuto reisen jidai no bei kuugun senryaku - Warden taisa no kokuu senryaku siso o chusin ni* (U.S. air strategy in the age of post-Cold War - based on colonel Warden's thoughts on air strategy), Shin Boei Ronsyuu (New Defense Studies), Vol. 28, No. 1 (2000).

CLAUSEWITZ AND THE NETHERLANDS
Paul Donker

On the eve of the French revolution there was also unrest in the Republic of the Seven United Provinces, the present-day Netherlands. Although a republic in name, the country was ruled in a fairly authoritarian manner by stadtholder William V. Like in France, the patriots demanded more democracy. When they briefly incarcerated Wilhelmina, William's spouse, on 28 June 1787, he had had enough. He asked her brother, King Frederick William II of Prussia, to launch a military intervention, upon which the latter dispatched an intervention force of approximately 25,000 men. This Prussian army was commanded by the Duke of Brunswick, who in 1792 was to command the invasion of France, an intervention that would be stopped by the revolutionaries near Valmy. In 1787, however, Brunswick managed to restore the authority of the stadtholder in less than a month.

Clausewitz studied Brunswick's campaign in the Republic of the Seven United Provinces in detail, and this case study, still very much worth reading today, forms part of the historical foundation on which his principal work *Vom Kriege* rests. Together with several other short studies the *Feldzug des Herzogs von Braunschweig gegen die Holländer in 1787* was incorporated in the last, the tenth volume of his posthumous works. His analysis has a modern ring to it; after all, it relates to a military intervention in a civil war. One of the most important conclusions Clausewitz drew from this case study was that a military intervention in a war-torn country may never be underestimated. He believed the Prussian cabinet had sent far too few troops in view of the chaotic situation, the option of the patriots to inundate the country and the possibility of France coming to their rescue. Also, an intervention should be based on a worst-case scenario and it could be assumed that the majority of the factions would be well-disposed towards the force.[1] Except for these inundations, there are many parallels with the recent operations in Bosnia, Iraq and Afghanistan, as will be seen below.

Conversely, there has been an interest from the Netherlands for Clausewitz's work from the very first. The first Dutch translation of *Vom Kriege* dates back to as early as 1846, and in that same year his entire posthumous works, except for the last two volumes, became available in Dutch. So, this was before the original work had gone through its second edition in Prussia. But, did this mutual interest and early availability in the native language mean that Clausewitz gathered a following in the Netherlands? Did he have a lasting influence on the political-military thinking and practice?

In order to answer these questions, this contribution will follow two subsequent approaches. First, it will be investigated how Clausewitz and his *Vom Kriege* have been cited in the military-scientific periodical *De Militaire Spectator* since 1832. This venerable periodical has been in existence for almost 180 years, and, by comparing the articles dealing with the subject, the extent of Clausewitz's following among the Dutch officers can be ascertained, and, by extension, his influence on the military thinking.

The second part of this contribution, subsequently, will focus on the extent of Clausewitz's influence on the political-military practice in the Netherlands. Of course, within the scope of this article it is impossible to cover all Dutch military operations since 1833. Therefore, this will be limited to three crucial political-military decisions of the past few years: the decision in 1994 to send an air-mobile battalion to the Srebrenica enclave; the decision to support the American-British invasion of Iraq politically but not militarily, and the decision in 2010 to terminate the mission in Afghanistan. As with the Prussian intervention of 1787 in the Netherlands, these three cases concern internally divided countries. In accordance with Clausewitz's method, it is possible to consider the fine-tuning of ends, ways and means.

The first Dutch translation

As is known, Clausewitz's widow published her husband's posthumous work in ten volumes between 1832 and 1837. The first three volumes together form *Vom Kriege*, the remaining seven are of an historical nature. At the same time the first issue of military-scientific periodical *De Militaire Spectator* was published on 29 January 1833.[2] Already in the first volume there was some brief attention for *Vom Kriege*, which the reviewer called the most scientific book so far on the art of war, praising the manner in which it was described by Clausewitz.[3] In the years to follow chief editor J. C. van Rijneveld repeatedly referred to *Vom Kriege* in his articles.[4]

The then librarian of the Royal Netherlands Military Academy, E. H. Brouwer, translated the first eight volumes of the posthumous work and they were published in a somewhat different composition between 1839 and 1846.[5]

What is striking is that he started with the more historical works and ended with *Vom Kriege*. Apart from that, it is not clear why he skipped the last two volumes, which oddly enough deal with the Prussian invasion of the Netherlands of 1787. One explanation for this is that Brouwer thought that there would mainly be interest in the then recent French Revolutionary and Napoleonic wars and not in the earlier campaigns described by Clausewitz in volumes 9 and 10. The overview below presents the first editions of the original and translated volumes. Shortly after the publication of this first Dutch translation First Lieutenant J. L. Wagner published a Dutch summary of *Vom Kriege* intended for a broader public.[6]

All in all, with this early translation by Brouwer and summary by Wagner the Netherlands was one of the first countries, if not the very first, to have the virtually complete works of Clausewitz available in the native language. In spite of this, this promising start was not to lead to a large influence during the nineteenth century. First of all, Brouwer was not very much interested in Clausewitz's thinking. Tradition has it that he had a large family and that translating military science works was a bitter necessity to sustain it. Apart from Clausewitz he also translated many other military science works and, as far as is known, always for a small audience. Secondly, the sales of the translation stagnated and in 1859 the publisher tried to rekindle the fire somewhat by issuing it under a new title.[7] There are no indications that this was a really successful move and today only a few copies of this Dutch translation have survived. Finally, in actual fact, there is only a modest number of references to Clausewitz's work in *De Militaire Spectator* between 1832 and 1870.

So, while in most European countries Clausewitz was discovered and translated rather late, after von Moltke had referred to him around 1870, he was noticed almost straightaway in Dutch military science circles and his work was translated almost immediately.

The period between 1870 and 1945

In the Netherlands, too, interest in Clausewitz increased after von Moltke had adopted him as his source of inspiration. The Prussian-German success against France in 1870 had of course not gone unnoticed and the concept of a war fought offensively, full of surprise and with all available force in order to be decisive, did not fall on deaf ears here. Still, even now there was no real breakthrough. Thus, up to World War II Clausewitz was referred to in the study books at officer education institutes, but Jomini received relatively more attention.[8]

One reason for this limited impact may well have been that in these years the Netherlands pursued a policy of non-interference with regard to the European major powers, which in times of crisis changed into a strict neutrality. After all, such a political strategy implied a purely defensive role of the armed forces, and offensive warfare, which was Clausewitz's hallmark, was the prerogative of the major powers. On top of that, this constant policy ensured that there would only be few new strategic challenges for the strategic thinkers in the Netherlands.

In a general respect, Clausewitz and his *Vom Kriege* were cited in *De Militaire Spectator* on a very regular basis until the outbreak of World War II. In articles and series of articles on strategy his name was never absent, and each time the reference was to the original German version of his work. Apparently, Brouwer's Dutch translation was not used. Between 1905 and 1909 then First Lieutenant C. C. de Gelder wrote an elaborate series, entitled *Strategische Studien*, in which numerous strategic problems of a general nature were discussed and in which Clausewitz was regularly cited.[9] Captain Wilson followed suit in 1931 with a series of four articles in which a general description was given of the military strategy.[10] In these and comparable articles the offensive conduct of war featured prominently and Clausewitz was consistently given his place in the line that runs from Frederick the Great to Napoleon, Jomini, von Moltke and von Schlieffen. As far as can be ascertained, the famous formula that war is a continuation of politics with other means was used for the first time in *De Militaire Spectator* in 1900.[11] Clearly, that aspect of his theory evoked less interest. Another striking absentee in the years leading up to World War II was his *wunderliche Dreifaltigkeit*. This important concept did not receive any attention although the relation between politics, society and the armed forces was an object of study. His views, too, on the chaotic side of war, the element of friction and his concept of *Schwerpunkt*, the subject of much present-day writing, were almost completely ignored.

An important strategic issue for the Netherlands between 1870 and 1940 was the question whether the defensive should be conducted fully statically (i.e. digging in behind the great rivers and inundations) or more dynamically (i.e. by means of an independently operating field army in front of the rivers). In the ongoing discussion on the topic in *De Militaire Spectator* there were frequent references to Clausewitz, needless to say to beef up the advantages of the latter option.[12]

Another topic in which Clausewitz was regularly quoted was the case study of the Prussian intervention of 1787, described above in the introduction. Both in the Netherlands and Germany new works on this invasion were published on a regular basis during this period and the reviews always contained references to his, by that time, almost 50-year-old study. Clearly, his view constituted a benchmark for Dutch readers.[13]

What is striking is that Clausewitz, in contrast to what happened in Great Britain, was not thrown on the dung heap of history after World War I. No articles were published that linked him to the dramatic course of that war. The problem of a direct versus an indirect strategy was not an issue here, and, besides, there were no first-hand experiences of the horrors of trench warfare. Also the fact that most Dutch officers at the time had a command of the German language, so had direct access to *Vom Kriege* without having to resort to a slanted translation, will have played a part in this. In *De Militaire Spectator*, Clausewitz was studied seriously against the background of World War I. His influence on von Schlieffen's and von Moltke's (the younger) strategies was recognized, but not censured.[14]

On the eve of World War II then First Lieutenant Calmeijer wrote a series of articles in which he presented his views on future warfare, and in which he repeatedly referred to *Vom Kriege*.[15] And already in the October issue of 1939 of *De Militaire Spectator* the Polish campaign was discussed and analyzed at length. The anonymous author was convinced that, "[t]he campaign in Poland will forever remain a classic example of the conduct of warfare, which the great German strategists (Clausewitz, Moltke, Schlieffen), emulating the wars waged by Frederick the Great and Napoleon, developed into a system, executed with the present-day munitions of war."[16]

The years of the Cold War

After World War II the Netherlands renounced its policy of non-interference and armed neutrality, gearing virtually its entire defence organization to the allied defence. As a consequence the NATO strategy became leading for the Netherlands armed forces and the need for strategic thinkers of their own diminished. Because the three Services, the Royal Netherlands Navy, the Royal Netherlands Army and the Royal Netherlands Air Force were each assigned their own area of operations, they began to diverge bit by bit. The Royal Netherlands Navy increasingly focussed on counter-submarine warfare in the Atlantic, the Royal Netherlands Army on large-scale land operations on the North German plains and the Royal Netherlands Air Force on the air war over the entire Western Europe. Only occasionally did the three organizations rub shoulders and for that reason there was little point in developing a joint military strategy.

Of course, some strategy was taught at the various staff schools but this was relatively modest and mainly directed at the existing NATO strategy. Nor was there any specific training for operational-strategic planners during this period. Needless to say that in such a restricted environment there was less attention for Clausewitz.

In fact, strategic thinking in the Netherlands during this period found its way to the civilian universities and similar institutions, where the so-called peace studies began to flourish, and within which there was some room for strategy and, by extension, for Clausewitz. In this context the names of H. W. Houweling, J. G. Siccama and P. M. E. Volten, in whose works *Vom Kriege* is often referred to, are certainly worth mentioning.[17] However, the focus of these studies during those years lay on preventing war rather than waging it. The horror of a global nuclear war caused the starting point to be maintaining peace. Clausewitz was mainly studied and quoted from this perspective, and his axiom that the political view prevails over the military one was the *Leitmotiv* in these studies. There was, however, also some attention for the thesis that defence is the strongest form of warfare, which served as a foundation for a completely passive NATO strategy, to be executed with purely defensive weapon systems. Another academic bone of contention was his concept of absolute war, which of course closely touches upon nuclear warfare.

It goes without saying that Clausewitz never disappeared completely from Dutch military thinking. Even during the Cold War he kept appealing to the imagination.[18] In 1971 then Lieutenant Colonel F. C. Spits, lecturer at the *Hogere Krijgsschool*, obtained his Ph. D. on a doctoral thesis in which *Vom Kriege* features prominently. In ten chapters the historical change in the conduct of war around 1800 and Clausewitz's related concept of absolute war were analyzed. Also his views on the primacy of politics were discussed and strongly defended against von Moltke's and Liddell Hart's erroneous interpretations of *Vom Kriege*.[19] What is typical for the Cold War days, incidentally, was that nowhere did the book mention that its author had a military background. Spits, incidentally, had a weekly radio column in which he commented on current military issues. He was also an extraordinary professor of miliary history at the University of Utrecht for a number of years.

Clausewitz was also cited on a regular basis in *De Militaire Spectator*. Officers, who had studied at German, British or American staff colleges became intimately acquainted with his works and referred to him in their articles. Thus, in this periodical there were quotes from the original German edition as well as the famed translation by Howard and Paret, but also earlier English translations. The Dutch translation by Brouwer, however, was not used anymore.

As for topics, 1985 saw a remarkable shift. Until that year Clausewitz had regained his historical place in military science, with the addition that there was now more interest in his political-military ideas at the expense of his more operational views.[20] Until 1985 there had been only one author to fall back on *Vom Kriege* in his study of an operational problem, in this case the defence behind the great rivers.[21] It is true, Clausewitz was mentioned in the study of the Sinai war of 1956 and the Vietnam war and like in the civilian world he was regularly quoted in connection with nuclear warfare. What was new in this period was, first of all, the communist-inspired views on Clausewitz, and a comparison, secondly, of his theories with Sun Tzu's. Finally, mention must be made of the article on the guerrilla against the Russian occupation of Afghanistan, if only because it was the only article in which also other work of Clausewitz was used, be it ever so modestly.[22] For the rest, during the Cold War period his entire oeuvre seemed to have been reduced to *Vom Kriege*.

As was said above, there is a clear watershed as of 1985, when Clausewitz was rediscovered as a source in operational and tactical problems, with a striking preference of authors for English translations of *Vom Kriege*, in particular Howard and Paret. One reason for this may be that the editors of *De Militaire Spectator* included several re-runs of articles by American authors, who, of course, used *On War*.[23] It is clear that the change of direction had everything to do with the change in thinking within NATO. When the 1980s saw an increase of interest in manoeuvre warfare, the step to Clausewitz was only a small one. In a series of articles the case was made for the introduction of the operational level between the existing strategic and tactical levels in order to create room there for manoeuvre, as, for instance, in the FOFA concept (Follow-on-Forces Attack).[24] What is interesting in this is that much earlier, in 1963 to be exact, a plea had been made in *De Militaire Spectator* for such a tripartite division, also on the basis of Clausewitz.[25] Then Colonel, the later Commander of the Land Forces, Lieutenant General M. Schouten, further elaborated this idea for the Royal Netherlands Army with R. J. van Vels, using, among others, Clausewitz's culmination point.[26] Their proposal invited a reaction from Lieutenant Colonel F. J. D. C. Egter van Wissekerke, who was to show himself one of the Netherlands' best experts on Clausewitz of the period. Egter van Wissekerke was a lecturer at the *Hogere Krijgsschool*, co-author of many doctrine publications and writer of many articles published in *De Militaire Spectator* and the *Carré* periodical. For support or illustration of his ideas he often referred to *Vom Kriege*, and it was thanks to his work that Clausewitz found his way into the Dutch army doctrine.[27]

Clausewitz was also discovered in those years by Air Force officers and they, too, linked his work to practice as well as doctrine. In 1991, the later Commander of the Air Force, B.A.C. Droste, analyzed the air war during the liberation of Kuwait and, among others, focused on Clausewitz's primacy of politics.[28] The Gulf War also featured regularly in later articles, but then there were more references to the more operational concepts of *Vom Kriege*, such as the centre of gravity.[29]

Clausewitz after the Cold War

When around 1990 the Cold War came to an end and the work on new Army and Air Force doctrines began, it appeared that they were in part inspired by Clausewitz's ideas. Various authors referred to *Vom Kriege*, in general sense as well as in the more specific embracing of concepts such as the trinity.[30] In his preface to the first *Landmacht Doctrinepublicatie* (LDP-1) the Commander of the Land Forces, Lieutenant General M. Schouten, states that it was in part inspired by Clausewitz and Fuller. In particular, this last name triggered a reaction by military historian J. W. M. Schulten, who explained that a reference to Fuller was unfortunate in view of his political ideas. Besides, Schulten disagreed with Schouten's view and that of others that there had been too little attention for manoeuvre warfare during the Cold War, and that for this reason the new doctrine fell back on Clausewitz.[31]

Schulten received little support and in *De Militaire Spectator* from 2000 onwards the authors kept seeing a clear relation between Clausewitz and the new way of warfare. Former U.S. Marine Corps colonel, N. Pratt, argued that we were living at a watershed comparable to that at the time of Clausewitz around 1800, and, taking this one step further, F. J. J. Princen and M. H. Wijnen claimed that his philosophical, non-linear way of thinking was the only way to hold firm in today's complex world.[32]

In particular, Air Force circles embraced the idea that it was not so much *Vom Kriege* as Clausewitz's philosophical method of studying the phenomenon of war that deserved a following. In his article entitled *The road to academic 'critical mass'* D. M. Drew described the co-operation of many years between the American and Netherlands Air Force Staff schools. Dutch air power lecturers were trained in America and in their tailor-made course both Clausewitz and his method of studying the phenomenon of war, called *'the Clausewitzian mindset'* by Drew, were given generous attention.[33] Two of these lecturers, F. H. Meulman and F. Osinga, testified of this mindset in the same theme issue of *De Militaire Spectator*.[34] A year later A. C. Tjepkema in his article on Boyd recognized a clear link with Clausewitz's thinking.[35]

Finally, Clausewitz became involved in the discussion on the present-day forms of warfare. M. W. M. Kitzen is of the opinion that his ideas constitute an important exponent of Western military culture and that this culture is at odds with modern counter-insurgency. B. W. Schuurman, on the other hand, argues that Clausewitz is discarded far too soon by several new war thinkers.[36]

Clausewitz in the Dutch military thinking

After this survey, which covers almost 180 years, it is time to make a preliminary weigh-up on the question of the extent of Clausewitz's influence on Dutch military thinking. Measured in terms of the number of references made in articles in *De Militaire Spectator*, it may be safely concluded that he has managed to acquire a position of his own. There are roughly two types of readers among Dutch officers; those who make an in-depth study of *Vom Kriege* and those who make occasional references to it. Although Clausewitz did not gather a following in the Netherlands, he and his *Vom Kriege* time and again manage to fascinate a number of officers and to inspire them to further study. The line-up of names like Van Rijneveld, Wilson, Calmeijer, Spits and Egter van Wissekerke shows that in particular officers with a certain intellectual curiosity know where to find him, irrespective of what their immediate environment thinks of that. That position is unequalled and the fact that the *'Clausewitzian mindset'* has enjoyed so much attention again since 2000 clearly shows that this will remain so for some time to come.

The group of officers not only studying *Vom Kriege* sec, but referring to him in their research, is obviously much larger. Clausewitz, his masterpiece and the ideas and concepts it harbours are a clear source of inspiration. In the Dutch military thinking a quote from *Vom Kriege* has the status of axiom that needs no further explanation. Also this position is unique, and, without reservations, may be called special after 180 years.

First of all, the way in which Clausewitz has been studied since 1832 has undergone some change, though. What is striking is that initially his historical works received more attention than his *Vom Kriege*, but the former have been completely forgotten since World War II. Needless to say, within those studies *"Der Feldzug des Herzog von Brauschweig gegen die Holländer 1787"* holds pride of place.

Secondly, just as in other European countries Clausewitz is clearly regarded as an exponent of a way of warfare. He is consistently given a place among Frederick the Great, Napoleon, Jomini, von Moltke (the elder) and the later German strategists. The adoration or revulsion, so noticeable in various other countries, is very rare here, possibly because of the strategic position of the Netherlands, which leads to purely defensive armed forces.

What is striking, thirdly, is that the interest for the more operational side of *Vom Kriege* seems to have waned considerably during the Cold War, only to return rather quickly after 1985. In contrast to Schulten's view, fairly little operational material was published in the forty years after 1945 by his colleagues. For that reason, the term re-discovery is justified for the situation after 1985.

In line with this, finally, it must be said that the political side of *Vom Kriege* received the most attention during the Cold War. Although as early as 1900 it was first pointed out that Clausewitz views war as a political instrument, the number of reference after this is not really great. In other words, for most Dutch officers *Vom Kriege* is mainly an operational book.

Clausewitz in the political-military practice

Now that Clausewitz's special place within the Dutch military *thinking* has become clear, it is time to consider the influence of his work on the political-military *practice*. As was said above, three important post-Cold War decision moments will be analyzed to that end, but before they are discussed, a brief survey of the changes within the Dutch armed forces will be presented. The so-called *Toetsingskader* (Assessment Framework) which is used in the Netherlands in the decision-making with regard to military missions abroad, will be dealt with in the process.

As was the case for other western militaries the Dutch armed forces had to undergo a process of re-orientation after the fall of the Berlin Wall, but compared to most other European countries, this transformation into a modern fully professional expeditionary organization, capable of being deployed across the entire spectrum of violence, was a relatively fast one.

To begin with, conscription was *de facto* phased out. As there was insufficient political support in 1997 for a change of the Constitution, conscription was, according to good Dutch political mores, retained legally but no longer executed in practice. Thus, conscripts were registered, but not called up or trained. Initially, this solution was chosen in order to be able to return to the large conscript army should the international situation give occasion for this. However, over time the entire infrastructure in the armed forces disappeared, making a re-introduction of conscription virtually impossible.

Along with conscription the phenomenon of the so-called mobilizable units became obsolete. This, too, was an extraordinary choice in the Netherlands. Nowadays, all units are ready or nearly ready and can be sent out on short notice. With the exception of a few CIMIC functions there are no mobilizable functions for the current service personnel when their contracts expire. As a result, all the time and energy spent on their education and specific training is lost. Even in case the armed forces are faced with a temporary increase of tasks, there are no reserve units that can be called up, as is the case of the United States of America.

Officially, the Dutch armed forces have three main tasks: protecting the integrity of national and Alliance territory; promoting the international rule of law and international stability; and supporting civil authorities in upholding the law, providing disaster relief and humanitarian assistance, both nationally and internationally. In practice the emphasis lies on the second task. The Netherlands is one among the few countries to even have incorporated this task in the Constitution.

Precisely because the military missions abroad have become so important and experience has shown that decision making in this area is extremely complex, a so-called *Toetsingskader* (Assessment Framework) has been developed. This important document is used to facilitate the communication between Government and Parliament and over time it has been adapted several times on the basis of experiences gained. In the context of the present study it is important to recognize that this *Toetsingskader* has a distinct Clausewitzian ring to it. The Assessment Framework has two main themes – the political advisability of a mission and its military feasibility. Here, *Vom Kriege* is just around the corner. It was Clausewitz, in particular, who taught us that ends, ways and means should be in line with each other in a (military) campaign. As is known, the bulk of Book 8 is devoted to that theme.

When dealing with the political aspects, the Framework examines the legal bases, the mandate, other participating countries, the possibilities for development aid and the room for the Netherlands to exert political influence on the mission. Apart from obvious considerations regarding weather and terrain, the military aspects pertain to the stance of the parties in the conflict, the concept of operations, the rules of engagement, the command structure, possible risks, duration of participation, availability of units and financial consequences. The Clausewitzian influence is evident, all the more so as the Assessment Framework assumes that the elements mentioned are considered in their mutual dependency.

In sum, it can be said that the transformed armed forces have given the Dutch politics a unique and extremely effective instrument in view of the nature of today's conflicts and threats. The *Toetsingskader* provides a Clausewitzian frame of mind to be applied in the political-military decision making on the actual use of that instrument.

Important aspects of the Dutch decision making

Still, the question remains whether Clausewitz would be entirely satisfied about the system that is currently applied in the Netherlands for taking strategic decisions. It is evident that he lived in a different political-societal climate from that 180 years later. As concerns political-military decision making, *Vom Kriege* broadly starts from fully sovereign states within which a small and selected group of people are fully responsible for this strategy. Thus, there is great freedom of action in determining ends, ways and means.

In 2010 the Netherlands is in a different position. First of all, currently there are much more precise international agreements, such as those in the UN Charter, which strongly limit the use of military power. Secondly, a Dutch effort will almost always take place under the auspices of an international organization such as the UN, NATO or the EU, or within a coalition of the willing. In such contexts the influence of The Hague on the mandate or strategy is limited, and, besides, the Dutch military contribution is only part of a larger effort. In short, Dutch decision making does not concern the entire strategy discussed in *Vom Kriege*, but merely partial aspects of it.

Also, within the Netherlands itself, the situation is totally different from that of Clausewitz's days. No more is there a limited number of decision makers. Only when the Netherlands is attacked directly, the Cabinet may act of its own accord, as a matter of urgency. In all other cases Parliament demands influence. Since 1990 there have been repeated differences of opinion between the Cabinet and Parliament on the borderline cases and the extent of influence. The current Constitution provides in a right of information, but many parliamentarians would rather see the realization of a right of approval, which would of course greatly decrease the decision power of the government.

So, where Clausewitz exclusively had in mind the strategic decision makers, in 2010 also parliamentarians play an important role. Needless to say, the consultations between the two are time-consuming and the transparency of the decision often comes under pressure in the search for compromise. This problem is reinforced in the Netherlands by the relatively large number of political parties, which always leads to the formation of coalition governments. As a mission abroad is a very serious matter, the government tries to find a large majority in Parliament. Therefore, attempts are made not only to get support for the mission from coalition parties, but also from the opposition or at least the bulk of it. Thus, all important decisions in the Netherlands inevitably imply compromise and military missions abroad are no exception. However, transparent military strategies do not go along well with compromise.

The last innovative aspect concerns the role of the media and the population. They, too, have acquired a much more prominent position over the past 180 years. An earlier version of the *Toetsingskader* still specifically took the societal support into account, but this is not the case anymore, the government being convinced now that it is itself expected to convince the public of the correctness of the decision to send out troops. And, of course, Parliament, as the ultimate representative body of the population, may be expected to ensure this support is adequately guaranteed.

The above observations show that, in spite of the Clausewitzian element of the *Toetsingskader*, it will be rather difficult in the Dutch political practice to arrive at a clear transparent strategy. So, although there may be an ambition to bring ends, ways and means in line, in accordance with Clausewitz's instrumentalist vision, the question is justified whether this can be attained in practice.

Three practical examples of political-military decision making in the Netherlands

After the end of the Cold War the Netherlands participated in many peace missions, most of which were successful, especially the (more classic) peace keeping operations. In a few cases, such as the 2001 UN mission in Ethiopia and Eritrea and operation *Amber Fox* a year later in Macedonia, the Netherlands even acted as lead nation. In other operations this role was fulfilled in cooperation with other nations, such as the deployment of the combined German-Dutch army corps headquarters in Afghanistan.

As long as missions were relatively free of violence, there were hardly any political-military problems in the Netherlands. However, when a mission had a more enforcing character this changed. As soon as there was an uncooperative opposing force which had to be brought under control with military means, things regularly went wrong at that level. This is striking, as a choice was made for armed forces that could be deployed across the spectrum of violence.[37] So, precisely in missions that approached Clausewitz's ideas, the decisiveness of The Hague seemed to dwindle.

In order to examine this extraordinary phenomenon, below three cases will be considered that caused some turmoil in the Netherlands as well as abroad.[38] They are the decision in 1994 to send an air-mobile battalion to the Srebrenica enclave; the decision to support the American-British invasion of Iraq in 2003 *politically*, but not *militarily*; and the 2010 decision to terminate the mission in Afghanistan. The former two cases have been investigated in the mean time by several commissions, which in the case of Srebrenica eventually led to the fall of the Cabinet, while also Afghanistan recently caused a government crisis.

In the three cases it will be examined whether the Netherlands used its armed forces as a Clausewitzian *instrument*. In an ideal situation an integral strategic assessment would have to yield a balance between ends, ways and means. What must not be forgotten in all this is that the armed forces are a *means of power*, and that consequently there is an opponent who may decide to put up a resistance. All things considered, Clausewitz's historical study of the Prussian intervention against the Hollanders in 1787 mentioned above may be used as a guideline.

Bosnia (Srebrenica)

The disintegration of Yugoslavia from 1991 onwards coincided with the first phase of the transformation to fully professional armed forces described above. The Netherlands shared the collective international indignation about the violent events and from the first took part in the various missions in the former Yugoslavia. Initially, this participation was limited, as the combat units were still manned by conscripts. Even before the first infantry battalion of the Air Mobile Brigade was fully operational by the end of 1993, strong pressure from politicians and from within the organization itself began to build to send them out immediately. Even before it was clear exactly where and how the battalion was going to be deployed in Bosnia, an official offer was made by the Minister of Defence to the UN. This came at a time when it was also still unclear politically and militarily what precisely the concept of *safe area* entailed. In the end, the unit was only allowed the means for self-protection and a vague promise of air support in case of an emergency.

In January 1994 the first air mobile battalion relieved a Canadian unit in the Srebrenica enclave, and gradually from this moment onwards the mismatch between the intended political objective and the means employed to achieve it became painfully clear. In vain, the new Minister of Defence, Voorhoeve, tried to change this situation. A year later the supply lines of the, by now third, battalion were cut off, followed by General Mladic's offensive in July 1995, during which the entire enclave was overrun, and an estimated 8,000 Muslim men lost their lives.

After the fall of Srebrenica there were several official investigations and when the bulky NIOD (Nederlands Instituut voor Oorlogsdocumentatie – Netherlands War Documentation Institute) report was presented, then Prime Minister Kok realized that a sweeping political gesture had to be made and, taking full political responsibility, he resigned.

The subsequent parliamentary inquiry commission was extremely critical of the political-military decision making in 1993. There had never been an integral assessment of the strategic situation. On the contrary, the decision making was incremental and strongly dominated by idealistic motives, while the military possibilities to realize the humanitarian objectives were pushed into the background. The commission ruled that more attention should have been paid to the criticism of the military leadership of the effectiveness of the mission. Finally, the Cabinet lacked a clear international negotiation strategy prior to the sending out of Dutchbat.[39]

In short, ends, ways and means were never in line, as envisaged by Clausewitz. Apparently, there was insufficient strategic awareness in the UN as well as in the Netherlands. Though the Dutch military leadership did foresee the problems, the urge among politicians to intervene prevailed. The Bosnians had a clear appreciation of this mismatch between objective and means and, in response, went on the offensive.

Iraq 2003

In 2002 the Americans and the British conceived the plan to oust Saddam Hussein and to ask their allies to support this, preferably with military means. Partly due to many internal problems, the decision making in The Hague on this issue was fraught with difficulties. On 16 April 2002 the second Kok government tendered its resignation following the above-mentioned NIOD report on Srebrenica. The subsequent election period was an extremely turbulent one, mainly due to the murder of the populist candidate Pim Portuyn. The elections caused a political landslide, upon which on 22 July the first Balkenende government took office. Its ministers, especially those from Fortuyn's party, had no or only very little political experience, and on 16 October of the same year this Cabinet fell, and remained outgoing until 27 May 2003. On 22 January 2003 for the second time early elections were held, won by the social-democrat PvdA party. In this same period of internal political turmoil the Americans and the British decided to invade Iraq on 20 March 2003 asking The Hague on several occasions to support this war with military means.[40]

As was the case with Bosnia, the Balkenende government did not draw up a negotiating strategy for itself, either. The directly involved ministers were in favour of the American-British line and up to the elections of 22 January 2003 they were supported by a parliamentary majority. As a result, this line became leading, but in view of the societal and later parliamentary resistance against military participation in the war, it was not followed consistently. From the summer of 2002 onwards the Cabinet had been searching for a compromise in order to be able to take the extraordinary decision on 18 March 2003 to support the invasion of Iraq *politically* but not *militarily*.

The recently published definitive report of the investigative commission into the Iraq issue mostly looked into the international legal aspects. The Davids commission concluded that at the time UNSCR 1441 offered an insufficient mandate for military intervention, so the Balkenende government was wrong to appeal to that resolution in making its decision. It also listened selectively to its own intelligence services, which produced a much more nuanced picture on the Iraqi weapons of mass destruction than the American and British governments.[41]

Apart from this criticism of the reasons for and international legal aspects of the decision, Davids also made several interesting observations on the more Clausewitzian question about the relation between the intended political objective and the employment of the military means, such as it was. First of all, the commission pointed at the absence of a fundamental debate in Parliament, society and actually also Cabinet. There was a generally-felt revulsion against Saddam Hussein, but opinions differed as to whether this warranted a war and whether the Netherlands should be military involved in that war. As from the summer of 2002 the Cabinet followed the trans-Atlantic policy line and would have preferred to support the war militarily. Opinion polls, however, showed that the majority of the Dutch population rejected a military contribution and also in Parliament there was insufficient support for such a course of action. Doing nothing, however, was not an option either for the Cabinet and for that reason a compromise was struck between proponents and opponents.[42] The formula adopted, therefore, should be interpreted first and foremost as an intermediate solution for internal use.

Secondly, Davids observed that, through its diplomatic and military channels, the Dutch government had constantly been in the picture about the American and British plans, being well-informed about both their nature and objectives. Still, no national strategic analysis was made. The commission was of the opinion that the Cabinet should have discussed its own policy line sooner and better. Even when the decision was taken in March 2003, the question about the exact meaning of the phrase *political but not military support* was not properly discussed, creating all sorts of misunderstandings as a consequence.[43]

A similar criticism relates to the objectives of a possible war. The Cabinet knew of the plan for a regime change in Baghdad, but did not think this was legitimate from an international legal perspective. That is why The Hague remained fully focussed on the dismantling of the weapons of mass destruction. The difference between those two war aims was not elaborated on and that is why the commission saw certain 'insincerity' in the Cabinet decision.[44]

In short, the Davids commission sketched an impression of an outgoing, somewhat inexperienced, Cabinet which in turbulent times went out of its way to please Washington, based on only scant support in Parliament as well as among the population. The Cabinet decision led to much political conundrum and, incidentally, also to persistent rumours in the media about secret military support in the guise of Special Forces, F-16s and submarines. The latter were even reinforced by the fact that simultaneously Patriot units were sent to Turkey to help that country cope with any possible Scud attacks. This mission, however, took place within the framework of the NATO treaty, a nuance that was lost on the media. After its investigation the commission subsequently disposed of all rumours as fiction.[45]

Although the adopted formula of political but not military support must be interpreted mainly in the complicated *internal* situation context of those days, what matters for the present study is the external result. Naturally, the Americans and the British were pleased with the political support and even reckoned the Netherlands among the *coalition of the willing*, although this was emphatically not The Hague's intention. Clausewitz, however, would have asked himself what the impact of the decision had been in Baghdad. Was the Netherlands for or against a military intervention? In the language of *Vom Kriege*: was the war a real instrument for the Netherlands to attain the intended objective, or was it not? The adopted formula left this entirely in the dark, and so Saddam Hussein in any case never worried about this Dutch decision.

Afghanistan 2010

The Dutch contribution to the ISAF mission (International Security Assistance Force) in Afghanistan caused major differences of opinion between the various political parties, too. The problem was there from the very beginning, the moment that The Hague received the request from Brussels to provide a unit for the southern province of Uruzgan. This time the controversy mainly concerned the *nature* of the mission. Virtually every party wanted to support the

Afghans in the reconstruction of their country and that is why in 2004 the Netherlands sent a *Provincial Reconstruction Team* (PRT) to the northern province of Baghlan, where the situation was relatively quiet. One year later NATO requested the Netherlands to assume a similar task in the much more turbulent Uruzgan. In Parliament, however, opinions were greatly divided on this issue. The left SP and GroenLinks parties saw far too many similarities with *Enduring Freedom*, which they so detested. For the Left-Liberal D66 party the Netherlands was running the risk of biting off more than it could chew, just like in Srebrenica, and also the Social-Democrat PvdA, the largest opposition party of the moment, had serious doubts. As a result, the second Balkenende Cabinet, a coalition government of the Christian-Democrat CDA, the Liberal VVD, and the above-mentioned D66, had a hard time finding a parliamentary majority for a mission in Uruzgan. D66 and PvdA held a key position and in order to get these two parties into the fold, the *resources* for the mission were heavily beefed up, while the emphasis in the *tasking* came to lie on reconstruction. In the Parliamentary Letter pertaining to the mission the PRT was central in the Dutch task force, which for the remainder consisted of regular combat troops, F16s and helicopters. Reconstruction, therefore, was at the core of the mission. However, risks were expressly mentioned, though deemed acceptable by the Cabinet. Especially compared to Srebrenica the unit was now equipped 'robustly'. Furthermore, it was pointed out that carrying out offensive actions might be required for the security of the PRT and that they would fall within the mandate.[46] After seven months of to-ing and fro-ing the mission finally got the go-ahead in February 2006 from a vast parliamentary majority.[47]

On 14 March 2006 the advance party was despatched and by the summer there were about 1,400 Dutch servicemen in *Task Force Uruzgan*, a number that in the following years was upped several times to around 2,000. During the mission it soon emerged that the situation in the province was extremely unstable and required more fighting than reconstruction. Although in previous missions the Dutch had suffered casualties and fatalities, this time the number increased steadily, to the extent that, soon, the soldiers were speaking of a Counter Insurgency (COIN) operation, while in the media and the Parliament doubts about the decision to go in resurfaced.[48] In short, the *nature* of the mission was clearly different than expected, or better still, hoped, and the political parties were divided on the issue.

In 2008 the, by then fourth, Balkenende Cabinet, a coalition of CDA, PvdA and Christian CU, had to take a decision for the first time on an extension of the mission. There was much resistance in the Parliament, as NATO had not lived up to its promise to find a successor for the Netherlands. Besides, the personnel volume had steadily been increasing and some parties had great difficulties with the nature of the mission. This discussion, too, dragged on and on, and it was only after the promise of this being the last extension that the PvdA reluctantly agreed.[49]

By this time a great divide had erupted among the Dutch population between support for the mission and support for the service personnel sent out. While the former had been continuously eroding, the majority of the population had been standing consistently behind its soldiers.[50] Incidentally, also politicians who were against the mission, always made a similar distinction. From the perspective of Clausewitz's *wunderliche Dreifaltigkeit* such a strict separation of the mission and those who are executing it is an interesting new fact.

In the Dutch media, there was ample appreciation for the manner in which *Task Force Uruzgan* carried out the mission. Like the politicians, the media avoided the term COIN, preferring instead the special *Dutch approach*, or the so-called 3D-concept (Development, Diplomacy and Defence), or, better still, capturing the *hearts and minds* of the Afghan population. Such characterizations went down well, whereas references to fighting were not popular in the Netherlands.[51]

Bearing in mind this state of mind, it is not surprising that President Obama's fundamental change of strategy for Afghanistan in December 2009 was not properly registered as such in the Netherlands. The only thing that came through was that an extra 30,000 troops would be sent temporarily. The fact that the Americans, as they had done for Iraq, changed their objectives for Afghanistan, and they moved their modus operandi towards the Dutch approach, largely went unnoticed. What did filter through to the media were the signals from the armed forces to the effect that the servicemen and servicewomen in Afghanistan themselves were eager to stay and finish the job. Also, all signs of international pressure were given ample attention in the press and Parliament.

From the beginning of 2009 onwards the Balkenende Cabinet was divided over the question of a second extension of *Task Force Uruzgan*, whether or not in an adjusted form. The CDA and CU ministers were in favour of such an extension, but those of PvdA were dead against. The various debates in the Parliament did not produce a majority. The proponents pointed at the international position of the Netherlands, at what had already been achieved and the requests from the various capitals. The opponents referred to the insufficient societal and political support and earlier agreement to leave Uruzgan at the end of 2010. According to reports, the most concerned ministers met on fourteen occasions in an attempt to find a compromise. For a brief period, a way out seemed to present itself when the PvdA ministers seemed prepared to consider a *civilian* mission. All the while, pressure from abroad to reconsider the departure was increased. Relations within the Cabinet, however, were steadily deteriorating and in the night of 19 and 20 February 2010 the Cabinet fell. After four years *Task Force Uruzgan* terminated its mission in the summer of that year, having suffered 24 fatal casualties.

As was the case with Srebrenica, Afghanistan was conspicuously absent in the subsequent election campaign, which focused exclusively on internal political issues, completely ignoring the occasion for the elections. Seen from the perspective of the *wunderliche Dreifaltigkeit*, this is somewhat odd. In conformity with Clausewitz, the societal support for the mission was presented as a crucial element in the political debate, but the entire mission received only luke-warm interest from the population.

In this issue, too, what became apparent was a great difference of opinion between the various political parties. The majority wanted to do their thing for the reconstruction of a war-torn Afghanistan, which again testifies of the Dutch idealism. That this was a high-risk mission was recognized from the beginning, and that is why *Task Force Uruzgan* was equipped so robustly. This explains why there were no military operational problems when, against expectation, COIN proved to be the actual main task. However, opinions differed greatly in The Hague about this shift in the *nature* of the mission. So, although the armed forces showed that they were up to such complicated operations, there was only limited political support in the Netherlands. In short, although the objective was deemed to be important, it was not important enough to fight for.

Clausewitz would probably not have understood the decision to withdraw and he would have pointed out to the politicians that warfare is always a mutual trial of strength and that its course is unpredictable. As in 1787, the Dutch politicians should have departed from the worst case and attributed an independent role to the Taliban.

Clausewitz in Dutch political-military practice

The three cases show the feeling of discomfort that many Dutch politicians have with the armed forces as an instrument of power. As long as the objective of a mission can be called 'idealistic' there is broad support, which, however, quickly dissipates when it comes down to the exercise of power. In the case of Srebrenica The Hague was completely taken by surprise by the aggressive Bosnians, in Iraq a national military contribution was still unattainable and in Afghanistan there was disappointment about the violent reaction of the local parties.

What is characteristic is the lengthy and cumbersome negotiations between the Cabinet and the political parties. The *Toetsingskader* suggests a Clausewitzian method, but in the Dutch practice coalition politics take pride of place. What is at stake is not a transparent strategy for the military mission, but sufficient political support. In order to obtain, maintain or strengthen it, major concessions must be made by the Cabinet, and from this often later problems ensue.

On top of that, foreign policy in general and military missions in particular are choice issues for political parties to create a distinct profile for themselves. They often adopt a 'principled' stance, keep a close eye on the opinion of the electorate and even do not shy away from a government crisis. This makes finding sufficient political support a risky undertaking for the Cabinet.

So, while the military strategy is best served by a stable political system, the actual situation is totally different. In the period covered there were several regular and intermediate elections that each time led to different coalitions, and every change had great consequences for the military policy. The Netherlands does not differ greatly from other European countries in this respect, but as the country is an eager contributor to military missions abroad, there are more problems here.

Unfortunately, the three recent examples of strategic decision making are not showpieces of a clear grasp of Clausewitz. Although it is evident that the armed forces are an instrument in the hands of politics, as it is perceived in *Vom Kriege*, it is often forgotten that it is an instrument of *power*. As long as the factions in the mission area welcome the Dutch troops or at least tolerate them, there is usually little trouble. After all, in such a situation ends, ways and means of the mission are in line. Peace missions, as the term implies, have a strong idealistic ring to them and that is precisely the image many Dutch politicians embrace.

But when there are missions with a clearly military character, so with an opponent, who, in Clausewitz's terms, must be subjected to our will with violence, the essence of *Vom Kriege* often seems to be insufficiently grasped in the Netherlands. Clausewitz explains that it is not merely the intended objective and the available means that determine the course of the battle, but first and foremost the effort of the opponent. After all, it is a showdown of strength, in which the will to carry it to its utmost consequence is the determining factor. In the Dutch political debate there is relatively much attention for own objectives, but little for the state of mind of the opponent. That Bosnians, Saddam Hussein and the Taliban may violently *resist* our noble intentions comes as an unpleasant surprise. It seems as if many Dutch politicians, opinion makers, journalists and scientists ignore precisely this aspect of *Vom Kriege* and refuse to see that Clausewitz is mostly speaking about an instrument of power.[52]

Clausewitz in the Netherlands

In order to determine the extent of Clausewitz's following in the Netherlands, the present study has gone into both his influence on the military thinking and the political-military practice. It seems there is a discrepancy in the Netherlands between thinking and acting.

From the very first beginnings in 1832 *Vom Kriege* was adopted in the Dutch military thinking and it is clear that his work was also known among civilian authors. In military circles Clausewitz almost continually had a small number of interested readers, who made a thorough study of his work out of scientific curiosity. Apart from that, *Vom Kriege* was used by several military authors to shore up their own theories or ideas. As for topics, continuous shifts can be observed, linked to the (strategic) issues of the day that the military thinkers were grappling with. Incidentally, attention for his more historical studies has disappeared almost completely since 1945. All in all, Clausewitz is a milestone in Dutch military thinking.

Also Clausewitz's influence on the *Toetsingskader* is remarkable, and in that sense the ideas from *Vom Kriege* can even be traced back in present-day political-military policy. It is, however, in their translation into practice that a discrepancy emerges, with more the idealistic motives conflicting with Clausewitz's instrumentalist vision on the armed forces.

Almost 180 years ago an unknown military reviewer wrote in *De Militaire Spectator* that "V*om Kriege* is possibly the most scientific book on the art of war written so far, and it offers an insight into the *internal nature* of the art of war, free from scholastic forms and principles." These wise words are still true today. However, there is every reason in the Netherlands to demand more attention for that internal nature.

Original version *Hinterlassene Werke des Generals Carl von Clausewitz über Krieg und Kriegführung*		Dutch translation E.H. Brouwer	
1. Vom Kriege	1832	Over den Oorlog	1846
2. Vom Kriege	1833		
		Over den Oorlog	1846
3. Vom Kriege	1834		
4. Der Feldzug von 1796 in Italien	1833	De Veldtogt van 1796 in Italie	1841
5. Die Feldzüge von 1799 in Italien und in der Schweiz	1833	De Veldtogten van 1799 in Italie en Zwitserland; Eerste deel	1843
6. Die Feldzüge von 1799 in Italien und in der Schweiz	1834	De Veldtogten van 1799 in Italie en Zwitserland; Tweede deel	1845
7. Der Feldzug von 1812 in Russland; Der Feldzug von 1813 bis zum Waffenstillstand; Der Feldzug von 1814 in Frankreich.	1835	De Veldtogt in Rusland, in het jaar 1812	1839
		De Veldtogt van 1813 tot op den Wapenstilstand en de Veldtogt van 1814 in Frankrijk	1839
8. Der Feldzug von 1815 in Frankreich	1835	De Veldtogt van 1815 in Frankrijk	1839

9. Gustav Adolphs Feldzüge von 1630-1632; Historische Materialien zur Strategie; Turenne; Die Feldzüge Luxemburgs in Flandern von 1690-1694; Einige Bemerkungen zum spanischen Erbfolgekriege.	1837	*Not translated*	
10. Sobiesky; Krieg der Russen gegen die Türken von 1736-1739; Die Feldzüge Friedrich des Großen von 1741-1762; Der Feldzug des Herzogs von Braunschweig gegen die Holländer 1787; Übersicht des Krieges in der Vendée 1793.	1837	*Not translated*	

Notes:

[1] Carl von Clausewitz, Der Feldzug des Herzogs von Brauschweig gegen die Holländer 1787. Strategische Beleuchtung mehrerer Feldzüge usw., *Hinterlassene Werke des Generals Carl von Clausewitz über Krieg und Kriegführung*, Zehnter Band, Zweite Auflage, Berlin 1863.

[2] The history of this oldest still published periodical in the Netherlands was recently described in: B. Schoenmaker en F. Baudet, *Officieren aan het woord, De geschiedenis van de Militaire Spectator 1832-2007*. Amsterdam, Boom, 2007. On the occasion of *De Militaire Spectator*'s 175th anniversary all volumes were digitalized on DVD, of which the author has gratefully made use.

[3] *De Militaire Spectator*, 1833, p. 63.

[4] See, for instance, *Bedenkingen over enkele punten van het Krijgskundig Onderwijs, en voornamelijk der Krijgsgeschiedenis*. MS, 1838, p. 55-65.

[5] Von Clausewitz, *Over den oorlog*. 2 deelen. 1846. *De oorlogen van 1796, 1798-99, 1812, 1814 en 1815*. 5 deelen. 1839-1845. Nagelaten werk door den generaal Karel Von Clausewitz. Uit het Hoogduitsch vertaald door E. H. Brouwer, Bibliothekaris bij de Koninklijke Militaire Akademie, Breda

[6] J. L. Wagner, *Grondstellingen over den oorlog, vrij gevolgd naar het werk* Vom Kriege *van den generaal K. von Clausewitz*. Maastricht, Burij Boekverkooper 1853.

[7] Translation by J.J. van Kesteren. Only one copy has survived at the museum of the Royal Netherlands Army at Delft.

[8] For an overview of these books see: G. Teitler e.a., *Militaire Strategie*. Amsterdam, Mets en Schilt, 2002, p. 21.

[9] C.C. de Gelder, *Strategische Studiën*. MS, 1905, p. 614-625 and 751-755. MS, 1906, p. 712-722 and 781-789. MS, 1907, p. 745- 759. MS, 1909, p. 581-598.

[10] J.J.C.P. Wilson, *Algemeen overzicht van de ontwikkeling der strategische denkbeelden in den loop der jaren*. MS, 1931, p. 237-251, 298-308, 351-370 and 438-457.

[11] H. Oolgaardt, *Eene inleiding tot de studie der krijgsgeschiedenis*. MS, 1900, p. 298-319.

[12] See, for instance, H.L. van Oort, *Actieve of Passieve Verdediging?* MS, 1892, p. 91-106.

[13] See also, L.M.A. von Schmid, *Oude en nieuwe literatuur betreffende den veldtocht van 1787*. MS, 1896, p. 652-662.

[14] B. van Slobbe, *Hedendaagsche strategische inzichten*. MS, 1929, p. 106-112. See also note 8.

[15] M.R.H. Calmeijer, *De verdediging in het verleden en heden met een blik in de toekomst*. MS, 1935, p. 131-132, and M.R.H. Calmeijer, *De oorlog van morgen*. MS, 1935, p. 179-181 and 267-269.

[16] Anonymous, *De Geschiedenis van den Oorlog, deel I. De veldtocht in Polen*. MS, 1939, p. 404-408.

[17] H.W. Houweling and J.G. Siccama, *Studies of war*. Dordrecht, Nijhoff, 1988. P.M.E. Volten, *De wonderlijke Drievuldigheid*. Inaugural lecture, Utrecht, 1985.

[18] See, for instance, A.J. Leijen, *Politiek, Strijd, Oorlog*. Research paper, KMA FMB 94-24, Breda, 1994.

[19] F.C. Spits, *De Metamorfose van de Oorlog in de achttiende en negentiende Eeuw*. Assen. Van Gorcum, 1971.

[20] R. A. Sleeuw, *Inleiding tot de krijgskunde*. MS, 1955, p. 209-216 and 270-283. H. Oolgaardt, *Eene inleiding tot de studie der krijgsgeschiedenis*. MS, 1976, p. 290-302.

[21] J. M. den Hartog, *De strategische waarde van grote rivieren*. MS, 1962, p. 425-436.

[22] C. H. Gelok, *Guerrilla in Afghanistan*. MS, 1984, p. 300-311.

[23] See, for instance, E. Alterman, *The uses and abuses of Clausewitz*. MS, 1988, p. 416-424.

[24] See also, D. Jablonsky, *Strategy and the operational level of war*. MS, 1988, p. 88-94 and 132-140. J. Langhenkel, R. Veger and H. P. Ueberschaer, *FOFA, optie voor de Koninklijk Landmacht*. MS, 1986, p. 572-580.

[25] G. Mensink, *Leer der operatiën*. MS, 1963, p. 546-551. Reprinted in MS, 1988, p. 506-511.

[26] M. Schouten and R. J. van Vels, *Operatieve kunst en tactiek*. MS, 1988, p. 512-522 and 561-570.

[27] See, for instance, F. J. D. C. Egter van Wissekerke, *Is aanvallen de beste verdediging van de Europese centrale sector?* MS, 1989, p. 130-140 and 197-209. F.J.D.C. Egter van Wissekerke, *Opdrachtgerichte commandovoering als leidend doctrinebeginsel van de Koninklijke Landmacht*. MS, 1996, p. 481-597.

[28] B. A. C. Droste, *De Golfoorlog, Breekpunt in de traditionele oorlogvoering?* MS, 1991, p. 521-525.

[29] A.K. Bijkerk, *Desert Storm, Air campaign versus Saddams strategie*. MS, 1994, p. 155-166.

[30] See F. H. Meulman, *De aard van crises en conflicten, De rol van air-power in een verander(en)de wereld*. MS, 1994, p. 5-10. J. Hardenbol, *Doctrine-aspecten van vredesoperaties, De toepasbaarheid van grondbeginselen*. MS, 1995, p. 83-89.

[31] J. W. M. Schulten, *Militaire Doctrine, minder nieuw dan het er uitziet*. MS, 2000, p. 464-468.

[32] N. Pratt, *Small Wars, The Past as Prologue, an Alternative Vision of Future Conflict*. MS, 2002, p. 381-399. F.J.J. Princen and M.H. Wijnen, *Defensie in beweging, Constante verandering door veranderende constanten*. MS, 2004, p. 215-224.

[33] D. M. Drew, *The road to academic 'critical mass'*. MS, 2003, p. 272-276.

[34] F. H. Meulman, *De luchtoorlog in Korea en Vietnam, Overeenkomsten, verschillen en lessen*. MS, 2003, p. 288-300. F. Osinga, *'Airpower' in het postmoderne tijdperk, Revolutie in de lucht*. MS, 2003, p. 338-357.

[35] A.C. Tjepkema, *Boyd: jachtvlieger en homo universalis.* MS, 2004, p. 301-314.

[36] M.W.M. Kitzen, *Westerse militaire cultuur en counter-insurgency, Een tegenstrijdige realiteit.* MS, 2008, p. 123-134; B. W. Schuurman, *Clausewitz en de new wars denkers, Een nieuwe kijk op het trinitaire concept en de critici.* MS, 2010, p. 33-43.

[37] In this context van Wijk speaks of a paradox in teh Dutch policy; R. de Wijk, *Defensiebeleid in relatie tot veiligheidsbeleid,* in E. R. Muller (e.a.), Krijgsmacht, Studies over de organisatie en het optreden. Alphen aan de Rijn, Kluwer, 2004.

[38] A fourth case could be the NATO operation *Allied Force* in 1999, where the Royal Netherlands Air Force belonged to the top three as for the number of sorties, but in which Dutch politics were hardly involved according to Van Wijk, hiding behind NATO. See De Wijk, p. 163.

[39] Parlementaire Enquêtecommissie Srebrenica, *Missie zonder vrede.* Eindrapport. 's-Gravenhage, Sdu Uitgevers, 2003. p. 420-432.

[40] Rapport Commissie van onderzoek besluitvorming Irak. Amsterdam, Boom, 2010, p. 79-123.

[41] Ibid., Conclusies nr. 8, 18, 20, 29 en 30, p. 425-427.

[42] Ibid., Conclusies nr. 2, 3, 4, 9, 31 en 43, p. 425-429.

[43] Ibid., Conclusies nr. 5, 6, 11 and 34, p. 425-428.

[44] Ibid., Conclusie nr. 7, p. 425.

[45] Ibid., Conclusies nr. 11, 36, 38, 39 and 45, p. 426-429.

[46] Tweede Kamer der Staten-Generaal, 27925, *Bestrijding internationaal terrorisme,* nr. 193, Brief van de ministers van Buitenlandse Zaken, van Defensie en voor Ontwikkelingssamenwerking, 22 december 2005.

[47] R. de Wijk, *Nederland en de NAVO-operatie in Afghanistan, Politieke besluitvorming en militaire uitvoering.* In B. Bomert e.a. (red), Jaarboek Vrede en Veiligheid 2006. Amsterdam, Rozenberg Publishers, 2006. B. Bomert, *Staten Generaal, 1 november 2005 - 31 januari 2006.* In Vrede en Veiligheid, Tijdschrift voor internationale vraagstukken, Jaargang 35 nummer 1, 2006, p. 72-74.

[48] R. de Wijk, *Nederland en de NAVO-operatie in Afghanistan,* p. 9-12. B. Bomert, *Staten Generaal, 1 mei 2006 – 31 oktober 2006.* In Vrede en Veiligheid, Tijdschrift voor internationale vraagstukken, Jaargang 35 nummer 4, 2006, p. 492-494.

[49] B. Bomert, *Nederlands defensiebeleid; meer met minder.* In B. Bomert e.a. (red), Jaarboek Vrede en Veiligheid 2008. Amsterdam, Rozenberg Publishers, 2008, p. 211-214.

[50] See P. Everts, *De Nederlandse publieke opinie over oorlog en vrede.* In Vrede en Veiligheid, Tijdschrift voor internationale vraagstukken, Jaargang 39 nummer 1-2, 2010, p. 105-108.

[51] See also G.R. Dimitriu and Dr. B. A. De Graaf, *The Dutch COIN approach: Three years in Uruzgan, 2006-2009.* In: Small Wars & Insurgencies, Volume 21, Issue 3, p. 429-458.

[52] An contemporary exception: H. Achterhuis, *Met alle geweld, Een filosofische zoektocht.* Rotterdam, Lemniscaat, 2008.

CLAUSEWITZ AND NORWAY – STARING AT A DISTANT SUN

Harald Høiback

At first glance you wouldn't think Norwegians and Clausewitz had much in common. Clausewitz spent his whole life in the service of Mars while modern Norway has apparently pursued peace at all cost. Norway is in fact one of the very few countries in the world to have gained independence without spilling a drop of blood. In 1905 Norway divorced Sweden under dramatic circumstances, but not a shot was fired in anger. Consequently, while other twentieth-century "newcomers", such as Finland and Poland, have generals as their founding fathers, in the shape of Carl Gustav Mannerheim and Jósef Pilsudski, the Norwegians have a road maintenance worker and a ship owner as their national father and grandfather, not to mention a range of polar explorers of course. Indeed, you would be hard pressed to find even a statue of a Norwegian general. They exist, but you have to know where to look. Ironically, the only military man on horseback in a public square in Norway is one of Napoleon's most dubious marshals, Jean-Baptiste Bernadotte who became king of Sweden and Norway in 1818.

To top it all, Norway's most renowned international brand is of course the Nobel Peace Prize. Even if the Prize for 2009 went to the Commander-in-Chief of a force in the middle of two wars, it is hard to imagine a candidacy for Clausewitz getting very far. Norway and Clausewitz are poles apart, apparently.

The aim of this essay is threefold. First we will map out Clausewitz's *Wirkungsgeschichte* in Norway. To what extent have the Prussian's ideas actually influenced the Norwegian discourse about war and peace? This question could of course be answered by an extensive research project, but the method here is simply to register Clausewitz's appearances in print. Secondly, we shall look at some important crossroads in Norwegian history in the light of *Vom Kriege*. In my opinion, central elements of Clausewitz's theories are vindicated by actual events in Norwegian history. Finally, we look at Clausewitz's impact on strategic thinking in contemporary Norway. Is the Old Prussian still relevant? Or more to the point, does Clausewitz still have important things to say to people willing to listen?

Clausewitz's Norwegian *Wirkungsgeschichte*

"The ideas of Clausewitz run like a subterranean river through all of modern military thought", according to Christopher Bassford.[1] To the extent this is so, it can be extremely difficult to demonstrate exactly where and how Clausewitz influenced Norwegian strategic thinking. And if he is everywhere, however veiled, it would be hard to pinpoint his philosophical bequest. Moreover, military writers have usually not operated with notes and bibliographies, so in both official manuals and in more private utterances you have as a rule to guess which sources the writer bases the arguments on. Our measuring method will thus be judged rather crude. In order to gauge Clausewitz's impact we will merely look for his name. To say something more substantial about his actual influence on Norwegian military discourse, directly and indirectly, is an order too tall for this particular undertaking.

For a start, Clausewitz's is by no means a household name to Norwegians at large. Certainly, you encounter it here and there, but rarely as more than a rather facile exercise in namedropping. For instance, an Internet search of more than 70 Norwegian papers and magazines published in 2009 retrieved only 7 articles with the term "Clausewitz". Britney Spears was mentioned in 537 and Jomini in 0, just for comparison.

On War has never been translated and published in Norway, except from a very abridged version issued in 1972, which has been out of print for decades.[2] To the best of my knowledge there has never been a book published about Clausewitz in Norwegian either, just a few research papers.[3] Not even large authoritative anthologies about "great thinkers", such as for instance the three-volume *Vestens tenkere* [*Western Thinkers*] from 1993, which covers almost 100 names spanning from Homer to Jean Baudrillard, have anything on Clausewitz. Contemporaries like Jefferson, Kant, Burke, Marquis de Sade, Blake, Goethe, Schelling and Hegel have all their own essays, but not Clausewitz.

There are some rare exceptions to Clausewitz's non-existence in a broader Norwegian discourse, as for instance the book *Myten og den irrasjonelle fornuft* [*Myth and the irrational reason*] by the poet Stein Mehren, Jan Ketil Arnulf's *Heltens ansikter: allmakt og heroisme* [*The face of the hero: Omnipotence and heroism*], and even in the song "Generalene" by Odd Børretzen. But the main conclusion remains: to the general public in Norway, Clausewitz is still a rather distant luminary whose work is read only by intellectual war buffs.

One of very few groups outside the military realm in Norway to have dealt with Clausewitz are probably the political radicals. In the socialists' own encyclopaedia, *PaxLeksikon* from 1979, praise of Clausewitz is unconditional: "Clausewitz [is] the most significant military theorist ever to have lived".[4] What's more, even a socialist could learn a lot from him, despite the awkward irony:

Clausewitz has long enjoyed very high status in socialistic thinking; even if it can be hard to praise a noble officer, particularly a Prussian, in circles of more or less true believers. Lenin appreciated Clausewitz immensely. And he is also the only thinker who gets the honour of being cited in the section about war and peace in "Quotations from Chairman Mao Tse-tung".[5]

That said, however, a cursory reading of a journal that certainly took both Lenin and Mao seriously, i.e. *Røde Fane* [*Red banner*], a periodical for communistic theory and debate, reveals very few references to Clausewitz. During the seventies and early eighties, when the magazine wrote extensively about wars of independence and the lurking danger of a third world war, you find conspicuously few leads to the allegedly greatest military thinker ever – but there are some:

The only scientific tenet about war is the one which originally made by the bourgeois philosopher of war Clausewitz: 'War is the continuation of politics by other means' [...] Lenin adopted and developed the tenet further based on the most advanced thinking in our time, the historical and dialectical materialism, the ideas about class struggle and history.[6]

The potted version of this became: "Lenin emphasised that politics and war are two sides of the same coin. War is politics by other means."[7] In other words, Clausewitz's ideas did play a part in the radicals' discussion, but his name was by no means ubiquitous.

Importantly, our interpretation of Clausewitz's position in strategic and military debates in Norway, especially outside the inner circle of military scholars, does not necessarily say very much about Clausewitz *compared* to other military thinkers. But it can tell us volumes about Norwegians' general lack of martial interest. If you don't bother about military thinking in general, Clausewitz would not be a central figure under any circumstances.

The situation is, of course, a bit different in the military discourse in Norway, but even there, it seems, Clausewitz is not as central as we tend to believe. The adage that Clausewitz is often quoted, but rarely read or understood, is not entirely correct in the Norwegian case. Not because he is widely read, but because he is quoted with some frequency. If you look through the major Norwegian military periodical *Norsk Militært Tidsskrift* (NMT), founded in the fateful year, for friends of Clausewitz, of 1831, you will find sporadic but far from excessive mentions of Clausewitz here and there, and he is hardly ever the main topic of the articles.[8]

The first article I found in the NMT mentioning Clausewitz was from 1840 and called "Om Krigskunst" [On Art of War]. Here Clausewitz is briefly quoted, but he is not given much room to roam: "War is, as Clausewitz states in his posthumous works, *On War*, more a mean for defense than for conquest."[9]

Fifteen years later there is a squabble between Lieutenant of the Cavalry Hagemann Brandt and Major General Jacob Gerhard Meydell about the merits of Heinrich Dietrich von Bülow. Cavallery Lieutenant Brandt instigated the row in 1855 by publishing a review of the book *Militärische und vermischte Schriften von Heinrich Dietrich von Bülow in einer Auswahl, Leipzig 1853*, to which Meydell responded. Brandt, he complained, had not given Bülow the credit he deserved. What is interesting here, however, is that Clausewitz, Bülow's chief assassin seen with our generation's eyes, plays no part in the discussion. People like Berenhorst, Tempelhof, Archduke Charles and Jomini are there in abundance, but not Clausewitz. Instead, it is Jomini who plays the part of the *enfant terrible* and Bülow's hardest, and for Meydell rather unfair, critic: "Jomini's critic of Bülow's theories lacks any sense of logic and is mostly unsubstantiated."[10] If Norwegian military thinkers had seen Clausewitz as an important thinker in the 1850s he should probably have been enlisted here. In his rebuttal to Meydell, Brandt leaves no doubt as to who the top dog was, and it was certainly not Clausewitz: "I already knew that in this country there still exist militaries that do not accept any suggestion about errors made by Bülow, and who regard such talk as almost blasphemy against this 'military science's Holy Spirit'."[11] If you encounter such snappy remarks today they are usually directed against the hero of this particular story, Clausewitz.

Meydell's own book, his 1837 *Lærebok i Krigskunsten* [*Textbook on the Art of War*], reinforces the impression of Bülow's legacy dominating Norwegian military thinking for decades after Clausewitz's "Bemerkung über die reine und angewandte Strategie des Herrn von Bülow," in *Neue Bellona* in 1805.

To pick just a few other places where today you would expect to find Clausewitz, but find only silence: In 1890 there was an article about Napoleon's genius for war, whose main argument was that not even Napoleon was a born leader. He had to go through both a practical and theoretical education to become "the Great Napoleon". The article ends with a discussion about the leap from *Wissen* to *Können*, and the even longer leap from *Nichtwissen* to *Können*.[12] Read with our "post-Howard-and-Paret's-translation-eyes" it is amazing anyone could write an article like that without even a tipping of the hat in Clausewitz's direction.

In 1908 Captain Sinding-Larsen published an article called "Krigen som regnestykke" ["The war as calculation"] where he wrote "The war is not a calculation. It is not numbers which decide the outcome, it is the moral strength. In that must a small nation trust."[13] Today I think it would be rather hard not to mention Clausewitz in such a discussion. Indeed, it would take an act of will not to do so. Not so in 1908, apparently. However, around the turn of the century something was about to happen in this regard.

In 1896 Lieutenant Gudmund Schnitler published an essay in *Norsk Militært Tidsskrift* called "Moltke, hans samlede skrifter og erindringer om ham" ["Moltke – his collected works and recollection of him"]. The essay is 15 pages long, but Clausewitz is noticeably absent.[14] However, in 1911 there is a short review of less than two pages of Moltke's *Kriegslehren*. It is signed "G.S.", which presumably is the very same Gudmund Schnitler. Now, Clausewitz has become the bedrock of Moltke's ideas: "Through a laborious study, primarily of Frederick the Great's and Napoleon's campaigns, Clausewitz's works, through ample experience and indefatigable work, Moltke has been among those who have proved the justification of the maxim: 'Genius is diligence' – the boundless ability to will."[15]

What had happened in between was that Schnitler had been in France and Germany from 1898 to 1900, conducting military historical research.[16] To what extent he actually met Clausewitz's ideas there I am in no position to tell. However, the thought is suggestive. Norwegian officers obviously read foreign military journals and Clausewitz's name was being increasingly invoked following Moltke's stunning victories, but Schnitler's personal encounter with the European debate may have been decisive.

The idea that Schnitler was in a process of granting Clausewitz a unique position among military thinkers is also vindicated by reading two editions of

Schnitler's book *Strategi*. The book was published as a draft in 1911 and then again in 1914. In the first edition Schnitler listed more than a dozen military authors, including Clausewitz, but without highlighting Clausewitz in any way. When we read the same passage in the 1914 edition, we recognize many of the names, but this time Clausewitz is given special treatment: "Clausewitz is perhaps the most influential military author. He succeeded in his wish to write a book that 'would not be forgotten after two or three years'."[17]

Given that Schnitler's ruled supreme as a military textbook in Norway until the Second World War, and that he personally lectured at the Staff College from 1903 to 1925, his endorsement of Clausewitz was in a sense the formal confirmation of Clausewitz's importance. Consequently, from the interwar years and beyond Clausewitz is, at least apparently, the philosophical kingpin of military thinking in Norway. When Norwegians take the time to write about military questions, you may therefore expect to find Clausewitz, even though he sometimes sparkles more by his absence than by his presence.[18] Indeed, Norwegian military authors, to the extent that they actually exist, may give the impression that Clausewitz is the only military thinker worth considering. To illustrate this desensitizing effect of the "Clausewitz-myopia" I will use the fate of his *bête noir*, Antoine de Jomini.

In 1998 Colonel Sverre Diesen issued a book called *Military Strategy*.[19] According to the publisher, this was the first Norwegian book about military strategy in 80 years. Its predecessor we have already discussed, i.e. Major Gudmund Schnitler's *Strategy* from 1914. In fact, even Schnitler made history. In a review of his book, it was claimed to be the first about strategy ever written in Norwegian.[20] If we compare Schnitler's and Diesen's treatments of Jomini we find, in my opinion, a rather discouraging tendency. Diesen mentions Jomini only once, and then in a very prejudiced and stereotypical way: "If we go back to Clausewitz, however, we find several of his contemporaries, among them the Swiss [military authority] Henri Jomini and the German [soldier] Heinrich von Bülow, claiming on the basis of the current faith in rationality to see nearly mathematical relations in strategy, with formulas for recommended angles between the base and lines of operations etc."[21]

Evidently, Jomini would hardly have accepted this as a fair description of his ideas, or at least not of his mature opinions. This was rather Clausewitz's impression of the man, but Jomini continued to publish long after Clausewitz's death. True, Jomini was a firm believer in rules for action and theory of war, but it was also "true that theories cannot teach men with mathematical precision what they should do in every possible case."[22]

Schnitler on the other hand was careful not to lump Jomini and Bülow together like his modern colleague does. He did not treat all thinkers except Clausewitz *en bloc*: "Others have opposed Bülow's opinions. Particularly the famous military author Jomini has with a great deal of pungency pointed out the erroneous overrating of outer lines. [Jomini] did not underestimate the mental spiral springs, morale and the power of personality."[23] Indeed, Schnitler's general description of Jomini is rather sympathetic:

Jomini - Ney's competent chief of staff and the famous military author - developed an artificial system for the art of war with meticulous and lined up axioms for guidance. In their solid and lucid form his works have still something extremely attractive to them. They appealed especially to the French spirit, which by its nature sharply distinguishes logically between the concepts.[24]

I think you would have to search long and hard to find anything resembling such effusive praise of Jomini in Norwegian today.

To conclude this section on Clausewitz's Norwegian Wirkungsgeschichte: around the Great War, defence intellectuals – at least those who left a visible historical trace – installed Clausewitz as the great authority of the philosophy of war. However, the Clausewitz legacy seems also to be of a rather sinister kind. On the one hand his positive influence has certainly not triggered a landslide of books and treatises about military strategy. The entire collection of published books, if we are a bit stingy, amounts to only two volumes in the last century. On the other hand, his "negative" influence has, unfortunately, been considerable. Clausewitz, through no fault of his own, has cast a long, dark shadow across a whole field of systematic thinking. Clausewitz was undoubtedly a great military thinker, possibly the greatest, but he is not the only one, and certainly not the latest.

Bernard Brodie, in a legendary remark, once said of Clausewitz's *On War*: "His is not simply the greatest but the only truly great book on war."[25] In Norway, there is an impending danger that "truly great" could disappear from the proclamation.

Intermezzo: Through Clausewitz's monocle

So far we have tried, in an admittedly rather offhanded way, to record and measure Clausewitz's early impact on Norwegian military discourse. Our conclusion was simple: he hasn't really stimulated learned strategic discussions in Norway, though he has monopolized the few that nonetheless took place. In this section we leave the question of Clausewitz's influence on Norwegian military thinking and deeds, and look at two seminal events in Norwegian history through the Clausewitzian monocle with a view to seeing whether Clausewitz can shed some new light on some defining moments in Norway's history.

In the last century Norway was on the brink of war on two occasions, in 1905 and 1940. On the first occasion the adversary was known and war avoided; in 1940, on the other hand, it came as a bolt out of the blue. Can Clausewitz make us see these affairs in a different light?

At the outset, it is important to remind ourselves that the idea of an imminent war between Sweden and Norway in 1905 is basically a myth.[26] Neither the Swedish nor the Norwegian government wanted war, and people on either sides of the border worked frantically for peace.[27] The question was rather whether Norway should make concessions on its way out of the Union, particularly regarding the Sweden's insistence that Norway demolish fortresses on the border. Eventually, the Norwegian Government agreed to demolish some of the fortresses, but was allowed to keep the ones with historical interest.

This compromise was like a red rag to military diehards. There were, in fact, officers around with a deep longing for war and saw this as a golden opportunity. To Colonel Henrik Angell, for instance, war was not as a curse, but a blessing: "to bleed for your country is an honour, a precious privilege."[28] He was not a little disappointed with the attitude of the "spineless" Norwegian government: "My people are weak, the mark of dependency is on their forehead."[29] We can continue down a similar road:

"I believe and confess that a people can value nothing more highly than the dignity and liberty of its existence. That it must defend these to the last drop of its blood. That there is no higher duty to fulfil, no higher law to obey. That the shameful blot of cowardly submission can never be erased. That this drop of poison in the blood of the nation is passed on to posterity, crippling and eroding the strength of future generations. [...] That a people courageously struggling for liberty is invincible. That even the destruction of liberty after a bloody and honourable struggle assures the people's rebirth. It is the seed of life, which one day will bring forth a new, securely rooted tree."[30]

To most readers of this essay, the passage above will be recognizable. It is not Angell speaking here, but Clausewitz. A tempting 'what if' is thus what would Clausewitz have done, or said, if he had been in Norway in 1905? Would he have chimed in with "the Angells" or hushed them down?

As is common with Clausewitz, protagonists on either side of a discussion can find ammunition in *On War* to hammer each other with; so even here. The quote indicates what Norway should have done: stand firm, make no concessions, and fight its way out of the union if need be. On the other hand, however, statements such as "there is a point beyond which persistence becomes desperate folly, and can therefore never be condoned"[31] point in the opposite direction.

That Norway actually achieved independence without the use of arms in 1905 indicates that there were other concerns than policy that drove Angell. For Angell, war with Sweden was presumably a golden opportunity to practice his profession, even if it was totally unnecessary to reach the desired political goal. Our temporary conclusion is thus that Clausewitz would have asked Angell to keep quiet and given him a lecture: "War is no pastime; it is no mere joy in daring and winning, no place for irresponsible enthusiasts. It is a serious means to a serious end."[32]

However, if we jump 35 years ahead and witness the incomprehensible degree of Norwegian gullibility and fumbling on the eve of war in 1940, we may perhaps have cause to reconsider. If Norway had won independence in 1905 with the use of arms, not just pens and diplomacy, the country would presumably have been differently disposed to defend its hard-earned independence. Germany could consequently not have envisaged a cakewalk up north, which was after all the expectation on which the whole operation was based.

Perhaps the rather congenial split of 1905 had left a "drop of poison in the blood of the nation" after all? Perhaps the Norwegians had indeed missed a golden opportunity to invest in the crucial patriotic spirit that can only be instigated by war? Indeed, once that spirit is kindled, it can, according to Clausewitz, serve the nation for generations:

"In short, the seed will grow only in the soil of constant activity and exertion, warmed by the sun of victory. Once it has grown into a strong tree, it will survive the wildest storms of misfortune and defeat, and even the indolent inertia of peace, at least for a while. Thus, this spirit can be *created* only in war and by great generals, though admittedly it may endure, for several generations at least, even under generals of average ability and through long periods of peace."[33]

It could be tempting to make a comparison with Finland, which fought a fierce civil war in conjunction with their separation from Russia in 1918, and which 20 years later stunned the world by almost holding the gargantuan Red Army to a draw. There are of course other explanations for this, but it is nonetheless thought provoking that Norwegians, who virtually live on an impregnable rock in the ocean, fell so easily to the conqueror, while Finland, sharing a long border with their enemy, stopped him in his tracks.

So, if we asked Clausewitz, whether he would have preferred a war in 1905 after all, in order to prepare the young Norwegian government for a stormy night in 1940, what would he have said? Now we have of course ventured rather far from what real "Clausewitzologs" deal with, but I think the answer would have been no. Clausewitz would not have opted for a war in 1905.

Presumably it is with war as with most other human activities, the best way to learn is by actually doing it. The best way to prepare for future wars is thus to fight. However, this does not mean that Clausewitz would have preferred to start a war in order to ignite the proper spirit and to train properly. The crucial point of war is to change the enemy, not ourselves: "*War is thus an act of force to compel our enemy to do our will.*"[34] War can never be treated as a live simulator or spectacular training ground. War is too serious and too unpredictable for that. War's *wunderliche Dreifaltigkeit* makes it utterly unwise to unleash a war simply to prepare for the next.

As I read Clausewitz, at least, the best thing to do is thus to avoid war altogether, as one did in 1905. And the best way to do that is to prepare thoroughly for it.

If actual warfare is out of the question the next best way to learn the art of war is to learn it from history. However, even if the past is far less uncertain and strenuous than battle, it offers no shortcuts:

"Anyone who feels the urge to undertake such a task [i.e. to teach the art of war entirely by historical examples] must dedicate himself for his labours as he would prepare for pilgrimage to distant lands. He must spare no time or effort, fear no earthly power or rank, and rise above his own vanity or false modesty in order to tell, in accordance with the expression of the *Code Napoleón, the truth, the whole truth, and nothing but the truth.*"[35]

It was here the Norwegians failed so fatally, especially the politicians. After 1905 they lacked the stamina or the honesty to learn from the past even if the experience of 1914-18 should have told them otherwise. The Norwegians should not therefore have provoked a war in 1905 in order to educate themselves, but they should have educated themselves in order not to provoke, however inadvertently, the war that came in 1940. All the major powers could, *unilaterally* speaking, have pulverized the Norwegian armed forces, but the race to the north cannot be seen in isolation. All major powers had bigger bones to pick than Norway, so a bit more strategic dexterity, on top of the already unfriendly Norwegian terrain, would probably have persuaded Hitler to look another way, at least for the time being.

After the war the Norwegian Commander-in-Chief General Otto Ruge wrote a book about the campaign. At the end of the book he says something particularly interesting in this regard. If he were given responsibility for teaching young officers again, he would concentrate even more on history.[36] The reason was simple: "Most people, even us military, are too inclined to accept the situation as it is at the moment, thinking it will be the situation for ever, and not remember that life goes on and the situation tomorrow will always be different from the one today, and there is therefore no reason to loose faith, even after a bad start. That is what we learn from history."[37]

The Norwegian armed forces' main problem was not their lack of training, lack of air defence capability or lack of anti-tank guns, but lack of historical knowledge and awareness. The crucial problem for the Norwegian Labour government was that it knew nothing about strategy and was proud of it. The foreign minister's iconoclastic statement that if you want peace you have to prepare for peace, became a classic for all the wrong reasons.[38] What brought war to Norway in April 1940 was therefore not lack of martial skills and military resources, but lack of strategic understanding.

So would modern Norwegian history have looked any different if Norwegian decision makers had known more history, and above all, known their Clausewitz? If they had managed to learn from books in peace what they were forced to learn through violence in war? I am inclined to think so, but realise that many of my fellow countrymen would only roll their eyes and shake their head had they heard me.

At least Clausewitz was proven right in his belief that the spirit created in war may last for several generations – even through bumpy times of peace. After the war, and in the shadow of the new threat from the East, Norway became a steadfast member of NATO, although not the most confrontational. Ever since 1945, Norway has kept soldiers abroad, either under the auspices of UN or NATO, and even under that, for Norwegian eyes, strange community called the EU.

The 1940 attack had finally taught Norwegians that if you want peace, you need to prepare for war. They also learned the value of honing the spirit of war, and of showing future generations that "our generation did its utmost to defend freedom."[39] General Ruge seemed to echo Angell when he said on April 10, 1940 that Norway had to continue the war, at least for the sake of national self-esteem.[40] The big difference was that Ruge pleaded for war *after* the attack, while Angell pleaded for war as a test of the nation and professional escapade.

Clausewitz and Norway in the 21st Century

So far we have strolled along a rather long and winding road to reach the main questions of this text: what about Clausewitz and Norway today? Do his ideas have any impact on Norwegian military discourse today, and in what way? What about the educational institutions? To what extent do they use *On War* or other texts by Clausewitz? And finally, does he get the attention he deserves? Is the Old Prussian still relevant for a small peace-loving country on the fringes of the civilized world?

Again, answering these questions in a properly academic way is outside the scope of this essay, and again I have to go for the next best thing. I shall measure Clausewitz's impact by checking his presence in military articles and in the curriculum of the military academies. I will also briefly check to what extent his name echoes in the corridors of the strategic decision makers in Norway.

As stated in the introduction, a very abridged version of *On War* was translated and published in Norway in 1972, i.e. in the middle of the Cold War. Worthy of note, this time it was not military men who brought Clausewitz to public attention, but political scientists. For most military minds it was hard to see how war could be the continuation of anything by other means, if those means included thermonuclear annihilation. However, Jens A. Christophersen, a political scientist and the editor of *On War,* saw matters differently: Here we are witnessing something modern strategy calls *deterrence.* Where war in a way ceases to be war, and where policy governs alone. And, we may add, the most important, and even the finest function weapons can have. Logically speaking we are here witnessing a continuation of one of Clausewitz's most essential thoughts, perhaps the most essential of his whole authorship.[41] Consequently, nuclear weapons had not made Clausewitz irrelevant, on the contrary.

We have to wait until after the favourable ending of the Cold War to find traces of military awareness of Clausewitz's continuing relevance. Not surprisingly perhaps, in the 1990s there was a small "surge" of Clausewitz-centred articles in *Norsk Militært Tidsskrift.* It could have been tempting to call this a Clausewitz renaissance, but that would have implied a former golden age of Clausewitz infatuation, of which I have found no evidence.

In the 1990s NMT printed four articles with headings mentioning Clausewitz.[42] We will take a closer look at the first one, Major General Odd Vincent Skjøstad's "Med Clausewitz inn i framtid, drøfting av fredskapende operasjoner" [Into the Future with Clausewitz. A Discussion of Peace Operations], because it encapsulates the main reasons why Norwegian military intellectuals should (re-)invigorate Clausewitz.

First and foremost, Skjøstad states that the dissolution of the Soviet Union had not yet made the world a more peaceful place.[43] This is the key to all that follows in the article. During the Cold War, Norwegians did not have to think strategically, to put it bluntly. By joining NATO in 1949, Norway had, in effect, become an appendix to greater nations' strategic considerations. During the Second World War, Norway had also disbanded its General Staff and with it much of the scholarly and reflective traditions that went with that institution. After 1945, to be an officer thus became a job for doers, not for thinkers. Now, however, after 1989, things were different. Even Norwegians had to (re-)learn how to think strategically: "It is only since the end of the Cold War the situation has changed. Today many again talk openly about war to reach political goals - we call it peace operations."[44] For 40 years Norwegians had prepared for the possibility of war coming to them, now they had to decide whether they wanted to join wars far from home: "Under what circumstances can we envisage Norway waging war, and what kind of considerations would we have to take into account in order to make such a consideration productive?"[45] In other words, strategy had again entered the scene.

Skjøstad's article also indicates how even in Norway the rediscovery of Clausewitz was inspired by the preceding American awakening. Another of the article's main messages is thus a Norwegian version of something Colin Powell discovered after the Vietnam War: "Clausewitz's greatest lesson for my profession was that the soldier, for all his patriotism, valor, and skill, forms just one leg in a triad. Without all three legs engaged, the military, the government, and the people, the enterprise cannot stand."[46] Clausewitz's trinity, taken the American Way, became even the Norwegian way to digest his theories: "Clausewitz established, at the outset of the last century, that war takes place between politics, armed forces and the will of the people. This view on war as a system applies in full even today."[47] Moreover, when Norwegians scrutinize other aspects of Clausewitz's heritage, as for instance the concept of *centre of gravity*, it is usually done in the light of a preceding American debate: "As we know, when there is debate in the USA it has repercussions for us all."[48]

Even in the first decade of the 21st century we encounter sporadic references to Clausewitz in *Norsk Militært Tidsskrift*, but he is rarely the main topic of discussion anymore.

The next question we posed was to what extent is he used to educate future officers in Norway today. In the following we will look briefly into that.

To start with, although Clausewitz has been on the shelf of the library of the Military Academy at least since 1863[49], that does not really say much about how he was used or read. Again, this is a question I have to leave to people better equipped in terms of time and expertise than myself. What I can do is to gauge the current state of affairs.

An informal survey of the three military academies in Norway reveals that Clausewitz's spirit is still around, but he is not a particularly towering figure. At the Naval Academy the cadets do not read Clausewitz as part of their curriculum at all, but they do read a few articles about him. At the Air Force Academy the cadets read Clausewitz, but only chapter 1 of Book 1, "What is War?", in addition to secondary literature. At the Army's Military Academy the cadets also read parts of Book 8, besides Book 1. The Army's cadets are also confronted with the content of Book 2 of *On War* "On the Theory of War". That the Army places Clausewitz higher than the Navy is presumably not surprising, given his rather landlocked perspective. This is also important to have in mind when measuring Clausewitz's impact on Norwegian military discourse as a whole. Norway is by nature, so to speak, a seafaring nation, and Clausewitz has no nautical aura.

At the Staff College, which is joint in Norway, Clausewitz is present in the sense of both he and Jomini being introduced from the lecturers, but neither is compulsory reading.[50] Nearly one in four Master's theses submitted to the Norwegian Defence University College from 2007 to 2009, mention Clausewitz in one way or another.[51] This rate of reference shows that Clausewitz is a central thinker, but it is presumably not excessive in any way. I would guess, without being in position to know for sure, that both Plato and Kant score similar, perhaps even higher, results in Master's theses in philosophy departments.

What is common to all my respondents at the academies, however, is the desire to have more time for Clausewitz. A cynic would of course say that all teachers would say that. *If* we only had more time we could cater to any hobbyhorse you may think of. Consequently, the fact that scholars want more Clausewitz on the reading lists is not very remarkable. Nonetheless, the reasons they give for wanting more Clausewitz are worth considering further.

The main argument to keep on exposing future officers to Clausewitz is the enduring need to thoroughly understand the philosophy and nature of war and armed conflict. Peace operations and wars of choice emphasise the military profession's political, ethical and cultural aspects, something a study of Clausewitz could help to provide. Some would of course maintain that Clausewitz said very little about politics, ethics and culture, and that if you want that kind of stuff you should go elsewhere. However, Clausewitz's contribution lies above such divisions. He provides instead a timeless philosophical underpinning of strategic thinking on which more multifarious, ephemeral or popular concepts can rest. In other words, Clausewitz can be a guide for the perplexed and for all those who want a deeper understanding of strategy.

Clausewitz's thought can also serve as a badly needed counterweight to the endless acronyms and relentless "more-for-less strategies". Whether called "manoeuvre warfare", "effect based approach to operations" or "network centric warfare", Clausewitz is there whispering the commander in his ear that in war everything is difficult, everything. Strategy offers few "Eurekas", but many possibilities to test moral stamina and political honesty. As such, preaching Clausewitz can thus in periods be a particularly ungrateful calling. Telling people who have seen the light that what they saw is probably the light of an oncoming freight train, just like all preceding visionaries who for a moment have thought that they have found the secret of easy victories, can be rather unpleasant and not a way to make friends in high places. Anticipated military cakewalks have a nasty tendency to end up like endless trials of fatigue.

Clausewitz also deserves more attention at the military academies because his main legacy is not his conclusions, but the way he gets to those conclusions. Clausewitz, taken this way, invites us to join him on a journey through a maze of considerations and a labyrinth of concerns. Where he eventually ends up is of relatively little importance, the journey is the goal. Consequently, one must read Clausewitz slowly in order to mature with the text. Presenting Clausewitz's main ideas as bullet points on a PowerPoint slide is thus prone to convey the wrong ideas, both of the man and of his thoughts.

Finally, spending more time to introduce Clausewitz to future military leaders could also be compared to introducing junior high school students to sex education. The point is not to teach you things you otherwise would not do, but to put you in a better position to reflect upon what you under all circumstances will come across. Even if you do not appreciate the genius of Clausewitz, it may be wise to give future officers some knowledge about the man, his time and his thoughts, because officers will, later if not sooner, encounter quotations and ideas allegedly belonging to the old master. By giving people the opportunity to think beforehand, so to speak, they may become a bit more immune to people hammering them with Clausewitzian wisdom, however tendentious or far fetched. This point was vindicated also by my respondent at the Norwegian MoD.

The problem with Clausewitz in the departmental corridors is not that his ideas are particularly evident in the daily business of strategy and policy-making, but that when occasionally his name does surface it is more often than not counterproductive because all those things Clausewitz said little or nothing about, but which are crucial to our own operations, get too little attention. As mentioned earlier in this essay, staring too intensely at Clausewitz does not make us wiser, but blind to all those theorists who have explicitly interestingly things to say about those situations we run into. As such, Clausewitz is in danger of being used as the proverbial lamppost. It lights up a certain area, but it does not help you a bit if you lose your car keys three blocks away. If you insist on searching where the light is brightest you will never find what you're looking for.

So, what is our conclusion so far? Did Clausewitz write a book that 'would not be forgotten after two or three years'? He certainly did, but his legacy is not as overwhelming as we may be led to believe. Has his eye-catching name, at least seen with Norwegian eyes, perhaps made him a bit more conspicuous than he actually is?

I will round off this essay by leaving the particular Norwegian context, and take a more generic look. The preliminary worry of this essay was that Clausewitz's influence has apparently been so all-pervading that it is next to impossible to put the finger exactly on where the impact has been greatest. John Shy makes a similar point: "No final word on a mode of thinking about warfare that has proved so durable, despite its flaws and momentous changes in the nature of war, seems possible. It has become, during almost two centuries, so deeply imbedded in Western consciousness that many adherents refuse to accept it as a 'mode' of thinking at all, but insist that [it] simply offer the Truth about war, or at least about strategy."[52]

Again, most readers of this essay will recognize that the innocently looking "[it]" in the quotation above does not refer to Clausewitz, but to Jomini.[53] So the reason why we do not encounter Clausewitz's name as often as we perhaps should in Norway, is either because Norwegians have assimilated his ideas so thoroughly it is virtually impossible to say where he ends and we begin, or because Clausewitz has not had that great an impact after all. Consequently, you could make a point that the reason we discuss Clausewitz more than we discuss Jomini is because Jomini created the paradigm of which we are still a part: "[Jomini's] general approach to the problem of war, abstracting it from its political and social context, emphasizing decision-making rules and operational results, turning warfare into a huge game of chess, has been surprisingly durable. Jomini, more that Clausewitz, deserves the dubious title of founder of modern strategy."[54] As the alleged creator of the paradigm, Jomini's footprints have been wiped out by all those subsequent theorists who have trodden the same path, however unconsciously. Clausewitz's footprints, on the other hand, are still vividly visible because almost no one has followed in his tracks, perhaps for good reasons.

That Clausewitz was a path-breaking military thinker is indisputable. However, if we were all like him and did as he did in 1812, that is, defect to the enemy instead of renouncing personal political convictions, and throw suspicion on the honest work of nearly all military educators but ourselves, the armed forces would be very hard to train, control and maintain. In a way

Clausewitz thus resembles Socrates. James Madison once said, "had every Athenian citizen been a Socrates, every Athenian assembly would still have been a mob."[55] Equally, had every soldier been a Clausewitz, every army would still have been a throng, or at least a bunch of capricious know-it-alls.

Clausewitz is relevant, still, and will presumably be so for the foreseeable future, not because we can build our armed forces and doctrine directly on his conceptual foundation or our military education directly on his philosophy of war, but because he offers a constant correction to the reigning way of thinking militarily.

Clausewitz is relevant in the same way as Plato and Shakespeare are. You rarely ask what can I use Plato for, or what can I gain by reading *Hamlet*. If that is your motivation for approaching them, you will leave them just as poor as you were when you came. You are far better off if you instead ask yourself what is my reaction to what I read? What does it make *me* feel given all that *I* have read and seen in world so far? Likewise, I think you are much better off if you come to Clausewitz to wonder and ponder, not just to grab something to have in your pocket in case of an academic emergency.

In a certain sense, then, Clausewitz is also *not* relevant, just like the sun, the rain or Elvis Presley are not relevant. If you ask a passionate bird watcher whether what he does is relevant, I think a sad look on his face is all you will get in return. Perhaps he too poses you a silent question: What kind of life are you living to make you ask such a question? The things in life we find most gratifying are not relevant, in any reasonable sense of the word. The same goes for a fondness for reading Clausewitz. His insights still give us food for thought, and if that is not reason enough to read and discuss him, then what is?[56]

Notes:

[1] Christopher Bassford, *Clausewitz in English, The Reception of Clausewitz in Britain and America 1815-1945* (Oxford University Press, 1994), p. 5.

[2] The book was issued in a series called "Practical philosophy" which included Nietzsche, Tocqueville, Weber, and Habermas, among others. At the moment of writing there is a process going on in Norway trying to finance a translation of *Vom Kriege*, but it seems very difficult to find anyone with both money to spend and a wish to see Clausewitz unfolded in Norwegian.

³ The closest we get to a book length treatment of Clausewitz and his legacy is presumably Rolf Hobson's *Fra kabinettskrigen til den totale krigen. Clausewitztolkninger fra Moltke til Aron*, Forsvarstudier nr 6, 1994 [*From cabinet wars to the total war. Clausewitz interpretations from Moltke to Aron*].

⁴ "Clausewitz (1780-1831), den mest betydelige militærteoretiker som noensinne har levd." Jens A. Christophersen, *PaxLeksikon* Bind 2 (Oslo: Pax forlag, 1979) p. 25. Christophersen had also edited the Norwegian translation of *Vom Krieg* in 1972.

⁵ Ibid. ("Innen sosialistisk tenkning har Clausewitz lenge hatt en meget høy status; selv om det rent konvensjonelt av og til kan være litt vanskelig å rose en adelig offiser, endog en prøyssisk sådan, i kretser av mer eller mindre rettroende. Lenin satte Clausewitz overmåte høyt. Og han er også den eneste tenker som får den ære å bli sitert i avsnittet om krig og fred i «Sitater fra Forman Mao Tse-tung»").

⁶ O. Fjørtoft "Imperialisme tyder krig" *Røde Fane, Tidsskrift for kommunistisk teori og debatt*, Nr 5 1975, p. 11. ("Den einaste vitskaplege tesen som finst om krig er den som først vart skapt av den borgarlege krigsfilosofen Clausewitz: 'Krig er eit framhald av politikken med andre middel.' […] Lenin tok over denne tesen og utvikla han vidare på grunnlag av den lengstkomne tenkinga i vår tid, den historiske og dialektiske materialismen, læra om klassekampen og historia.")

⁷ O.F. "Sovjet truer Norge" in *Røde Fane*, Nr. 4, 1976, p. 6. ("Lenin understreka at politikk og krig er to sider av samme sak. Krig er politikk med andre midler.")

⁸ Obviously, one has to read a lot more than *Norsk Militært Tidsskrift* to fully map Clausewitz's impact on Norwegian military debate, but that periodical is chosen here as the most likely place to find articles on Clausewitz. The consequence of that choice is that parts of the debate, particularly the naval part of it, must be left to future researchers.

⁹ "Krig er nemlig," som Clausewitz i hans efterladte Skrifter, "vom Krige," siger, "meer et Middel til Forsvar end til Erobrin". "Om Krigskunst og deri i senere Tider gjorte Fremskridt" by Christiania militaire Samfunds Committee for Krigkunsten, in *Norsk Militairt Tidskrift 9de Bind eller 17de og 18de hefte*, Christiania 1840-1841, p. 6.

[10] "Jominis Critic over de bülowske Theorier mangler al mulig Logik, og bestaar meest i Paastande uten Beviis." Meydell "Bemærkninger angaaende Bülows Schriften" *Norsk Militairt Tidskrift 2den Hæfte. 9de Bind* Christiania 1855, p. 343.

[11] "Jeg vidste forud, at der hertillands endnu gives Militaire, som ikke taaler den mindset Tale om Feil hos Bülow, som ansee saadan nær sagt som Gudsbespottelse mod denne 'den militaire Vitenskabs Helligaand'". Kr. Hagemann Brandt "Svar paa Generalmajor Meydells 'Bemærkninger' i Anledning af min Anmeldelse af H. von Bülows vermischte und militairische Schriften." in *Norsk Militairt Tidskrift 19de Bind eller 3die Række: 1ste Bind*. Christiania, 1856) p. 105.

[12] "Napoleons feltherregeni" based on *Mil. Wochenblatt's* treatment of general Pierron's study *Comment s'est formé le génie militaire de Napoléon I?* (Paris, 1889) *Norsk Militært Tidsskrift*, 53. Bind, 1890.

[13] Captain Sinding-Larsen, "Krigen som regnestykke" in *Norsk Militært Tidsskrift*, 71.bind, Kristiania 1908, p. 563. ("Krigen er ikke noget regnestykke. Det er ikke tallet som bestemmer utfaldet; det er den moralske kraft. Og den må de små nationer bygge på.")

[14] Premierløjtnant G. Schnitler, "Moltke, hans samlede skrifter og erindringer om ham" in *Norsk Militært Tidsskrift* 59. Bind, Kristiania, 1896, p. 574-589.

[15] G.S. "Moltkes Kriegslehren" i *Norsk Militært Tidsskrift* 74 Bind, Kristiania, 1911, p.405. ("Gjennem et flittig studium, fornemlig av Fredrik den store og Napoleons felttog, Clausewitz's verker, gjennem rike erfaringer og utrættelig arbeide har Moltke været en av dem, hvis liv og levnet synes at bevise sandheten av det ord: 'Geni er flid' – den ubegrænsede evne til at ville."

[16] Smith, Sven-Erik Grieg, "Gudmund Schnitler – en norsk Clausewitz?" [G.S – a Norwegian Clausewitz?] in *Norsk Militært Tidsskrift* nr.7, 1987 p. 17.

[17] Gudmund Schnitler, *Strategi* (Kristiania: Grøndahl & Søns Forlag, 1914), p. 16. ("Clausewitz er kanskje den som har øvet størst betydning som militær forfatter. Det er lykkedes ham at opnaa sit ønske at skrive en bok som 'ikke vilde være glemt i løpet av to eller tre aar.'").

[18] An article by the signature S.B. called "The relationship between the art of government and the art of war", for instance, was published in 1922, without mentioning Clausewitz with a word. (S.B. "Sammenhengen mellom statskunst og krigskunst" *Norsk Militært Tidsskrift*, 85. Bind 1922.)

[19] Sverre Diesen *Militær strategi, En innføring i maktens logikk* (Oslo: Cappelen, 1998). For the record: Diesen was later promoted to four stars general and has served as Chief of Defence.

[20] "Den er bemerkelsesværdig ogsaa av den grund, at den er første strategi, der er utgit paa norsk" *Norsk Militært Tidsskrift*, 74. Bind, Kristiania 1911, p. 405.

[21] Diesen, *Militær strategi* p. 41. ("Går vi tilbake til Clausewitz var det imidlertid flere av hans samtidige, bl a sveitseren Henri Jomini og tyskeren Heinrich von Bülow, som med utgangspunkt i datidens fornuftstro mente å kunne se tilnærmet matematiske sammenhenger i strategien, med formler for anbefalte vinkler mellom operasjonsbasis og operasjonslinje osv.")

[22] Antoine Henri de Jomini *The Art of War* (1838), (London: Greenhill Books, 1992), p. 323.

[23] Schnitler, *Strategi*, p.112 ("Han undervurderte ikke de aandelige drivfjære, de moralske faktorer og personlighetens makt.")

[24] Ibid., p. 323. ("Jomini – Ney's dygtige generalstabschef og den kjendte militærforfatter – utvikler i sine arbeider et kunstig system for krigskunsten med opstillede bestemte grundsætninger for deres ledelse. I sin faste, klare form har hans skrifter dog noget særdeles tiltalende ved sig. Særlig maatte de virke paa den franske aand, i hvis væsen det ligger at sondre skarpt logisk mellom begrepene").

[25] Bernard Brodie "The Continuing Relevance of *On War*" in Carl von Clausewitz, *On* War, edited and translated by Michael Howard and Peter Paret (Princeton University Press, 1976), p. 53.

[26] Gunnar Åselius "Sverige – motvillig småstat i imperialismens tidsålder" in Rolf Hobson, Sven G. Holtsmark and Tom Kristiansen (eds) *Stormaktene, Sverige og Norge 1905-1907* (Oslo: Cappelen, 2006) p. 40.

[27] By 1900 there were 425 Peace Organisations in the world; no less than 211 of those were in Scandinavia. Michael Howard, *War and the Liberal Conscience* with a new foreword (London: Hurst & Company, 2008), p. 44.

[28] Henrik Angell, quoted in Roy Andersen, *Henrik Angell – en nordmann på tvers* (Oslo: Aschehoug, 2000), p. 165.

[29] "Mit folk er veigt, lydrigsstemplet staar paa dets pande" Angell quoted in ibid., p. 166.

30 Clausewitz's "Bekenntnisdenkschrift" from 1812, quoted in Hew Strachan *Clausewitz's On War, a Biography* (New York: Atlantic Monthly Press, 2007), p. 53.

31 Clausewitz, *On War*, p. 252.

32 Ibid., p. 86

33 Ibid., p. 189.

34 Ibid., p. 75.

35 Ibid., p. 174.

36 "If I ever again become involved in the education of young officers, I will thus put even more emphasis on historical studies than I previously did." Otto Ruge, *Felttoget* [The Campaign] (Oslo: Aschehoug, 1989, p. 206) ("Får jeg igjen noe å gjøre med oppdragelsen av de unge offiserer, vil jeg derfor legge enda mer vekt på studiet av historien enn jeg har gjort tidligere.")

37 Ibid. ("Folk flest, også vi militære, er altfor tilbøielige til å akseptere situasjonen som den er i øieblikket og gå ut fra at den situasjonen blir den endelige, i stedet for å huske på at livet går videre og at situasjonen imorgen alltid vil være en annen enn idag, og at det derfor ingen grunn er til å miste troen, selv om det går galt i første omgang. Det er det vi lærer av historien.")

38 Halvdan Koht in a parliament meeting, March 1936, quoted in Nils Ørvik, *Norsk sikkerhetspolitikk, 1920-1939*, vol. II, *Vern eller Vakt?* [Norwegian Security Policy, 1920-1939, vol. II, Guard, or Watch?] (Oslo: Tanum, 1961), p. 125. For the record: Outstanding historical knowledge does not imply outstanding military and strategic understanding. Foreign minister Koht was in fact a professor in history, but his crisis management was less than adequate.

39 King Haakon 7th, quoted in Ruge, *Felttoget*, p. 206.

40 "Regardless of how it was going to end, we had to pick the fight now with regard to the future. To surrender without a fight would be devastating for the nation's self-esteem." Ibid., p. 20 ("Men hvordan det enn så kom til å gå, måtte vi i hvert fall ta op striden nu av hensyn til eftertiden. Det å gi oss uten kamp ville være ødeleggende for nasjonens selvaktelse.")

41 "Her er vi over på det omfattende felt som med et uttrykk fra moderne strategi er kjent som *deterrence*, eller avskrekking. Hvor krig på sett og vis opphører å være krig, og hvor politikken rår grunnen alene. Og vi kan vel innskyte, den viktigste, og også den fineste funksjonen våpen i det hele tatt kan ha. – Rent

logisk står vi her overfor en videreføring av en vesentlig tanke hos Clausewitz, kanskje også det mest essenielle i hele hans forfatterskap." Jens A. Christophersen, "Clausewitz og vår egen tid" ["Clausewitz and our own era"] in *Om Krigen,* p. xxiii.

[42] Odd Vincent Skjøstad "Med Clausewitz inn i framtid, drøfting av fredskapende operasjoner" ["Into the Future with Clausewitz, considering peace operations"], *Norsk Militært Tidsskrift* 1994, nr 3; Robert Mood "Karl M. von Clausewitz (sic) vs Sun Tzu" *Norsk Militært Tidsskrift* 1995, nr. 8-9; Harald Høiback "Clausewitz og det Postmoderne" [Clausewitz and Postmodernism] *Norsk Militært Tidsskrift* 1996, nr. 11; Henning-A. Frantzen "Er Clausewitz's 'Om Krig' apolitisk?" [Is Clausewitz's 'On War' apolitical?] *Norsk Militært Tidsskrift* 1998, nr. 2.

[43] Skjøstad "Med Clausewitz inn i framtid, drøfting av fredskapende operasjoner", p. 26.

[44] "Det er først etter avslutningen av den kalde krigen at situasjonen har forandret seg. I dag snakker mange igjen åpent om krigen for å oppnå politiske mål – vi kaller det fredskapende operasjoner." Ibid., p. 27.

[45] "Under hvilke forutsetninger kan vi tenke oss at Norge vil føre krig og hvilke faktorer må vi minimum ta med for å gjøre en slik drøfting fruktbar?" Ibid.

[46] Colin L. Powell, *A Soldier's Way, An Autobiography* (London: Hutchinson, 1995), p. 208.

[47] Skjøstad "Med Clausewitz inn i framtid, drøfting av fredskapende operasjoner" p. 29. ["Clausewitz slo fast, ved starten av det forrige århundre, at krig finner sted i et forhold mellom politikk, stridskrefter og folkeviljen. Denne oppfatning av krig som et system gjelder uavkortet også i dag."]

[48] Terje Bruøygard, "Tyngdepunkt og begrepsforvirring" [Center of Gravity and confusion of ideas] in *Norsk Militært Tidsskrift*, 2004, nr. 5, p. 13 ("Som vi vet, når det er en debatt i USA får den gjerne konsekvenser for alle").

[49] Katalog over Den kongelige norske krigskoles bibliothek, Christiania 1863, p. 40.

[50] In danger of breaching "client confidentiality", I quote an anonymous note from one of the staff college's former students: "It is unfortunate that *On War* is not included in our syllabus, since it is claimed that this is the most quoted, but least read book. When shall we (officers) then read/study Clausewitz?" To be a bit impertinent; both the salary and the time Norwegian officers spend off

duty should allow for an encounter with Clausewitz, if they want to have one, even without the employer's encouragement and support.

[51] Just for the sake of comparison; Jomini is mentioned in less than 5% of the Master's theses and Liddell Hart in less than 10%. (The Master's programme commenced in 2007.)

[52] John Shy, "Jomini" in Peter Paret, *Makers of Modern Strategy, from Machiavelli to the Nuclear Age* (Oxford, 1986), p. 184.

[53] The [it] substitutes "–correctly understood–Jomini and latter-day Jominians". Ibid., p. 185.

[54] Ibid., p. 144.

[55] James Madison quoted in Gordon S. Wood, *The Purpose of the Past, Reflections on the Uses of History* (New York: The Penguin Press, 2008), p. 151.

[56] The author wants to thank Håkan Edström, Øistein Espenes, Tor-Erik Hanssen, Rune Haugdal, John Andreas Olsen, Karl Rommeteveit, Bjørn Tore Solberg and Hans Jørgen Wiborg, for stimulating discussions about Clausewitz, Mette Guderud for helping out in The Norwegian Armed Forces Museum's library and archives, and especially Gullow Gjeseth, Chris Saunders and Anita and Frank Carroll who made several suggestions for the article's improvement.

CLAUSEWITZ IN A POST-COMMUNIST STATE: A CASE STUDY OF SLOVENIA

Vladimir Prebilič and Jelena Juvan

Introduction

When discussing the influence and importance of the prominent military theorist Carl von Clausewitz, we can easily compare him and his findings with Sigmund Freud in the field of psychology, Adam Smith in economy, Justice Marshall in law, Thomas Jefferson or Karl Marx in governance. The 19th century Prussian soldier and theorist is regarded a prophet whose views on the character and nature of war have held up over the past two centuries.[1] However, for the intent of this paper we will not focus on his work on understanding and waging war, but on the so-called Clausewitzian trinity: the relationship between the state, the army and the people.[2] Certain extremely successful defence systems were organized (e.g. USA) on his conclusions, and they represent a role model for developing countries. The Republic of Slovenia (hereafter RS) underwent an extremely intense period in which it reformed its national defence system. However, in order to understand the continuity of the reformation of the Slovene defence system, one has to keep in mind the very intense historical development on the territory of RS.

The Republic of Slovenia is one of the youngest and smallest states in Europe. It ensured its independence and sovereignty through a legitimate and legal use of force that lead to the rapid recognition of the newly formed state and full membership in the United Nations in 1992. Even though military conflicts and wars are not likely to occur on this territory today, the area was marked by numerous conflicts, many of which have changed the political map of Europe. The first conflicts reach back even before the rise of the Roman Empire, while the last took place as late as 1991. The reason behind these conflicts lies in the geostrategic importance of the territory of the Republic of Slovenia, for these 20.500 km represent the meeting point of four basic geomorphologic units: the Mediterranean, the Alps, the Dinaric-Karst and the Panonian plains. Each one of them is defined by its own physical geographic characteristics such as relief, climate, vegetation and soil. This is why contemporary geo-politicians include the territory of the Republic of Slovenia amongst the contact areas, i.e. areas of transition between larger geostrategic regions.

Cohen[3] defines this territory as a bridge between the various regions that enables a direct and indirect communication between them. As a consequence the geostrategic value of the area was on a constant increase, which continuously led to conflicts for dominance between the various regional forces. Numerous defence lines were constructed. The first amongst them was the Claustra Alpium Iuliarum that was built as early as the 3rd century AD.[4] The border role of the area was also clear as the Frankonian Empire was emerging under Charles the Great and continued to be clear as it saw the rise of the Austrian Empire. With the fall of the Austro-Hungarian monarchy, its border role changed. This territory no longer represented the southern edge of Western Europe, but the northern edge of the newly founded Kingdom of Yugoslavia. This position became even more important in the post 1945 period, when the Socialist Republic of Slovenia represented the western most part of the new social order and ideology – socialism and communism. Today, when RS is a full member of the European Union and NATO, the situation has not really changed. Its position and role has once again obtained the before mentioned geopolitical connotation – it represents the south-eastern edge of the Central European community, which is often perceived by European politicians as the gateway into the restless western Balkans.

The changing security environment and the Slovenian defence system

All of the mentioned geostrategic characteristics had a direct influence on the formation of the current defence system in the independent RS. It is clear that the first origins of the Slovenian armed forces reach back to the fall of the Austro-Hungarian monarchy in 1918. On 1st November 1918 general Rudolf Maister took command of the military units that were returning from the various fronts and used them to create the Slovenian army. The 4,000 soldiers and 200 officers were sufficient for the disarmament of the German security guard and taking over Slovenian Styria and Carinthia (cover the Slovenian national border). Until the peace treaty was signed this also represented the border between the Republic of Austria and the Kingdom of Yugoslavia. During World War II the territory of Slovenia saw the formation of the resistance movement that consisted of partisan units. These units gained in strength right up to the liberation when they were organisationally transformed into the Slovenian army. The liberation was followed by great disappointment, for the formation of the People's Federative Republic of Yugoslavia also saw the formation of a single military force – the Yugoslav army - which meant that the Slovenian army was incorporated into the joint army. The 1948 period of tension between the blocs which saw the Socialist Federative Republic of Yugoslavia step out of the Soviet bloc, the extreme tension in relations between 1948 and 1953, the promotion of the third political and development option (the formation of the movement of independence) from 1961 onwards and the 1968 military intervention of the Soviet Union in Czechoslovakia, all represented reasons behind the restructuration of the Yugoslav defence capabilities. In 1968 the Yugoslav federal assembly adopted the legislation which transferred a part of the defence responsibilities to the republics.[5] This change also led to the formation of the Slovenian Territorial Army (TA). This opportunity to form a limited armed force was rigorously enforced by the Slovenian political leadership. Even though TA units were foreseen as a territorial component that would offer support in the defence off a certain territory to the Federative Yugoslav People's Army (YPA), great differences existed between the various TAs. SR Slovenia was the most diligent in putting aside funds for constant training, education, armament and organisation of its TA. Thus, the Slovenian TA was qualitative leaps ahead of other TA organisations in the other republics. At the beginning of 1990 the Slovenian TA units consisted of approximately 75,000 reserves that could be called in at any time.[6]

Independence and the birth of the Slovenian Armed Forces

Independence was a long-lasting Slovenian desire that peaked with the first Slovenian multiparty elections at the beginning of 1990, which lead to the SFRY leadership declaring a state of alert. In May 1990 the Territorial Army of Slovenia received an order to hand over its weapons, ammunition, mines and explosives to the YPA. Through this YPA managed to confiscate the TA's weapons that were stored in military barracks, but not much more of the remaining weaponry, for TA blocked the removal of weapons from their warehouses wherever this was possible. Following the ten days of war (which saw 72 battles and three ceasefire agreements) the defence forces of Slovenia achieved victory. The war cost 76 lives and 326 wounded on both sides.˙ 31 tanks, 22 armoured transporters, 172 transport vehicles, 20 all terrain vehicles and 6 helicopters were destroyed or damaged.[7]

However, during the first steps of the newly formed independent country the opinions as regards the future development of the defence system varied considerably. Immediately after the May 1990 elections the political option that called for the demilitarisation of Slovenia was relatively strong. This initiative was mainly linked to the withdrawal of YPA from Slovenia in the near future, but it also announced the opposition of a part of the public to any armed forces in Slovenia. The same period also saw the emergence of the political option that wanted to see the establishment of the Slovenian army, which would represent direct competition to YPA in establishing the right to legitimate use of armed forces on the territory of Slovenia. This decision was a result of the obvious supremacy of YPA[8] and the fear that a war on a greater scale might erupt, for this could greatly and in all aspects endanger the newly formed country. This also represented a confrontation of two entirely different concepts: the classical state model with a strong military structure and a state without an army in the classical sense. In October 1990 a public opinion poll carried out in Slovenia showed that 25.2% of all respondents were opposed to Slovenia having an army, while in January 1991 as many as 48.8% of all respondents were in favour of a demilitarised Slovenia. The option in favour of the Slovenian army had the advantage of the support of a part of the government, especially the Ministries of Defence and Interior, while the demilitarisation option had strong support in the RS presidency, the opposition and the general public. The difficulty in establishing demilitarisation mainly lay in the accordance of the neighbouring countries – for it was the security systems of the neighbouring countries that could ensure the demilitarisation of RS and not public opinions. The various threats and the YPA's military intervention certainly reduced the tendencies for demilitarisation, for Slovenia and the Slovenes were faced with the realistic threat of war and social poverty.[9]

The post-independency period (1991-1994) was based on the formation of the national defence as practiced by Western states. This meant that the primary goal of the defence system became the establishment of a partially professional army and the commencement of military duty in its full scope as soon as possible. In 1993 the inclusion into NATO became a strategic goal for the first time. In the following years this goal was included into all development strategic and normative solutions and measures. This resulted in the 1994 Defence Act, which normatively defined the organisation of the defence system and the Slovenian Army. With this Act the Slovenian armed forces (SAF) were de facto established along with its new structure that was divided into the manoeuvre and territorial part. The final act in the establishment of the army was the formation of the conscript system and general military obligation that accompanied the professional core. Similar to other states with parliamentary democracy the jurisdictions of individual bodies within the defence leadership and administrative system were defined and civil supervision of the armed forces was ensured. The inclusion into NATO became the goal of all Slovenian parliamentary parties, the opposition as well as the governing parties.[10]

The period between 1994 and 2004 was marked by vast organisational changes that took place throughout the Slovenian defence system. Following 2001 the structural and organisational changes were essential for the development of SAF which was influenced by a number of factors: the increase in global terrorism, the spread of arms for mass destruction, the wars in Afghanistan and Iraq and consequentially the increased need for cooperation in defence (between resources as well as states). The otherwise solid and majority public opinion support as regards Slovenian NATO membership was tested in 1999 when the allies attacked Serbia without a UN mandate. Up until 2001 the armed forces grew (in 2001 there were 73,000 military conscripts in the Slovenian armed forces), the years 2002-2003 saw a sharp fall in the number of conscripts (to 39,000 conscripts). This led to the decision that the armed forces should consists entirely of professionals. Thus the last generation of conscripts performed its military duty in 2003.[11]

The period following the inclusion into NATO[12] led to a new structure and organisation of the Slovenian army, for it became a professional army (with a contractual reserve) in 2003. At this we were not merely dealing with the change in the manner of filling the numbers, but also with foreseen functional changes – the various systems for educating and training professional soldiers and members of the contractual reserves.[13]

Through the years the ratio between the representatives of the permanent and reserve forces changed in favour of the permanent forces.

Alongside these structural changes a functional transformation of the SAF also took place. In the 1990s the armed forces were divided with a simple division into manoeuvre and territorial forces, in 2001 the SAF was divided into mediating forces, main and additional forces, and once we joined NATO in 2004 total NATO standardisation and classification took place.[14]

Year	Armed forces	Permanent forces
1999	76,000	4,500
2000	70,000	5,000
2001	51,000	5,150
2002	39,000	5,600
2003	26,000	6,300
2004	18,000	6,950
2007	14,665	7,105
2010[15]	9,237	7,576

Source: O Slovenski vojski (On Slovenian Army).

The Republic of Slovenia has at its disposal 7,500 soldiers, while the war time forces established themselves at a total of 14,000 soldiers. Due to NATO membership we have renounced the right to develop certain defence capabilities, for the defence of RS is based on the use of the shared allied forces, which also incorporate the SAF forces. This led to Slovenia being dedicated to the modernisation process of the armed forces which lead to better efficiency, shared operations and easier deployment. The transformation to professional defence forces has also transformed the reserve forces. Thus the SAF currently has a voluntary contractual reserve[16], which in 2010 consists of 1,661 members which is below the 5,500 contractual reserves planned for this year. (On Slovenian Army, *Programme* for the *Development* and *Equipment* of the Slovenian Army).

The applicability of Clausewitz in Slovenia

There is no doubt that the importance of Clausewitz's contribution to the theory of military interventions surpasses his practical contribution, and yet both, the practical experience as well as theory are inseparably linked as the experience gained on the battlefield encouraged Clausewitz in his intense contemplation as regards the nature of warfare. Clausewitz is believed to be the founder of the classical political war theory and it is this theory that kept Clausewitz a common name studied and lectured at educational institutions even today. His main work *On War* is considered a classic, which »is in a certain sphere of human activity so important that the coming generations of scientists use it as a basis for the construction of their theories, while the experienced and established scientists consider it a standard that enables them to evaluate their own work«.[17] One could say that the work *On War* is for military science what Machiavelli's *The Prince* is for politics, Thucydides' *History of Peloponnese Wars* for history and Smith's *The Wealth of Nations* for economy.[18] In the opinion of certain authors the greatness of Clausewitz's work lies in the fact that it is interdisciplinary[19] as it reaches into the field of philosophy, epistemology, methodology of social sciences, history, political theory, psychology, military strategy as well as tactics. »The concepts of strategy, military force, military organisation, all of which are usually considered to be self-evident were in fact defined by Clausewitz«.[20] Until Clausewitz all dealings linked to war and politics remained partial and did not reach the level of unified scientific theory. »What the renown philosophers and wise men could not construct, was established by the almost unknown (during his lifetime) Prussian professional solider Carl von Clausewitz«.[21] By gathering and comparing data on a number of different wars Clausewitz wanted to learn about the true face of war, ascertain its basic characteristics and laws. Through this he wished to compile a theory that would offer a key for scientifically led wars.[22] Clausewitz's work can be divided onto two levels: on the first level he leaned upon the findings of the military history until then and his personal observations of military practice; on the second level he originated from the classical German philosophy revelations that were at his disposal.[23] Following fifteen years of work he reached the conclusion that the logic of war cannot be sought in the military activities. He realised that »war does not have its own logic and that politics (i.e. the complex human social activity that is oriented and defined by the control of the public power) are hiding behind it«.[24] Only politics can link the various appearance forms of wars into one type and it is politics that give these various forms of armed violence the inner logic and unity. »Politics define the intention, means and scope of wars«.[25]

Clausewitz studied the multidimensional relations between war and politics. In his opinion politics define all basic characteristics of war, and war is and »will always remain a dependent, secondary expression of politics«.[26] Undoubtedly the best known postulate, but also the most commonly misinterpreted one is the main postulate of his theory which reads as follows: »War is a political act and an efficient political tool, a continuation of political relations with other means«.[27] Following Clausewitz's death the Prussian generals and field marshals Moltke, Schlieffen, Seekt and Ludendorf were considered to be his followers in military science and expertise. However, according to Bebler[28] the four of them lacked the political and philosophical depth and dialectics of thought that was so typical for Clausewitz. All four rejected Clausewitz's warnings as regards the supremacy of politics during war, and interpreted the previously mentioned postulate in such a way that politics have (once the war has started and until it ends) to allow the war to do the talking. In the work of Schlieffen, Clausewitz's term »absolute war« became the basis for developing the extremely intense attack strategy of total war, a war that leads to the final destruction of the enemy, while his differentiation between strategy and tactics, defence and attack were in the later German military school changed into a rigid pattern.[29] In his discussions on war Clausewitz stated that war is nothing more but a duel on a larger scale. The first and main goal of war is to dominate over the opponent and make him incapable of any further resistance,[30] make it impossible for him to defend himself.[31] War forces our opponent to fulfil our will. The main task of the armed forces is to protect the country, i.e. defend it.[32]

The work *On War* consists of a collection of eight books. Clausewitz finished the first six books before his death and they were given the final editing and were published by his widow Marie von Clausewitz. The last two books, books seven and eight, were merely outlined by Clausewitz, and were also published as such. When studying the applicability of the Prussian military theoretician for the Slovenian defence system one needs to take into account certain specifics. Due to the short period in which RS has been independent the war experience of its defence forces are relatively limited - mainly to the defence during the liberation of Slovenia, i.e. a period during which the defence system was only emerging. Thus Clausewitz's theory that is linked to the study of the war phenomenon cannot be applied directly in its entirety. His discussions that deal with the organisation and operation of the defence system present something else of use. As the military and political priority of RS on the break of the millennia was to become full NATO members the architects of our defence system have found themselves under the influence of our recent experience and the various advisors from the member states in the North Atlantic Treaty Organisation. The conglomerate of these influences contributed to the current situation of the Slovenian defence system.

In his theoretical starting point Clausewitz[33] views armed forces as regards their strength and composition, its state outside of combat, their supply and their general attitude towards land and territory. He defines the dominance of the forces in numbers as the key factor; »the principle to be as strong as possible in the decisive combat has to now be placed slightly higher than it was placed in the past«.[34]. He talks about »that division and formation of the different arms into separate parts or sections of the whole Army, and that form of general position or disposition of those parts which is to be the norm throughout the whole campaign or war«.[35] This consists of the arithmetic and geometric element of division and positioning. The division arises from the permanent peacetime organisation of the armed forces, which consists of battalions, squadrons, regiments, etc. If necessary these individual parts are joined into larger parts, to the whole. Clausewitz ascertained that the unit becomes rigid if it does not have a sufficient number of elements. On one hand the top leadership is weakened if the parts of the whole are too large, and on the other hand the strength of the order is weakened in two ways with every new commanding level: firstly due to the loss that occurs as a result of the new transition and secondly due to the prolonged time the order needs to travel.[36] "The order of **battle** of an **army** is therefore the organisation and disposition of it in **mass ready** prepared for **battle**".[37] »The main principle as regards the organisation is that anywhere where a confrontation can be imagined, across the entire war territory, the armed forces are disposed in such a way that the units are at any given point capable of independent confrontation«.[38] According to Clausewitz the precondition for this is fulfilled by merging three military units, with an organic division of the whole and an appropriate command.[39]

In war the battle is not a battle man on man, but a much more diversified whole. Two types of units can be distinguished in this large whole: the first are defined according to the subject and the second by the object.[40] All war activities are thus directly or indirectly connected to combat. »The army is recruited, dressed, armed, trained, it sleeps, eats and is marched, just so that it would fight on the right side, at the right time«.[41] In combat all activities are oriented towards the destruction of the opponent or to the destruction of his armed forces. »to conquer and destroy the armed power of the enemy is always one of the main means of warfare «.[42]

However, warfare is accompanied by a myriad of activities, the main purpose of which is not to destroy the enemy but to serve the war. These activities are linked to the maintenance of the armed forces.[43] Activities and objects that belong to the battle itself are marches, camps and cantonments. Other activities that belong merely to maintenance are feeding, hospital care, and the supply of weapons and equipment. One of the most important ideas in Clausewitz's theory is his clear distinction between strategy and tactics. He defines strategy as the »is the employment of battle to gain the end of the war; it must therefore give an aim to the whole military action, which must be in accordance with the object of the war, and to this end it links together the series of acts which are to lead to the final decision...«.[44] In his opinion the best strategy is: to always be superior, generally as well as at the decisive point.[45] The key to success lies in the concentration of forces. »Nothing should be separated from the bulk, if this is not demanded from the purpose«.[46] Clausewitz sees the strategic reserve as an important element of successful warfare. This reserve has a double role: firstly it prolongs and revives the battle, and secondly it can be used in unforeseen cases. He divides the reasons that condition the use of combat into various elements: moral, physical, mathematical, geographic and statistical elements. It is interesting that Clausewitz places great stress on moral forces. He ascribes moral forces as one of the most important objects of war.[47]

As already previously stated the main and only task of the defence forces is to protect the country, i.e. defend it. Book six is dedicated to defence. By dedicating an entire book to defence he indicated the great importance he ascribed to it. In his opinion the actual notion of war does not emerge with the attack, for this does not have combat nor appropriation as its final and absolute purpose, the notion of war only emerges through defence, for this has combat as its direct goal, for defence and combat are obviously two sides of the same coin. Any defence is oriented merely against the attack, it therefore assumes combat, while attack is not necessarily aimed at defence, but towards the appropriation and does therefore not necessarily assume combat. Thus it is in the nature of things that whoever is the first to trigger the act of war also sets the first laws for war, and this is always the defender.[48]

When these theoretical starting points are used to confront the current Slovenian defence system, we can expose certain similarities as well as certain differences. As already stated in the introduction, the RS defence system has based its legitimacy on the defensive war for independence and sovereignty. This 1991 confrontation was recognised by the international community as an example of respecting all rules of international warfare as well as humanitarian law[49]. RS legally limited its operation also in the process of forming its defence capabilities. As the carrier of defensive or military power the Slovenian army has a very clear task – the defence of the territorial entity and sovereignty of

RS[50]. The constitutional norms (Constitution of RS) restrict the international activities of the Slovenian armed forces, for it defines that its operation in international operations and missions is only possible if they are supported by the UN Security Council[51].

However, since the Slovene armed forces have first cooperated in international operations and missions in 1997 a number of tasks have been added. Today RS represents a reliable partner in ensuring international security through various international operations and missions, with which it is consistently moving away from its defined task. Thus, it is not unusual for the citizens of the RS and individuals in the Slovenian political elite to be asking themselves[52] whether the Slovenian armed forces are a necessary element for ensuring national defence and security.

Following the introduction of the professionalization of the Slovenian armed forces a few important changes in the organisation of the defence capabilities were indicated by the move away from Clausewitz's theoretical starting points. The first change is linked to the direct responsibility of defending the state or its cooperation in the defence of the state. It is true that today's security challenges are different to what they used to be and that the defence systems are thus organised differently – they are based on small, professional and highly trained armed forces, however the tie or relation between the defence system and the inhabitants of RS (the Prussian theoretician paid great attention to the tie between the armed forces and the inhabitants), is undergoing important changes. This can be noticed on three levels: the interest for working in Slovenian armed forces is small, the youth is less and less likely to opt for voluntary service in the military service, and the public opinion is less inclined to support the activities of the Slovenian armed forces in international operations and missions. Authors such as Moskos[53] and Haltiner[54] have drawn attention to such events in a period when the Western countries were increasingly opting for the abandonment of the conscription system.

Research has also noticed gradual changes in the relation between the defence system and the state or the political elite that administrates with it. As stated by Clausewitz, politics have to lead the army and this is one of the main postulates of contemporary democracy that is also backed by international organisations. However, the professionalization process is increasingly standing in the way of this relation. Parliamentary control is legislatively founded, however, its de facto execution is often considered less important than it truly is. To a certain degree this state can be ascribed to the following factors: the young democracy and with it the political elite are still learning about true political responsibility, the defence sector is becoming less and less important in the daily political events and with this the opportunities for promoting the work of the legislative and in this case supervisory branch of power are diminishing, at the same time the defence sector has ever better cadre at its disposal (due to the professionalization), that (un)intentionally shows its capabilities also by avoiding direct control. We can state that the legislative basis in RS enables such control; however a lot more needs to be done in this field if we want to raise the awareness of the political elite, civil society and the media in this area.[55]

Slovenian military education and Clausewitz

Military education and the education of officers are of key importance for the operation of the armed forces. Already Clausewitz recognised the importance of the education of officers. When judging the position and deciding as regards war one of the officer's central and most important characteristics is his ability to create a strong link between the intellect, moral and physical courage and strong will.[56]

When discussing Slovenian military education we need to first o all define this term. While numerous other countries have based their education on military academies (that as a rule represent the beginning of the officer's career and are as a system excluded from the civil educational system), RS represents an exception, for it does not have a system of military academies. In Slovenian armed forces the officers' education is entirely incorporated into the civil educational system, right to the very end of university education and the appropriate title (B.A.). In other words, the basic expert knowledge, as well as the socialisation process of the youth, is entirely in the hands of civil education and could be compared to the American model for officers at the Reserve Officer Training Course. At this the Defence Studies[57] programme at the Faculty of Social Sciences is an exception, for it has (in cooperation with the Ministry of Defence of RS and the Slovenian armed forces) created a military module. This university programme is the only one in RS, in which entirely military contents are included within the civil system.

Within this programme Clausewitz appears in the lectures at numerous subjects, for his theoretical findings and understanding of war and defence systems are essential for any defence studies student. They encounter

Clausewitz at the subject *Polemology*, which is a compulsory subject for 1st year defence studies students, and an optional subject for the students of other courses at the faculty (in higher grades). This subject pays a lot of attention to Clausewitz as he presents one of the more important themes in the first, introductory part of the lectures, in which the students are getting acquainted with the great thinkers, who have dealt with the theory of warfare throughout history. An important component of the lectures is represented by Clausewitz's biography, for his military career was an important factor that influenced the development of his line of thought and the formation of his theory. Clausewitz is mentioned as an example of an 18th century individual, who - in a period in which noble descent was demanded if one wanted to make it through the rank of officers in the armed forces - managed to establish himself at the top military positions, even though he was assumed to be of middle class descent[58].

At the subject Polemology Clausewitz is treated as one of the great military theoreticians, and the students are acquainted with some of the basic terms that he defined, such as: military force, social force, the nature of war. The importance of preparing for war is emphasised, and the goals of war are discussed, as are the means used in a war in order to achieve these goals. A part of the focus is dedicated to defence, the relation between defence and attack within the tactics, the relation between defence and attack in the strategy, and the reciprocal effect between defence and attack.

On the 1st level of studies Clausewitz is also mentioned in the subject *Military History*, in which his role in the professionalization of the Prussian armed forces is discussed (for he was one of the key authors of the military reforms under the leadership of the Prussian defence minister Scharnhorst and an exceptionally important military pedagogue). His research work is also important as an example of the studies of combat and its analysis. The subject *Military History* is a compulsory subject for the 1st year defence studies students, and an optional subject for the students of other courses and higher grades.

3rd year defence studies students encounter Clausewitz within the subject *Theory of Tactics*, in which great attention is paid to the tactics (many of them are still applicable in the contemporary military organisation) of various military theoreticians, amongst which the most visible role is taken by Clausewitz. In the 4th year the students encounter the Prussian theoretician once again at the subject *Military Logistics*, in which they analyse his findings in the field of military logistics and his understanding of its position within the military organisation. At this it should be emphasised that his views in the field of military logistics are faced with the views and findings of his contemporary in the field of military theory – Antoine-Henri Jomini.

The expert education and training of future officers in the Slovenian armed forces begins with their entry into the program at the School for Officers which is performed by the Doctrine, Development, Education and Training Command. The precondition for their entrance into the school for officers is a completed university course at one of the civilian faculties. The School for Officers trains the candidate as a platoon commander which represents the starting point in the career of an officer. A military career can be further pursued with various other courses carried out by the Doctrine, Development, Education and Training Command: with the headquarters school, the higher headquarters school and the general staff school.

Before the candidates can start with their education at the School for Officers, they have to successfully pass the selection process and the basic military training. The School for Officers lasts for one year and provides the candidates with military knowledge suitable for performing basic officer's responsibilities. In order for an officer to be promoted to captain, he has to successfully complete the headquarters programme (five months), he can become a major after successful completion of the higher headquarters course, and a colonel (or higher) once he has successfully completed the highest level of military education – general staff school.[59]

Discussions on the appropriateness of the existing education programme for officers in Slovenian armed forces appear every now and then. And yet when all factors and specifics of Slovenia, its armed forces, the changing security measures in the international security environment and finally also the needs of the Slovenian armed forces are taken into account, the current concept of the basic education of officers at civil universities (which is with the necessary special higher education and specialist knowledge and skills parallel or added to by the military organisation with its educational capabilities) seems to be sufficient.[60] This system has a number of important advantages. Firstly, with the education in various university courses the necessary diversity in the composition of officers is ensured. This ensures that the military organisation will efficiently perform the various tasks in various work posts, and it will be capable of selecting the most appropriate individuals in the increasingly changing (operative) circumstances. Secondly, this ensures the important continuous cooperation between the military organisation and the various national intellectual centres, which in turn contributes to the strengthening of the civil-military cooperation and partnership and ensures greater general public support. Thirdly, it is of key importance for the officers to obtain a degree in a profession that is acknowledged and highly sought after in the civil workforce market, for once they retire from their military career this will enable them to perform a stress-free and successful re-socialisation into the civil environment (regardless of the increased competitiveness in the civil labour market) and will lead to successful re-employment.[61] These findings should be joined by the note that Clausewitz's theory is not encountered by the future officers of the Slovenian armed forces during their basic military education and training. Thus it is slightly unusual that the role and importance of this military theory (and consequentially Clausewitz) is not dealt with by a military institution but a civil one.

Conclusion

In 100 years the territory of the current Republic of Slovenia has seen five states that differed from each other in all aspects. The empire, kingdom and socialist republic have all fallen. However, regardless of the differences in the state organisation, political systems, size, living standards and national homogeneity, certain similarities in the formation and operation of the defence systems of the various states could be noticed. This is where one can feel the important components of Clausewitz's understanding of the defence system and especially the armed forces as its most important component. Even more, the period in which SFR Yugoslavia and its defence system existed, offers a surprising transfer of Clausewitz's findings into the world of reality. The defence of the homeland was the basic postulate of all citizens who were included in the Yugoslav defence system in its various forms. Similar holds true for the status of the defence system itself and its cooperation with the civil surroundings. In Yugoslavia the civil-military relations were established according to the principles of close cooperation, and this provided the defence system with an exceptionally high level of legitimacy right up to the moment when the defence system was politicised and manipulated in order to achieve unification in an otherwise nationally and ethnically inhomogeneous state. A part of the experience gained by the Yugoslav defence system could be (in a modified version) transferred to the level of the new state, i.e. the independent and sovereign Republic of Slovenia and its defence system. However, due to the emphasised discontinuity of the young Slovenian political elite this was not realised. The

Slovenian defence system was thus funded on completely different postulates, based on the examples of certain Western European states. Many an attempt to transfer these experiences to the level of the Republic of Slovenia has proven to be unsuccessful. However, we can conclude that the Slovenian defence system is organised efficiently and that it functions successfully, regardless of its smallness. The question is how many Clausewitz's principles have been preserved within this system? The international security challenges have changed the security architecture in numerous aspects, and this is reflected in the defence systems. Thus, we could foresee the transience of Clausewitz's findings. However, certain principles discussed in this article can still be applied to contemporary defence systems, especially in the field of civil and military relations. Unfortunately, the study carried out by the Prussian military theoretician and his conclusions are moving further and further away from the defence system itself. The only exception is represented by the defence studies, which preserve his importance in the pedagogical process or at least indirectly ensure the understanding of Clausewitz and the basics of his military theory.

Notes:

[1] Scales H. Robert, Clausewitz and World War IV. *Armed Forces Journal*, 2006, p. 1. Accessible at:

http://www.armedforcesjournal.com/2006/07/1866019 (viewed on 25th August 2010).

[2] New D. Larry, Clausewitz' Theory: On War and Its Application Today. In *Airpower Journal*, fall, 1996, p. 1. Accessible at:

http://www.airpower.maxwell.af.mil/airchronicles/apj/apj96/fall96/lnew.pdf (viewed on 25th August 2010).

[3] Cohen, Bernard. 2003. Geopolitics of the World System, Rowman & Littefield Publishers Inc., New York

[4] Frelih, Marko, *Longaticum in rimski obrambni sistem – Claustra Aplium Iuliarum* (Longaticum and the Roman defence system– Claustra Aplium Iuliarum), Matformat d.o.o., Logatec 2003, p. 32.

[5] Prunk, Janko, *A brief history of Slovenia*. Ljubljana 2000: Založba Grad.

[6] Kladnik, Tomaž. 2007. Slovenian Armed Forces in the Service of Slovenia, Defensor d.o.o., Ljubljana

⁷ Mikulič, Albin, *Defending Democratic Slovenia 1991*, Republic of Slovenia, Ministry of Defence, Slovenian Armed Forces Museum 2005, p. 22.

⁸ YPA had approximately 22,000 soldiers only in the territory of Slovenia, while the entire 5th area – Slovenia and Croatia – was covered by 45,000 soldiers, 1,160 tanks, 3,000 pieces of artillery and 500 anti-aircraft guns (Kladnik 2007).

⁹ Jelušič, Ljubica. 2005. Military Reforms in Slovenia, In: Kernic, Franz (Hsg.), Klein, Paul (Hsg.), Haltiner, Karl (Hsg.) The European armed forces in transition: a comparative analysis, Peter Lang, New York, seiten, 129-144.

¹⁰ Prebilič, Vladimir, Von der Staatsgründung bis zur EU-und NATO-Mitgliedschaft: permanente Reformierung der slowenischen Streitkräfte? In: Rudolf Jaun, Michael Olsansky (ed.), *Strategische Wende – Technologische Wende: die Tranformation der Staitkräfte am Übergang zum 21. Jahrhundert*, Zürich: Militärakademie an der ETH, pp. 19-32.

¹¹ Grizold, Anton, Slovenija v spremenjenem varnostnem okolju: k razvoju obrambno-zaščitnega sistema: izzivi in spodbude (Slovenia in a changed security environment: the development of the defence and protection system: challenges and encouragements), Ljubljana 2005: FDV, p. 131.

¹² Post 2004

¹³ Svete, Uroš / Ljubica Jelušič, NATO-Kompätibilität aus der Sicht des Kleinstaates: Das Beispiel der slowenischen Armee. Welche Armee hat Zukunft?, Sicerheitspolitische Arena vom 12. Mai 2007, Winterthur, *Beilage zur Allgemeinen Sweitzerischer Militärzeizschrift*, Nr. 7/8, Juli 2007, p. 15.

¹⁴ Grizold, ibid., pp. 135-6.

¹⁵ Data for June 2010

¹⁶ Any individual, a citizen of the Republic of Slovenia, without dual nationality, can become a member of the voluntary contractual reserves. As a rule the contracts are signed for a period of 5 years (see *How to become a contractual reserve?* Accessible at:

http://www.postanivojak.si/index.php?id=33. (viewed on 25th August 2010).

¹⁷ Krajlah, Dejan, Clausewitz in vojskovanje v Evropi v XVIII in v začetku XIX. stoletja: diplomska naloga (Clausewitz and warfare in Europe in Kladnik, Tomaž 2006. Slovenian Armed Forces in the Service of Slovenia, Defensor d.o.o., Ljubljana, p. 4.

[18] Handel, I. Michael, Masters of War – Classical Strategic Thought. London-Portland 2001: Frank Cass., p. 1.

[19] See ibid.

[20] Brglez, Alja, O vojni naposled tudi pri nas doma (On war also in our backyard). In: *O vojni (On war)*, Carl von Clausewitz, 311-335. Ljubljana 2004: Studia Humanitatis, p. 317.

[21] Bebler, Anton. Carl von Clausewitz in klasična politična teorija vojne (Carl von Clausewitz and the classical political theory of warfare), *Časopis za kritiko znanosti*, No. 75/76, 1985, p. 4.

[22] Ibid., p. 6.

[23] Ibid., p. 7.

[24] Ibid.

[25] Ibid.

[26] Ibid., p. 9.

[27] Ibid., p. 8.

[28] Ibid., p. 10.

[29] Summarised from Ibid..

[30] Clausewitz, von Carl, *O vojni* (On war). Ljubljana: Studia Humanitatis 2004, p. 17.

[31] Ibid., p. 18.

[32] Ibid., p. 32.

[33] Ibid., p. 167.

[34] Ibid., p. 169.

[35] Ibid., p. 171.

[36] Ibid.

[37] Ibid.

[38] Ibid., p. 174.

[39] Ibid.

[40] Ibid., p. 37.

[41] Ibid.

[42] Ibid.

[43] Ibid., p. 72.

[44] Ibid., p. 103.

[45] Ibid., p. 126.

[46] Ibid.

[47] Ibid., p. 107.

[48] Based on ibid..

[49] ITCY has studied several assumed cases of violations of international warfare and humanitarian law, but no prosecution was started against anybody involved in the 1991 liberation war of RS.

[50] The tasks of the Slovene army are defined in Article No. 37 of the Defence Act which states: "The tasks of the Slovenian army are the following: perform military education and training for armed combat and other forms of military defence; ensure the necessary or demanded readiness; perform military defence in the event of an attack on the state; in natural and other disasters participate in the protection and rescue efforts in accordance with its organisation and equipment; perform obligations adopted by the state through international organisations and treaties." (Defence Act).

[51] Due to the aforementioned legislative restrictions RS was not permitted to cooperate in the 2003 military action of the coalition forces in Iraq. Legally questionable was also the permission given to the allied air force to fly through the Slovenian airspace during their 1999 attack on Serbia, as this NATO operation was not backed by the UN Security Council. (Türk, Danilo, *Temelji mednarodnega prava* (Basics of international law). Ljubljana 2007: GV založba, p. 523).

[52] In spring 2010 the Slovenian weekly magazine Mladina published a call to sign the petition »Abolish the armed forces« on its homepage. The petition received a great response. By the end of August 2010 the petition was signed by almost 9,000 individuals, including certain opinion makers and renown intellectuals. A detailed look at the contents of the petition reveals that it is not a call for the Slovenian armed forces to be completely abolished, but a call for its reorganisation in the sense that the armed forces are preserved in the form of individual units, the basic task of which is to contribute in international operations and missions. (See petition *Abolish the armed forces*)

[53] Moskos, C. Charles, Recruitment and Society after the Cold War. In: Eitelberg, Mark J. and Stephal L. Mehay (ed.): *Marching Toward 21st Century: Military Manpower And Recruiting.* Greenwood Press, Westport, Connecticut, pp. 139-148; Moskos, C. Charles, John Allen Williams and David R. Segal, Armed Forces after the Cold War. In: Moskos, Charles, John Allen Williams and David R. Segal (ed.). *Postmodern Military.* Oxford University Press 2000, pp. 1-13.

[54] Haltiner, Karl W., The Definite End of the Mass Army in Western Europe?. In: *Armed Forces and Society* 25 (1), 1998, pp. 7-26.

[55] Prebilič, V., Civilno-vojaški odnosi po vstopu v Nato in EU - praktični vidik civilnega nadzora nad oboroženimi silami z analizo razmerij med zakonodajno in izvršno oblastjo ter evroatlantskimi povezavami (Severnoatlantsko zavezništvo in EU). Raziskovalni projekt (šifra: M5-0187) (Civil and military relations following the inclusion into NATO and the EU - practical aspect of the civil control over the armed forces and the analysis of the relation between the legislative and executional power and the Euro Atlantic connections (NATO and EU). Research project). Ljubljana 2007: Obramboslovni raziskovalni center.

[56] From Žabkar, Anton and Uroš Svete, Šolanje vojaških profesionalcev med tradicionalnimi izhodišči in (post)modernimi izzivi (Educating military professionals between traditional starting points and (post)modern challenges. In: *Bilten Slovenske vojske.* 1., 2008, pp. 183-208.

[57] The study of defence studies has been educating the cadre for the national security system already since 1975. Later on the defence studies have seen great changes and the course was adjusted to fit the international security studies, the Slovenian needs for military and defence knowledge. In the war for the liberation of Slovenia its graduates found themselves at the very top leadership of the armed conflict. In 2005 the defence studies programme offered two new Bologna programmes. The first, the so-called general defence studies, is aimed at educating for political and international security competencies, while the second, the military defence studies, offer more contents from the field of military practice, skills, training, military science and the use of the armed forces. It includes knowledge from the fields of defence studies, international security, political science, sociology and anthropology. It was formed so that it is comparable to the programmes of military academies in Western Europe

who have transformed their programmes for officers in accordance to the Bologna reform (Jelušič, Ljubica, Kaj lahko obramboslovje prispeva k povečanju profesionalnosti častnikov in častnic Slovenske vojske (razprava) (What can defence studies contribute towards the increase in the professionalism of officers in the Slovenian armed forces (discussion)). In: *Bilten Slovenske vojske*. 1., 2008, pp. 176-177).

[58] Bebler (Ibid., p. 4) stated that the noble descent was questionable; however it opened the gateways to the military profession to the young Clausewitz.

[59] Poles, Ljubo. 2008. Koncept vojaškega izobraževanja častnika slovenske vojske – Stanje in vizija (The concept of military education of the officers of the Slovenian armed forces – the current condition and vision. In: *Bilten Slovenske vojske*. 1., 2008, pp. 121 – 129.

[60] Kotnik, Igor, Kakšen naj bo sodobni častnik Slovenske vojske in kako do njega (What should a contemporary officer of the Slovenian armed forces be like and how to get him). In: *Bilten Slovenske vojske*. 1., 2008, p. 90.

[61] Summarised from ibid., pp. 90-91.

Bibliography:

Bebler, Anton, Carl von Clausewitz in klasična politična teorija vojne (Carl von Clausewitz and the classical political theory of warfare), *Časopis za kritiko znanosti*, No. 75/76, 1985, pp. 3-17.

Brglez, Alja, O vojni naposled tudi pri nas doma (On war also in our backyard). In: *O vojni (On war)*, Carl von Clausewitz, pp. 311-335. Ljubljana 2004: Studia Humanitatis.

Clausewitz, Carl von, *O vojni* (On war). Ljubljana 2004: Studia Humanitatis.

Handel, I. Michael, Masters of War – Classical Strategic Thought, London-Portland 2001: Frank Cass.

Cohen, Bernard, *Geopolitics of the World System,* Rowman & Littlefield Publishers Inc., New York 2003.

Frelih, Marko, *Longaticum in rimski obrambni sistem – Claustra Aplium Iuliarum* (Longaticum and the Roman defence system – Claustra Aplium Iuliarum), Matformat d.o.o., Logatec 2003.

Grizold, Anton, *Slovenija v spremenjenem varnostnem okolju : k razvoju obrambno-zaščitnega sistema: izzivi in spodbude* (Slovenia in a changed security environment: the development of the defence and protection system: challenges and encouragements), Ljubljana2005: FDV.

Haltiner, Karl W., The Definite End of the Mass Army in Western Europe?. In: *Armed Forces and Society* 25 (1), 1998, pp. 7-26.

Jelušič, Ljubica, Military Reforms in Slovenia, In: Kernic, Franz (Hsg.), Klein, Paul (Hsg.), Haltiner, Karl (Hsg.) The European armed forces in transition: a comparative analysis, Peter Lang, New York 2005, pp. 129-144.

Jelušič, Ljubica, Kaj lahko obramboslovje prispeva k povečanju profesionalnosti častnikov in častnic Slovenske vojske (razprava) (What can defence studies contribute towards the increase in the professionalism of officers in the Slovenian armed forces (discussion)) . In: *Bilten Slovenske vojske*. 1., 2008, pp. 175-183.

How to become a contractual reserve soldier? Accessible at:

http://www.postanivojak.si/index.php?id=33. (viewed on 25th August 2010).

Kotnik, Igor, Kakšen naj bo sodobni častnik Slovenske vojske in kako do njega (What should a contemporary officer of the Slovenian armed forces be like and how to get him). In: *Bilten Slovenske vojske*. 1., 2008, pp. 75-96.

Krajlah, Dejan, Clausewitz in vojskovanje v Evropi v XVIII in v začetku XIX. stoletja: diplomska naloga (Clausewitz and warfare in Europe in Kladnik, Tomaž. 2006. Slovenian Armed Forces in the Service of Slovenia, Defensor d.o.o., Ljubljana.

Mikulič, Albin, *Defending Democratic Slovenia 1991,* Republic of Slovenia, Ministry of Defence, Slovenian Armed Forces Museum 2005.

Moskos, C. Charles. Recruitment and Society after the Cold War. In: Eitelberg, Mark J. and Stephal L. Mehay (ed.): *Marching Toward 21st Century: Military Manpower And Recruiting*. Greenwood Press, Westport, Connecticut, pp. 139-148.

Moskos, C. Charles, John Allen Williams and David R. Segal, Armed Forces after the Cold War. In: Moskos, Charles, John Allen Williams and David R. Segal (ed.). *Postmodern Military,* Oxford University Press 2000, pp. 1-13.

New D. Larry., Clausewitz' Theory: On War and Its Application Today. In *Airpower Journal*, fall 1996. Accessible at:

http://www.airpower.maxwell.af.mil/airchronicles/apj/apj96/fall96/lnew.pdf (viewed on 25th August 2010).

On Slovenian armed forces. Accessible at:

http://www.slovenskavojska.si/o-slovenski-vojski/ (viewed on 25th August 2010).

Papaj J. Christopher, Clausewitz and 21st Century Warfare, Strategy Research Project, U.S. Marine Corps, U.S. Army War College, Carlisle Barracks 2008., Pennsylvania.

Petition *Abolish the armed forces.* Accessible at:

http://www.mladina.si/mladina_plus/peticije/ukiniti_vojsko/ (viewed on 25th August 2010).

Poles, Ljubo, Koncept vojaškega Izobraževanja Častnika slovenske vojske – Stanje in vizija (The concept of military education of the officers of the Slovenian armed forces – the current condition and vision). In: *Bilten Slovenske vojske*. 1., 2008, pp. 121-129.

Prebilič, V., *Civilno-vojaški odnosi po vstopu v Nato in EU – praktični vidik civilnega nadzora nad oboroženimi silami z analizo razmerij med zakonodajno in izvršno oblastjo ter evroatlantskimi povezavami (Severnoatlantsko zavezništvo in EU).* Raziskovalni projekt (šifra: M5-0187) (Civil and military relations following the inclusion into NATO and the EU – practical aspect of the civil control over the armed forces and the analysis of the relation between the legislative and executional power and the Euro Atlantic connections (NATO and EU). Research project)). Ljubljana 2007: Obramboslovni raziskovalni center.

Prebilič, Vladimir, Von der Staatsgründung bis zur EU-und NATO-Mitgliedschaft: permanente Reformierung der slowenischen Streitkräfte?, In: Rudolf Jaun, Michael Olsansky (ed.), *Strategische Wende – Technologische Wende: die Tranformation der Streitkräfte am Übergang zum 21. Jahrhundert.* Zürich: Militärakademie an der ETH 2008, pp. 19-32.

Prunk, Janko, *A brief history of Slovenia,* Ljubljana: Založba Grad 2000.

Resolution of the general long-term programme of the development and equipment of the Slovene armed forces, 2004. Accessible at:

    http://www.uradni-list.si/1/objava.jsp?urlid=200489&stevilka=4023 (viewed on 25th August 2010).

Scales H. Robert, Clausewitz and World War IV. *Armed Forces Journal,* 2006 Accessible at:

    http://www.armedforcesjournal.com/2006/07/1866019 (viewed on 25th August 2010).

Svete, Uroš und Ljubica Jelušič. NATO-Kompätibilität aus der Sicht des Kleinstaates: Das Beispiel der slowenischen Armee, Welche Armee hat Zukunft?, Sicherheitspolitische Arena vom 12. Mai 2007, Winterthur, Beilage zur Allgemeinen Sweitzerischer Militärzeizschrift, Nr. 7/8, Juli 2007, pp. 14-17.

Türk, Danilo, *Temelji mednarodnega prava* (Basics of international law), Ljubljana 2007: GV založba.

Zakon o obrambi RS (uradno prečiščeno besedilo) (Defence Act of the Republic of Slovenia, official version). Accessible on

    http://zakonodaja.com/zakoni/i/2/10/zobr_upb1/zobr_upb1 (viewed on 25th August 2010).

Žabkar, Anton and Uroš Svete, *Šolanje vojaških profesionalcev med tradicionalnimi izhodišči in (post)modernimi izzivi* (Educating military professionals between traditional starting points and (post)modern challenges. In: *Bilten Slovenske vojske.* 1., 2008, pp. 183-208.

CLAUSEWITZ, 'THE PEOPLE IN ARMS' AND THE LIBERATION STRUGGLE IN SOUTH AFRICA: CAN THEY BE LINKED?

Thean Potgieter and Francios Vrey

The relevance of Clausewitz reflects a long and winding history as proponents for and against Clausewitz continues to dot the literature. Between those rejecting Clausewitz and those arguing for his continued relevance, reside a wide spectrum of opinions, yet his work remains integral to debates attempting to explain, explore or describe contemporary war, strategy, and armed violence.[1] Clausewitz has influenced the thoughts of military decision-makers across the globe and the interpretation of Clausewitz continues to cut across ideological and cultural divides. Although not influential in every country, *On War* certainly continues to stimulate debate. Historically the focus was on the conventional side of war, but currently more emphasis is being placed on the application of Clausewitz to "small wars".

In their struggles against colonialism, African societies have historically used unconventional tactics to fight colonial forces. After the Second World War political, socio-economic and psychological elements were included to form a cohesive new approach, often referred to as revolutionary warfare. In 1948 the apartheid government came to power in South Africa and as a result of its colonial legacy and the rise of white-minority rule it lacked legitimacy. Resistance to apartheid quickly gained momentum and eventually developed into a revolutionary struggle that drew strongly upon the support of the people.

Due the discrepancy in force between the apartheid government and those wishing to destroy it, the conflict that followed was not only military in nature, but included economic pressure, subversion, diplomacy and psychological actions. As it was essentially a political war waged for the power of the state, the stakes were high – it was about achieving the overthrow of the incumbent government and bringing about a total or revolutionary change. Apartheid's response was known as "total strategy" and it was a pragmatic approach relying on lessons learned and adapting skills and techniques over close to 20 years of conflict. Yet, despite militarily successes the apartheid government lacked legitimacy and, unlike the liberation forces, it failed to provide an acceptable political alternative to the masses.

This paper is not a narrative of the liberation struggle in South Africa. It is rather an endeavour to note aspects of Clausewitz's conceptions of "the people in arms" and their continuing theoretical impetus for those engaged in such struggles.

Clausewitz: A Relevant Legacy?

Clausewitzian thought as an explanatory theory on war has limitations that stem from the unique set of circumstances of his time. Gray[2] maintains that Clausewitz remains the pre-eminent theorist on war and strategy as his views have best withstood the test of time, but acknowledges that they are not perfectly suited to explain contemporary strategy and war in their entirety. Both Angstrom and Kinross list a number of rather influential strategic theorists who question the contemporary relevance of Clausewitz. Keegan, Lutwak and Van Creveld are mentioned as prominent critics in this regard.[3] Given the changes in the wars of the late twentieth and early twenty-first centuries, much of the criticism evolves from explanations of major interstate wars as opposed to the significant growth and prevalence of irregular armed conflicts in recent times.[4]

In opposition to the critics, are those who defend the continuing relevance of Clausewitz. Contemporary theorists such as Gray, Angstrom, Smith, Kinross and Heuser argue for the continued relevance of Clausewitz. This debate between the critics and proponents shows the typical coexistence of two competitive explanatory paradigms that each draws its own constituency of supporters.[5] The proponents and critics of the continued relevance of Clausewitz appear to coexist, with each holding and defending their views. The almost disproportionate contemporary prevalence of low-intensity conflicts forms one particularly salient matter that drives the polemics between the proponents and critics of Clausewitz's contributions in *On War*.[6] This particular matter therefore requires closer scholarly attention.

Brodic in *The Continuing Relevance of On War*[7] also addresses the controversies that surround the durability of Clausewitz's thought and in an evenhanded manner points out those aspects of the work that are still of relevance and those that are of diminishing relevance. Brodie quite harshly sets out the voids or irrelevance of some parts of the work to the present. This acknowledgement must, however, not be exploited to also undermine the continued utility of the work. For example, the war-politics nexus and the rise of the so-called "lesser" forms of warfare, known today as guerrilla warfare or people's war, remain topical. The war-politics connection is well known, but the aspect of lesser forms of war is perhaps less visible, although it grew in stature during the first decade of the twenty-first century. Daase, in turn, offers a more updated and enthusiastic argument for the continued relevance of Clausewitz and in particular his contributions to a better understanding of contemporary, irregular armed conflicts.[8] Through study and experience Clausewitz understood small wars better than most of his contemporaries and instances of traditional small wars, national insurrection by guerrilla warfare, and people's war are depicted in *On War*.

The setting, or unique circumstances of his time, is a point of criticism, but the debate and differences of opinion offer an opportunity to once again learn from some of the enduring insights Clausewitz offers. Although the debates for and against Clausewitz for some time tended to cluster around so-called major wars,[9] low-intensity conflicts now stand at the centre of one strand of the dispute. Although seen as a point of entry to challenge the relevance of Clausewitz, the literature portrays that Clausewitz did not ignore or snub this particular form of war, and, in fact, contributed much at a point in time when general Prussian military thought left little room for innovative ideas.[10]

Clausewitz was exposed to, participated in, lectured and wrote on matters related to what we now term low-intensity conflict, insurgency and terrorism. Just as is the case today, during the time of Clausewitz, several terms denoted the irregular manifestations of war as displayed by references to small war, partisan warfare, and as noted by himself in *On War*, The People in Arms.[11] In a sense, the realities of major war as illustrated by the conquest of most of Europe by Napoleon, dominated the strategic landscape of the time. A second, and perhaps less spectacular range of events materialised that did not leave the military untouched. A range of political, economic and social challenges were set in motion across the European continent that required from armed forces to maintain internal order, prevent revolution and even prop up unpopular regimes.[12] A third phenomenon relates to a gradual movement to bring war, soldiering and society closer together and make war the concern or an affair of the people or broader population as well.[13] In a sense Europe moved into a phase of social and political revolution that tended to sweep aside embedded political and military preferences for major wars between the political entities of the time.

Clausewitz and the irregular side of war show a nexus that runs along two broad lines. Firstly, irregular operations and resistance that took place in Prussia as well as on the wider European continent during the time of Clausewitz. Secondly, his own thought and scripts about people's war and its eventual inclusion in *On War*. Of interest is also that during Clausewitz's very first introduction to soldiering, he formed part of a regiment that fought in an irregular mode against the French.[14] His first exposure (at the age of twelve) to war thus entailed operations that comprised raids, ambushes and smaller detachments that at the time were viewed as part of a small war. The sociopolitical setting of war at the time of Clausewitz must, however, also be considered.

Geoffrey Best describes Europe of 1770-1870 – a period coinciding with the life of Clausewitz (1780-1831) – as "Revolutionary Europe".[15] One influence during this period stemmed from thought and efforts to involve broader society more closely in defending the homeland – well beyond that of participation only in strict Prussian-styled conventional combat formations.[16] By the turn of the eighteenth century broader changes in the social and economic spheres also allowed for shifts in the Prussian military, in particular shifts that brought the Prussian military and society closer together.[17] The notion of a nation in arms slowly began to take shape in Prussia. This was initially viewed as a threat to the Prussian status quo, rather than a pathway to build a better Prussian military by the involvement of broader society. The ideas propounded by Clausewitz, that society indeed has a more influential role to play during war and should be integrated more closely into the military effort, were unfortunately not well received.[18]

The French occupation of Prussia and surrounding Europe, however, gave rise to several uprisings.[19] The salient outcomes of this period are a better understanding by, and a determined drive for the physical entry of, broader society into the Prussian military. Simultaneously a rising climate calling for some liberation from French domination swept across Europe. This anti-French climate gave rise to insurrections by small groups against the regular French forces of occupation. It is therefore not strange that Best ends his discussion on revolutionary Europe with *"People's wars of national liberation"*[20] – a period that overlaps with the life of Clausewitz and continues after his death. It was a time when major wars in Europe had to coexist with the growth of domestic insurrections and wars of a lower intensity fought in a different manner by soldiers not viewed as professional regulars.

As for Prussia, the "*Aufruf an mein Volk*" by Frederick William (March 1813) created the impetus to move beyond the normal conventions of warfare.[21] The window of opportunity did not slip past reform-minded Prussian officers like Clausewitz, but the call did not only apply to ideas relevant to irregular forces fighting in more irregular ways. Opportunities for change in the regular and irregular domains were on offer. This is where the prospect for change tied in with the view of Clausewitz that society must be more involved in fighting wars. War no longer stood as a matter of concern for the military only.[22] By reforming the state, opportunities to make the armed forces more effective and legitimate unfolded. Pressure on the political level created the leeway for changes to a bureaucratic Prussian military that had to adjust to adaptations that had made its major foe, France, militarily much more effective.

Other events and developments also influenced Clausewitz and his ideas on more irregular forms of warfare. Both Hahlweg and Heuser expounded on these matters.[23] The American Revolution and the French Revolution both showed how armed forces could fight differently and be more effective. As other European countries reacted to the French occupation of most of Europe, regular forces that operated in the "*Kleinkrieg*" mode became more common and successful. The Vendee fighting, the Tyrolian case and the Spanish uprising against the French all served to underline French vulnerabilities.[24] Although they were not very strong in military terms, irregulars augmented regular forces to deal more effectively with the occupying French and their allies. The regular-irregular combination that drew society into the fighting in several ways was not lost upon Clausewitz. While the irregular fighting initially seems to denote regular forces fighting in a somewhat irregular mode, it appears that over time the forces themselves assumed an irregular profile and sought out irregular tactics to employ against the regulars.

The growth in partisan and people's wars that stemmed from the practice of small wars conducted on the fringes of regular wars is significant. As a concept and a practice, small wars as small-scale military operations conducted by small 'detachments' comprised of irregular forces on the fringes of major operations where regular forces dominate as primary actors predate the ideas of Clausewitz.[25] The real contributions of smaller irregular detachments were, however overshadowed by the preference of the period to have regular forces, often consisting of foreign or mercenary elements, to do the fighting. Some interplay between major and small wars thus took place, although major or regular warfare remained privileged in the literature and in fact serves as rationale for Heuser's contribution on *Small Wars in the Age of Clausewitz* that highlights the more irregular side of war that drew Clausewitz's attention.

Manifestations of small wars during the time of Clausewitz are important. In greater Europe several examples underline the fact that another form of warfare in fact coexisted with major war. Rulers employed certain ethnic groups with skills in horsemanship, mountain warfare and local languages to gather information. Thus the use of military contingents that play a different role to that of primary fighting units to bring about an outcome through armed violence against a military opponent becomes apparent. It remains, however, a matter of scale or choice on just how different the two contingents were. Heuser nonetheless attributes guerrilla and partisan modes of warfare to these small war contingents as they exemplify how today's special forces and guerrilla fighters tend to operate.[26]

Clausewitz was initially more familiar with small war (*kleiner Krieg*) than guerrilla warfare for he studied the former as a military, not a political manifestation, and as part of special operations by regular forces (not guerrilla warfare) to conduct reconnaissance, patrols, raids and ambushes.[27] Guerrilla warfare (that stands closer to people's war or insurgency) on the other hand, brings the political affiliation closer. Clausewitz does make the political connection between politics and war a central tenet of his views and particularly so in arguing that without politics war is in fact meaningless and serves no purpose.[28]

A second exposure to a tighter triad of war, politics and people also influenced Clausewitz. People (broader society) became generally more closely involved in war and began to serve in active fighting in particular. The American War of Independence and the French Revolution are two meaningful events depicting how American and French societies were recruited or herded into the military machinery. The foreign or mercenary elements did not disappear as such, but people from all levels of society began to augment the regulars and initiated irregular fighting tactics. Irregular or small war tactics accordingly became part of the overall fighting regime and featured alongside or in tandem with the tactics of the regular forces.[29] The Spanish resistance to the French reinforced the idea that people outside the formal military structures (hereafter often called guerrillas) are able to augment the war effort through irregular tactics that eventually can be orchestrated into a broader campaign.[30]

Kinross[31] maintains that Clausewitz's deeper understanding of irregular warfare stems from his *Bekenntnisdenkschrift* and his exposure to small wars, partisan warfare in Russia and the mobilisation of the *Landwehr* against the French in 1813. Whether as an introduction or mere departure, Clausewitz studied the irregular side of war at a time when strategic reality and what governments (Prussia in particular) wished to see, appeared not to coincide. Reality in fact is portrayed by much of what appears in Book 8 of *On War* about the changing face of war over time as a product of the nature of states and societies, time and prevailing conditions.[32] Rulers and societies portray different preferences on how to conduct war, who to involve and what aims to pursue, and Clausewitz understood that the Prussian preferences were strong, but had become outdated.

In addition to exposure to instances of small wars over a period of time, Clausewitz also actively studied and published or lectured on the topic. In addition to The People in Arms in *On War* (Book 6 Defence), other publications and bodies of thought also emerged.[33] Clausewitz is most explicit in viewing guerrilla war "as a people's war of liberation or resistance"[34] with the people's uprising showing tactics found in guerrilla warfare. Although a last resort, guerrilla warfare is now placed within the realm of the general theory of war. This move to maturity by involving society in the framework of war also offers the opportunity of broad resistance by the social order to external occupation – not just by building larger regular forces, but by broadening the scope of opposition to any foe in direct and indirect ways. Although seemingly comprehensive in appearance, Clausewitz acknowledges that his views are perhaps not authoritative due to people's war still being uncommon and (at the time) not open to comprehensive study.[35]

In his analysis of two of Clausewitz's documents, Hahlweg manages to isolate some important thoughts on Clausewitz and guerrilla war.[36] From the *Bekenntnisdenkschrift* (a document more focussed upon liberating Prussia from French occupation), the following salient thought arises. A people's war of liberation and resistance includes a general uprising using guerrilla war and tactics reflecting reconnaissance, raids, ambushes, and terror by employing popular forces to augment the regulars. It is the *Bekenntnisdenkschrif* that shaped Clausewitz's thought on what was often considered the lesser form of war. Although he does not offer a comprehensive theory of guerrilla warfare as an independent way of warfare, Clausewitz accurately sets guerrilla warfare in the theory of war, outlines its ways and means and conveys its utility of resistance by the people, at a time when the institutional barriers to this very notion began to crumble.[37]

The chapter titled "The people in arms" in *On War* attends to guerrilla warfare more comprehensively within the realm of defence against an invader. The chapter sets the scene for people's war by explaining the context of opportunities to involve society in a war effort within a wider framework of general war, facilitating population and geographic features in a country and how to avoid defeat.[38] Important for survival is that the irregular forces must avoid set battles with the regular forces and operate on the periphery of the main theatre of war, thus forcing the enemy to divert a disproportionate effort towards containing the insurgents. The chapter also covers the vulnerabilities of this strategic defensive way of war.[39] Understanding that insurgent actions are fought by irregular troops, Clausewitz notes the danger of entrapment by regular forces that holds the real possibility of military defeat for the insurgent. Whether as an addition on the fringes of the main military effort, or as a last stance to survive, insurrection and armed resistance by the people through lesser military means grew in importance in Clausewitz's outlook.

Notes on the Liberation Struggle in South Africa

The above discussion indicates that the relevance of Clausewitz continues to receive scholarly attention. As the focus is more often upon different manifestations of war, Clausewitz's applications to African countries such as South Africa might perhaps be rare, but it is not irrelevant. Given the prevalence of irregular wars on the African continent and of liberation movements claiming the successful conduct of people's wars in Southern African countries, the relevance of Clausewitz cannot be ignored. It is therefore not strange that Daase[40] points out that the African National Congress (ANC) in South Africa succeeded in surviving politically against superior military odds by employing the concept of people's war. In the South African case the weak political position, but rather solid security position of the incumbent apartheid government resulted in no small way from its hold over the defence establishment. The South African liberation movements embarked upon an armed struggle that reflected discernable political and military pathways. The importance of drawing in society became apparent over time and quite early in the history of the armed resistance, the utility of Clausewitz and guerrilla warfare featured quite prominently.[41]

After the Second World War armed resistance against colonialism was fused with political, social-economic and psychological elements to form a cohesive new approach, often referred to as revolutionary warfare. European colonial powers therefore became engaged in various such wars in their colonies. In South Africa the situation was somewhat different; the colonial government was replaced by a local government that in 1948 instituted apartheid – a political system based on race, with the majority excluded from direct participation in political processes and a series of racial discriminatory laws. Apartheid had no legitimacy amongst the masses and in due course it became the scorn of the international community. For decades a complex and multi-dimensional anti-apartheid struggle was waged in South Africa, in the African region and across the world.

The 1950s saw an upsurge in popular protest against the apartheid system under the banner of the African National Congress (ANC) and other organisations. Mass action included protests, boycotts, stayaways, strikes, defiance campaigns and civil disobedience. The most notable protest action was the Sharpeville shootings in March 1960. During a peaceful march to the police station, organised by the Pan Africanist Congress (PAC), nervous constables alarmed by the size of the crowd, panicked and fired into the crowd. Sixty-nine people died and 180 were wounded, many shot in the back. Sharpeville was a dramatic turning point. The government declared a State of Emergency, detained many ANC and PAC leaders and banned both organisations. To those opposing apartheid Sharpeville indicated that non-violent resistance had achieved nothing, while apartheid was condemned internationally and calls for sanctions against South Africa were made in the United Nations.[42]

Clausewitz reminded us that to understand the nature of the conflict is the "first of all strategic questions and the most comprehensive".[43] For many years an effort to understand the nature of the conflict and design an appropriate strategic response was part and parcel of the struggle history of South Africa, and it is reflected in the efforts of both the liberation forces and the apartheid government. Furthermore, as the strategies of the opposing forces are dialectically linked, both sides tried to adapt to the unique political, socio-economic, topographical and operational conditions.

Nelson Mandela explains that when peaceful campaigning against apartheid policies did not succeed, he realised it is the oppressor that defined the nature of the struggle, and the only recourse the oppressed had was to use methods mirroring those of the oppressor. This implied that they had no alternative but to resort to an armed struggle, specifically as the non-violent weapons they used – such as speeches, deputations, threats, marches, strikes, stay-aways and volunteer imprisonment – were met with an iron hand. Non-violence has failed and "violence was the only weapon that would destroy apartheid".[44]

In 1961, the ANC and the South African Communist Party (SACP) established an underground guerrilla army, *Umkhonto we Sizwe* (MK), the Spear of the Nation. With its establishment the MK high command made its commitment to the liberation struggle clear and emphasised that its decision to embark on an armed struggle, was not reached easily, but emanated from the lack of success of peaceful protests and the repression by the oppressor.[45]

After the creation of MK, Mandela studied the literature on warfare, revolutions and guerrilla warfare. Specifically the creation and sustaining of a guerrilla force was of interest. Some of the sources he found particularly interesting were *Commando* by Deneys Reitz, on the guerrilla tactics the Boer generals applied during the Anglo-Boer War; Edgar Snow's *Red Star Over China*, on Mao's determined approach and non-traditional thinking; while *The Revolt* by Menachem Begin was of interest as it showed how to conduct a guerrilla campaign in a country without mountains or forests. He also studied the theories of Mao Tse-tung, Fidel Castro and Ché Guevara. Clausewitz, Mandela stated, was particularly interesting as Clausewitz's central thesis, that war was a continuation of politics by other means, "dovetailed with my own instincts".[46]

MK now had four alternatives, sabotage, guerrilla warfare, terrorism and revolution. Due to its fledging status Mandela regarded revolution as inconceivable, while terrorism "inevitably reflected poorly on those who used it" and might undermine public support, guerrilla warfare was a possibility but the sensible place to start was sabotage. He preferred it, as sabotage would inflict "the least harm against individuals" and offered the best hope of reconciliation between races afterwards. The MK strategy was to "make selected forays against military installations, power plants, telephone lines and transportation links; targets that would not only hamper the military effectiveness of the state, but frighten National Party supporters, scare away foreign capital and weaken the economy".[47] It was hoped that this would induce the government to negotiate, but if sabotage did not work, the struggle had to move onto the next phases, guerrilla warfare and terrorism.

On 11 July 1963 the headquarters of MK in Rivonia were raided. Its leadership was arrested and sentenced to life imprisonment on Robben Island. During the 1960s both the ANC and PAC faced major difficulties as exiled organisations. Despite being welcome in a number of African countries, it was difficult to infiltrate South Africa because of the terrain, the strength of the security forces and the fact that South Africa's northerly neighbours (the Portuguese colonies of Mozambique and Angola as well as Rhodesia) provided a protective cordon. Military action therefore remained limited and much attention was focussed on attempts to develop underground structures and train insurgents, but there was little opportunity to carry out operations.[48]

The ANC leadership understood that though much could be learned from theorists such as Mao Tse-tung, Che Guevarra, Regis Debray and others, as well as from the examples of the revolutionary struggles in China, Vietnam, Latin America and others, the South African situation must be seen as unique. As Joe Matthews explained, the people had to be armed for "the problems posed by the South African revolution ... learn from the revolutionary experience all over the world, but ... applied to the South African revolution".[49]

At the Morogoro conference in 1969 the ANC decided to adopt a new strategy calling for a protracted armed struggle and mass mobilisation. Guerrilla warfare was considered to be the best method for the materially weak to fight against the materially strong as its unique attributes (such as surprise, mobility, stealth and tactical retreat) would stretch the resources of the government's conventional forces. Influenced by Mao, the strategy emphasised the countryside as the primary theatre of the insurgency, supported by urban actions.[50] As the ANC had to conduct this rural action from beyond the borders of the country and did not have a secure base within the country or immediately across the border, the struggle was fraught with problems. Not only was a significant segment of society urbanised, but much of the resistance against apartheid was concentrated in urban areas and few rural areas could sustain an insurgency.

The decolonisation of Mozambique and Angola changed the situation dramatically as the new pro-Soviet governments provided sanctuaries and made it possible for guerrillas to infiltrate South Africa. Though MK also developed guerrilla cells in urban areas, they were, in essence, seen as an extension of the countryside approach. Not much occurred in terms of the armed struggle and when the large-scale Soweto riots occurred in 1976, the ANC and MK were surprised. They were not really ready to fully exploit the situation and only limited acts of sabotage occurred. However, the Soweto uprisings challenged MK's emphasis on the rural approach and by 1979 a policy shift to "people's war" dictated a focus on urban guerrilla warfare, specifically in the townships, with the guerrilla linking up with mass political organisations. International support for the struggle was also deemed important and as a result the revolutionary strategy now rested on four pillars, international support, mass action, underground activity and the armed struggle.[51]

As the apartheid state had to confront a variety of challenges, the rigid apartheid model was breaking down and it was in decline during the late 1970s and the 1980s. These challenges had to do with the requirements of an industrial economy, labour and urban resistance and the changing geopolitical situation in Southern Africa due to the independence of Mozambique and Angola in 1974 and the political settlement in Zimbabwe. As the spiral of resistance and repression deepened, the South African state reacted.

The apartheid government realised that change was necessary due to changing economic and social conditions and commenced with a process to reform apartheid incrementally, while still retaining political power. It interpreted the challenges it faced in terms of a "total onslaught", which was closely linked to the broader Cold War as the apartheid government professed to be a bastion against communist expansion and the perceived threat posed by revolutionaries from inside and outside the country. This "total onslaught", it believed, was inspired from abroad and coordinated by communist powers.[52] The Minister of Defence, Magnus Malan, explained that many African states had "promised their absolute support … to the communist-inspired terrorist organisations such as the ANC, the PAC and SWAPO in their so-called liberation struggle … The Russian aim is to build up a force in this way to be able to attack South Africa … [they] train terrorists within and outside Africa … We cannot permit Russia to proceed unhindered with its diabolical plans in our subcontinent …"[53].

The outcome was a policy known as "total strategy" and the Defence White Paper of 1977 was the blueprint: A "Total National Strategy" had to be formulated at the highest level to secure the government and its institutions; identifying, preventing and countering subversion and revolution; and countering any form of revolutionary action. The national security structure had to develop a counter to any threat; emphasis was placed on the permanent force as the nucleus of the SA Defence Force; while counterinsurgency techniques, intelligence networks and the capacity to operate throughout the region had to improve. The SA Police was responsible for countering the internal unrest, but the SA Army would provide countrywide support. Politically a process of incremental reforms had to take place. Total strategy essentially rested on two pillars, a political programme and the security component. These military, political, and economic aspects of the government's response were further understood to be in constant need of adaptation to meet changing situations.[54]

The inspiration for total strategy came from a variety of sources, most notably the French theorist General André Beaufre. Based on the French counterinsurgency experiences in Indochina and Algeria, Beaufre advocated that coordinated total onslaughts demand total, indirect counter-strategies coordinating military with political and economic policy. Strategy should achieve its results through a series of methods, with the military playing "… no more than an auxiliary role".[55] To Beaufre, strategy was not a single doctrine but a "method of thought" and to select the best course of action requires a thorough understanding of the situation as every situation requires a specific strategy. A strategy that might be effective in one specific situation might be disastrous in another. Beaufre indicated that countries often go to war with tactics alone – a military approach based on false premises. In Indo-China the French lost although their tactics were excellent, but they were defeated by enemy strategy. Despite this experience, the same mistakes were repeated in Algeria as the approach did not fit the situation. Ignorance of strategy is therefore often the most fatal error.[56]

If a military victory is unattainable in a specific struggle, other methods must be used to great effectiveness as twentieth century revolutionary, irregular, and asymmetrical struggles have shown. Beaufre emphasised that strategy provides a whole series of means, which includes everything from the application of hard military power to propaganda, economic and psychological measures. As the desired outcome of any conflict is to force the enemy to accept your will, the aim of strategy is to achieve policy objectives by using all possible resources, including those available in the multidimensional revolutionary warfare environment. As this type of war is total and is "carried on in all fields, political, economic, diplomatic and military", strategy must also be total and it should no longer be the exclusive domain of the military.[57] It all seemed very appropriate to the Apartheid planners.

In essence total onslaught reflected the mindset of apartheid leaders, their notion of the challenge to their authority, and it shaped the response – total strategy. The rationale was quite clear: South Africa was the target of a total onslaught which must be combated with a total strategy combining effective security with a policy of reform. Reform was aimed at removing the grievances the revolutionaries could exploit, while society had to be restructured in line with the requirements of industry and the economy, the political interest of the government and the security interests of the military and security forces. Total strategy in actual fact combined political and military action.

Many reforms that addressed grievances in the fields of industry, economy, labour, education, pass laws and petty apartheid followed. Constitutional development was an inherent part of total strategy. In an attempt to co-opt sections of society that were previously excluded from government, the tricameral constitution of 1983 created a parliament with three separate assemblies, one for White, one for Coloured and one for Indian Members of Parliament. But the overall authority was effectively still with the white House of Assembly. As the system clearly made no provision for African participation, a system of Black local authorities was instituted to elect local governments. The tricameral system and token Black local authorities in effect had very little appeal for the population and was resented. It was seen as not real reform and a ploy of the apartheid government to maintain authority. It led to much protest action and caused a legitimacy crisis for the apartheid reform process.[58] With the political pillar of total strategy thus unsuccessful, only the security pillar remained.

The security establishment (police and military in particular) had an important role to play in the total strategy. A National Security Management System was created with the State Security Council at its head. The State Security Council, an advisory body to Cabinet, soon gained much influence as it controlled the security situation and in many ways, according to some observers, it became an alternative Cabinet.

In their counterinsurgency approach the SADF and its generals initially drew from French and British experiences. Soon, and within the context of total strategy, it developed a counterrevolutionary response with much emphasis on the fact that it was a struggle for the people. The American theorist J.J. McCuen, who placed the accent on mirroring Maoist style revolutionary guerrilla warfare based on a protracted, phased struggle, was well studied.[59] The counterrevolutionaries had to arrest the progression of the struggle in every phase, implement a counter-phase, and force it back into an earlier phase.

By the late 1970s and the 1980s, due to the changing geopolitical situation and the support anti-apartheid forces received from many countries in the region, the SADF became embroiled in the conflict in Angola. This conflict, conducted across the Namibian-Angolan border, involved the liberation forces (such as the SWAPO and the ANC), Angolan and Cuban forces, Soviet advisors, as well as UNITA. In addition the SADF also operated across the region, often neutralising targets in countries harbouring guerrillas, which affected the stability of those countries adversely. Inside South Africa it supported and even supplanted the SA Police.

With its practical, instinctive approach, the SADF achieved much military success. It often discounted theory and relied on experience as much of its theory was in any case determined by the experience in Namibia and Angola.[60] Military leaders recognised that local conditions made it unwise to narrowly follow theories and models, as a former Chief of the SADF explained: "I had too much experience of people who have certain models and then they apply those models, come hell or high water, they apply those models ... I would like to get the facts and the figures and listen to everybody, analyse situations and decide on what would be the best approach ..."[61]. So, despite the notions echoed by the political leaders that such a struggle is 80% political and 20% military, without a clear and legitimate political alternative, the political problem was addressed by the application of military power.

Coinciding with the establishment of the tricameral parliament and the Black local authorities, internally the conflict entered a new phase in popular resistance by the middle 1980s. From 1984 onwards primary resistance against the government grew and by 1985 a township revolt had spread to most parts of the country. In many townships civil government collapsed and was replaced by alternative structures, those supporting or working for security forces and local authorities were isolated, student and labour unrests as well as rent and consumer boycotts were common and there were calls to make South Africa ungovernable and create a revolution. The exiled ANC received increased support, while guerrilla infiltration and attacks on state installations increased.

South Africa was now reaching new heights in popular resistance and state repression and there was a widespread but mistaken belief that the state was about to collapse. Despite the open rebellion and chaos, the state reacted with force and made it clear that the revolution was not about to occur. The Army and Police deployed in the townships from October 1984 onwards. In July 1985 the government declared a State of Emergency in many regions and in the following year a full State of Emergency came into effect (only lifted in 1990). The entire resources of the state were mobilised in the internal struggle. Coordination of counter-revolutionary measures improved and the security forces managed to effectively crush the internal uprising by 1987.[62]

At the Kabwe Consultative Conference in June 1985, the ANC reappraised its strategy of "people's war" and "making the country ungovernable" as this policy had shown a specific weakness due to the focus on urban operations. The result was more operations in rural areas, landmines and attacks on white farms. If operations were conducted in border areas, guerrillas could retreat back across the border. Though the harsh nature of the State of Emergency led to a large number of detentions, and harmed the operational capability of MK, many operations still occurred during the late 1980s.[63]

South African society was paying the price for the fact that there was no credible political solution. The State Security Council seemed to dictate government policy, while through the National Security Management System a web of strict security controls were instituted.[64] The defence budget was huge and much militarization took place amongst the white segment of society. The media was also curtailed and in general South Africa became a security state. The international condemnation of apartheid and economic sanctions had caused a profound economic crisis. Popular protests, on the other hand, continued. In such conditions an increasing spiral of worsening poverty, disaffection and continued repression was inevitable.

A stalemate therefore existed. The dissidents could not overthrow the hegemony of the state, while the state had lost the initiative and its legitimacy. The cost of the war was unacceptable and without a political solution there was no way out. The application of military power, or "war", therefore ceased to be a political tool, but had become an objective on its own.

Change occurred suddenly. On 2 February 1990 F.W. de Klerk, the new President of South Africa, announced sweeping changes that included the unbanning of the ANC and other parties and organisations, as well as the release of many political prisoners, including Nelson Mandela. Soon key sections of apartheid legislation were repealed and formal multiparty negotiations, leading to a new political dispensation and a democratic South Africa commenced. The notion of a clear and acceptable political outcome, instead of the mere application of force, again entered the equation and paved the way towards a negotiated settlement.

Though the relationship between war and politics is obvious to all students of Clausewitz, its relevance to lesser forms of war is less evident. If politics is the "guiding intelligence" and war is only the "instrument", then political constraints will inherently moderate the conduct of war. This is specifically relevant to this type of conflict. For example, if an uprising is brutally suppressed by force, it would leave a bad legacy and create much animosity which could undermine efforts to seek a solution. In this sense suppression and the Sharpeville uprising in 1960, the Soweto uprising in 1976 and the State of Emergency in the 1980s created vast resentment against the apartheid government and caused many potential recruits to join the ranks of the liberation forces. Only a changed political situation provided an outcome.

A clear political programme is very important in a revolutionary struggle. In 1955 the Congress of the People (various liberation movements) accepted the Freedom Charter which demanded an end to apartheid, equality before the law and the creation of a righteous society based on the will of the people. The Charter became the foundation of ANC ideology, a blueprint in the liberation struggle and a beacon of hope for many. Mandela likened it to other political manifestos such as the American Declaration of Independence, the French Declaration of the Rights of Man and the Communist Manifesto.[65] Despite much criticism of the Charter, it must be seen as a revolutionary document because it propagated radical changes to the economic, social and political structure of South Africa and served as a benchmark for opposition to apartheid into the 1990s.

In his study of Clausewitz, Lenin highlighted that by analysing the psychological and sociological makeup of an enemy and its reactions, crucial weaknesses can be identified. The soundest strategy is then "to postpone operations until moral disintegration of the enemy renders a mortal blow both possible and easy". As a revolutionary Lenin saw political action as psychological. It was not military action (as Clausewitz emphasised) that had to break the moral of the enemy, but political action.[66] Within the Leninist framework state power should be seized by insurrection and the transformation of society should then take place. These ideas were pleasing to the ANC as they placed much emphasis on the leadership, making the revolutionary struggle a calculated and precisely executed affair. The ANC saw state power as central to the process and Oliver Tambo (former President of the ANC) explained it as follows: "All revolutions are about state power … 'power to the people' means … to destroy the power of apartheid tyranny and replace it with popular power with a government whose authority derives from the will of all our people, both black and white." In the same context, Thabo Mbeki saw the ANC as the "vanguard" of "national liberation", working towards mobilising all groups and classes for the "destruction of the apartheid system" with victory of the "national democratic revolution" as the objective.[67]

As a result of the unique political situation experienced in the time of Clausewitz, in his conception, war and soldiering increasingly became a concern of the people and the notion of a nation in arms gradually developed. Clausewitz maintained that the link between war and society should be closer, which was vindicated by the fact that insurrections against French domination were sweeping across Europe showing that war was no longer a matter for only the military.[68] The notion of the nation in arms is relevant for acting against an invader or foreign domination as was the case with French influence in the time of Clausewitz. In Africa the invader and foreign domination were encapsulated in colonial power and apartheid. Again, in Prussia it was possible to bring to fruition the nation under arms in the conventional sense and confront Napoleon on the battlefield, whereas in Africa the levels of available physical force between the opposing sides were disproportionate. Hence, the concept of the nation in arms was relevant as it had to prepare the nation for a people's war – to mobilise and organise everybody for resistance on all levels of society in a protracted multidimensional struggle. In fact, if it was not possible to defeat the occupier or the target government, the cost of the war had to become unacceptable and change had to be forced upon it.

What Clausewitz did not anticipate, also due to the uniqueness of the circumstances of his time, is that guerrilla tactics and the notion of the people's war would become infused with politics. Also, that this new type of war would not only be war waged for political objectives, but that politics would become the war. The people's war in essence became a struggle for the "hearts and the minds" of the people. Revolutionary wars are therefore not decided on the battlefield, but as the Brazilian theorist Abraham Guillen emphasised, "rather by winning the political support of the people".[69]

The struggle for the "hearts and minds" in South Africa was a more complex process than it might seem. For the disenfranchised black masses resistance was a logical choice, but those resisting apartheid were not only black, and from the beginning they included defective voices from other groups. In many senses the dissatisfaction of many white South Africans contributed much towards the eventual political solution. This was evident in a number of developments. By the 1980s South Africa experienced a "virtual civil war" in many parts of the country and the SA Army occupied the townships in support of the SA Police and retained control through military power, detentions and increased repression. The soldiers that had to perform these tasks were mostly white conscripts who did two years, compulsory military service, fought in the "Border War" and were internally deployed in the townships. Many resented their role – it was not the principle of military service that caused the resentment, but the fact that they were fighting internally. Their lives and schools were also infused with security force propaganda and they were susceptible to various security controls. This did not go unopposed. Objection by conscripted servicemen occurred, while the End Conscription Campaign gained much wider support after the deployment of troops in townships.[70] Furthermore, the spectacle of young soldiers losing their lives in a poorly defined "Border War" raised many questions about its purpose amongst the white electorate. Internationally condemnation also grew, South Africa became a pariah state, sanctions and disinvestment caused economic decline, taxes increased and constant labour unrest disrupted normal economic activities. The cost of the war had simply become unacceptable.

Regarding guerrilla warfare Clausewitz's focus is more on it as a tool in defence within the wider framework of a general war. This is comprehensible against the background of his time as much military effort could be diverted to contain guerrilla forces. However, Clausewitz's recognition of the salient nature of guerrilla warfare as a tactic of choice for the militarily inferior or "the people" and the fact that he emphasises geographic features and warns that guerrilla forces should avoid direct battle with regular forces are important and relevant. In contrast with other parts of the world a rural-based peasant revolt or a guerrilla campaign waged from the countryside, was not successful or the best option in South Africa. A landed peasantry in the Chinese sense did not exist and it was not possible to create base areas in forests and mountain ranges where the guerrillas would have sufficient sanctuary from government forces. Though a countryside approach was initially favoured, the emphasis moved to an urban insurrection with support from rural areas. MK appreciated that the armed forces should not be tackled directly, and the conflict became a politico-socio-economic struggle waged in various dimensions. It was therefore a move from guerrilla warfare, as the most important tool, to a complex popular revolutionary struggle with guerrilla warfare interspersed with acts of terrorism as a tool. The armed struggle and urban violence was not of major significance or at all militarily decisive, yet in political terms its impact was vast.

Conclusion

The model for the liberation struggle in South Africa is not to be found in the literature produced by Clausewitz. In contrast with some of the great wars of the past, the influence of Clausewitz was also not instrumental to the liberation struggle in South Africa. Yet, the contribution Clausewitz made to our understanding of conflict, including this one, was omnipresent.

Certainly, war is not only a continuation of politics in great wars, but those waging irregular wars or conducting revolution must always take cognisance of it. If military actions do not take place to support a clear and legitimate political goal, they are doomed to failure. A common threat therefore visible in the history of colonial wars or wars of national liberation is that military power in itself is not enough; clear political goals must be in place.

In the South African example the struggle waged by the liberation forces had a clear political objective with which the majority identified, while the military actions of the apartheid regime lacked political credibility. It was therefore a revolutionary struggle waged for a desired political outcome, against counterrevolutionary warfare lacking political legitimacy. The liberation forces thus understood the nature of the conflict and mobilised their array of forces quite appropriately, although their military wings remained somewhat peripheral at times. The then South African government also understood the nature of the conflict, but their success with military counter-measures accentuates their failure on the political and socio-economic levels. Not heeding Clausewitz by losing sight of the political imperative to guide the security campaign is the single fatal blunder of the apartheid government.

Clausewitz certainly did not emphasise this type of conflict and it is easier to search for his influence in the great wars of the last two centuries. Yet, applicability exists and the fact that the work of Clausewitz promotes an understanding of a type of conflict that essentially developed and was raised to saliency long after his death, pays testimony to the following: How thorough and deep his understanding of war and conflict as a complex phenomenon was, the inter-relationship of war in its various guises and the fact that Clausewitz still holds supreme as a philosopher of war.

Notes:

[1] See Stuart Kinross, 'Clausewitz and Low-Intensity Conflict', *Journal of Strategic Studies*, 27(1), (March, 2004); M.L.R. Smith, 'Guerrillas in the Mist: Reassessing Strategy and Low Intensity Warfare, *Review of International Studies*, 29, (2003), p. 21 and Hew Strachan and Andreas Herberg-Rothe, (eds), *Clausewitz in the Twenty-First Century*, Oxford: Oxford University Press, 2007, pp. 6-8.

[2] Colin Gray, Clausewitz rules, OK? The future is the past – with GPS, *Review of International Studies*, 25. (1999), p. 180.

[3] Jan Angstrom, "Introduction" in Isabella Duyvesteyn and Jan Angstrom, *Rethinking the Nature of War*, London: Frank Cass, 2005, p. 9; Kinross, Clausewitz and low-intensity conflict, p. 36.

[4] See Hew Strachan and Andreas Herberg-Rothe, Introduction, in Strachan and Herberg- Rothe (eds), *Clausewitz in the Twenty-First Century*, p. 11.

[5] Thomas Kuhn, *The Structure of Scientific Revolutions*, 2nd Edition, Chicago: University of Chicago Press, 1970, p. 198.

[6] Christopher Daase, "Clausewitz and Small Wars" in Strachan and Herberg-Rothe (eds), *Clausewitz in the Twenty-First Century*, p. 182.

[7] Bernard Brodie, "The continuing relevance of On War" in Peter Paret and Michael Howard, (eds), *On War*, Princeton: Princeton University Press, p. 45.

[8] Daase, Clausewitz and Small wars, p. 192.

[9] Gray, 1999, Clausewitz rules, p. 177.

[10] Kinross, Clausewitz and low-intensity conflict, p. 36.

[11] Clausewitz, "The people in arms" in Peter Paret and Michael Howard (eds), *On War*, Princeton: PUP, 1984, p. 479.

[12] Geofrey Best, *War and Society in Revolutionary Europe*, 1770-1870, Fontana, 1982, pp. 253-254.

[13] Clausewitz, "Interdependence of the elements of war" in Paret and Howard (eds), *On War*, p. 592.

[14] Peter Paret, "Clausewitz", in Peter Paret (ed), *Makers of Modern Strategy: From Michiavelli to the nuclear age*, Princeton: Princeton University Press, 1986, p. 188.

[15] See Best, *War and Society in Revolutionary Europe*.

[16] Best, *War and Society in Revolutionary Europe*, pp. 50-51.

[17] Best, *War and Society in Revolutionary Europe*, p. 157.

[18] Paret, Clausewitz, pp. 192 and 195.

[19] Best, *War and Society in Revolutionary Europe*, p. 159.

[20] Best, *War and Society in Revolutionary Europe*, p. 257.

[21] Best, *War and Society in Revolutionary Europe*, pp. 162-163.

[22] Paret, Clausewitz, p. 192.

[23] Hahlweg, Clausewitz and guerrilla warfare in Michael Handel, *Clausewitz in Modern Strategy*, London: Frank Cass, 1986 and Beatrice Heuser, Small wars in the age of Clausewitz: The watershed between partisan war and people's war, *The Journal of Strategic Studies*, 33(1), February, 2010.

[24] Hahlweg, Clausewitz and guerrilla warfare, p. 127.

[25] Heuser, Small wars in the age of Clausewitz, p. 141.

[26] Heuser, Small wars in the age of Clausewitz, p. 146.

[27] Kinross, Clausewitz and low-intensity conflict, p. 37.

[28] Clausewitz, What is war? in Paret and Howard (eds), *On War*, pp. 80-81.

[29] Heuser, Small wars in the age of Clausewitz, p. 148.

[30] Heuser, Small wars in the age of Clausewitz, p. 150.

[31] Kinross, Clausewitz and low-intensity conflict, pp. 37-38.

[32] Clausewitz, Interdependence of the elements of war in Paret and Howard (eds), *On War*, p. 586.

[33] Hahlweg, Clausewitz and guerrilla warfare, p. 129.

[34] Hahlweg, Clausewitz and guerrilla warfare, p. 129.

[35] Clausewitz, People's war in Paret and Howard (eds), *On War*, p. 483.

[36] Hahlweg, Clausewitz and guerrilla warfare, p. 129.

[37] Hahlweg, Clausewitz and guerrilla warfare, pp. 129-130.

[38] Clausewitz, People's War in Paret and Howard (eds), *On War*, p. 480.

[39] Clausewitz, People's War in Paret and Howard (eds), *On War*, pp. 482-483.

[40] Daase, Clausewitz and Small wars, p.182.

[41] Mandela, N.R. Nelson Mandela's statement to the court during the Rivonia trial, 20 April 1964, p. 11.

[42] Nigel Worden, *The Making of Modern South Africa: Conquest, Segregation and Apartheid*, Oxford: Blackwell, 1994, p. 107.

[43] Carl von Clausewitz, *On War*, Howard and Paret (trans. and eds.), p. 88.

[44] Nelson R. Mandela, *Long Walk to Freedom. The Autobiography of Nelson Mandela*, London: Abacus, 1994, pp. 182 and 194.

[45] Mashudu G. Ramuhala, 'Guerrilla Warfare from an MK Perspective', in Deane-Peter Baker and Evert Jordaan, *South Africa and Contemporary Counterinsurgency. Roots, Practices, Prospects*, Claremont: UCT Press, 2010, p. 126.

[46] Mandela, *Long Walk to Freedom*, pp. 325-326 and 329.

[47] Mandela, *Long Walk to Freedom*, p. 336

[48] Rocky Williams, 'The Other Armies: Writing the History of MK', in Ian Liebenberg, et al. (eds), *The Long March. The Story of the Struggle for Liberation in South Africa*, Pretoria: HAUM, 1994, pp. 25-26.

[49] Joe Mathews as quoted in Ramuhala, Guerrilla Warfare, p. 127.

[50] Kevin O'Brien, 'A Blunted Spear: the Failure of the African National Congress/South African Communist Party Revolutionary War Strategy 1961-1990', *Small Wars and Insurgencies* 14 (Summer 2003), pp. 27-70 and 30-32.

[51] Ramuhala, Guerrilla Warfare, pp. 130-131.

[52] See the discussion in Chris Alden, *Apartheid's Last Stand. The Rise and Fall of the South African Security State*, London: MacMillan, 1996, pp. 36-41.

[53] *Debates of the House of Assembly,* South Africa: Friday 20 May 1983, cols. 7538-7541.

[54] Department of Defence (DOD), *White Paper on Defence 1977*, South Africa: DOD, 1977, pp. 1-2, 6, 7, 20-24 and 25. See also Rocky Williams, 'The Role of the Truth and Reconciliation Commission in the Re-Professionalisation of the South African Armed Forces', *Strategic Review for Southern Africa,* 21 (1999).

[55] André Beaufre, *Strategy of Action*, London: Faber and Faber, 1967, pp. 111-112. See also Gavin Cawthra, *Securing South Africa's Democracy. Defence, Development and Security in Transition,* London: Macmillan, 1997, pp. 33 and 47-48.

[56] André Beaufre, *An Introduction to Strategy*, London: Faber and Faber, 1961, p. 13.

[57] André Beaufre, *Introduction to Strategy*, pp. 13-14 and 24.

[58] Worden, *Making of Modern South Africa*, p. 124-125.

[59] See John J. McCuen, *The Art of Counter-Revolutionary War. The Strategy of Counter-Insurgency,* London: Faber and Faber, 1966.

[60] Chris Alden, *Apartheid's Last Stand*, p. 219.

[61] General Jannie Geldenhuys, former Chief of the SADF, quoted in Anita M. Gossmann, 'The South African Military and Counterinsurgency: An Overview', in Baker and Jordaan, *South Africa and Contemporary Counterinsurgency*, p. 90.

[62] See the discussion in various sources, notably Ellis and Sechaba, *Comrades against Apartheid. The ANC and the South African Communist Party in exile,* 173-174; TRC of South Africa Report, National Overview, (164); and Worden, *Making of Modern South Africa*, p. 136.

[63] T. Motumi, 'Umkhonto We Sizwe - Structure, Training and Force Levels (1984 to 1994)', *African Defence Review*, nr 18, August, 1994, p. 3.

[64] Worden, *Making of Modern South Africa*, p. 131.

[65] Mandela, *Long Walk to Freedom*, p. 203.

[66] Andre Beaufre, *Introduction to Strategy*, pp. 23-24.

[67] Oliver Tambo and Thabo Mbeki quoted in Ramuhala, Guerrilla Warfare, pp. 126 and 127.

[68] Peter Paret, "Clausewitz", in Peter Paret (ed.), *Makers of Modern Strategy: From Machiavelli to the nuclear age*, Princeton: PUP, (1986), pp. 192 and 195.

[69] Abraham Guillen quoted in Max G. Manwaring, *Shadows of Things Past and Images of the Future: Lessons for the Insurgencies in our Midst*, Carlisle: US Army War College, 2004, p. 3.

[70] Worden, *Making of Modern South Africa*, p. 132.

CLAUSEWITZ, SPAIN AND THE 21ST CENTURY
Miguel Alonso Baquer

Clausewitz never visited Spain, nor did he study the country's war history. This was not so for Antoine-Henri Jomini of Switzerland, who was a member of Marshal Ney's general staff during our war of independence.

Clausewitz let the opportunity pass to join the King's German Legion, which operated under the command of Wellington since 1809. Those were the months of Napoleon's operations on the Iberian Peninsula (October 1808 to January 1809). And it was the time when Clausewitz returned from Paris via Switzerland to Berlin, eager to enter into marriage with Marie von Brühl.

In the final years of his life he must have come to regret his not taking part in the so-called Peninsular War (1808 to 1814). Even before that time, he had made himself a name as a researcher of the *guerrilla* or "small war" and the supporting role of the town militias.

It took many years before the works of Clausewitz came to the attention of the Spanish military. Quotes of Clausewitz are conspicuously absent from 19th century essays. One way to correct this state of affairs would have been to include in the libraries of the General Staff schools either the original works or translations into other, more accessible languages.

In 1870, the situation improved under conditions marked by the dethroning of Queen Isabel II de Borbón. The strong man during that revolution, General Juán Prim, eventually suggested that Leopold of Hohenzollern should be made king, much to the chagrin of the empire of Napoleon III. At the time, there was a considerable interest in German politics and strategies. The General Staff had accumulated precise studies of the campaigns of the Austro-Prussian War and the Franco-Prussian War in Italy and France. And through Nicolás Marselli, the Italian General, knowledge was received of the enormous reputation enjoyed by Carl von Clausewitz and his masterpiece.

Reflections on the French Revolutionary Wars and the Napoleonic Wars written in German focused on the works of Archduke Charles of Austria (1771 to 1847) and the "Principles of Strategy" of the most able commander of operations in mountainous terrain of that era. As early as in 1831, the year Clausewitz died, his four volumes had been translated into Spanish.

A text that was accepted at our military academies of the 19th century was *Die Theorie des großen Krieges: Der russisch-polnische Feldzug des Jahres 1831* (The Theory of Major Warfare: The Russian-Polish Campaign of the Year 1831). The book was written by the Prussian general staff officer Colonel Wilhelm von Willisen (1790 to 1879) – who at the time served as a lecturer at the Prussian War Academy in Berlin – and was published in Barcelona in 1850.

It was translated by Major Ambrosio Garcés de Mantilla of the Spanish Engineer Corps, and dedicated to the scientist and Chief of Engineers Antonio Remón Zarco del Valle. It was fairly successful, yet proved to be detrimental to Clausewitz's reputation. It was directed against everything that had been proposed by the strategist Heinrich von Bülow (1757 to 1805). The most consulted book, after all, probably was *Précis de l'Art de la Guerre: Des Principales Combinaisons de la Stratégie, de la Grande Tactique et de la Politique Militaire* by Baron Antoine Henri de Jomini (1779 to 1869), sent to print in 1839 for the Spanish military, titled *Cuadro Analítico de las principales combinaciones de la guerra*.

Clausewitz was not unknown to the Spanish generals Evaristo San Miguel (1785 to 1862), Manuel Gutiérrez de la Concha (1808 to 1874), and Francisco Villamartín, an infantry major, who were avid readers of essays written in foreign languages. They knew the *Betrachtungen über die Kriegskunst, ihre Fortschritte, ihre Widersprüche und ihre Zuverlässigkeit* (*Observations on the Art of War, Its Progress, Its Contradictions, and Its Reliability*) by Georg Heinrich von Berenhorst (1757 to 1805), and were instrumental in the discreditation of Ernst Wilhelm von Büchel (1754 to 1823). It was only the glorious victories achieved by General Moltke (1800 to 1891) and the critiques by Theodor von Bernhardi (1802 to 1887) that promoted the acceptance of Clausewitz by our military academy, the *Escuela Superior de Guerra* (1893 to 1936).

In 1908, two students of that very *Escuela Superior*, first lieutenants Abilio Barbero and Juan Seguí, translated some parts of the treatise *On War* selected by themselves. The printing shop of the *Sección de Hidrografía*, located at Calle de Alcalá No 56 in Madrid, published a book of 268 pages in the quarto format. And there were enough Spanish military authors who – distressed by the so-called "Disaster of 1898" in Cuba and the Philippines – disseminated the teachings of the great Prussian writer of treatises. Yet, they kept looking for what could not be found in the work of Clausewitz: An obsession with infantry tactics and guidelines for colonial warfare and the protectorate wars in Africa.

The complete Spanish text of *On War* was not available until the beginning of the Second World War (though there were paper editions owned by the *Círculo Militar Argentino* in Buenos Aires). References to Clausewitz were made frequently in the lectures given at the academy of the army (*Escuela Superior del Ejército*, established in 1940), the older naval school (*Escuela de Guerra Naval*) and the more recently established academy of the air force (*Escuela Superior del Aire*). Yet, the critical stance taken by the British Liddell Hart and the French André Beaufre was widely spread.

The clearest and most praising attention was bestowed in two volumes of the five-volume edition of the *Historia de la Infantería Española* (History of Spanish Infantry), titled *Entre la Ilustración y el Romanticismo* (Between Enlighenment and Romanticism), dated 1994 (II), and *La época de los ejércitos Nacionales* (The Era of National Armies), dated 1998 (III).

The great thinker Carl von Clausewitz is lauded in chapter I, 'Los tratadistas militares del siglo XVIII' (Military Writers of the 18th Century) of the first volume, and in chapters II 'En la hora de las Academias Militares' (In the Hour of Military Academies) and IV 'Los tratadistas militares del siglo XIX' (The Military Writers in the 19th Century) of the second volume, all edited by General Miguel Alonso Baquer, who coordinated the entire work.

What had already been read were other original works in the French language and collections of private letters which revealed the melancholy condition of the Prussian general, a condition the occurrence of which among other important career officers of various traditions might be a subject worthwhile studying. In Spain, Carl von Clausewitz came to be fully embraced after Raymond Aron's near-encyclopedic study *Clausewitz: Philosopher of War* had been translated for the *Escuela de Guerra Naval*.

Finally, the Spanish Army Staff's Military Publication Service and, somewhat later, the Ministry of Defense (1999) concerned themselves with some excellent translations of *On War*. In 1978, a very precise critical piece was published in the army journal *La Revista Ejército*, with a foreword written by the journal's director, General Juan Cano Hevia. Those were the years of transition from an authoritarian system of government to a formal democracy. In two thick volumes, the Ministry of Defense compiled the translations of the writings of two British authors, Michael Howard and Peter Paret, with an introductory essay by Bernard Brodie.

So, the figure of Clausewitz had finally made its appearance in Spain, entering into the 21st century with ease, while the works of Hans Delbrück (1887), Carl Schwartz (1887), W. M. Schering (1935), W. Hahlweg (1957), Raymond Aron (1976) and Peter Paret (1979) enjoyed new-found appreciation.

In this consolidation of interest, a preeminent role was played by the *Escuela de Estado Mayor* (where I myself lectured as a professor on the history of warfare in the years 1976 to 1983), and I would like to take the liberty to expound on how this actually came to pass.

There was the erroneous impression that the abstract ideas of Clausewitz applied only to major wars, and both during the lectures I gave and in my later works under the auspices of the *Instituto Español de Estudios Estratégicos* (Spanish Institute for Strategic Studies) (1986-2001) his accurate teachings were frequently applied. And, from my viewpoint, I explained what we, Spanish civilian and military researchers alike, should consider to be most impressive.

My contribution is focused on the young Clausewitz's deliberations on mountain warfare; the special position he held among the intellectuals of his epoch in his mature years; and on considerations as to his ideas and beliefs. Naturally, differing opinions may be found among my students, but I think that this summary of interpretations of one Spaniard may sufficiently serve to outline the horizon of the 21st century.

On Mountain Warfare

My essay titled *Clausewitz y la guerra de montaña* (Clausewitz and Mountain Warfare) was published in Bulletin No. 211-IV, July/August 1988, under the auspices of the *Centro Superior de Estudios de la Defensa Nacional* (CESEDEN) (Academy of National Defense Studies).

Based on four texts, I explained the thoughts developed intuitively by Clausewitz's mind that showed the traits of a genius:

- Notes on strategy (1804)
- Lectures on the small war (1810-1811)
- Treatise (1818), to include the earliest mention of mountainous terrain

- Study on the campaign of 1799, dedicated to Archduke Charles of Austria, in the form it was published between 1828 and 1830, yet without being disseminated.

My colleagues and students came to the conclusion that, had Clausewitz gained direct insights from the war of independence, this would have been helpful in understanding the vicissitudes Spain experienced in the wake of that conflict.

On his Position among the Intellectuals

The CESEDEN monograph titled *Clausewitz y su entorno intelectual* (Clausewitz and his intellectual surroundings) published in 1990 included the particular attention bestowed on the concepts by Kant, Jacques Hippolyte Guibert, Fichte, Moltke, Schlieffen and Lenin (in this order). While my own contribution shared in this endeavor to elucidate the history of Clausewitz's fame, I garnered the support of German scientist Martin Kutz and Colonel Antonio de Querol Lombardero, a member of the Spanish Marines.

My own views are expressed in four short essays:

a) *Los intelectuales y la estrategia* (The Intellectuals and the Strategy)

This is a brief article, with some critical allisuions to the most prestigious intellectuals of the period from 1898 to 1936, illustrating the deplorable indiferende towards the ideas of strategic value of the Spanish military authors.

b) *Guibert, un oficial progresista al servicio de la revolución* (Guibert, a Progressive Military Officer in the Service of the Revolution)

This essay contrasts Napoleon's (rather cursory) ideas on the nature of the modern state with all that which Clausewitz committed to writing on the subject when he returned vom Paris in 1808.

c) *Nacionalista y místico* (Fichte: Jacobin, Natonalist and Mysti)

This is another essay illustrating Clausewitz's mental autonomy with respect to the great movement of German idealism so as to highlight his approaching the style of Montesquieu, actually on the basis of aphorisms.

d) *Marie von Brühl, esposa de Clausewitz* (Marie von Brühl, the Wife of Clausewitz)

A third essay on the person of Clausewitz, who – having turned more humane since his radical melancholy – is surprised by the ideas and convictions that actually came from the religiosity of Friedrich D.E. Schleiermacher.

The attractiveness of the figure of Clausewitz for Spain was already guaranteed in the last decade of the 20th century. There was an obvious risk of his falling into disregard or oblivion, though, because Spanish military men of the 21st century are facing a situation radically different from that of the past. So it was to be anticipated that, after the return of Clausewitz's thoughts to the Spanish centers of study of war and peace, abandon would ensue. And this is exactly what has happened over the past years.

My personal answer to that phenomenon was clear – though one cannot say how accurate – without my selecting other answers provided by my military and scholarly colleagues. For I undertook two complementary interpretative tasks titled the "ideas and beliefs", seeing in my minds eye the figure of Clausewitz.

On Ideas and Beliefs

What continue to be of interest in Clausewitz are - separately from each other - his ideas and beliefs. In Spain it is not easy to put them in precise terms because, for quite some time now, they have been ascribed to two schools of thought which I think have deviated from the straight line pursued by the evidently melancholic mind of that ingenious German romantic.

Melancholy is a sentiment that usually affects modern-day soldiers, sailors and aviators when they know themselves to be superior or distinguished. It grows as they become aware of the enormous distance between what things are and what they should be like. Melancholy dwells next to informed knowledge but hardly ever next to the hope for salvation. And, in the medium term, the melancholic individual feels himself to be discredited as a leader of his fellow soldiers and their successors in his time. He writes a lot, yet little is published.

In 1986, I published the essay *Las ideas y las creencias de Clausewitz* (The ideas and beliefs of Clausewitz) in RECONQUISTA, the periodical of *Espíritu*

Militar Español (a publication the production of which was terminated in 1993 after about fifty years of existence). It was a dialogue between me and Raymond Aron.

The French humanist had written: "How come I feel this deep familiarity, a sympathy towards a man from whom everything should keep me apart?" "Romantic and rational, merciless in his analyses and of a touching sensitiveness, Clausewitz belongs to the lineage of those like Thucydides and Macchiavelli who, through failing in action, found the leisure and sufficient resolve to elevate to the level of clear science the theory of an art which they practiced imperfectly."

As a Spanish military man who already has entered into the third millennium of the Christian era, I do not consider Clausewitz to be "a man from whom everything should keep me apart". For me, Clausewitz is a being that is rather close. My sympathy with him and with those like him is spontaneous. But my respect for the influence which he accepted from his wife Marie von Brühl goes deeper. In its roots, that influence is of a religious nature.

Rather than as a melancholic military man, I would see Carl in the nostalgia of a chivalry lost in the times of revolution. And that is also how I wish to see the military in the Western Europe of the 21st century.

I agree with Raymond Aron in that Clausewitz pertains to the, still numerous, lineage of those "who, through failing in action, found the leisure and sufficient resolve to elevate to the level of clear science the theory of an art which they practiced imperfectly."

So it is with tenderness that I pick up a fragment of the letter sent from Paris to his fiancée Marie on 5 October 1807. "Even the most sublime creations of humanity, for as many centuries as they may exist and work in harmony; bear within them the element of their own destruction." And it is so that the letters of Marie von Brühl, perhaps under the influence of her godfather, F. Schleiermacher, alluded to other creations not necessarily like the works of humanity; for example: Creation.

Conclusion

The short essay on *Las ideas y las creencias de Carl Clausewitz*, takes up the line of interpretation which give him validity for the entire 21st century, also in Spain. I view him steeped in suffering after the violent death of the poet Heinrich von

Kleist; I view him in his seeking to understand the mysticism of Fichte (or Hölderlin) while not abandoning what he admired most in Montesquieu and what he was able to learn from Marqués de Santa Cruz de Marcenado, a Spanish author of the 18th century.

The problem as to the survival of his mastery stems from the intellectual abuse which I studied in my last essay of the CESEDEN monography, *Clausewitz y su entorno intelectual*.

I referred to the two schools of thought deviating from a correct interpretation of his reasoning: The positivistic school of French and German military authors of treatises, which dominated in the period between two major wars (1918-1939), and the materialistic school of the civilian theoreticians in the service of a different revolution, which pursued a series of armed interventions directed against tradition, especially the armed intervention in Russia in 1917.

It was these two schools of thought, with exceptions, that refused to reflect on the deep roots of the dialectic of hostile will and intention. Clausewitz the thinker was a theoretician of moderation, who was against extremism and in favor of waging a tough war (a defensive war that is) against the spirit of conquest. This was not so for the intellectuals with whom I dealt with in my essay in the monograph *Las dos estirpes desviadas del pensamiento de Clausewitz*.

It is urgent that the work of Clausewitz be extracted from these two trajectories. By preferring to apply maxims over principles, Clausewitz was superior to those who considered strategy as a means of short-term total victory.

Clausewitz recognized that the phenomenon of "war" went beyond the geometric synthesis of things military, mechanical, physical etc.... He immersed himself into the political and cultural aspects, yet without drifting into the transcendent or religious sphere. He was rather an agnostic than a believer. This, however, was not true of his loving and cultivated wife Marie von Brühl.

Also, he avoided the dialectics of a radically violent will as appear in Friedrich Schiller, who was a revolutionary rather than a reformist. He never confounded war and revolution, combat and commotion. He accorded to the phenomenon before him the treatment it deserved, that is, to be treated as "war".

For this reason, he deserves to remain what he has come to be in Spain: a classical author, who should not be forgotten but remembered more every day.

CLAUSEWITZ IN SWEDEN
Lars Ericson Wolke

In January 1833 a reviewer in the Journal of the Swedish Academy for Military Sciences wrote that "A just published work, with the title: *Vom Kriege* ... has resulted in a lot of attention, which with reference to the part of the text we have seen, is highly justified.". In December the same year, the editor-in-chief of the Journal, Johan August Hazelius, meant that this new book could be regarded as "one of the most excellent that our profession owns".

These two quotations imply that Clausewitz and *Vom Kriege* had a vast impact on Sweden and Swedish military thinking already from the very beginning.[1] Nothing could be more false. The review in 1833 could be seen as a lonely, although very positive, public mention of the book. But then it was not mentioned again in this Swedish military journal until 1856, a quarter of a century later. This long silence very much reflects the destiny of Clausewitz and his great book in Sweden; sometimes it was highly regarded, sometimes almost forgotten in silence.

However, Clausewitz was read in Sweden also during the "decades of silence". The two most influential military theoreticians in Sweden during the first half of the 19th century were Johan Petter Lefrén and Johan August Hazelius. They both wrote influential books and manuals and for decades taught young officers at the War Academy at Karlberg's castle. We know that both of them studied the works of Clausewitz and Jomini, but the influence of the later was higher than the Clausewitzian influences. Both Lefrén and Hazelius discusses the importance of the "enthusiasm of the people" and the importance of moral factors. Especially by Hazelius we can trace obvious influence from Clausewitz in these matters.

In 1809 a large military disaster in a war against Russia led to Sweden's loss of Finland. Finland had for some 650 years been an integrated part of Sweden, and the military collapse in 1809 led to, among other thing, a revival for studies in military theory, in order to initiate reforms within the army and navy. In this respect the situation in Sweden was similar to that in Prussia after the disastrous defeats against Napoleon and before the war of 1813.

But it was Antoine Henri Jomini that became the most influential international military theorist in Sweden during the first half of the 19th century, not Clausewitz. However, during the 19th century Sweden more and more became oriented towards Germany, away from her traditional military ally and inspiration, France. This process was more evident after 1870-71. For the next decades, until 1918, yes, to large extends all the way to 1945, Germany was the by far most important professional inspiration for the Swedish army; the navy and later the air force tended to look more towards Great Britain. The first foreign language studied in Swedish schools was, until 1945, German, and much of the cultural and scientific world in Sweden was oriented towards Germany. In the late 19th and early 20th century Swedish officers were used to read military books in German. All this of course paved the way for an introduction of Clausewitz, although it was somewhat delayed.

The man who reviewed *Vom Kriege* in 1831 was Johan August Hazelius, one of Sweden's most influential officers and military theorists throughout the 20th century. He wrote several books on military theory and also started a private school for young officers as a complement to the War Academy at Karlberg outside Stockholm. However, not even the influential Hazelius could guarantee a continuous success for Clausewitz and his book.

But in 1856 Clausewitz was once again mentioned in the Journal of the Academy for Military Sciences. A new book by an influential infantry officer and writer, Julius Mankell, was reviewed in the Journal. In his text the reviewer says that the earlier works of Clausewitz "are so well known, that nothing have to be mentioned about then here". Despite the silence about it, Clausewitz's book seems to have been read and discussed in Sweden during the 1830's to the 1850's. In the coming decades Clausewitz would inspire not only the development of military theory in Sweden, but also military historians.

Step by step Clausewitz made entrance in the Swedish military education system. Around 1880 he was a much read writer at the Artillery and Engineers College. In his education the teacher in art of war and war history, Carl Warberg made the following reference when he discussed the "popular war": "… I allow myself to quote the by myself several times mentioned military writer Clausewitz".

In 1883 Carl Otto Nordensvan, then teacher in tactics and war history at the War College in Stockholm wrote about *Vom Kriege* also in the Journal of the Academy for Military Sciences. He meant that the book described "not that one would like to learn, but what can not be learned. My whom, who will learn the basics of war, not be tired and, as good as he can, make himself familiar with the great war philosopher" (i.e. Clausewitz). Nordensvan was also the editor of Helmuth von Moltke's letters and orders from the war 1864-1871, so he can be regarded as Sweden's best expert in contemporary German military theory and practice.

The officers that studied at the War College (founded in 1878) obviously didn´t read Clausewitz as a part of their curriculum, but they got familiar with him through the lectures given by their teachers, or by quotations of Clausewitz in the much read *Kriegskunst des neunzehnten Jahrhunderts* by Friedrich Wilhelm Rüstow.

In the first autumn semester of the new War College in 1878 several of the students chose to write papers about the subject "A short overview of the literature in war science". Not so few of them highlighted Clausewitz as a central writer in military theory, but they also regarded him as very philosophical and difficult to read. The Prussians ideas about the relationship between war and politics were discussed by many of the students. Also writers as Jomini, von Bülow and Rüstow were mentioned in the student papers. But all the students pointed out the British 18th century theorist Henry Lloyd as the first one who tried to make a systematic writing about the war. "He forces the reader to think more than read", as one of the students describes his experience of Lloyd. That could also have been said about Clausewitz.

During the following years we can see a process in the use of Clausewitz. In papers written by students at the War College in 1907 and 1911 many of them discussed Clausewitzan thoughts about the importance of defeating the main forces of the opponent or just described the war as the outmost form of politics.

Both in these papers as in several editions of the tactical manuals of the army written by the general Lars Tingsten, we can trace a development towards more stressed demands that the military leadership should be given more strategical freedom of movement by the politicians.

Tingsten was teacher in general staff service at the War College, and later became both chief of the College, minister of war and, finally, chief of the general staff. The first edition of his book *Taktikens grunder* ((*The fundaments of tactics*) was published in 1892-1893 and it came in constantly new editions until the 1920's. For the Swedish army Tingsten's book was *the* tactical manual, with large parts also about operational and strategical matters.

In his book Tingsten discusses military theory in a way that clearly is influenced by Clausewitz. According to Tingsten all decisions about war should be made by the political leadership after advice from the military leadership, while the later should lead the military operations. "There should from the very beginning of the war be an appropriate interaction between politics and warfare", he writes. The influences from Clausewitz, and to an even higher degree from contemporary German thinking, can also be traced in a text where Tingsten describes the way to a "decisive victory in field". This decisive victory was not only a possibility, but desirable aim.[2]

When he discussed the borderline between politicians and the military in his book *Kriget och krigsinrättningarna* (*The War and the war institutions*) in 1893 the above mentioned Carl Otto Nordensvan quotes Clausewitz. But in his 1907 published book *Krigsföringen i dess olika former* (*Warfare in it's different forms*) Nordensvan has abolished Clausewitz and instead refers to Helmuth von Moltke.

So we can establish as a fact that Clausewitz was discovered and read in Sweden at a very early time, but it was not until after the victorious Germans wars during the 1860's and 1870's that he became more intensively studied in Sweden, especially at the War College. But after the turn of the century 1900 Clausewitz more and more came in the background. Instead it was the more or less perverted version of Clausewitz's text about the relationship between politics and war that was put forward by Moltke and his colleagues in the German general staff that was studied. However, this change should probably be seen as an independent Swedish development, and not a nondependent Swedish imitation of the German development. As late as in 1915 students at the War College, that "underestimated" the importance of a form the political leadership independent military operations were corrected by their teachers. This very Clausewitz- and even more Moltke-inspired view of the relationship between the political and military spheres began to change just a couple of years later.

We can say that Clausewitz during the three last decades of the 19th century was very much red and discussed in Sweden; yes to some extent he dominated the theoretical discussion within the military. But his *Vom Kriege* was never translated to Swedish, partly because most Swedish officers were expected to read and understand German. His ideas about the relationship between politics and war were debated, but in general Clausewitz and his Magnus Opus never became an integrated part of the terminology of military science in Sweden, in contrary to the conceptions and ideas of Jomini and, to an even greater extent, of Alfred Thayer Mahan.

After the end of the Great War in 1918 the interest for military theory declined dramatically in Sweden, and especially that in Clausewitz, whom for many was regarded as the very symbol of the collapsed Prussian militarism. Instead theories about the new technological "machine war" were discussed in the military journals.

In 1939, when the dark clouds once again gathered over Europe, a Swedish naval officer, G E F Boldt-Christmas, published a book with the title *Från Clausewitz till Liddell Hart. A strategical study.* In this book, published in November 1939, he uses Clausewitz and the contemporary Liddell Hart to understand the strategical situation in Europe and the world after the Collapse of Poland but before the German invasion of Scandinavia and Western Europe. Boldt-Christmas belonged to the pro-British circles in the Swedish officer corps, a then minority especially in the army. In 1945 he published a much debated book in which he argued that Sweden's neutrality during World War Two was far too friendly towards Nazi-Germany. Now, in 1939, Boldt-Christmans meant that the Swedish armed forces still were too much influenced by Clausewitz's thoughts, and as a consequence of that by Prussian militarism. Bold-Christmas argued that many Swedish army officers, in accordance with Clausewitz's fundamental ideas, wanted to muster as large units as possible in order to destroy the enemy's main force. For Boldt-Christmas this could never be a rational purpose for a small nation's army. Instead he argued that all the effort should be focused on stopping an invader at the beaches or along the land border, not necessarily do destroy his main forces.[3]

A short selection of minor parts of *Vom Kriege* was translated into Swedish and published in Sweden in 1942. This edition was made by one of the most skilful, Swedish speaking, Finnish historians Jarl Gallén.[4] But his edition and its preface is, not so surprisingly, very much influenced by the political and military situation for Finland in the year 1942.

The decline of military theory in general and Clausewitz in particular became even more after 1945. The Cold War meant for Sweden, among other things, that the interest in military theory almost totally disappeared. Only a handful of officers and scholars kept the interest going. One of the few were the historian Gunnar Artéus, who in his dissertation 1970 discussed the influence from war theory by Clausewitz, Jomini and the influential German historian Hans Delbrück on the way a number of Swedish historians between 1855 and 1935 analysed and discussed the invasion of Russia by Charles XII and the Swedish army in 1707-1709. His result was that many historians were influenced by military theory, not the least by the one of Clausewitz, and this affected the way we study and understand their books on military history.[5]

But the general view was that the Swedish defence force very well knew who the enemy was, his capabilities and his equipment. It was only a question of if, when and where an eventual war should be fought. Instead of looking for guidelines in military theory it was for many Swedish officers, at all levels, only a matter of being on the right landing beaches in time to stop and threw back the Soviet invader. You didn't have to read Clausewitz in order to accomplish that.

But after the end of the Cold War 1989-1991 and the collapse of first the Warsaw Pact and then the Soviet Union all this changed. The traditional enemy disappeared, and in order to keep the orientation in a changed world, Sweden's armed forces began to read and discuss military theory again. This was especially true for the National Defence College (the former War College), where the department for Military History became an important actor in this revival of theoretical studies in war and warfare.

In 1991 *Vom Kriege* was translated to Swedish for the first time in the 160 years it had existed. The translation was made by Colonel Hjalmar Mårstenson – in 1975-1981 Sweden's military attaché in Bonn – with comments written by the two distinguished historians Klaus-Richard Böhme and Alf W. Johansson.[6] The 670 pages thick book made it suddenly possible for Swedish officers and students, to study Clausewitz's text despite how good the English or German was. This meant a lot for the military theory revival and debate in Sweden in general and at the National Defence College in particular. One can note that the edition of the book was made by a commercial publishing company, and since 1991 this Swedish edition has arrived in several more printings.

In order to promote the study of Clausewitz and his book, the three men behind the translation in 1995 published a guide to the study of *Vom Kriege* including the translation of a paper by the American professor Bernard Brodie.[7]

Alf W. Johansson at that time published a much read book about war and warfare in Europe during the 19th and 20th century, in which he discusses Clausewitz and the role that Clausewitz's ideas has played in the European military development during some 150 years since the time of Napoleon. This book has been used and is still used in most of the courses at the National Defence College since its first edition and has also been a large commercial success.[8]

As a consequence of that edition of *Vom Kriege* the National Defence College in 1994 arranged a minor seminar about Clausewitz. Two lectures discussed Clausewitz's role for a number of Swedish military historians in the decades around 1900 and the perception of Clausewitz's ideas in Sweden before 1914.[9] This indicates a new born interest in Clausewitz and *Vom Kriege* in Sweden, and from that time Clausewitz has been read and discussed in the courses at the National Defence College.

Since the autumn 2009 the National Defence College has been giving courses on a higher level than before, a so called "Higher Staff Education", i.e. a kind of general staff course. In these courses advanced military theory has a very important role. That moment includes a lot of reading about the historical development of military theory, but also, and that is important, original texts written by thinkers like Clausewitz, Jomini, Mahan, Corbett, Douhet, Warden and others. The purpose is twofold. First it gives the student a first hand notion about the texts and their writers, i.e. our historical heritage. Secondly and most important is for the students to discuss in written and in verbal presentations how they regard the actuality of theses texts. Do they have anything to give to today's officer to develop his professional skills, and if so (or not) how do they motivate that? Here we of course come very close to the very essence of military theory, namely its usefulness, direct or indirect, for the military profession.

It is not *what* Clausewitz says that is in focus today, rather more *how* he says it that is of importance. By reading Clausewitz officers and students try to find (if possible) terms and thoughts from the text that can help us as a tool to shred light upon the reality of warfare of today. This is the principal way Clausewitz is used today at the National Defence College in Stockholm. Lectures and studies about his writing discuss to what extent his texts can be used to analyse the modern theatre of war, especially with regard to counterinsurgence warfare (COIN). In short: the question asked to Clausewitz's text is the following: "Has Clausewitz anything to tell those who today conduct operations – conventional, COIN or PRT – for example in Afghanistan?" Whatever the answer on this question may be the very existence of it shows that

Clausewitz still plays a role in the military theory debate in Sweden, some 180 years after the first Swedish review of *Vom Kriege*.

Notes:

[1] For a general overview of the development of military theory in Sweden in general and Clausewitz's role within that process see Lars Ericson Wolke, *Krigets idéer. Svenska tankar om krigföring 1320-1920* (Published in Swedish: *The Ideas of War. Swedish thoughts about Warfare 1320-1920*), Stockholm 2007, pp. 279-285.

[2] See Lars Tingstens manuscript *Avgörande seger i fält* (*Decisive victory in field*), kept at the Military Archives, Stockholm, **Lars Herman Tingsten´s collection** volume 4.

[3] G. E. F. Boldt-Christmas, *Från Calusewitz till Liddell Hart. En strategisk studie* (*From Clausewitz to Liddell Hart. A Strategical Study*), Stockholm 1939, pp. 38-39 and passim.

[4] Carl von Clausewitz, *Krig och krigföring* (*War and Warfare*). Edited and translated by Jarl Gallén, Stockholm 1942.

[5] Gunnar Artéus, *Krigsteori och historisk förklaring. I. Kring Karl XII:s ryska fälttåg* (*War theory and historical explanation. I. About the Russian Campaign of Charles XII*), Göteborg 1970.

[6] Carl von Clausewitz, *Om kriget* (*On War*). Translated and commented by Hjalmar Mårtenson, Klaus-Richard Böhme and Alf W. Johansson, Stockholm 1991.

[7] Hjalmar Mårtenson, *von Clausewitz om kriget. Kommentarer, definitioner och register* (*von Clausewitz about war. Commentaries, definitions and register*), Stockholm 1995.

[8] Alf W. Johansson, *Europas krig. Militärt tänkande, strategi och politik från Napoleontiden till andra världskrigets slut* (*Europe's war. Military thinking, strategy and politics from the Napoleonic Era to the end of the Second World War*), Stockholm 1988 and several later editions.

[9] Gunnar Artéus, Clausewitz och forskningen om Karl XII:s ryska fälttåg (Clausewitz and the research about Charles XII's Russian Campaign) and Gunnar Åselius, Clausewitz-receptionen i Sverige intill första världskriget (The Reception of Clausewitz in Sweden before World War One), in *Militärhistorisk Tidskrift 1994,* pp. 24-34 and pp. 35-53.

CLAUSEWITZ IN SWITZERLAND
Roland Beck

Carl von Clausewitz (1780-1831) visited Switzerland in June 1807 as a war prisoner of the victorious Emperor Napoleon. This followed the terrible defeats of the Prussian army at Jena and Auerstedt, the disaster of Prussian-Eylau and the defeat of Russia's ally at Friedland.

Clausewitz was a young staff captain with no real military perspectives, who was far from his home and family. Is it no wonder, then, that Clausewitz had a bleak world view during this dark phase of his life.

His picture of Switzerland

In a letter to his beloved bride, Countess Marie von Brühl, Clausewitz wrote that villages in western Switzerland were unremarkable. He remarked that no village had a festive tower and no city a grand cathedral. Towns and villages had gray and nondescript appearances, he wrote. This is all the more astonishing because the landscape Clausewitz described has long been praised for its natural beauty and architecture.

"The beautiful city of Geneva takes her place at sea without grace or dignity. Houses are placed with economic accuracy around the centre. The Evangelical Church has a dry appearance. The towers are just high enough to earn the name and only a few feet higher than the houses. Lausanne is not much better. The small towns along the beautiful lake, Coppet, Rolle and Morges, disappear under the fruit trees and gardens."

At Castle Coppet on Lake Geneva

Clausewitz arrived with Prince August of Prussia at the magnificent Castle Coppet on Lake Geneva on 11 August 1807. His mood improved considerably due to the Peace of Tilsit, which brought the two prisoners of war a break from their internment. The Prince and Clausewitz were allowed freedom of movement throughout the French territory, which included Switzerland. After French revolutionary troops invaded in March 1798, Switzerland lost its independence and neutrality and became a vassal state dependant on Napoleon's grace.

The Prince used the relaxed internment to travel to Switzerland – home to the glorious Alps – a particular trend of the time, common amongst the aristocracy: a romanticism of nature and most especially the mountains. Examples of this romanticism can be found in the early works of scientist and writer Albrecht von Haller (1708-1777), who wrote a poem on the Alps, or the work of Swiss historian Johannes von Müller (1752-1809), who chronicled and glorified the Swiss Confederation in Europe.

The Prince's preference for the great romantic literature of his time and its exponents played an important role in choosing to travel to Castle Coppet, for the renowned writer and poet Germaine de Staël (1766-1817) resided at the castle.

A second factor in the Prince's preference of Switzerland and Castle Coppet was the parallel visit of the charming Juliette Récamier (1777-1849). The Prince had already met Récamier in Paris and sought to make her better acquaintance. Récamier, who was painted by the great Louis David so memorably on a chaise longue, did not just happen to be in Coppet. She was considered pro-German and an enemy of Napoleon; subsequently, she left Paris to stay with her close friend, Germaine de Staël.

Clausewitz little understood the Prince's weaknesses for the softer sex and described the young Juliette Récamier as an "ordinary coquette". At sixteen Juliette had married one of the most influential bankers in Paris and had a widespread network of contacts. In effect, she had the men of Paris at her feet!

The advances of Prince August of Prussia were unsuccessful - in spite of a written marriage promise that is carefully preserved in the archives of the Castle Coppet. The reasons for the failure of these advances are little known. One might presume it had something to do with Juliette's status as a married woman already, her lack of nobility and her Catholicism.

When the passports for their departure to Prussia on 7th October 1807 arrived, the two internees were allowed to move forward toward their freedom. And the Prince ended this romantic chapter of his life.

Encounter with August Wilhelm von Schlegel

In the summer and autumn of 1807 Lake Geneva awakened back in Clausewitz his feelings for the beauty of nature and life. He wrote to his wife: "From

Coppet we overlook the lake from its whole length on one side and to Geneva on the other. We see the most secret corners of the earth from the gates, from the homes, and from the Rhone River. 'It's like a garden is looking to the country', William Tell says to his son ... and I never go for a walk without seeing natural splendour. No spot of even a few inches is uncultivated. Everything is fenced with green hedges. The frequent vineyards, where wine is cultivated in the Italian way, multiply the elegance of rich flavor. From the soft lighting of the wonderful alpine white heads, and above all the surfaces of the water in these beautiful autumn days, I dare not say a word ... "[1].

In these days of autumn 1807, despite all adversities, Clausewitz succumbed to the beauty of nature. This was reinforced by his acquaintance with the poet and philosopher, August Wilhelm von Schlegel (1767-1845), who also was staying at Castle Coppet. After the early death of Baron Eric Magnus de Staël-Holstein in 1804, Schlegel resided at Coppet permanently. He accompanied the great writer on her frequent trips to Italy, France, Scandinavia and England.

Clausewitz was allowed to sit at the table next to Schlegel, where he enthusiastically wrote to his beloved bride in Berlin. Schlegel influenced Clausewitz not only by his romantic sense of nature, but also with his unadulterated, pure nationalism and patriotism. At this point, all those assembled belonged to Germaine de Staël's circle of friends. They longed for a liberated Germany and promoted a new German nationalism, these should provide the courage and strength for the Prussian liberation struggle after the earlier ignominious defeats.

Through his acquaintance with Germaine de Stael, Clausewitz became more enthusiastic, he wrote in a letter to his bride, of German literature. Germaine de Staël herself was taken with the two Germans, calling them "les deux Allemands par excellence"[2].

In the circle of Germaine de Staël

Germaine de Staël was a Swiss citizen with German roots. Coppet is a castle on Swiss soil and this piece of land belonged to the young, French-speaking canton of Vaud since 1804. But Germaine de Staël was born the daughter of the great French statesman and theorist Jacques Necker (1732-1804), a finance minister. Her father, in turn, was born in Geneva, but his father was Mark Brandenburger, professor of constitutional German law at the University of

Geneva. These were the strong German roots of Germaine de Staël, which perhaps help the reader understand why she was so deeply connected to German culture and why her work "De l'Allemagne" in two volumes was such a resounding success[3].

Germaine de Staël promoted the image of Germans and Germany throughout France. Thus it was good for a common understanding between the two great nations. As the Bismarck era ended, however, Bismarck rightly feared that the southern German states and the rest of the former Confederation of Rhine States could close a bilateral alliance with France or Austria and thwart its war plans.

Clausewitz has dealt intensively with the chatelaine of Coppet and reached the following judgement: "Madame de Staël is a woman of much fantasy. She has a strong German spirit, but otherwise she is very French. That is to say: everything she thinks and speaks is marked by her German spirit; however she lacks the practicality of the mind and the quiet, gentle dignity of German womanhood what I need so much to find a woman interesting. In Madame de Staël this falls on me less uncomfortable, because she talks almost always about matters of literature, and therefore more contact with their advantageous side is in. It gives me pleasure, to see so sincere homage among strangers to the German spirit, to the German feelings."[4]

His picture of the Swiss population and their spirit of resistance

Though Clausewitz was also involved with the Swiss population of the surrounding area, his verdict was not very positive. He stated the following in his travel journal: "Nothing catches the men's attention, they are almost like Germans, at least a lot is missing that they have French loquacity and vivacity; one also sees many blondes. The second (female) sex is excellent. Usually the women are all very dark, but because all the people look sickly, the women also look pale and very yellow. They do however often have beautiful, black, but usually even more beautiful dark blue eyes, beautiful teeth, a pleasant, subtle and witty countenance. All in all they give off an impression of melancholy, which gives them all even the ugly ones, some interesting allure." He continued: "The clothes are shabby, but something picturesque, somewhat naive-poetic. The whole nation has a rare degree of good-natured politeness."[5]

In fact, Switzerland was in those years (during the periods of French occupation), a dirt-poor country, plundered, starved, mistreated and humiliated by the French occupation troops. These French troops followed the Napoleonic principles of the country, and refrained from hawser. Since 1803, Switzerland had a mediation agreement with France, but the occupation was not forgotten, and such deep scars do not heal. Switzerland still had to make significant duties and military service for France. For the augmentation of the Swiss regiments into Napoleon's troops, 18,000 Swiss were permanently sent to serve under the French.

If the mood in Coppet and Geneva was not so oppressive, it was because the French revolutionary troops liberated Canton of Vaud from the rule of Bern. The Canton of Vaud had been a free country and had every reason to be in a euphoric mood.

This situation was quite different from the situation in central Switzerland. The central cantons, especially Nidwalden, have never been subjected to the French conquerors. As such, they represented the myth of "William Tell" and have remained strongly against any foreign power to subjugate them. The consequences were inevitable. Central Switzerland has been repeatedly hit by the severe punitive actions. The population was decimated systematically and Johann Heinrich Pestalozzi (1746-1827) had to take care of the destroyed families and the many orphans.

Inspired by the Romantics

Clausewitz wanted nothing more than to see Central Switzerland, when he was returning to Germany. In his letter to Marie von Brühl, he wrote: "When I return, I hope to see the German Switzerland, it is classic in so many regards. In particular, I would have been happy to see the lake of Vierwaldstätten. Although I would not have been so happy to travel across, where Tell lay in the ship, tied with ropes, a derelict man to see, defenceless, what he tells us...."[6].

Clausewitz had in fact taken the pathos of Friedrich von Schiller (1759-1805). The national epic of Switzerland, published in 1804, provided Clausewitz the spiritual nourishment that he urgently needed after the catastrophic collapse of Prussia. In this respect, the visit to Switzerland meant for Clausewitz internal collection and development of psychic forces for the liberation struggle. The example of William Tell and the freedom struggle of the

Confederates against murderous tyrants provided a great welcome. Clausewitz showed the example of the Swiss Confederation, which depicted a freedom struggle in a seemingly hopeless situation against a far superior adversary. This example showed that in the end this kind of situation could lead to a worthwhile, independent and sovereign state of existence.

Balance of the visit in Switzerland

In summary, we can say that Clausewitz's visit in Switzerland in 1807 was extremely important for his spiritual and mental development. These experiences helped him to fight for a liberated Germany, a state of freedom and independence. Moreover this stay, the visit in Coppet, enriched its social and literary education considerably and enabled him to gain important friends like the poet and philosopher August Wilhelm von Schlegel. Unfortunately, he didn't gain any friends from the women's society. He remained in the hearts of Coppet, connected by his faithful Marie von Brühl.

Development of the theory on the little war

Back in Berlin, he developed his lectures on the little war at the new "Kriegsschule", the first Prussian General Staff College in Berlin. These were inspired by the many impressions and experiences from the visit in Switzerland; Clausewitz brought these basic thoughts on paper. They are to this day of great importance, even for the defence doctrine of Switzerland.

Many countries today lead wars outside their borders, such as the world power USA and its allies in Iraq and Afghanistan. But Switzerland, as a neutral and independent small state, has to conduct the war within its borders and therefore needs to know the principles of "the little war."

Switzerland excellently accomplishes through its strict enforcement of general compulsory military service and in view of its geographical conditions, the conditions that Clausewitz calls for a successful management of "the little war". In his sixth book about the arming of the people, he notes: "The conditions under which the people's war can be effective alone are as follows:

1. that the war occurred in the interior of the country,
2. that the war will not be decided by a single disaster;
3. that the war theatre occupies a considerable area of land;
4. that the people support the measure;

5. that the country is very divided and inaccessible, either by mountains and through forests and swamps or by the nature of the soil culture."[7]

Only the third requirement does not apply to Switzerland. The country is relatively small, but some helpful factors are the mountains, the forests, many rivers and lakes, and the dense colonization of the plateau. All these aspects favour "the little war".

Clausewitz said next that "a poor class, accustomed to hard work and privation class" also shows strong military power[8]. This is not true for the Swiss population in the modern major conurbations. But the inhabitants of the mountain valleys, of the lofty mountain farms and the rural areas generally meet these requirements even in the high mass. The old fighting spirit still lives in them, as we know from the Swiss military history.

Clausewitz provides a first approach for a defence doctrine of Switzerland, by saying that the people's war would be in a first phase "like a fog and cloudlike-being"[9] that could never concretize to a resisting body. Otherwise the enemy would focus an adequate force to this core, destroy it and make a large number of prisoners. "Then the courage would drop, everybody believes, the main question would be decided, and that a further effort would be in vain, and their arms would fall from the hands of the people"[10].

Clausewitz goes on to say that the more passive first phase of defence had to be supplemented by a strong offensive and aggressive second phase of defence. He firmly believes the following: "From the other side, it is nevertheless necessary, that this dense fog shrinks to masses at certain points and forms threatening clouds, which can create strong lightning"[11].

To simplify, Clausewitz encourages "the little war" for a defensive doctrine, which weakens and wears the opponents with many small pins and needles, and which shatters and destroys the enemy with massive counter-attacks like lightning from a clear sky. This gives the basic structure of "the little war" in the strict sense of the word.

Clausewitz adds a further consideration: He calls for this "little war" either "as a last resort after a lost battle or as a natural support before a decisive battle is to be delivered"[12]. With this statement he asks, that strong defence forces must be ready after weakening the enemy to finally beat and destroy them in key areas. This idea has further consequences for a Swiss defence doctrine.

Arming of the people as the basic of the Swiss defence doctrine

The transfer of these basic considerations to the present day is not easy. Of course, the threat is not comparable with the time when Switzerland faced Prussian forces in the great wars of liberation from the 1813/14. The armament and equipment of today's armed forces is not comparing with those earlier armed forces. Therefore, we can only speak of basic considerations and the level of reference to the construction of a defence doctrine can only be strategic.

With the formation of the Army XXI in the nineties, Switzerland has added many new elements in its defence doctrine. Unfortunately these elements are suitable for "the great war" or better for wars of intervention abroad and less intended for the conventional defence in the interior of the country. The current development of the political situation in Switzerland shows that the failed operations abroad (for example, the wars in Iraq and Afghanistan), caused a loss of acceptance in the large war, while the classic little war in national defence gained importance. Strong political forces ask the complete abandonment of operations abroad and therefore they will put a stop to the Swiss engagement in Kosovo. Defence should not be practised in the future in the strategic areas of interest outside of Switzerland, but within its borders, perhaps in cooperation with friendly powers.

The new postulated security concept of "Security through Cooperation" confirms this trend as well. The cooperation is to be, however, mainly in the field of education, intelligence, disaster relief and peace promotion, while there are still no concrete plans visible for the area of defence. As long as the Swiss Federal Constitution defines Switzerland as a neutral and independent state, the intentions for the defence case cannot become a public issue. Given the threat of terrorism, of ballistic missiles from the Middle East, and of nuclear weapons, cooperation intentions could soon become an important political issue.

Initiatives threaten the principle of the arming of the people

Recently, the further development of the Swiss Army has been risked by two initiatives from a known political fringe group that advocates the abolition of the army. Both initiatives are directed against the arming of the people, as

Clausewitz calls in his sixth book for the defence in the interior of the country. The initiative to protect against weapon's violence undermines the credibility of the militia soldiers and threatens the shooting outside of the military service and, more generally, the private shooting clubs in their existence. The other initiative for the abolition of general compulsory military service simply undermines our traditional armed forces and therefore the principle of the arming of the people.

We are not allowed saw the name of this political fringe group. Characteristic of this group is that it eliminates things that exist, without creating something new. So this fringe group urges the abolition of the general compulsory military service, without saying how, for example, the recruitment of a voluntary militia should occur, or what the implications on the composition and quality of the army will be.

Countries, who have left the traditional national defence and therefore also the general compulsory military service and engage their armed forces abroad almost exclusively, provide us with the necessary experience. Accordingly, the recruitment of voluntary militiamen in Switzerland with a comparatively low unemployment rate and a pronounced prosperity will be realizable only with high salary payments. Already a miniature army would cause labour costs of approximately an additional 20,000 federal employees. If we consider that not even the doubling of full-time instruction Corps, what the Army XXI concept envisaged, was possible in life, we see how illusory such an intention is. In short, the abolition of general compulsory military service would have a dramatic impact on military budget and federal budget and would, as a result, prevent investments to modernize the Swiss army.

Even the composition of the Swiss army would change. The army would no longer be a reflection of the people, but a rallying point for citizens, who don't have a civil job, or for military enthusiastic Secondos, who expect with the completed military service better prospects in the civilian labour market, or for violence enthusiastic Rambo's and other marginalized groups in society. The political control of such an army would increasingly become a problem. Sooner or later, such an army would be a burden or a threat for the country's own citizens.

We can therefore conclude that the initiative to abolish general compulsory military service in Switzerland is not sufficiently resolute and can be rejected. This does not prevent us from constantly checking our armed forces and military law. For example, the Swiss Officer Society recently developed a position paper to give new impetus to the development of the militia army.

For a politically viable development of the army, only the Federal Constitution and the framework of the executive Swiss Federal Counsellors should be allowed to form a basis. It is therefore necessary in the future that the core competence of the Swiss army remains in the area of defence against a military attack on Switzerland. The Swiss army should be organized after the principle of a militia army, to make sure that we have a strong professional and militia officer corps, and that we bend or break the hold on the conscription.

Consequences on the tactical-operational level

On the tactical-operational level, it is difficult to derive principles for the Swiss defence doctrine. It can be said for certain that strong infantry forces in the border area need to weaken the opponent. On the other hand, in the key areas of Zurich, Bern and Lausanne and in the Alps, strong defence forces are called for to make the final decision and to destroy the opponent.

These forces have to be organized, trained and equipped after the latest findings from today's wars. This includes not only heavy weapons like as tanks and artillery, but also a powerful air force and air defence. Without temporary and localized air superiority in key areas, no military success on the ground will succeed in future. That is why modern and efficient forces of air force and air defence are of such overwhelming importance.

The hunting fight of the infantry in the border area should be lead freely and not have solid blocking positions. On the other hand, the defence in key areas needs locally defined dispositives with assigned troops where they can lead the defensive struggle from prepared positions and assigned application areas. The idea in the current doctrine of the Army XXI is that a few brigades can form heavyweights to lead the defence wherever necessary and in any terrain. Otherwise they would be overwhelmed by the capacities of a militia army and would thus inadequately utilize the strengths of the terrain.

We can thus derive further conclusions. Switzerland needs combat units, which are allocated in key spaces and which have the necessary equipment and training. While professional armies respond quickly to new threats and can be reorganized accordingly, a militia army of a small state with only a year short service needs decades or years to develop a new defence doctrine and to make sure that the troops are trained and equipped accordingly. To think a militia army only at emerging threats could, with the help of two or three combat brigades, grow to the maximum war strength, is a most dangerous and deceptive illusion.

Defence readiness also in peacetime

Politicians fear the high cost of a quantitatively and qualitatively well-armed militia army in peacetime. But security has its price and without security, or even with the loss of the own country, all other political efforts are in vain. Some politicians claim that the army has to be prepared only for the current likely threat case, which is terrorism. A threat to Switzerland by a foreign power, that would create dispute in the land, cannot be foreseen. From past historical experience we know that no one can predict threats for the next ten or twenty years. So, for example, the Social Democrats previously rejected the defence of Switzerland four years before the outbreak of the Second World War. After the war many politicians overturned the then-current world view of respecting the territorial integrity of nations. This was not the case when the Russian army invaded Georgia.

Switzerland is well advised if it follows the goal of a warlike militia army even in peacetime, so that the entire world acknowledges its sovereignty, autonomy, independence and inviolability of its territory.

General compulsory military service and militia as eternal cornerstone

Carl von Clausewitz left his imprint over two hundred years ago on Switzerland and on Castle of Copped in the circle of Germaine de Staël. It was here that he experienced spiritual dimensions of education first-hand and learned many proposals. But the main impetus he gained was from Switzerland with its stubborn will to autonomy, independence and freedom. Clausewitz's own personal experience led him to conclude these values can be obtained only with an aggressive attitude and a strong army. Then he built his theory of war and especially that of "little war", gave lectures at the appropriate young war-school at Berlin and prepared the future elite for the Prussian War of Liberation against Napoleon.

His theory of "little war" is still of great importance for Switzerland today. Militarization of the people, as described in his sixth book, is still the basic principle of the defence of a neutral and independent small state. General compulsory military service and the militia are cornerstones of Switzerland's defence today and hopefully the future.

Notes:

[1] Linnebach, Karl, *Carl and Marie von Clausewitz. A picture of life in letters and diary sheets.* Berlin, Warneck 1916, p. 145.

[2] Schramm, Wilhelm von, *Clausewitz. Life and Work*, Esslingen am Neckar 1976, p. 193.

[3] Staël, Germaine de, *De l'Allemagne.* 2 vols, Paris, Garnier-Flammarion 1968.

[4] Linnebach, ibid, p. 146.

[5] Schramm, ibid, p. 178f.

[6] Linnebach, ibid, p. 148f.

[7] Clausewitz, Carl von, *On War*, 19th edition, Dümmler Verlag, Bonn 1980, p. 801.

[8] *On War*, op cit, p. 801.

[9] *On War*, op cit, p. 803.

[10] *On War*, op cit, p. 803.

[11] *On War*, op cit, p. 803.

[12] *On War*, op cit, p. 805.

Literature:

Clausewitz, Carl von, *On War*, 19th edition, Dümmler Verlag, Bonn 1980.

Clausewitz, Carl von, *Writings-essays, letters, studies*, edited by Werner Hahlweg, Volume 1, Göttingen 1966, and Volume 2, Göttingen 1990.

Clausewitz, Carl von, *Scattered small fonts*, compiled, edited and introduced by Werner Hahlweg, Osnabrück 1979.

Clausewitz, Carl, *Selected by military writings*, edited by Gerhard Forster and Dorothea Schmidt in collaboration with Christa Gudzent, Berlin-Ost 1980.

Linnebach, Karl, *Carl and Marie von Clausewitz. A picture of life in letters and diary sheets.* Berlin, Warneck 1916.

Schramm, Wilhelm von, *Clausewitz. Life and Work*, Esslingen am Neckar 1976.

Staël, Germaine de, *De l'Allemagne.* 2 vols, Paris, Garnier-Flammarion 1968.

CLAUSEWITZ IN AMERICA TODAY
Christopher Bassford

"You say 'to paraphrase Clausewitz.' What is that? What is 'Clausewitz'?" "I apologize for the analogy, which is obscure. The book, I have to say, is impenetrable, and I think the only part of it that is - that anybody mostly has ever read is the one line that "war is the continuation of policy by other means"'.[1]

Since the 1890s, there has been considerable interest in Clausewitz in the United States on the part of various individuals, some of whom - Dwight Eisenhower, George Patton, Albert Wedemeyer, Colin Powell - had some influence on official American policy and strategy. Unfortunately, it is normally quite impossible to credibly determine or demonstrate in any very clear way precisely how these individuals' reading of any such book translates into practical action. Especially in the decade or two after the Vietnam War, there was a great deal of official interest in *On War*, and discussions of Clausewitz figured very prominently in U.S. professional military education. Clausewitz's name and some of his thoughts, in one form or another, came to appear in some key doctrinal or policy statements. While a very lively investigation of Clausewitz by a number of thoughtful American academics has continued since that era, however, it would be hard to say that Clausewitz's writing has any notable direct impact today on American soldiers or policy makers. Among contemporary American military affairs writers there is a distinctly negative attitude towards his name. Accounting for the ups and downs in Clausewitz's reputation and impact in America is inevitably a speculative venture - writing intellectual history is always a bit like trying to nail jelly to the wall. I will not shrink, however, from voicing my own personal views as to why even Americans who actually read Clausewitz's writings (or, at least, are *assigned* to read them) seem to get very little out of the exercise.

A Short History of Clausewitz in America
While there have been many attempts to project Clausewitz's impact on American thinking back into the 19th century - especially to ascribe a Clausewitzian inspiration to President Abraham Lincoln's and/or General

Ulysses S. Grant's conduct of the American Civil War - these efforts are based on pure speculation. There is in fact no evidence of any American reading of *On War* before the 1890s. While the American naval theorist Alfred Thayer Mahan expressed - late in his career - a very high opinion of Clausewitz, we have no good evidence for the reasoning behind that opinion or for any actual influence on Mahan's thinking. There is a distinctly American tradition of individual military scholars or practitioners commenting significantly on Clausewitz, starting with General John McAuley Palmer (1870-1955). Palmer was from a political family and was a believer in mass, popular armies. Following World War I, he inspired the passage of Congressional legislation - which proved futile - to create a large Swiss-style mass reserve army system in the United States. Palmer found inspiration for his views in Clausewitz's equation of war and politics. He argued, essentially, that American organization for war should be a continuation of America's organization for politics. But Palmer's stunned reaction c.1892 to the notion that war is a political phenomenon is revealing of the broader American mindset: "In browsing through [*On War*] I found the striking statement that 'war is not a separate thing in itself but is merely a special violent phase of human politics.' This truth was so startlingly simple that I could not grasp it at first. But it gradually dawned upon me that here was a fundamental military concept which I had never heard about in my four years at West Point."[2]

A similar enthusiasm for Clausewitz ran through Harvard historian Robert M. Johnson, the aristocratic Hoffman Nickerson (Palmer's opposite in terms of military policy, a believer in elite professional armies), political scientist Bernard Brodie, and commanders like Patton and general, later president, Eisenhower.[3]

Despite the intense interest of individual soldiers like Eisenhower and Patton, American military institutions overtly rejected the fundamental assumptions of *On War*. While the philosopher had insisted that war was "the expression of politics by other means", the traditional attitude of American soldiers was that "politics and strategy are radically and fundamentally things apart. Strategy begins where politics end. All that soldiers ask is that once the policy is settled, strategy and command shall be regarded as being in a sphere apart from politics."[4] In the wake of Vietnam, however, *On War* was adopted as a key text at the Naval War College in 1976, the Air War College in 1978, and the Army War College in 1981. Clausewitzian arguments are prominent in the two most authoritative American statements of the lessons of Vietnam: the

1984 Weinberger Doctrine and Army Colonel Harry Summers' seminal *On Strategy: The Vietnam War in Context* (first published in 1981).[5] Colin Powell, a junior officer during the war in Vietnam and a beneficiary of the boom in Clausewitz studies during the 1970s and 1980s, made many favorable and seemingly well-informed references to Clausewitz. The U.S. Marine Corps's brilliant little philosophical field manual *FMFM 1: Warfighting* (1989) was essentially a distillation of *On War*, with strong dashes of Sun Tzu and an un-Clausewitz-like emphasis on maneuver. The later MCDP series of USMC publications was eclectic but thoroughly permeated with Clausewitzian concepts.[6] It would be very difficult to understand the evolution and meaning of US service and joint doctrine since the 1970s without reference to Clausewitz's influence, however poorly his actual ideas may be reflected therein.

The sudden acceptability of Clausewitz in the wake of Vietnam is not difficult to account for, for among the major military theorists only Clausewitz seriously struggled with the sort of dilemma that American military leaders faced in the aftermath of their defeat. Clearly, in what had come to be called in scathing terms a "political war", the political and military components of the American war effort had come unstuck. It ran against the grain of America's military men to criticize elected civilian leaders, but it was just as difficult to take the blame upon themselves. Clausewitz's analysis could not have been more relevant. Many of America's soldiers found unacceptable any suggestion that they had failed on the battlefield, but they were willing to admit that policy had been badly made and that they had misunderstood their role in making it.

Unfortunately, while recognition of the debacle in Vietnam in many ways created an opening for fresh political-military thinking, and certainly led to a genuine American enthusiasm - some called it "a craze" - for Clausewitz, it also greatly distorted the way his ideas were received. Encouraged by some infelicities in the then-new Paret translation, Summers's treatment turned on a rigid interpretation of Clausewitz's trinity as a concrete set of social structures - people, army, and government. That interpretation had a powerful appeal at the time. In America's traumatic war in Vietnam, those social elements had come thoroughly unstuck from one another. Summers' interpretation of this trinity was a positive doctrine, highly prescriptive: A nation could not hope to achieve success in war unless these three elements were kept firmly in harness together.

The post-Vietnam fashion for Clausewitz was widely associated with the American military reform movement, which came to seemed blasé in the wake of the *Desert Storm* victory of 1991. That is consistent with the historical pattern of military-institutional interest in Clausewitz. Established institutions tend to find the complexities of *On War* tempting only when spurred by the shock of severe military embarrassment - e.g., Prussia itself after 1806, then 1848; France after 1871; Great Britain after the inglorious Boer War. Military institutions basking in the glow of success are not inclined to wrestle with such challenging material. As early as 1995, then-Major (U.S. Army Intelligence) Ralph Peters noted that the US Army War College's bust of Carl von Clausewitz "has been moved from a prominent, shrine-like alcove to an off-center auditorium entrance, where it has a status somewhere between that of a Hummel figurine and a hat-rack."[7]

As a result of all these factors, the tremendous amount of attention paid to Clausewitz in professional military education and in military doctrine came to have a very limited payoff. To a great degree, Clausewitz's impact became limited to a small number of discrete concepts that have individually found their way, in severely dumbed-down form, into service or joint military doctrine: the "center of gravity" (the hunt for which became a quasi-theological quest in military classrooms and elsewhere during the 1980s),[8] the "culminating point of the offensive", and Harry Summers's version of the "remarkable trinity". The connections between these concepts, their larger context, and even the meaning of Clausewitz's links between policy, politics, and war, were most frequently lost. Moreover, the difficulty of reading *On War* is so great, and so notorious, that students and faculty alike tend to await the mandatory classes on Clausewitz with mind-numbing dread. The content of those classes tends increasingly to be abbreviated and shallow. The task of presenting them is delegated to hapless junior faculty who, unable to pick up much of Clausewitz's actual argument on short notice, find the assignment unrewarding.

The wars in which the American military found itself engaged after 11 September 2001 did not seem to offer much application for the operational-level Clausewitzian concepts that had been shoe-horned into U.S. military doctrine in the 1980s. There has been little effort to adapt other aspects of *On War* that are highly relevant to the current wars, notably the arguments concerning the people in arms and the inherent strengths of the defense. These are almost completely ignored by American military thinkers. The famous counterinsurgency manual, FM 3-24, makes no meaningful reference to Clausewitz other than to say that "Clausewitz thought that wars by an armed populace could only serve as a strategic defense; however, theorists after World War II realized that insurgency could be a decisive form of warfare. This era spawned the Maoist, Che Guevara-type focoist, and urban approaches to insurgency."[9]

Part of the problem is that Americans have a hard time conceding that the enemies they are fighting thousands of miles from American shores might in any sense be the "defenders". In any case, the writings of Martin van Creveld and John Keegan have created the illusion that Clausewitz was blind to anything beyond conventional warfare and the uniformed, goose-stepping armies of mirror-image European states, and thus couldn't possibly have anything useful to say about insurgencies. A curious fact about smart insurgents, however, is that they tend to consider themselves to be the legitimate states of the societies they intend to rule. Thus the revolutionary Mao Zedong had no difficulty understanding the relevance of Clausewitz's ideas on popular warfare to his own situation.[10]

Until recently, most serious American academic work on Clausewitz has been stimulated by German emigres who made English translations or wrote specifically about Clausewitz, most notably Hans Rothfels, Hans Gatzke, Herbert Rosinski, O. J. Matthijs Jolles (a Schiller scholar), and Peter Paret. Others, like Alfred Vagts and Henry Kissinger, offered sophisticated insights on Clausewitz in the course of writing on other subjects.[11] In any case, it has been the German emigres who have contributed by far the larger part of what is available in English of Clausewitz's *Werke*. There have been three full translation of *Vom Kriege* into English. The first and only credible non-emigre translation, that published in 1873 by British Colonel J.J. Graham, is honest but ponderous, overly literal, often obscure, and now entirely obsolete. The most accurate translation is Jolles's, done in 1943 at the University of Chicago, but the copyright is held by Random House, which has failed to exploit it. The standard version today is that published through Princeton University Press by Sir Michael Howard and Peter Paret in 1976, though it is coming under increasing criticism for missing many important subtleties and for having perhaps excessively "clarified" Clausewitz's thinking. Gatzke translated *Die wichtigsten Grundsätze des Kriegführens zur Ergänzung meines Unterrichts bei Sr. Königlichen Hoheit, den Kronprinzen* in 1942 as *Principles of War*; before falling into obscurity it was widely misunderstood to be a summary of *Vom Kriege*. Other bits and pieces of Clausewitz's *Werke* have been translated into English, especially by Paret and his American student Daniel Moran, but these have had little impact on Clausewitz's reputation and none on American professional military education. Of Clausewitz's historical campaign studies, only two have been published in English in complete form. *The Campaign of 1812 in Russia* was translated anonymously by a member of the Duke of Wellington's circle in 1843 and frequently reprinted.[12] In collaboration with two American colleagues, I myself recently published a translation of *The Campaign of 1815* in a book,[13] intended for a popular audience that included a great deal of material from Wellington and his circle and their views on Clausewitz. Books about Clausewitz - e.g., Paret's outstanding *Clausewitz and the State* (by far the best biography of Clausewitz available in English) and my own *Clausewitz in English: The Reception of Clausewitz in Britain and America* - have little impact on military education, which focuses solely on *On War*.[14]

There has, unfortunately, been little love lost between these German emigre academics and their American counterparts. It is probably true that the German Clausewitz scholars were frustrated by their American students' cultural resistance to basic aspects of Clausewitz's world view (on which, more later), though there were less creditable sources of friction. For instance, the World War II-era German expatriates reportedly regarded Brodie as *"dieser Auswurf des Chicagoer gettos."*[15] Rosinski, who lectured at both the Army and Navy war colleges, lost his jobs there and descended into messianic paranoia. Rothfels and Gatzke made only very limited forays into publishing in English about Clausewitz. Jolles had very little interest in military affairs and made his excellent translation of *On War* largely to avoid active military service by supporting the University of Chicago's wartime military studies program. Paret's fundamental interests are in the history of aesthetics, not military history or theory. Consequently, his work on Clausewitz, beyond the translation of *On War*, is too aridly intellectual to appeal to the American military-affairs audience.

Currently, the two most active and influential American writers on Clausewitz are Antulio (Tony) Echevarria and Jon Tetsuro Sumida. They rarely see eye-to-eye, however. Echevarria, a former armored cavalry officer who, like Gen. David Petraeus, has a Princeton Ph.D., is sophisticated and well informed. As Director of Research at the U.S. Army's Strategic Studies Institute, he tends to write for a military or military-academic audience. He and I tend to be in substantial agreement on most matters so I will focus my comments on Sumida.[16]

Originally a naval historian, Sumida is a civilian professor of history at the University of Maryland who tends to write for other civilian military historians. His 2008 book *Decoding Clausewitz: A New Approach to* On War focuses on two vital aspects of *On War* that have heretofore largely been ignored in the English-speaking world. These are Clausewitz's argument that defense is inherently the stronger form of war and his ideas concerning the use of history as a tool for military education.[17] These are very important arguments that relate both to policy and to education, and they deserve a great deal of attention. I find Sumida's explication provocative and engaging. His contention that these two aspects alone constitute the purpose and core of *On War*, however, is not convincing, and his tone has been taken by some as more than a bit self-aggrandizing. As Jennie Kiesling puts it (in a review that is ultimately quite positive), "Almost everything in *On War* is very simple, but the simplest things are so difficult that no previous reader has comprehended Carl von Clausewitz. Or so Jon Sumida would have one believe. The fundamental thesis of *Decoding Clausewitz* is that, a great deal of "intelligent, rigorous, and productive" study notwithstanding, previous interpreters of Carl von Clausewitz's masterwork have missed the point. Or rather, three points: that Clausewitz had virtually completed *On War* by the time of his death, that the superiority of defense to offense is the work's dominant idea, and that Clausewitz sought to present not a comprehensive theory of war but a scientific method by which each individual can prepare himself to practice war knowledgeably. *On War* is a practical handbook for the peacetime education of wartime commanders, and the essence of that education is "the mental reenactment of historical case studies of command decision."

It would be unfortunate if these stylistic issues were to inhibit a very desirable debate, which might have the potential for revolutionizing the American understanding of Clausewitz.

Despite the importance of Echevarria's and Sumida's work, however, what I personally regard as the most important piece published on Clausewitz since c.1980 is Alan Beyerchen's brilliant 1992 article, "Chance and Complexity in the Real World: Clausewitz on the Nonlinear Nature of War."[18] Beyerchen teaches 19th- and 20th-century German history at Ohio State University. His primary focus is on the history of science. In this article, Beyerchen addressed what may be the fundamental source of resistance to Clausewitz in the English-speaking world - the unspoken source of the divide that separates those who think they "get" Clausewitz from those who find him opaque. To people with a world view engendered by linear math, an engineering mentality, a 19th-century "Newtonian" understanding of science (from which Newton himself did not suffer), or the artificialities of social "science", Clausewitz's seeming obsession with chance, unpredictability, and disproportionalities in the cause/effect relationship are baffling charlatanry; they smack of mysticism. Beyerchen, a historian with a rare understanding of mathematics, explains the implications of nonlinear math and the "new sciences" of Chaos and Complexity for our understanding of "real-world" phenomena like fluid dynamics, market booms and busts, "complex adaptive systems", and war. Chaos and Complexity are not the products of "new age" or mystical thinking. They derive from very, very "hard" science and mathematics. While these two particular terms now seem rather faddish, in fact the concepts they represent are fully emblematic of the direction that all modern science and mathematics took in the second half of the 20th century as computers began making it possible to study natural systems that the old tools simply couldn't handle. It is quite impossible to grasp the meaning of Clausewitz's trinity (which, in turn, is crucial to any attempt to tie together all of the many threads of *On War*) without grasping the scientific implications of his imagery of "theory floating among these three tendencies, as among three points of attraction." He was describing a classic example of "deterministic Chaos".

I have focused thus far on writers and actors with a positive view of Clausewitz. There has, of course, been a great deal of hostility to Clausewitz in the United States, much of it deriving from the work of British writers. Anglo-American resentment towards Clausewitz largely originated in anti-German feelings deriving from World War I and not ameliorated by the Nazi era. It was given coherent though highly disingenuous[19] form by British military historian B.H. Liddell Hart, whose private opinion of Clausewitz was far more positive than the views he normally chose to express in print. In the wake of the Korean War, Liddell Hart's consciously false portrayal of Clausewitz as the "Mahdi of Mass" and the "Apostle of Total War" was remedied with many American academics, especially political scientists, by Robert E. Osgood's widely read 1957 book, *Limited War*, which provided the first truly important, historically grounded, and theoretical discussion of the concept that enlisted Clausewitz's authority.[20] By 1979, Osgood was calling Clausewitz "the preeminent military and political strategist of limited war in modern times", a new image for the military philosopher radically different - if almost equally disputable - from the image that had previously held sway. But Liddell Hart's treatment was resurrected and amplified in 1968 by the editor of a popular abridgement of *On War*, American biologist and musician Anatol Rapoport, whose antagonisms were directed primarily towards Henry Kissinger and the Westphalian international system; Clausewitz was a secondary target at best. Rapoport regarded Clausewitz's expressed belief in the superior power of the defense as essentially a sham, enabling him to save space by deleting all of Book VI as irrelevant.[21]

This tradition has been given new life in the United States by Israeli historian Martin van Creveld and Britons John Keegan and Mary Kaldor, who have planted a powerful but almost entirely false image of Clausewitz in Western military literature. In particular, van Creveld and Keegan have sought to entomb Clausewitz's theories in a vanished - and largely ahistorical - world in which war was exclusively the province of all-powerful Weberian-style states engaged in purely conventional military struggles with one another. In Creveld's hostile and influential assault, Clausewitz's description of a dynamically interacting trinity of passion, chance, and reason in war becomes a rigid, formulaic prescription for a lumbering, incompetent, dinosaur-like caricature of the early-20th-century Western state.[22] As Paret's American student Daniel Moran puts it, "The most egregious misrepresentation of Clausewitz ... must be that of Martin van Creveld, who has declared Clausewitz to be an apostle of 'Trinitarian War', by which he means, incomprehensibly, a war of 'state against state and army against army', from which the influence of the people is entirely excluded."[23]

These delusory treatments of Clausewitz have culminated in a recent string of anti-Clausewitzian articles and books.[24] The nature of these attacks is perhaps best characterized by Stephen Melton's *The Clausewitz Delusion: How the American Army Screwed Up the Wars in Iraq and Afghanistan*.[25] There is little point to analyzing Melton's views here, however, for his criticisms of "Clausewitz" and the "neo-Clausewitzians" makes no reference to the historical Clausewitz or his actual writings. This "Clausewitz" is simply the personification of an obtuse style of purely conventional, technology-dependent, firepower-dependent, state-on-state warfare.

Why Americans Struggle with Clausewitz

In my experience, American military and governmental students get very little out of reading Clausewitz. I have nothing to do with designing the relevant course or teaching it (the vast majority of my energies over the last several years have been devoted to information technology crises and other administrivia). But I do conduct the preparatory workshops for instructors assigned to teach our core course on military history and theory (with two seminar sessions devoted exclusively to Clausewitz). Nonetheless, a good 80 percent of the students I interrogate in the subsequent oral examinations can speak of Clausewitz's theories only in terms of keeping the "Remarkable Trinity's" components of People, Army, and Government tightly bound together in lock-step pursuit of a policy of Total War. While students sometimes associate the notion of "limited war" with Clausewitz, the actual meaning of "limited objectives" seems poorly understood, e.g., "Well, as you know, our objectives during the 2003 invasion of Iraq were quite limited." They seem to believe that the "limited" in "limited war" refers to <u>means</u> - consequently, even wars aimed at the most radical forms of "regime change" still qualify as limited so long as nuclear weapons are not employed.

Unfortunately, it would be completely unrealistic to suggest that our instructors and students should be able to handle Clausewitz with ease. While the trepidation and often outright terror that instructors sometimes telegraph to students is immensely counterproductive, the fact remains that *On War* is an extraordinarily difficult book. Fundamentally, this is true because the subject itself is inherently difficult. But brilliant, fascinating, and important as it is, *On War* is also very long and densely written in a style completely unfamiliar to American readers. Its dialectical approach, so essential to achieving its profundity, is intensely confusing to Anglo-American readers who expect a book to contain a "thesis statement" supported by 2-300 pages of proof unsullied by contradictory evidence. It contains innumerable digressions of limited interest to most potential modern audiences. The existing book is based on an unfinished set of draft papers and incorporates ideas from different and sometimes contradictory stages of Clausewitz's intellectual evolution. While I personally believe that *On War* is internally more consistent and closer to completion than many commentators do, the book's frozen evolutionary features remain problematic. Various translation problems muddy many of its broad concepts. Few Americans can place Clausewitz into any meaningful historical context, and *On War*'s profusion of historical examples, instructive to specialists on 18th and 19th-century Europe, is generally useless for readers to whom the phrase "That's history" is just another way to say "That's utterly irrelevant." These older, exclusively European examples leave many readers with a false impression that the ideas they illustrate are themselves obsolete, culturally circumscribed, exclusively oriented on the state, and thus irrelevant to the modern world. Its lack of reference to sea- and aerospace forces requires modern readers to use rather more imagination than is commonly required - or available - when seeking to grasp its modern implications. The Paret translation is particularly problematic in its unilluminating determination to translate *Politik* as "policy" whenever possible. Without devoting a great deal more effort to preparing American students to read *On War* effectively, and giving ourselves much more time for intensive discussion of its context, arguments, and implications, scholars should not expect to achieve much by assigning it to the mass of students. We would do better to absorb its crucial concepts and put our energies into conveying them in a form unburdened by the liabilities of Clausewitz's own, unfinished presentation. As it stands, however, American scholars remain so divided over the book's meaning (both broadly and in detail) that we are in no position to do that.

These problems with the existing text are so great that once, only half-joking, I floated a proposal to completely re-write it using modern examples, up-to-date scientific imagery, and an editorial meat-cleaver to reduce the book to digestible length. Those concepts that have proved most incomprehensible to American readers in their current presentation would be freely rewritten to address the sources of confusion and misapprehension. I actually received a number of offers to fund this project, but these invariably came with unacceptable strings attached - e.g., "The new work will demonstrate that Clausewitz supported the concept of NetCentric Warfare....".

At the root of American problems with Clausewitz, however, lie the seemingly ineradicable pathologies of American strategic culture. British writer Colin Gray penetratingly captured these in a list including indifference to history, the engineering style and dogged pursuit of the technical fix, impatience, blindness to cultural differences, indifference to strategy, and the evasion of politics.[26] I would add to that an essentially economic rationality and a perverse pseudo-Clausewitzian conviction that war is "merely the continuation of unilateral policy" - or, better yet, a convenient way to keep bad policy going a little bit longer through the admixture of "other means".

But American strategic culture is what it is, for a host of historical reasons. It seems unlikely that the study of Clausewitz is going to change it. And however annoying or pathological it often seems in the cold light of academic analysis, viewed over the long term the American approach to war and politics has been stupendously successful. As Churchill noted, after trying everything else the Americans do tend to do the right thing. At its best, America's strategic success reflects more than the failures of its adversaries - it represents the triumph of character over intellect.

Nonetheless, one cannot help but wonder if the application of a little more intellect, of the Clausewitzian variety, might not help.

Notes:

[1] House Appropriations Committee, Thursday, March 13, 1997. Exchange between Committee Chairman Congressman Herbert Leon 'Sonny' Callahan and Undersecretary of Defense for Policy Walter B. Slocombe.

[2] I.B. Holley, Jr., *General John M. Palmer, Citizen Soldiers, and the Army of a Democracy* (Westport, CT: Greenwood Press, 1982), 66.

[3] Asked in 1966 what book (other than the Bible) had had the greatest effect on his life, Eisenhower answered, "My immediate reaction is that I have had two definitely different lives, one military, the other political. From the military side, if I had to select one book, I think it would be ON WAR by Clausewitz." Letter, Dwight D. Eisenhower to Olive Ann Tambourelle, 2 March 1966. Eisenhower Post-presidential Papers, Special Name, Box 8. There is considerable evidence to back up Eisenhower's claim, but none of it points to Clausewitz's influence on any particular military or political decision he ever made.

[4] Command and General Staff School, *Principles of Strategy for an Independent Corps or Army in a Theater of Operations* (Fort Leavenworth, KS: U.S. Army Command and General Staff School Press, 1936), 19.

[5] Prior to the American debacle in Vietnam, few thinkers writing in English had paid much serious attention to Clausewitz's trinity as a distinct concept. The term first achieved prominence in skewed form in Harry Summers, *On Strategy: A Critical Analysis of the Vietnam War* (Novato, CA: Presidio Press, 1982), written in 1981 while Summers was a student at the U.S. Army War College.

[6] I think I can safely say that, since I wrote a number of them.

[7] Ralph Peters, review of Bassford, *Clausewitz in English*, *Parameters*, Winter 1994-95.

[8] Each of the American armed services (and, separately, the Joint Staff) evolved narrow, distinct, specialized, and usually quite incompatible doctrinal definitions of "center of gravity" - a phrase that, except for a small number of very

specific but quite varied discussions - was essentially a verbal tic on Clausewitz's part. See Dr. Joe Strange, *Centers of Gravity & Critical Vulnerabilities: Building on the Clausewitzian Foundation So That We Can All Speak the Same Language* (Quantico, VA: Marine Corps University, series "Perspectives on Warfighting" number four, 1996) for a hilarious but highly accurate discussion of this doctrinal train-wreck.

[9] *FM 3-24: Counterinsurgency*, Headquarters, Department of the Army, December 2006, p. 1-4.

[10] See Christopher Daase, "Clausewitz and Small Wars," in Hew Strachan and Andreas Herberg-Rothe, eds., *Clausewitz in the Twenty-First Century* [Proceedings of a March, 2005 conference at Oxford] (Oxford University Press, 2007). But Daase is a German working in Britain--very little is being done on this subject in America.

[11] Although a substantial part of Hans Delbrück's *corpus* has been translated into English, it seems to have had little direct influence on American military historical writing.

[12] A far better though only partial translation appeared in Carl von Clausewitz, *Historical and Political Writings*, eds./trans. Peter Paret and Daniel Moran (Princeton: Princeton University Press, 1992).

[13] Carl von Clausewitz and Arthur Wellesley, 1st Duke of Wellington, *On Waterloo: Clausewitz, Wellington, and the Campaign of 1815*, ed./trans. Christopher Bassford, Daniel Moran, and Gregory W. Pedlow (Clausewitz.com, 2010); another translation, by Peter Hofschröer, appeared almost simultaneously, with the odd title of *On Wellington: A Critique of Waterloo* (University of Oklahoma Press, 2010).

[14] Peter Paret, *Clausewitz and the State: The Man, His Theories, and His Times* (Princeton: Princeton University Press, 1976; reprinted 2007); Christopher Bassford, *Clausewitz in English: The Reception of Clausewitz in Britain and America, 1815-1945* (New York: Oxford University Press, 1994). A complete list of Clausewitz's work available in English translation can be found at *http://www.clausewitz.com/bibl/CwzBiblEnglish.htm#Cwz*.

[15] Bassford, *Clausewitz in English*, p. 174.

[16] See Echevarria, *Clausewitz's Center of Gravity: Changing Our Warfighting Doctrine - Again!* (Strategic Studies Institute, September 2002); *Clausewitz and Contemporary War* (New York: Oxford University Press, 2007).

[17] Jon Tetsuro Sumida, *Decoding Clausewitz: A New Approach to* On War (Lawrence, KS: University Press of Kansas, 2008). Reviews have been numerous and mixed. See especially West Point professor Eugenia Kiesling's lively review in *Army History*, Summer 2010, pp. 46-48 – also

http://www.clausewitz.com/bibl/KieslingReviewsSumida.htm.

[18] Alan D. Beyerchen, "Chance and Complexity in the Real World: Clausewitz on the Nonlinear Nature of War", *International Security*, Winter 1992/1993, pp. 59-90.

[19] See John Mearsheimer, *Liddell Hart and the Weight of History* (Ithaca: Cornell University Press, 1988).

[20] Robert Endicott Osgood, *Limited War: The Challenge to American Strategy*. Chicago: University of Chicago Press, 1957; *Limited War Revisited*. Boulder: Westview Press, 1979.

[21] Carl von Clausewitz, *On War,* ed. and with an introduction by Anatol Rapoport (Baltimore: Penguin Books, 1968).

[22] Ironically, Creveld's anti-Clausewitzian interpretation of the trinity derives not from *On War* itself but from the very much pro-Clausewitz work of U.S. Army Colonel Harry G. Summers, Jr.

[23] Daniel Moran, "Clausewitz on Waterloo: Napoleon at Bay," Clausewitz and Wellesley, *On Waterloo: Clausewitz, Wellington, and the Campaign of 1815*, p. 242, referring to Martin van Creveld, *The Transformation of War: The Most Radical Reinterpretation of Armed Conflict Since Clausewitz* (New York: The Free Press, 1991), 49.

[24] See the critique of this anti-Clausewitz literature in Bart Schuurman, "Clausewitz and the 'New Wars' Scholars", *Parameters*, Spring 2010, pp. 89-100. For examples see Bruce Fleming [Professor of English at the U.S. Naval Academy], "Can Reading Clausewitz Save Us from Future Mistakes?" *Parameters*, Spring 2004. pp. 62-76; Tony Corn [U.S. Department of State], "Clausewitz in Wonderland", *Policy Review* (Web Exclusive), September 2006; Phillip S. Meilinger [Ph.D., Colonel, USAF, ret.], "Busting the Icon: Restoring Balance to the Influence of Clausewitz", *Strategic Studies Quarterly* (Fall, 2007), pp. 116-145, and "Clausewitz's Bad Advice", *Armed Forces Journal*, August 2008. The primary target appears to be the arrogance of self-proclaimed Clausewitzians, since these critiques touch only tangentially (at best) on Clausewitz himself and his actual arguments. See also the responses by the pro-Clausewitz camp: Nik

Gardner [Air War College], "Resurrecting the 'Icon': The Enduring Relevance of Clausewitz's *On War*", *Strategic Studies Quarterly*, Spring 2009, pp. 119-133; responses to Fleming by myself, Tony Echevarria, and Michael David Rohr in *Parameters*, Summer 2004.

[25] Stephen L. Melton, *The Clausewitz Delusion: How the American Army Screwed Up the Wars in Iraq and Afghanistan (A Way Forward)* (Minneapolis: Zenith Press, 2009).

[26] Colin S. Gray, "History and Strategic Culture", in Williamson Murray, MacGregor Knox, and Alvin Bernstein, Editors, *The Making of Strategy: Rulers, States, and War* (New York, NY: Cambridge University Press, 1994), pp. 592-598. I've listed six characteristics out of Gray's eight.

AUTHORS

Austria

RAUCHENSTEINER, Manfried, Dr. phil., Prof., born 1942. Since 1975 Professor for Austrian and Contemporary History at the University of Vienna and the Diplomatische Akademie, Vienna. He taught Military history and War theories at the Austrian Military Academy, Wiener Neustadt and the Landesverteidigungsakademie (General Staff Academy), Vienna. Prof. Dr. Rauchensteiner was from 1988-1992 Head of the Military Historical Service Department, Ministry of Defence, and 1992-2005 Director Heeresgeschichtliches Museum, Vienna. Since then Advisor Militärhistorisches Museum der Bundeswehr, Dresden. He is author of 14 books on Austrian and Military History, numerous articles, TV productions etc. The last publications: Stalinplatz 4. Österreich unter alliierter Besatzung 1945-1955 (2005) and Zwischen den Blöcken. NATO, Warschauer Pakt und Österreich (ed., 2009).

E-mail: manfried.rauchensteiner@univie.ac.at

Belgium

COLSON, Bruno, Dr. Pol. Sc., Dr. Hist., is Professor of War and Strategy in Modern History and History of International Relations at the University of Namur (Louvain Academy) and senior research fellow at the Institut de Stratégie comparée in Paris (Ecole pratique des Hautes Etudes). He has served as an adviser to the President of the Parliamentary Assembly of the OSCE in 1994-1995 and has lectured on strategy and international affairs at the Royal Institute for Defence Studies in Brussels and at the Collège interarmées de Défense in Paris. He has published numerous books and articles on American strategy, transatlantic relations, the Napoleonic wars, Jomini and Clausewitz, including *La culture stratégique américaine. L'influence de Jomini* (Economica, 1993), *L'art de la guerre de Machiavel à Clausewitz* (Presses universitaires de Namur, 1999), *Le général Rogniat, ingénieur et critique de Napoléon* (Economica, 2006). He is currently working on an anthology of Napoleon's military writings following the table of contents of *On War* by Clausewitz. He is also researching on Clausewitz's participation in the campaign of Waterloo.

E-mail: bruno.colson@fundp.ac.be

WASINSKI, Christophe, Ph.D in International Relations, is Lecturer at the University of Namur and at the Université Libre de Bruxelles (ULB), where he is a member of the research centre REPI (Recherche et Enseignement en Politique Internationale). He is also a member of the Réseau multidisciplinaire d'études stratégiques (rmes.be). Christophe Wasinski has published in the *Annuaire Français de Relations Internationales*, *Cultures & Conflits*, *Les Champs de Mars*, *Stratégique* and *International Political Sociology*. His master's thesis was about the reception of Clausewitz in the United States from 1945 until the end of the 20th century (http://www.stratisc.org/pubelec.html).

E-mail: christophe.wasinski@fundp.ac.be

China

YU TIEJUN is Associate Professor in the School of International Studies and general secretary for the Center for International and Strategic Studies at Peking University. Previously, he served as visiting fellow at the Center for International Security and Cooperation at Stanford University in 2005, and also as visiting scholar at the Fairbank Center for East Asian Research at Harvard University in 2005-06. Dr. Yu has published a variety of articles focused on international relations theory and military alliances in East Asia. He is also the Chinese translator of *Myths of Empire* by Jack Snyder (Beijing: Peking University Press, 2007) and *Discord and Collaboration: Essays on International Politics* by Arnold Wolfers (Beijing: World Affairs Press, 2006), among other works. He teaches International Security and Strategic Studies at Peking University. His research interests include IR theory, East Asian Security, and Military History. Dr. Yu received a Ph.D., M.A. and B.A. from the School of International Studies at Peking University.

E-mail: yutiejun@pku.edu.cn

Denmark

CLEMMESEN, Michael Hesselholt, MA (hist.) Brigadier General (ret. Danish Army), was Director Strategy Department and Course Director of the Danish Joint Senior Command and Staff Course at the Royal Danish Defence College from 1991 till 1994 and creator and first Commandant of the Baltic Defence College from 1998 till 2004. He has since the late 1980's been lecturing military history, strategic theories and the realities of doctrinal development at staff and war college levels. Clemmesen is currently a senior research fellow at the Royal

Danish Defence College Center of Military History. He has published numerous books and articles. His latest publication is (with the title translated from Danish): *The Long Approach to 9. April. The History about the Forty Years prior to the German Operation against Denmark and Norway.* Odense: The University Press of Southern Denmark, 2010).

E-mails: michael@clemmesen.org & cfm-21@fak.dk.

Finland

VISURI, Pekka, Dr. Pol. Sc. is a retired Finish Army Colonel. He has worked 15 years as researcher at the Finnish Institute of International Affairs in Helsinki, and from 2008 as project researcher at the Aleksanteri Institute of the University of Helsinki. He currently is adjunct professor at the National Defence University in Helsinki and specialized in security policy and strategy. His dissertation: (in English) *From total war to crisis management. The evolution of defence doctrines in Western Central Europe and Finland 1945-1985* (University of Helsinki 1989). His latest publications include: *Sverige och Finland vid skiljevägen 1808-1812* (co-author, Esbo: Fenix, 2009), *Suomi kylmässä sodassa* (*Finland in the Cold War.* Helsinki: Otava, 2006), *Suomen turvallisuus- ja puolustuspolitiikan linjaukset* (ed. 2. edition, Engl. *Guidelines for the Finnish Security and Defence Policy*, Helsinki: Otava, 2003) and *Suomi ja kriisit* (coeditor with Tuomas Forsberg et al, Engl. *Finland and Crises*, Helsinki: Gaudeamus, 2003).

E-mail: pekka.visuri@kolumbus.fi

France

COUTAU-BÉGARIE, Hervè, Dr. Pol. Sc., is professor of History of Strategic Thought at the Ecole pratique des Hautes Etudes (Sorbonne) and professor of Strategy at the Ecole de guerre (Joint War College). He was President of the French Commission of Maritime History from 1990 to 1992 and President of the French Commission of Military History from 2000 till 2005. He currently is President of the Institut de Stratégie et des Conflits – Commission Française d'Histoire Militaire. His books are mainly related to naval strategy: recently: *L'Océan globalisé* (2007), *Le Meilleur des ambassadeurs* (2010) and to general strategy: *Traité de stratégie* (1999, 7th ed. 2011). He also co-authored: *Darlan* (1989), *Mers el-Kébir 1940* (1994), *Dakar 1940* (2004) and edited various collective books.

E-mail: herve.coutau-begarie@academie.defense.gouv.fr

Germany

HARTMANN, Uwe, Dr. phil., is Colonel (with General Staff education) in the German Armed Forces (Bundeswehr). He served in the politico-military department and in the Planning and Advisory Staff in the Ministry of Defence as well as in several military assignments on battalion up to Corps level. Since December 2009, he has been the Commander of the students' regiment of the Helmut-Schmidt-Universität / University of the Bundeswehr Hamburg. Uwe Hartmann published books and articles on philosophy of science, educational theory, the leadership philosophy of the Bundeswehr ("Innere Führung") and on Carl von Clausewitz, including: Carl von Clausewitz. Erkenntnis, Bildung, Generalstabsausbildung, München 1998; Carl von Clausewitz and the Making of Modern Strategy, Potsdam 2002. Together with Claus von Rosen, he has been editing the "Jahrbuch Innere Führung" since 2009. Uwe Hartmann is a graduate of the University of the Bundeswehr Hamburg and of the Naval Postgraduate School in Monterey/CAL.
E-mail: uwe.hartmann@bundeswehr.org

ROSEN, Claus Freiherr von, Dr. phil., Lieutenant Colonel (ret.), is Professor of military pedagogy at the National Defence Academy in Tartu/Estland. He served in the German Armed Forces (Bundeswehr) from 1963 until 2001. He had several assignments in training and education of staff officers, officers, and non-commissioned officers. Since 1993, he has been the official holder of Wolf Graf von Baudissin's bequest. In 2002, he was appointed as the leader of the "Baudissin Dokumentation Zentrum" at the Command and General Staff College of the German Armed Forces in Hamburg. Dr. von Rosen published several books and articles on training, didactics, leadership, leadership philosophy, tradition, and on Carl von Clausewitz in educational and sociological perspective, including: Bildungsreform und Innere Führung, Weinheim/Basel 1981; Nie wieder Sieg. W. Graf v. Baudissin: Programmatische Schriften 1951 - 1981, München 1982; Die "heutigen Kriege" - nach Clausewitz. Zum Verständnis der neuen Kriege heute. In: Hammerich, Helmut, Hartmann, Uwe, Rosen, Claus von (ed.), Jahrbuch Innere Führung 2010. Die Grenzen des Militärischen, Berlin 2010, pp. 201-239. Together with Uwe Hartmann, he has edited the "Jahrbuch Innere Führung" since 2009.

E-mail: claus.rosen@gmx.de

Israel

KOBER, Avi, Dr., is Associate Professor at the Department of Political Studies and Senior Research Associate at the BESA Center for Strategic Studies, Bar-Ilan University. His main areas of research are military theory, Israeli military thought, and the Arab-Israeli wars. His recent publications include "Targeted Killing during the Second Intifada: The Quest for Effectiveness," *Journal of Conflict Studies*, Vol. 27, No. 1 (Summer 2007); "The IDF in the Second Lebanon War: Why the Poor Performance?" *Journal of Strategic Studies* Vol. 31, No. 1 (February 2008); *Israel's Wars of Attrition* (New York: Routledge, 2009); and "Technological and Operational Incentives and Disincentives for Force Transformation," in Stuart Cohen (ed.), *The Decline of the Citizen Armies in Democratic States: Processes and Implications* (London: Routledge, 2010).

E-mail: avik@doubt.com

Italy

BOZZO, Luciano, is Professor of *International Relations* and *Theories of International Politics* at the Department of Political Science and Sociology of Politics (DISPO), University of Florence. He is Director of the Master in "Leadership and Strategic Planning", a joint program of the Italian Air Force and the University of Florence, where he teaches *Strategic Studies* and *International Politics*. He taught various academic disciplines at the Universities of Triest, Pisa and Bologna, and, from 1990 to 1996, was Professor of *Global Strategy* at the War College of the Italian Air Force. He is a member of the International Institute for Strategic Studies (IISS), London, and Director of the Centre for Strategic and International Studies (CSSI) at the Political Science Department of the University of Florence. His research activity is focused on the theory of action; the relationship between conflict, communication and culture; the concept of strategic culture and the evolution of military thought.

E-mail: bozzo@unifi.it

ILARI, Virgilio, Prof. Dr., holds since 1991 the Chair for History of Military Institutions at the Catholic University of Milan. He had taught before History of Roman Law at Macerata. He is President of the Italian Society for History. Ilari has published numerous books and articles. His latest publication concentrated on the military history of Ancient Italian States during the French Revolution and Napoleonic Wars.

E-mail: virgilio.ilari@tiscali.it

GIACOMELLO, Giampiero, is Assistant Professor of International Relations with the Facoltà di Scienze Politiche Universita' di Bologna (Italy) and Adjunct Professor of Policy Analysis in the European Studies MA Program, James Madison University, Firenze. He was post-doctoral associate with the Peace Studies Program at Cornell University in 2004. In 2002, he was Social Science Research Council Summer Fellow in Information Technologies and Security at Columbia University, where he worked on methods for measuring cyberwars. Dr. Giacomello's research interests cover strategic theory, cyberterrorism, and European defense policies. His most recent publications include a textbook on strategic studies (in Italian) with Gianmarco Badialetti, the volumes *Security in the West* (edited with Craig Nation) and *Italy's Military Operations Abroad* (with Piero Ignazi and Fabrizio Coticchia, forthcoming), as well as several articles in *International Studies Review, European Security, Contemporary Politics, Small Wars and Insurgencies* and other peer-reviewed journals.

E-mail: giampiero.giacomello@unibo.it

Japan

OKI, Takeshi, M.A. taught military history, international relations and contemporary German history at the Tsukuba University and other Japanese universities; 1999-2001 advisor of the National "Showakan Museum" (Museum for the pre war history of modern Japan). 2002-2004 lecturer in military history at the National Institute for Defense Studies (Japanese Self Defense Force). He has published numerous books and articles as an independent researcher and author. His latest book is *"Tetsujuji no Kiseki"* (The trail of the Iron Cross: Wehrmacht in the Second World War). 2010.

E-mail: dr191939@gmail.com

Netherlands

DONKER, Paul, Drs. is lecturer at the Department of Military Studies of the Netherlands Defense Academy. He taught strategy at the Instituut Defensie Legrangen (Netherlands Defence Command and Staff College). His military career includes almost ten years of active service as an infantry officer. He holds a Master's Degree in philosophy from the University of Amsterdam and ins working on his PhD thesis "Clausewitz on Zweck und Ziel". Currently he is finalizing a monograph on Clausewitz and the French Revolutionary Wars. Donker is co-editor of the "Militaire Spectator".

E-mail: P.Donker.02@NLDA.NL

Norway

HØIBACK, Harald, Lieutenant Colonel, Ph.D., is currently employed as a faculty advisor at the Norwegian Defence Command and Staff College. He is an officer in the Royal Norwegian Air Force, trained as a fighter controller, and his military record includes duties as a crew chief, interceptor controller and instructor. He has also served as advisor to the Norwegian Ministry of Defense. He is a graduate of the Royal Norwegian Air Force Academy, holds a master's degree in philosophy (cand. Phiol.) from the University of Oslo and a master's degree in history from the University of Glasgow (M.Phil.) He is the author of Command and Control in Military Crises (2003) and has also published numerous articles on military history and military thought.

E-mail: hahoiback@fhs.mil.no

Slovenia

JUVAN, Jelena, Ph. D. in defence science, is an assistant at the Defence Studies department and a graduate research assistant at the Defence Research Centre at the Faculty of Social Sciences, University of Ljubljana. She holds a B.A. in political science (2001) and a Ph. D. (2008) in defence science, both from the Faculty of Social Sciences University of Ljubljana. She is an assistant lecturer for the courses: Sociology and political science of the armed forces, Polemology and Foreign and security policies of the European Union. Her research fields include: military families, peace operations and human factor in the armed forces. Selected publications: MOELKER, René, JELUŠIČ, Ljubica, JUVAN, Jelena. News from the home front: communities supporting military families. In: CAFORIO, Giuseppe (ed.). Armed forces and conflict resolution: sociological perspectives, (Contributions to conflict management, peace economics and development, vol. 7). 1st ed. Bingley: Emerald, 2008, pp. 183-210; JUVAN, Jelena. Usklajevanje delovnih in družinskih obveznosti v vojaški organizaciji. Soc. delo, avg. 2009, vol. 48, No. 4, pp. 227-234.

E-mail: jelena.juvan@fdv.uni-lj.si

PREBILIČ, Vladimir is holding since 2007 the Chair of Defence Study Department at the Faculty of Social Sciences University of Ljubljana and has conducted different research projects for the Slovenian MOD and Slovenian Government. After his studies of history and geography at the University of Ljubljana he finished an M. A. thesis on the conversion of former military sites. He received the Manfred-Wörner Scholarship of the German MoD and the COST A10 Scholarship of the EU Commission and attended the course: Conducting Military and Peacekeeping Operations in Accordance with the Rule of Law, at the Defence Institute of International Legal Studies, Newport, Rhode Island, USA. Prebilic recently has published: *Theoretical aspects of military logistics.* Defense & security analysis, Jun. 2006, vol. 22, no. 2, pp. 159-177; *Defense system and ecology - the North Atlantic Treaty Organization role,* Polemos, siječanj/prosinac 2005, sv. 8, br. 1/2, pp. 183-203. *Von der Staatsgründung bis zur EU- und NATO-Mitgliedschaft: permanente Reformierung der slowenischen Streitkräfte?* in: JAUN, Rudolf (ur.), OLSANSKY, Michael (ur.). *Strategische Wende - Technologische Wende: die Transformation der Streitkräfte am Übergang zum 21. Jahrhundert,* (Schriftenreihe, MILAK Schrift Nr. 9). Zürich: Militärakademie and der ETH, 2008, pp. 19-32. *Foreign politics of Yugoslavia: an important factor of informbiro confrontation* in: JAKUS, János (ur.), SUBA, János (ur.). *A baranyai államhatár a XX. században: a Pécsi Tudományegyetemen 2008.* Pécs: HM Hadtörténeti intézet és Múzeum, 2008, pp. 78-90.

E-mail: vladimir.prebilic@fdv.uni-lj.si

South Africa

POTGIETER, Thean, Dr., is Director of the Centre for Military Studies, Faculty of Military Science, Stellenbosch University (South African Military Academy). He previously served as Chair Military History Department (Faculty of Military Science), at SA Naval Staff College, onboard *SAS Protea* (SA Navy hydrographic survey ship), at Armscor (Armaments Corporation of South Africa) and at the University of Johannesburg (formerly RAU). He holds degrees in the Human Sciences, Military History and Strategic Studies, while his doctorate (Stellenbosch) focussed on defence against maritime power projection. He has vast teaching experience at universities and colleges and is a regular participant at international academic events. He has published widely (books, chapters in books and articles) in a large number of countries on topics ranging from military history to maritime defence and security issues. He serves on numerous academic boards, on editorial boards and is also the Secretary-General of the South African Chapter of the ICMH (International Commission of Military History). He has acted as principle organiser of various international conferences, including the ICHM Congress (Cape Town, 2007) and a maritime security conference (Stellenbosch, 2008), and has received a number of academic and military awards.

E-mail: Thean@ma2.sun.ac.za

VREÿ, Francois, Dr. Since 1995 lecturer in Military Strategy at the Faculty of Military Science, Stellenbosch University. Teaches on Low-Intensity Conflict, New Security Agenda of Africa and Research Methodology at the under and post-graduate levels. He obtained his PhD from Stellenbosch University with a thesis on *An Analysis of the Military Futures Debate: Explaining Alternative Military Futures for the SANDF*. He is the current editor of the journal *Scientia Militaria: South African Journal of Military Studies*. His latest publications include a chapter on security in the Gulf of Guinea in *Maritime Security in Southern African Waters* (2009) and a chapter on future insurgency in the forthcoming publication *South Africa and Contemporary Counterinsurgency: Roots, Practices, Prospects* (2010, UCT Press).

E-mail: francois@ma2.sun.ac.za

Spain

ALONSO BAQUER, Miguel, Ph. D., Brigadier General (Ret.). Spanish Institute for Strategic Studies (Ministry of Defense of Spain - Madrid). Ph. D. History and Geography (Universidad Complutense - Madrid). He taught History of the Art of War in the Staff College of the Spanish Army, in the Naval War College, in the Army High Studies College and in the Spanish Center for National Defense Studies. He has published numerous books and articles. In relation to Carl Clausewitz, the following publications can be highlighted: "Ideas and believes of Carl Clausewitz", "Marie von Brühl, Clausewitz's wife", "Clausewitz and the Mountain Warfare", "Spanish Military Organization during the last three Centuries".

E-Mail: ieee@oc.mde.es

Sweden

ERICSON WOLKE, Lars, Ph. D. and Professor in Military History at the Swedish National Defence College, Stockholm and Assistant Professor in Military History at Åbo Academy (the Swedish University at Turku, Finland). He is president of the Swedish Commission for Military History and since 2005 member of the Board of the International Commission for Military History (since 2009 its 2nd Vice President) He is also a member of the Royal Swedish Academy for Military Sciences. He has published some 25 books, including *The Ideas of War. Swedish thoughts about warfare, 1320-1920* (Published in Swedish in 2007 as *Krigets idéer. Svenska tankar om kring 1320-1920*). His latest books are: *Swedish Sea Battles. A Naval History through 500 years* (2009); and *Bomb and Burn them. Tactic and Terror in Aerial Warfare during 100 Years* (2010) both published in Swedish. He currently is working on a Study of Sweden's Operational and Tactical Experiences from its participation in the International Operations in former Yugoslavia, 1992-2007.

E-mail: lars.ericsonwolke@fhs.se

Switzerland

BECK, Roland, Dr. phil., Colonel of the Swiss General Staff, born 1949. Since 2008 he has been Chief editor of the General Swiss Military Review. 1975-76 Clausewitz studies at the University of Münster/Westfalen (Germany). 1981 he finished his dissertation about political-military aspects of the conflict between Prussia and Switzerland in the years 1856/57. Since 1982 he has taught military science in the courses of Swiss General Staff and in the years 1994-1996 he was personal collaborator of the Chief of Swiss General Staff. 1997-2001 he served as Commander of the officer school and as Chief instructor of the Swiss Tank Forces. 2002-2007 he was Chief of the Operational Training in the Army Staff. Beside the professional work he established the Swiss Section of the Clausewitz-Gesellschaft in 2001. Since this time till 2009 he was the president of this section of the Clausewitz-Gesellschaft. He has published numerous articles and books. His latest book deals with the 175 years of the Swiss Officer

Society (2008). Beck is also project leader of the work: History of the Swiss General Staff. Up to this day 11 volumes of this work have been published.

E-mail: roland.beck@asmz.ch

USA

BASSFORD, Christopher, Dr., has been Professor of Strategy at the U.S. National War College since 1999. He is a former U.S. artillery officer and the author of inter alia, *Clausewitz in English: The Reception of Clausewitz in Britain and America, 1818-1945* (New York: Oxford University Press, 1994) and *MCDP 1-1; Strategy* (a U.S. Marine Corps Doctrinal Publication, 1997). He is the editor of The Clausewitz Homepage, http://www.clausewitz.com/ and has taught at Purdue University, the Ohio State University, the U.S. Marine Corps Command and Staff College, and the U.S. Army War College.

E-mail: BassfordC@NDU.edu

Editor

POMMERIN, Reiner, Prof. Dr. phil. habil., Colonel Res (German Air Force), was holding from 1992 till 2008 the Chair for Modern and Contemporary History at the University of Dresden. He had taught before at Cologne, Mainz, Erlangen and Jena. He was Kennedy Fellow at Harvard University 1979/80, German Visiting Professor at St. Antony's College Oxford 1994/95 and holding the Fulbright Distinguished Chair for German Studies at Vanderbilt University 1996/97. Pommerin is a member of the Clausewitz-Gesellschaft, the German Commission for Military History and of the Board of the International Commission for Military History. He also is Co-Editor of the Militärgeschichtliche Zeitschrift (MGZ). Pommerin has published numerous books and articles. His latest publication is: *Maritime Security in Southern African Waters* (co-editor with Thean Potgieter, Stellenbosch: Sun Press, 2009).

E-mail: reiner.pommerin@t-online.de

Index

Absolute War	51, 88, 117, 179, 215, 270	Böhme, Klaus-Richard	325
Afghanistan	74-75, 85-86, 93, 98, 111, 210-211, 223, 227, 229-231, 326, 333, 335, 349	Boldt-Christmas, G.E.F.	324
		Bollati, Ambrogio	180
		Barbero, Abilio	312
Ancona, Clemente	181	Barbieri, Michele	183
Andersen, Claus Eskild	60, 67	Bassford, Christopher	107, 183, 240
Andersen, John Erling	71-72	Baudrillard, Jean	240
Angell, Henrik	246-247, 250	Beaufre, André	85, 89-91, 110, 299, 313
Angstrom, Jan	288	Bebler, Anton	270
annihilation	26-27, 89, 115, 204, 251	Begin, Menachem	296
		Berenhorst, Georg Heinrich von	242
Araya, Akashi	206	Berg, Nils	64, 67
Archenholz, Johann Wilhelm von	176	Bernadotte, Folke	64
Arnulf, Jan K.	240	Bernadotte, Jean-B.	239
Aron, Raymond	37, 52, 86, 89, 107-109, 112, 115-116, 118, 125-126, 159, 176, 182-183, 312-314, 317, 330	Bernard, Henri	32-33
		Bernard, Vittorio	183
		Bernhardi, Theodor von	312
Artéus, Gunnar	324	Bismarck, Otto v.	331
Austria, Archduke Charles of	16-18, 21, 242, 311, 315	Blanch, Luigi	177, 181
		Blaschke, Richard	124
Baggesen, August	60-61	Bosezky, Sascha	22
Baldini, Alberto	179	Botti, Ferruccio	182
Baquer, M.A.	313	Boyen, H. von	17
Bobbio, Norberto	184	Brandt, Hagemann	242
Bode, A. W.	124		

Bravo, Gian M.	184	Colson, Bruno	35-36, 115-116
Brodie, Bernard	52, 245, 288, 313, 325, 342, 346	Concha, Manuel Gutiérrez de la	312
Brühl, Marie von	31, 60, 311, 316-318, 328, 332,-333, 365	conscription	66, 95-96, 206, 220, 273, 305, 337
Brustlein, Corentin	112	Corbett	207, 326
Büchel, Wilhelm von	312	Cormier, Pierre-Yves	114
Bülow, Heinrich Dietrich von	157, 242, 244-245, 312, 322	Corvisier, André	110
		Coutau-Bégarie, Hervé	115
Buschmann, Klaus	126		
Caemmerer, Rudolf von	123	Creuzinger, Paul	123
		Creveld, Martin van	27, 35, 206, 288, 345, 349
Canevari, Emilio	178-180		
Canfora, Luciano	177	Cristoforis, Carlo de	177, 181
Castro, Fidel	296	Csicserics, Maximilian	124
centre of gravity	217		
Ceola, Paola	184	Curi, Umberto	183
Ceva, Lucio	182	Daase, Christopher	289, 294
Chagniot, Jean	110	Dalpane, Federico	183
Charles, Jean-Léon	32	Dayan, Moshe	158
Christopherson, Jens A.	251	Debray, Regis	297
		Delbrück, Hans	184, 314, 325
Churchill, Winston	351	Derbent, Thierry	36-37, 111
civil war	94, 181, 210, 248, 305, 342	Desportes, Vincent	115
		Diesen, Sverre	244
Clausewitz, Marie von	60, 123, 270	Dill, Günter	126, 129
		diplomacy	229, 247, 287
Cochenhausen, Friedrich von	124, 144	Dobry, Michel	109
		Dongsheng, Zhai	48
Cohen, B.	264	Douhet	23, 76, 326
COIN	228-230, 326	Drago, Antonino	184
Colombo, Alessandro	185	Drew, D.M.	218
colonialism	287, 295		

Durieux, Benoît	107, 114-115	French Revolution	117, 206, 210, 212, 292, 311, 328, 332
Echevarria, Antulio J.	346-347	Freund, Julien	109, 184
effect based approach to operations	253	Frigo, Gianfranco	183
Eimannsberger, Ludwig von	21	Frost, Lucia Dora	111
		Fuller, J. F. C.	93, 217
Eisenhower, D. D.	175, 342	Freud, Sigmund	118, 263
Eisenkot, Gadi	162	Freyberg	64
Elias, Norbert	117	Gaja, Filippo	182
Elze, Walter	123-124	Galet, Emile	31-33, 37
Engelberg, Ernst	129	Gallén, Jarl	324
Engels, Friedrich	16, 45, 89, 125, 131, 166, 178	Gallie, W. B.	182
		Gandolfi, Antonio	178
Entrèves, Ettore Passerin d`	183	Garde, Hans Jorgen	65
		Garibaldi, G.	178, 181
Enze, Su	52	Gassen, Helmut	126
epistemology	112, 139, 181, 269	Gatzke, Hans	345-346
Etzersdorfer	25	Gelder, C.C. de	213
Evola, Juius	179	Gentili, Alberico	174
Fabian, Franz	126	Giáp, Vö Nguyên	23
Falkenhayn	180	Girard, René	116-118, 184
Faltz, Walter	124	Glucksmann, André	107, 182
Farinacci, Roberto	178, 180	Gneisenau, N. von	176
Feltrinelli, Giangiacomo	182	Goethe, J. W. von	240
		Gooch, John	173
Fichte, J.	33, 315, 317	Graham, J.J.	345
Folard, J.C.	110	Gramsci, Antonio	178
Foucault, M.	184	Grant, Ulysses S.	181, 342
Franzosi, Piergiorgio	183	Gray, Colin	76, 288, 351
Frederick the Great	31, 87, 210, 213-214, 219	Griffen, A.	114
		Grünberg, Jan	137
Frederick Wilhelm III.	291	Guerzoni, Luciano	183

Guevara, Ernesto Che	25, 37, 111, 296, 345	Hinsley, F. H.	64
Guibert, Jacques Hippolyte	107, 110, 315	Hitler, Adolf	24, 180, 184, 249
		Hohenzollern, Leopold von	311
Guillen, Abraham	304	Homer	240
Guineret, Hervé	112	Honig, Jan Willem	206
Guiscardo, Rodolfo	182	Houweling, H.W.	215
Guss, Kurt	127	Howard, Michael	52, 63, 65-66, 69, 80, 89, 107, 109, 159, 182, 216, 243, 313, 345
Gustenau, Gustav	20		
Guth, Ekkehard	128		
HaCohen, Gershon	158	Huaruo, Guo	46
Hale, John Rigby	175	Huntington, Samuel	117
Haller, Albrecht von	329	Hussein, Saddam	225-227, 232
Haltiner, K. W.	273	**I**nnere Führung	126
Halutz, Dan	156, 161-162, 166	insurgency	167, 289, 345
Hackl, Othmar	127	irregular wars	117, 294, 306
Hahlweg, Werner	14-16, 19-21, 27, 67, 110, 112, 122, 125-127, 129-130, 139, 180, 182, 291, 293	Ishizu, Tomoyuki	206
		Jean, Carlo	182-185
		Jefferson, Thomas	240, 263
		Johansson, Alf W.	325
Handel, Michael	33-34, 49, 52, 133, 173	Johnson, Robert M.	342
Hannibal	158	Jomini, Antoine Henri	13, 16-18, 23, 27, 32-35, 45, 61, 72, 77, 79, 89, 107-110, 113, 116, 122, 127, 140, 157-158, 174-178, 180-181, 185, 207, 213, 219, 240, 242, 244-245, 253, 255, 276, 311, 320, 322, 324, 326, 356
Hartmann, Uwe	133-134, 137		
Hazelius, Johan August	320-321		
Hegel, G.W.F.	107, 123, 138, 178-179, 184, 240		
Henrotin, Joseph	34, 36		
Herberg-Rothe, Andreas	13, 183		
Heuser, Beatrice	110, 136, 288, 291-292	Jolles, O.J. Matthijs	345-346
		Joseph, Franz	17
Hevia, Juan Cano	313	Joxe, Alain	109, 115
Hindenburg, Paul v.	180		

Kalckreuth, F.A. von — 179
Kaldor, Mary — 349
Kant, I. — 23-24, 179, 240, 253, 315
Kahn, Herman — 21
Kawamura, Yasuyuki — 206
Keegan, John — 288, 345, 349
Kessel, Eberhard von — 123
Kiesling, Jennie — 347
Kinross, Stuart — 288, 293
Kissinger, Henry — 345, 349
Klerk, F.W. de — 302
Kleemeier, Ulrike — 27, 132
Klein, Alexander — 23-24
Kleist, Heinrich von — 317
Kohlhoff, Jörg — 19, 137
Korfes, Otto — 240
Kroon, Helge — 63-65
Kutz, Martin — 137, 315
Labanca, Nicola — 183
La Barre Duparcq, Edouard Nicolas de — 177
Lange, Rudolf — 132
Langendorf, Jean-Jacques — 132
leadership — 21, 63-64, 66, 71, 73-74, 76, 90, 97-98, 126, 128, 136, 139, 152, 158, 173, 225, 265, 267, 275, 297, 303, 322-323, 359
Lebovici, Gérard — 108, 110
Lefrén, Johan Petter — 320
legitimacy — 155, 166, 272, 277, 287-288, 295, 300
Lenin, V. — 18, 37, 43, 45-47, 64, 72, 89, 111, 120, 181-182, 205, 241, 303, 315
liberation movements — 20, 294, 303
Liddell Hart, B. H. — 23, 35, 48, 51, 72, 108, 163, 184-185, 206-207, 215, 313, 324, 348
Liebknecht, Karl — 111
Lincoln, Abraham — 181, 341
Linnebach, Karl — 123
Livni, Tzipi — 162
Lloyd, Henry — 322
Lombardero, Antonio de Querol — 315
Loreto, Luigi — 185
Loretoni, Anna — 183
Lossau, Johann Friedrich Konstantin von — 112
low-intensity conflict — 288-289, 364
Ludendorff, Erich — 33, 179, 206
Luhmann, Niklas — 132, 135-136
Luraghi, Raimondo — 181
Luttwak, Edward N. — 35, 90, 156
Lyng, Jorgen — 64, 70, 75
Machiavelli — 35, 65, 72, 179, 185
Macho, Thomas — 27
Madison, James — 256, 361
Mahan, Alfred Thayer — 21, 23, 72, 76, 176, 181, 207, 324, 326,

	342	Mehring, Franz	178
Maister, Rudolf	264	Menicocci, Marco	184
Maizière, Ulrich de	181	Metzsch, Horst von	124
Malan, Magnus	298	Meulmann, F.H.	218
Malis, Christian	115	Meydell, Jacob Gerhard	242
Mandela, Nelson	295-296, 302-303		
Mankell, Julius	321	Miguel, Evaristo San	311, 313, 364
Mannerheim, Carl Gustav	95, 239	Millotat, Christian	128
		military strategy	21, 111, 129, 213, 231, 244-245, 269, 364
manoeuvre warfare	216-217, 253		
Mantilla, Ambrosio Garcés de	312	Mini, Fabio	185
		Mitchell	23
Mao Zedong	25, 42, 45-47, 53, 72, 89, 107, 111, 182, 241, 296-297, 300, 345	Miyake, Masaki	206
		Molinari, Andrea	183
Marcenado, Marqués de Santa Cruz de	318	Moltke, Helmuth von	89, 128, 166, 206, 212, 214-215, 219, 243, 270, 312, 315, 322
Marselli, Nicolás	178-179, 181, 311	Moltke, Johann	24
Marshall, Justice	263	Montecuccoli	21-22
Martel, André	110	Montesquieu	315, 318
Maruhata, Hiroto	206	Moran, Daniel	345, 349
Marwedel, Ulrich	107, 122, 124, 127	Mori, Massimo	183
Matthews, Joe	297	Mori, Rintaro	204
Marx, Karl	45, 47, 64, 87, 108, 125, 178, 181, 263	Moskos, Charles	273
		Motte, Martin	115
Maschke, Gunther	112	Müller, Johannes von	329
Matuszek, Krzysztof C.	132	Müller, Lutz	111, 114
		Müller, Martin	26
Mazzarino, Santo	185	Münkler, Herfried	21, 131-132
Mbeki, Thabo	304	Murray, Williamson	206
McCuen, J.J.	300	**N**apoleon	31-33, 35-36, 61, 77, 85, 87-88, 91, 93, 150, 152, 173, 176, 206-
Meckel, Jacob	204		
Mehren, Stein	240		

	207, 212-214, 219, 243, 289, 304, 311, 315, 320, 326, 328-329, 332, 338, 356, 361
network centric warfare	86
Neuens, Jean N.	110, 177
Nève, Alain de	36
Newton	347
Nickerson, Hoffman	342
Nohn, Ernst August	125
Nordensvan, Carl Otto	321-323
Osinga, F.	218
Osgood, Robert E.	348
Overstraeten, Raoul Van	32-33
Owens, William	173, 175
Palmer, John McAuley	342
Panebianco, Angelo	183
Paret, Peter	16, 21, 33, 51, 52, 63, 72, 107, 109, 125-126, 132, 181-182, 216, 243, 313, 343, 345-346, 349
Parker, Geoffrey	175
partisan warfare	289, 293
patriotism	252, 330
Patton, George	341-342
peace	9, 16-17, 19, 22, 25, 69, 78, 88, 95-97, 125, 128-129, 154, 183, 219, 223, 231, 239, 241, 246, 248-251, 253, 264, 271, 295-296, 316, 328, 335, 338, 361-363
Pedroncini, Guy	9
Peischel, Wolfgang	22
people	24-25, 42-44, 47, 68, 89, 94-95, 99, 116, 126, 154, 173, 203, 221, 239, 242, 246-247, 249, 252, 254, 263, 265, 287-295, 297-298, 300-305, 320, 331, 333-336, 338, 343-344, 347, 349-350
Pestalozzi, Johann Heinrich	126, 332
Peter, Ralph	344
Petraeus, David	346
Pezzullo, Francesco	184
philosophy	44, 67, 76, 87, 92, 100, 107, 123-125, 127, 132, 176, 245, 253, 256, 269, 359, 362
Picaud-Monnerat, Sandrine	111
Pickert, Wolfgang	127
Pieri, Piero	181
Pilsudski, Jósef	239
Plato	253, 256, 276
Plenge-Trautner, Jeppe	78
Pontecorvo, Gillo	179
Portuyn, Pim	225

Powell, Colin	252, 341, 343
Pratt, N.	217
Princen, F.J.J.	217
Prezzolini, Giuseppe	178
Prim, Juán	311
Primicerj, Giulio	183
Proektor, Daniel M.	16, 18
professionalization	273-275
psychology	66, 263, 269
Ragionieri, Ernesto	181
Rapoport, Anatol	348-349
Reber, Gérard	110
Récamier, Juliette	329
Reiter, August	22
Reitz, Deneys	296
Regele, Ludwig	24
revolutionary warfare	36, 287, 295, 306
Rid, Thomas	18
Rijneveld, J.C. van	211, 218
Ritter, Gerhard	127, 181-182
Rizzi, Loris	183
Roberts, Michael	175
Rosen, Claus von	137, 359
Rothfels, Hans	65, 123, 180, 345-346
Rosinski	111, 115, 345-346
Rusconi, Gian Enrico	184-185
Rüstow, Friedrich Wilhelm	174, 176, 178, 322
sabotage	296, 298
Sade, Marquis de	240
Sanfelice	184
Scharnhorst, Gerhard	17, 124, 132, 176, 275
Scheler, Wolfgang von	129
Schelling, Wilhelm v.	240
Schering, Walther Malmsten	123-124, 179, 314
Schiller, Friedrich von	318, 332, 345
Schleiermacher, Friedrich D.E.	133, 138, 316-317
Schlegel, August Wilhelm von	329-330, 333
Schlieffen, Alfred von	24, 43, 89, 114, 123, 180, 184, 204, 206, 213-214, 270, 315
Schmitt, Carl	112, 117, 131, 179, 181, 183-184
Schnitler, Gudmund	184, 243-245
Schössler, Dietmar	16, 126, 131
Schouten, M.	217
Schramm, Wilhelm Ritter von	126-127
Schrehardt, Carsten Wilhelm	114
Schulten, J.W.M.	217, 219
Schuurman, B.W.	218
Schwartz, Karl	123
Schwarzkopf, Norman	158
Schwendi, Lazarus	21
Seeckt, H. von	206, 270
Seguí, Juan	312
Shakespeare	256
Sharon, Ariel	159

Shimuzi, Takichi	206	Tell, William	330
Snow, Edgar	296	Terray, Emmanuel	109, 115
Shy, John	255	theory of war	16, 22, 25, 67, 111, 132-133, 137-140, 182, 244, 252, 279, 293, 338, 347
Siccama, J.G.	215		
Simpkin, Richard	23		
Sinding-Larsen	243		
small wars	10, 80, 125, 287, 289, 291-293, 361	Thucydides	269, 317, 330
		Tingsten, Lars	322-323
Smith, Adam	137, 263	Tjepkema, A.C.	218
Smith, Rupert	117	total strategy	89-90, 287, 298-300
Socrates	256	trinity	34-35, 48, 50, 89, 99, 135, 217, 252, 263, 343-344, 348-350
Spannocchi, Emil	21		
Spits, F.C.	215, 218	Trummer, Peter	126, 137
Staël, Germaine de	330	Türpe, Andrée	16, 126
Stadler, Christian	26	Unterseher, Lutz	27
Stamp, Gerd	127, 181-182	Vad, Erich	126
Stern, Elazar	156	Vagts, Alfred	345
Stiebellehner, Markus	20	Valle, Antonio Remón Zarco del	312
Strachan, Hew	115, 179, 183-184		
Stübig, Heinz	126	Vels, R.J. van	217
subversion	184, 287, 298	Villamartín, Francisco	312
Sullivan, Brian	173		
Sumida, Jon Tetsuro	346-347	Vilnai, Matan	166
Summer, Harrry	343-344	Volten, P.M.E.	215
Sun Tsu	21, 23	Vos, Luc de	32-33
Suzuki, Tadashi	206	Wagner, J.L.	212
Swetschin, A.	136	Waldstätten, Alfred von	21
Swielande, Tanguy Struye de	36		
		Wallach, Jehuda	27
Taboni, Pier Franco	183	Warberg, Carl	321
Tambo, Oliver	303	Warden, John A.	23, 76-77, 326
Tamura, Iyozo	204	Wasinski, Christophe	31, 35-36, 115, 357

Wedemeyer, Albert	341
Wellington	311, 346
Weniger, Erich	125
Wenzel, Paul	25
Wijnen, M.H.	358
Will, Thomas	128
Willisen, Wilhelm von	312
Wissekerke, F.J.D.C. Egter van	217-218
Wörner, Manfred	122, 363
Xianzhong, Niu	49
Yaalon, Moshe	162
Ye Jianying	44
Yinan, Jin	52
Yinhong, Shi	48
Yong, Li	52
Yuanlin	18

Carola Hartmann Miles-Verlag

Politik, Gesellschaft, Militär

Uwe Hartmann, *Innere Führung. Erfolge und Defizite der Führungsphilosophie für die Bundeswehr,* Berlin 2007.

Peter Heinze, *Bundeswehr „erobert" Deutschlands Osten,* Berlin 2010.

Reinhard Schneider, *Neuste Nachrichten aus unseren Kolonien. Pressemeldungen von den Aufständen in Deutsch-Ostafrika und Deutsch-Südwestafrika 1905-1906,* Berlin 2010.

Dieter E. Kilian, *Politik und Militär in Deutschland. Die Bundespräsidenten und Bundeskanzler und ihre Beziehung zu Soldatentum und Bundeswehr,* Berlin 2011.

Hans Joachim Reeb, *Sicherheitskultur als kommunikative und pädagogische Herausforderung – Der Umgang in Politik, Medien und Gesellschaft,* Berlin 2011.

Reiner Pommerin (ed.), *Clausewitz goes global. Carl von Clausewitz in the 21st Century,* Berlin 2011.

Hans-Christian Beck, Christian Singer (Hrsg.), *Entscheiden – Führen – Verantworten. Soldatsein im 21. Jahrhundert,* Berlin 2011.

Dieter E. Kilian, *Adenauers vergessener Retter – Major Fritz Schliebusch,* Berlin 2011.

Ingo Pfeiffer, *Gegner wider Willen. Konfrontation von Volksmarine und Bundesmarine auf See,* Berlin 2012.

Eberhard Birk, Heiner Möllers, Wolfgang Schmidt (Hrsg.), *Die Luftwaffe zwischen Politik und Technik. Schriften zur Geschichte der Deutschen Luftwaffe, Bd. 2,* Berlin 2012.

Eberhard Birk, Winfried Heinemann, Sven Lange (Hrsg.), *Tradition für die Bundeswehr. Neue Aspekte einer alten Debatte,* Berlin 2012.

Holger Müller, *Clausewitz' Verständnis von Strategie im Spiegel der Spieltheorie,* Berlin 2012.

Dieter E. Kilian, *Kai-Uwe von Hassel und seine Familie. Zwischen Ostsee und Ostafrika. Militär-biographisches Mosaik,* Berlin 2013.

Angelika Dörfler-Dierken, *Führung in der Bundeswehr,* Berlin 2013.

Peter Heinze, *Berliner Militärgeschichten*, Berlin 2013.

Cornelia Fedtke, Kai-Uwe Hellmann, Jan Hörmann, *Migration und Militär. Zur Integration deutscher Soldaten mit Migrationshintergrund in der Bundeswehr*, Berlin 2013.

Reihe: Jahrbuch Innere Führung

Uwe Hartmann, Claus von Rosen, Christian Walther (Hrsg.), *Jahrbuch Innere Führung 2009. Die Rückkehr des Soldatischen*, Eschede 2009.

Helmut R. Hammerich, Uwe Hartmann, Claus von Rosen (Hrsg.), *Jahrbuch Innere Führung 2010. Die Grenzen des Militärischen*, Berlin 2010.

Uwe Hartmann, Claus von Rosen, Christian Walther (Hrsg.), *Jahrbuch Innere Führung 2011. Ethik als geistige Rüstung für Soldaten*, Berlin 2011.

Uwe Hartmann, Claus von Rosen, Christian Walther (Hrsg.), *Jahrbuch Innere Führung 2012. Der Soldatenberuf zwischen gesellschaftlicher Integration und suis generis-Ansprüchen*, Berlin 2012.

Uwe Hartmann, Claus von Rosen (Hrsg.), *Jahrbuch Innere Führung 2013. Wissenschaften und ihre Relevanz für die Bundeswehr als Armee im Einsatz*, Berlin 2013.

Einsatzerfahrungen

Kay Kuhlen, *Um des lieben Friedens willen. Als Peacekeeper im Kosovo*, Eschede 2009.

Sascha Brinkmann, Joachim Hoppe (Hrsg.), *Generation Einsatz, Fallschirmjäger berichten ihre Erfahrungen aus Afghanistan*, Berlin 2010.

Schwitalla, Artur, *Afghanistan, jetzt weiß ich erst… Gedanken aus meiner Zeit als Kommandeur des Provincial Reconstruction Team FEYZABAD*, Berlin 2010.

Erinnerungen

Blue Braun, *Erinnerungen an die Marine 1956-1996*, Berlin 2012.

Harald Volkmar Schlieder, *Kommando zurück!*, Berlin 2012.

Harald Volkmar Schlieder, *Opa Willy. 1891 Dresden – 1958 Miltenberg. Von einem, der aufsteigen wollte. Eine sächsisch-deutsche Lebensgeschichte in Frieden und Krieg*, Berlin 2012.

Harald Volkmar Schlieder, *Mein Vater – Musiker und Offizier. 1918 Dresden – 1998 Miltenberg,* Berlin 2013.

Reinhart Lunderstädt, *Aus dem Leben eines Hochschullehrers. Persönlicher Bericht,* Berlin 2012.

Wulf Beeck, *Mit Überschall durch den Kalten Krieg. Mein Leben für die Marine,* Berlin 2013.

Monterey Studies

Uwe Hartmann, *Carl von Clausewitz and the Making of Modern Strategy,* Potsdam 2002.

Zeljko Cepanec, *Croatia and NATO. The Stony Road to Membership,* Potsdam 2002.

Ekkehard Stemmer, *Demography and European Armed Forces,* Berlin 2006.

Sven Lange, *Revolt against the West. A Comparison of the Current War on Terror with the Boxer Rebellion in 1900-01,* Berlin 2007.

Klaus M. Brust, *Culture and the Transformation of the Bundeswehr,* Berlin 2007.

Donald Abenheim, *Soldier and Politics Transformed,* Berlin 2007.

Michael Stolzke, *The Conflict Aftermath. A Chance for Democracy: Norm Diffusion in Post-Conflict Peace Building,* Berlin 2007.

Frank Reimers, *Security Culture in Times of War. How did the Balkan War affect the Security Cultures in Germany and the United States?,* Berlin 2007.

Michael G. Lux, *Innere Führung – A Superior Concept of Leadership?,* Berlin 2009.

Marc A. Walther, *HAMAS between Violence and Pragmatism,* Berlin 2010.

Frank Hagemann, *Strategy Making in the European Union,* Berlin 2010.

Ralf Hammerstein, *Deliberalization in Jordan: the Roles of Islamists and U.S.-EU Assistance in stalled Democratization,* Berlin 2011.

Ingo Wittmann, *Auftragstaktik,* Berlin 2012.

Neue Reihe: Standpunkte und Orientierungen

Daniel Giese, *Militärische Führung im Internetzeitalter – Die Bedeutung von Strategischer Kommunikation uns Social Media für Entscheidungsprozesse, Organisationsstrukturen und Führerausbildung in der Bundeswehr,* Berlin 2014.